FAMILY PSYCHOLOGY

Theory, Therapy and Training

Luciano L'Abate
Georgia State University

UNIVERSITY
PRESS OF
AMERICA

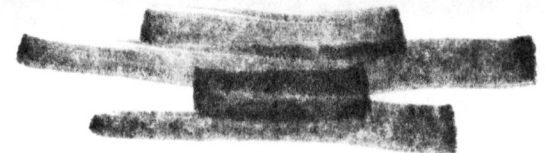

Copyright © 1983 by

University Press of America, Inc.

P.O. Box 19101, Washington, D.C. 20036

All rights reserved

Printed in the United States of America

Library of Congress Cataloging in Publication Data

L'Abate, Luciano, 1928-
   Family psychology.

   1. Family psychotherapy. 2. Family. 3. Psychology--
Study and teaching. I. Title.
RC488.5.L3 1983   616.89'156   82-20255
ISBN 0-8191-2883-X
ISBN 0-8191-2884-8 (pbk.)

ACKNOWLEDGMENTS

I am grateful to various publishers who have graciously consented to the reprinting of articles in this collection.

Chapter 1 is currently in press in the <u>Academic Psychology Bulletin</u>. A request to reprint has been made and permission is pending.

Chapter 2 was originally published in <u>Teaching of Psychology</u>. Permission to reprint was granted by the editor, Robert S. Daniel, Ph.D.

Chapter 3 was published as a book (<u>Understanding and Helping the Individual in the Family</u>). Permission to reprint graphs contained in the original was granted by the publisher, Grune & Stratton, Inc.

Chapter 4 was originally published in <u>Family Therapy</u>. Permission to reprint was granted by Martin Blinder, M.D., Editor-in-Chief.

Chapter 5 was originally published in <u>International Journal of Family Counseling</u> (now <u>American Journal of Family Therapy</u>). Permission to reprint was granted by the editor, Richard S. Sauber, Ph.D.

Chapter 6 is reprinted from Volume 1, Number 1 of <u>Journal of Marriage and Family Counseling</u> (now <u>Journal of Marital and Family Therapy</u>), copyright 1975, American Association of Marriage and Family Therapy. Reprinted by permission.

Chapter 7 was originally published in <u>International Journal of Family Counseling</u> (now <u>International Journal of Family Therapy</u>). Permission to reprint was granted by the editor, Gerald H. Zuk, Ph.D.

Chapter 8 is "Marriage: The Dream and the Reality" by L. L'Abate and B. L. L'Abate, <u>Family Relations</u>, 1981, Vol. 30, No. 1, pp. 131-136. Copyright 1981 by the National Council for Family Relations. Reprinted by permission.

Chapter 9 was published originally in the <u>International Journal of Family Therapy</u> (now the <u>American Journal of Family Therapy</u>) and is reprinted here with the permission of the publisher, Brunner/Mazel.

Chapter 10 is reprinted from Volume 3, Number 2 of Journal of Marriage and Family Counseling (now Journal of Marital and Family Therapy), copyright 1977 by the American Association of Marriage and Family Therapy. Reprinted by permission.

Chapter 11 was published originally in the Journal of Marital and Family Therapy and is reprinted with the permission of the publisher, the American Association of Marriage and Family Therapy.

Chapter 12 was published in Family Therapy and is reprinted here with the permission of Martin Blinder, M.D., Editor-in-Chief.

Chapter 13 was published originally in the Journal of Marital and Family Therapy and is reprinted here with the permission of the publisher, the American Association of Marriage and Family Therapy.

Chapter 14 is "The E-R-A Model: A Heuristic Framework for Classification of Skill Training Programs for Couples and Families" by D. Ulrici, L. L'Abate, and V. Wagner, Family Relations, April 1981, Vol. 30, No. 2, pp. 307-315. Copyright 1981 by the National Council on Family Relations. Reprinted by permission.

Chapter 15 is being published in Family Therapy and is reprinted here with the permission of Martin Blinder, M.D., Editor-in-Chief.

Chapter 16 was originally read as a paper.

Chapter 17 was published originally in the Journal of Marriage and Family Counseling (now the Journal of Marital and Family Therapy) and is reprinted here with the permission of the American Association of Marriage and Family Therapy.

Chapter 18 was published originally in Family Therapy and is reprinted with the permission of Martin Blinder, M.D., Editor-in-Chief.

Chapter 19 was published originally in Family Therapy and is reprinted with the permission of Martin Blinder, M.D., Editor-in-Chief.

Chapter 20 was published as a chapter in Group Therapy: An Overview, 1975 and is reprinted here with the permission of the Stratton Intercontinental Medical Book Corporation.

Chapter 21 was published originally in *International Journal of Family Counseling* (now *American Journal of Family Therapy*) and is reprinted here with the permission of the publisher, Brunner/Mazel.

Chapter 22 was published originally in the *American Journal of Family Therapy* and is reprinted here with the permission of the publisher, Brunner/Mazel.

Chapter 23 was published originally in the *American Journal of Family Therapy* and is reprinted here with the permission of the publisher, Brunner/Mazel.

Chapter 24 was published originally in *Family Process* and is reprinted with the permission of the Business Manager, Judith Lieb.

Chapter 25 was published originally in *Family Therapy* and is reprinted with the permission of Martin Blinder, M.D., Editor-in-Chief.

Chapter 26 was published originally in *Professional Psychology* and is reprinted here with the permission of the American Psychological Association.

Chapter 27 was written expressly for this collection.

Chapter 28 was also written for this collection.

Chapter 29 was published originally in the *Journal of Marriage and Family Therapy* and is reprinted here with the permission of the American Association of Marriage and Family Therapy.

Chapter 30 was written expressly for this collection.

I acknowledge the help of all my students, now colleagues, who have helped me in this journey. Without them, I doubt that I could have traveled this road alone. I am also grateful to Mrs. Marie Morgan for her caring, considerate, and careful typing and editing of my garbled hieroglyphics and to her husband, Gene Morgan, for distracting me from these chores with an occasional game of tennis.

L.L.

TABLE OF CONTENTS

Acknowledgments iii
Foreword ix
Preface. xi

INTRODUCTION

1. The Family as a Unit of Psychological Theory and Practice. 3
2. The Family Taboo in Psychology Textbooks. . 17

SECTION I. THEORY AND METATHEORY

3. A Theory of Personality Development in the Family 23
4. The Differentiation of Resources 47
5. Psychopathology as Transaction: A Historical Note 57
6. Pathologic Role Rigidity in Fathers: Some Observations 63
7. Protectiveness, Persecution, and Powerlessness. 75
8. Marriage: The Dream and the Reality . . . 81

SECTION II. FEELINGS AND INTIMACY

9. Of Scapegoats, Strawmen, and Scarecrows . . 87
10. Intimacy is Sharing Hurt Feelings: A Reply to David Mace. 101
11. Intimacy is Sharing Hurt Feelings: Comparison of Three Conflict Resolution Models . . 105
12. The Paradoxes of Intimacy. 113

SECTION III. THE ROLE OF FEELINGS IN THERAPY

13. The E-R-A Model: The Role of Feelings in Family Therapy Reconsidered: Implications for a Classification of Theories of Family Therapy. 125
14. The E-R-A Model: A Heuristic Framework for Classification of Skill Training Programs for Couples and Families 133
15. Toward a Classification of Family Therapy Theories: Further Elaborations and Implications of the E-R-A-Aw-C Model. 143

TABLE OF CONTENTS
(Continued)

SECTION IV. LINEAR METHODS IN FAMILY THERAPY

16. The Laboratory Evaluation of Families. . . . 159
17. The Laboratory Evaluation and Enrichment of Couples: Applications and Some Results. 169
18. Forced Holding: A Technique for Treating Parentified Children 177
19. The Role of Family Conferences in Family Therapy. 187

SECTION V. CIRCULAR APPROACHES IN FAMILY THERAPY

20. A Positive Approach to Marriage and Family Therapy 195
21. Paradox as a Therapeutic Technique: A Review 209
22. A Compilation of Paradoxical Methods . . . 221
23. Enrichment and Written Messages with Couples. 237
24. The Use of Paradox with Children in an Inpatient Setting 247
25. Coping with Defeating Patterns in Family Therapy. 253

SECTION VI. IMPLICATIONS FOR TRAINING

26. Training Family Psychologists: The Family Studies Program at Georgia State University. 269
27. Training in Family Psychology 277
28. Structure and Gradualness in the Clinical Training of Family Psychologists . . . 287
29. Enrichment Role Playing as a Step in the Training of Family Psychologists . . . 301

SECTION VII. CONCLUSION

30. Family Psychology: The Present and the Future 311

FOREWORD

Something strange has been happening (or not happening) in the field of clinical psychology: while in every other mental health discipline, family theory and family therapy have taken a strong foothold, in clinical psychology there is barely any recognition that systemic thinking about human dilemmas exists. The roots of this phobic avoidance of the transactional perspective are uncertain but probably have quite a lot to do with the fact that most of the leading theorists in family therapy have been psychiatrists and that most of the practitioners of family therapy have been, and are, social workers. Neither of these professions have ever endorsed the kind of "scientist-practitioner," "Boulder Model" training that is so widely espoused by (the teachers of) clinical psychology, and perhaps this has been sufficient reason for clinical psychologists, in academic circles at least, to disregard developments in those fields. Family-oriented thinking has made substantial inroads into the training of clinical psychologists only in a few clinical training programs with a strong social learning theory orientation to clinical work. But the teaching of family therapy in these programs focuses on family therapy as a collection of techniques rather than as the applied clinical expression of a way of thinking about human experience and its vicissitudes that is a radical departure from traditional theories and models.

It is no surprise, then, that there are few clinical psychologists in the forefront of family therapy. And it is sad to note that most among this handful of visible clinical psychologists-family therapists identify themselves more with the family movement than with psychology.

Given this foreboding context, Lu L'Abate has achieved a pedagogical and administrative miracle in creating a family studies specialization in a clinical psychology doctoral training program. This course of study and practice is itself described here, but what is more important is that this volume brings together the seminal writings of the only clinical psychologist to date who has succeeded in establishing a truly viable family therapy program within academic clinical psychology.

What is especially impressive about Lu L'Abate's

work in the field is that, unlike many in-vogue family therapists of the 1980s who seem not to believe that families are made up of persons, he has never lost sight of what family therapy was originally all about: bridging and transcending the falsely constructed dichotomies between individual and interactional experience and change. In so doing, L'Abate sends an enormously important message to the field of clinical psychology about the dangers in its continuing history of artificially cutting itself off from the fields of sociology, cultural anthropology, and philosophy. Clinical psychology has not had an easy time in the last three and a half decades establishing its autonomy and right to exist as an independent profession. But in many ways it has become so well differentiated that, if it continues on this developmental trajectory, it may die. L'Abate's book, then, is much, much more than a mere collection of the papers of a creative thinker, talented teacher, and gifted clinician: it is the most life-inspiring book for the conceptual growth of clinical psychology in a long, long time. It's so good, I wish I had written it myself.

                                        Alan S. Gurman, Ph.D.
                                        Professor of Psychiatry
                                        University of Wisconsin
                                              Medical School

PREFACE

The purpose of this book is to assemble the papers published by the author and his co-workers in a variety of professional journals during the last decade. These papers address a variety of areas, ranging from theory to specific applications in marital and family enrichment and therapy. A series of chapters at the conclusion of the text describe a training program in family psychology, which, as far as the author knows, is unique in this country. There are many training programs in psychiatry, social work, home economics, and various family therapy institutes; however, this program is the only one with a <u>complete</u> curriculum leading to a Ph.D. in <u>family psychology</u>. Family psychology is that branch of psychology which, as a science and as a profession, deals with the relationship between the individual and his/her family. As made abundantly clear in the first section of this book, this branch has been forgotten and is a relative newcomer in psychology, an offspring of the process of differentiation that psychology has undergone and is undergoing, as any structure or organization usually does. The trend of this collection remains consistent throughout the book, i.e., how to relate individual functioning and dysfunctioning to its most natural context, the family. The family as a whole has been the subject of sociology, whereas the individual has been the subject of psychology. In this volume, these papers attempt to link both fields theoretically as well as practically. We may not have succeeded, but we have attempted this linkage. Because of its clinical bent, a great many papers in this book deal directly with issues and problems of dysfunctionality rather than functionality. Functionality has been examined in greater detail in a previous publication (L'Abate, 1976) and will be referred to throughout this book.

The main audience for this book would be: (a) clinical psychologists in training instructions, who are seeking a more innovative approach to theory, practice, and training; (b) their students; (c) trainers in the field of family psychiatry, social work, and education, who are seeking a framework in theory and practice; and (d) professionals involved in family therapy.

It should be clear from the outset that the major focus of this book is <u>clinical</u>, or <u>applied</u>, family psychology. Within this overall rubric, the major points of emphasis have been theory (Sections I, II, and III), practice (Sections IV and V), and training (Section VI). As the reader will also surmise very quickly, the dividing line between theory and practice is oftentimes very thin indeed, and the overlap between these two areas is at times great, as it should be.

In considering theory (Section I), the reader should keep in mind the difference between theory and metatheory. Very likely, a great many of the papers in this section could be classified as metatheoretical rather than as belonging to a specific theory. Most of these papers pertain to the major assumption that the individual is a subsystem of a larger system, the family. Although systems thinking pervades many of these papers, the focus remains the same: What is the relationship of the individual to his/her family? What kind of family relationships produce functionality and dysfunctionality in the individual? How does the individual add to or subtract from the family functionality or dysfunctionality?

The chapters in Sections II and III bear upon the main issue of family relationships, i.e., the negotiation of <u>distance</u> between and among intimates. Intimacy represents the state or position of being between loving and caring individuals, leading to a feeling of contentment and well-being, even though this state or position may have been achieved with considerable pain. <u>Intimacy is the most difficult state or position to achieve in one's life and in one's family</u>. Hence, it is important in personality development in the family. These two sections place considerable emphasis on the role of feelings and emotions in the relationship between the individual and the family. As considered in greater detail elsewhere (L'Abate & McHenry, in preparation), emotions modulate, deal with, and are mainly responsible for how we come close and break apart in intimate as well as not-so-intimate relationships. Human relationships are governed by emotionality to a much greater extent than we would like to acknowledge. Furthermore, academic psychology has usually relegated emotions to a secondary position vis-a-vis "cognition." Hence, cognitivism and its therapeutic derivates have acquired a primary position in psychology. The chapters in this section are clearly aligned on the contrasting side of that position, maintaining that emotionality is primary to cognition, developmentally, emprically, and theoretically. This position is clearly controversial and likely to remain so until the weight of empirical evidence becomes sufficiently overwhelming to make this position either more or less tenable.

The first 15 chapters of this book are loosely theoretical-clinical; the remainder, from chapter 15 to the end, is definitely more applied in its practical elaborations. This emphasis should not blind the reader to the necessity for a nonclinical, mostly academic, research-oriented family psychology. There is room for such a specialization separate from clinical practices and techniques. Nevertheless, psychology, as a science and as a profession, for reasons alluded to in the first two chapters, has not as yet seen fit to expand in this direction. Family psychology as an academic discipline, like many scientific developments, is still in the process of evolving from clinical applications (L'Abate, 1964).

A major distinction that separates Section IV from Section V is the linear-circular dichotomy often used in the jargon of family therapists. <u>Linear</u> refers to a straightforward, step-by-step, gradually progressive approach; <u>circular</u> refers to a circuitously cryptic, suddenly surprising, unexpected approach, such as the one used in a positive reframing of a symptom or of a stigmatized "patient." Change in families is based in part on the skillful and timely use of <u>both</u> approaches, which gives us another dichotomy familiar to family therapists: the digital-analogic distinction. <u>Digital</u> means either-or, true-false, black-white, right-wrong distinctions, whereas <u>analogic</u> means continuous, uninterrupted sequence or dimension (both-and). The former is exemplified by the digital watch; the latter is exemplified by the traditional watch with two hands. The light switch is an on-off digital mechanism; how much light there can be in the room is an analogic measure. These two distinctions will appear frequently throughout these chapters.

The linear-circular distinction highlighted by Sections IV and V clearly indicates that dysfunctional relationships are characterized by negativity, digitality, and linearity. A variety of strategies is necessary to intervene with such relationships. Some interventions can be gradual, step-by-step sequences (linear). Some interventions can be circular, dealing with presenting symptoms or issues from the sides, as it were, rather than face to face, as in linear interventions.

The section on training (VI) relates mostly to

clinical training, despite the acknowledgment that the academic aspect is just as important even though it is neglected by many clinicians devoted to helping families (just as research is important to the whole clinical enterprise).

A word needs to be said about the use of the term "family psychology" rather than the more generic term "family therapy." Members of the former profession can teach the latter; very seldom can the reverse occur. A well-trained family psychologist should be able to combine theory with practice, research with training, and prevention with therapeutic interventions. S/he should be able to evaluate a family, using a variety of diagnostic tools, and to intervene using a variety of approaches. S/he should not be limited to conducting family therapy and, to that extent, should be able to supervise most family therapists without the previously mentioned qualifications.

Finally, some prognostications about the status of and the prospects for family psychology will be made in the last chapter.

REFERENCES

L'Abate, L. <u>Principles of clinical psychology</u>. New York: Grune & Stratton, 1964.

L'Abate, L. <u>Understanding and helping the individual in the family</u>. New York: Grune & Stratton, 1976.

L'Abate, L., & McHenry, S. <u>Adjustment and personality: An interpersonal perspective</u> (MS in preparation).

INTRODUCTION

CHAPTER 1

The Family as a Unit of Psychological Study and Practice

Luciano L'Abate and Lyn Thaxton, Georgia State University

> Abstract. The family taboo in psychological theory and practice is related to the overuse of terms that avoid considering the family, such as "situation," "context," "environment," and other generic and vague terms. Such an avoidance is found in clinical practice as well. Reasons for such an avoidance may be found in atomistic and reductionistic emphases. Hopefully, corrective signs that the family is becoming a legitimate unit of psychological theory and practice are present.

It is the thesis of this paper that a new paradigmatic shift is facing us. This paradigm shift is neither strictly ideological nor methodological; rather, it constitutes a change from intrapsychic and intraindividual perspectives to interindividual and intrafamilial perspectives. It implies a transactional perspective (L'Abate, Weeks, & Weeks, 1978) that makes the family the unit of study and of intervention.

As a science and as a profession we are generally unprepared to deal with individuals within the family systems; we are unprepared (a) theoretically; (b) methodologically; (c) in our training programs; and (d) in our clinical methods. The family, the major and most immediate context of human development and personality, has received little attention in most psychological writings. The individual in vacuo without his immediate context, the family, is still the dominant focus of psychological study. This bias can be objectively measured in textbooks (Dunne & L'Abate, 1978), and is clearly seen in theories, research, clinical practice, and methods of training.

The family has been neglected in psychological thinking partly because of atomistic-analytic emphases, narrow empiricism, and limited conceptual frameworks that currently pervade the field. There are hopeful indications that such a change in orientation is slowly taking place in clinical practice, theory, and research.

The Family "Phobia" in Psychology

Psychology as a science and a profession has seldom dealt directly with the family. This problem is revealed in (a) the limited number of references in textbooks and (b) emphasis on general concepts, such as "situation," "environment," and "community." In an analysis of 60 textbooks in six different areas (child, adolescent, exceptional child, personality, social, and abnormal), it was found (Dunne & L'Abate, 1978) that the last three areas had at most 8 percent coverage of family-related terms and concepts. In their emphasis on generalities, psychologists have for the most part avoided references to the family. A great many papers published in major psychological journals and collections (Bem & Funder, 1978; Craik, 1978; Ekehammer, 1974; Endler & Magnusson, 1976) have focused on the organism-situation interaction but have usually failed to describe the specific "situation." As regards "environment" and "community," there are entire divisions of the APA structure devoted to environmental and even population psychology, another division dedicated to community psychology, and a Society for the Study of Social Issues. There is not, however, even a section of a division dedicated to the major "mediator" between the individual and "society," the family.

This academic and scientific avoidance is paralleled in clinical practice. Psychologists are clearly still oriented toward testing, assessing, measuring, and interviewing individuals with emphasis primarily on intraindividual variables that more often than not show a complete lack of relationship to family variables (Barker, 1968).

Avoidance in Theory

Psychology has failed to consider the family as a system because of restricted conceptual and methodological tools. S-R or S-O-R language and Reinforcement language fail to deal with the complex transactions of family life that are in fact more appropriately describable by communication-information systems and transactions (L'Abate, 1969). Recent representative articles (Bem & Allen, 1974; Bowers, 1973; Ekehammer, 1974) concerned with the person x situation controversy have suggested the need to look at both influences on behavior from statistical as well as logical and empirical viewpoints. It is argued that the person and the "situation" influence each other in a two-way interaction. We have not, however, reached the goal of recognizing (a) that most "situations" are human; (b) that these human situations are, more often than not, familial; and (c) that these situations are transactional in nature.

The Family as Situation and Context

"Situation" is defined as that aggregate of stimuli that produces a noticeable change in behavior. These stimuli can be human as well as nonhuman and inanimate. Furthermore, this situation encompasses the dimensions of both space and time, and is, in the final analysis, defined by the intersection of these continua. Thus, stimuli that compose the context have their place in the spatial dimension and are related to the topography and territoriality of behavior as well as to its temporality (L'Abate, 1976). The physical situation is mostly spatial, related to movements and nonverbal behavior. The human situation, with its heavy emphasis on verbal behavior, is mostly temporal. From a spatial-temporal viewpoint, any situation is in a process of continuous flux and change as long as human beings continue to move in time. Consequently, we are continuously changing to the extent that our situations change, and our situations change as we change.

Development is a process of change in the continuous relationship between an individual and the context. Changes take place in the individual, in his context, and within the relationship between the two. The major context of the infant, from the viewpoint of biological survival, is his caretaker. Attachments during this stage of life will determine, in part, the nature of attachments to other intimates on which the child and the adult will be dependent for emotional survival during his lifetime. The home and family is the context for emotional survival. The family still maintains its position as the societal institution with major responsibility for the emotional support and emotional training of individuals, despite the fact that it has delegated much of what previously was its venue to other institutions.

What we know as personality is not without cognitive and intellectual components as well as affective ones. The familial context provides important influences here as well. For example, Zajonc and Markus (1975) demonstrated that level of intellectual functioning is directly related to family size and birth order, and Lynn (1969) provided strong evidence for a curvilinear relationship between parental distance from children of the same sex as the parent and children's cognitive style and problem-solving ability. Yet, despite such evidence for the importance of familial factors in both emotional and cognitive areas, most recent personality theories disregard marriage and family, partly because of the substantial shift in thinking that different orientation requires. As Haley (1975) indicated, the change from an individual to a family viewpoint necessitates a change in thinking about behavior causations: "...the 'cause' of behavior no longer resides within the person, but in the context of other people" (p. 4).

Jackson (1967), in elaborating a familial context approach to understanding personality and psychopathology, stated:

> We will move from individual assessment to analysis of the contexts, or more precisely, the *system* from which individual conduct is inseparable...Since the family is the most influential learning context, surely a more detailed study of family process will yield valuable clues to the etiology of such typical modes of interaction (p. 139-140).

A change in approaches to both assessment and treatment is beginning in the mental health field. Framo (1975) commented on this shift in perspective.

> ...it's very difficult to change individuals solely through the one-to-one relationship with a professional; it is necessary to change contexts, especially intimate ones...Symptoms come to be viewed as by-products of pathological relationship events (p. 16).

We are in need of new theoretical, statistical, and practical approaches to the study of person x situation transactions. Ekehammer (1974) gave some suggestions for greater statistical refinements in the study of interactional patterns. Yet, this statistical rigor may well be premature in view of the need for more advances in conceptual frameworks and methods of information-gathering. Some indicators of paths to follow are seemingly naive naturalistic observations as in the frame analysis of Goffman (1974), global clinical reports by Spiegel (1971), and global qualitative ecological and naturalistic descriptions by Barker (1968), Moos (1974, 1976), and Patterson (1974).

Bronfenbrenner (1979) proposed a new approach to child development that takes into consideration the child's ecological environment. He conceives of this environment as a set of nested structures, from the microsystem, e.g., the home or classroom, to the macrosystem, the belief systmes or ideology of a specific culture. Bronfenbrenner's theory of human development concentrates on the process of understanding and controlling the environment, which gradually shifts from adult to child. The author describes existing research studies that take a descriptive, naturalistic approach: Children's institutions, day care, and preschool are among the areas considered. Bronfenbrenner's pioneering work has profound implications for the study of the family in its natural setting.

Avoidance in Methods

Traditional methodological practices have led to at least two unsatisfactory results: (a) artificiality and narrow empiricism, the study of individuals apart from the variables of affecting and being affected by them, and (b) atomism, the breakdown into smaller and more molecular variables within these individuals. To achieve rigorous control of subjects, we have studied them apart from their families and living systems. We have used artificial and atomistic languages, such as S-R, that fail to deal with the complexity and circularity of familial behavior. When the family has been studied at all, it has been approached in a fragmentary manner: Parent-child relationship, mothers, fathers, father-child relationship, and parents have been separately considered. There has been little significant study of the family as a whole (L'Abate, 1976).

Artificiality and Narrow Empiricism

In reconsidering the two disciplines of scientific psychology, experimental control and systematic correlation, Cronbach (1975) spoke of the importance of context:

> Instead of making generalization the ruling consideration in our research, I suggest that we reverse our priorities. An observer collecting data in one particular situation is in a position to appraise a practice or proposition in that setting, observing effects in context; in trying to describe and account for what happened he will give attention to whatever variables were controlled, but he will give equally careful attention to uncontrolled considerations, to personal characteristics and to events that occurred during treatment and measurement (pp. 124-125).

Empiricism for empiricism's sake is just as irrelevant as untestable theory. Cronbach's statement is reflective of a new turn in understanding of empiricism. Ideally, there will be more consideration of contextual effects and less use of methodology to discount these effects, as suggested by Broffenbrenner (1979).

Atomistic-Analytic Emphases

Traditionally we continue to split the person and environment; however, this split has been only the beginning. Persons are then divided into various intrapsychic variables, traits, and characteristics, and these in turn have been further subdivided into smaller and more "pure" variables, for the sake of getting closer to man's true "essence." In this process the object of study has become no better understood as a functioning human being.

The pendulum is swinging back and forth between atomism and holism. It is presently swinging away from the atomistic bias of the behaviorists. The new holism must be one which adequately describes and accounts for individual-environmental transactions in the immediate environment, that is, marriage and the family.

Avoidance in Training Procedures

At present, many factors are interacting to preserve the status quo in regard to considering the family as a legitimate unit of study and practice. Most classroom training follows directly from textbooks. Consequently, it is difficult to expect that in giving or receiving training, there will be much time or energy for presenting a viewpoint contradictory to that in the textbooks.

The bias in favor of individual treatment approaches that exists in traditional clinical practices perpetuates graduate training built around the same bias. The transactional relationship between mental health service agencies and the universities presently serves to promote sameness. Mental health centers want personnel trained most thoroughly in techniques of individual assessment and treatment, and this is what graduate schools produce. As a result, for mental health agencies that want a change in approach, well-trained family therapists are hard to find. Family approaches are still taught as a tangential or "special" topic in most graduate schools. Courses in individual assessment techniques are still mandatory and the major mode of training. By the time the student has mastered these skills, he is faced with foreign language exams, dissertations, and the like, and has little time left over for gaining knowledge and experience in family research and practice.

Avoidance in Clinical Practice: Evaluation and Therapy

Clinical procedures have not fared much better than experimental methodologies. Diagnostically, a psychiatric model has been followed; virtually all tests and other methods of assessment are oriented toward an intrapsychic view rather than an interactional one. Objective assessment techniques involve, almost solely, assessment for self-definition, as the examinee gives it. If and when we attempt to extrapolate from the individual to familial

context, it is done through a long chain of questionable
inferences; for example, by trying to ascertain the individual's view of his/her relationship to his/her family of
origin through his/her responses to Rorschach cards or TAT
pictures. Tests constructed to evaluate individuals have
been inappropriately used to assess dyadic relations, either
between mates or between parent and child. Instruments
such as parental ratings or children's family drawings have
been used to get information on how the family context more
directly; such attempts are still unidirectional and fail
to show the multidirectional complexity of family transactions (Broffenbrenner, 1979).

Therapeutically, the majority of patients are treated
with individually-oriented techniques or brought together
in therapy groups, isolated from the family contexts. In
behaviorally-oriented interventions as well, the viewpoint
is still strictly reactive. One example is found in the
report of Engeln, Knutson, Laughy, and Garlington (1968),
who trained a mother to obtain greater compliance and cooperation from her child. The authors candidly pointed out
that this improvement was accompanied by a deterioration in
the husband-wife relationship which, by the very nature of
the limited intervention, had to be disregarded. Unfortunately, behaviorally-oriented therapists usually fail to
report these kinds of results, so there is no way of knowing how many "successful" behavioral treatments may have
produced this kind of "system correction." Only when the
notion of system is considered (Jones, Reid, & Patterson,
1974; LeBow, 1972; Patterson, 1974) will behaviorists and
other practitioners become aware of and be able to take
steps to overcome limitations on the impact of "successful"
interventions.

The Family as a Quantum Jump

Moving from individuals to a consideration of their
relations with their families is a quantum jump that we are
not ready to make, theoretically, empirically, or applicatively. Perhaps the fear of such a leap arises partly from
frustration with intraindividual variables. Despite intense efforts, we have been frustrated even at the individual
level; the feeling may be that a more molar family level of
investigation is too complex to approach. Though common
sense and an increasing body of theory and data on family
relations point to the efficacy of this orientation, the
cognitive shift required will not be easy to make. Such a
jump will necessitate throwing away a baggage of concepts,
ideas, and techniques in going from the individual to his

most basic dyad (either husband-wife or parent-child) and then to his most immediate context, his family.

Hopeful Signs: Change for the Future

This shift in orientation calls for major conceptual evolution, amounting to what Kuhn (1962) referred to as a paradigm shift. The methodological and conceptual retooling required, both in the clinic and the laboratory, is so great that considerable time may elapse before such a change can occur. Presently, it is clear that clinical applications, as seen in the field of family therapy, are moving ahead of theoretical and methodological advances (Foley, 1974; Glick & Kessler, 1974). Still, advances are being made in all these areas.

In Theory. The family therapy movement has increased interest in theoretical approaches that can encompass both the individual and his family (L'Abate, 1976). Communication theory (Watzlawick, 1967), systems theory, and the like are the direct outcome of clinical applications. Marriage and the family have received greater attention from psychologists in the last few years, as evidenced by the works of Foá and Foá (1974), Murstein (1971; 1974), Bengston and Black (1973), Hartup and Lempers (1973), and Rausch et al. (1974).

Gilmore (1974) devoted 36 pages out of 291 to a discussion and review of the family as a factor in personality formation, self-esteem, and in the backgrounds of productive persons high in academic achievement, creativity, and leadership. McNeill's book (1969) also contained a number of references to the role of the family in the socialization process. Hopefully, with the increase in contributions of this type, the integration of the family approach into the mainstream of academic psychology and its textbooks will be soon in coming (Kantor & Lehr, 1975).

In Research. There are a great many difficulties in research on the family, as was well documented by Jacobs' (1975) review. Yet, as a result of clinical applications and theoretical advances, an increase in research activities is bound to be forthcoming. A significant step will have taken place in this area when the methodological sophistication of American social psychology, as well as its concepts and theories (Deutsch & Kraus, 1965; Shaw & Costanzo, 1970) are applied to the study of the family. The family will then become the real testing ground for many of these abstract theories and concepts. As life's most important unit of continuously interacting personalities, the family is the matrix for many of social psychology's conceptual entities, even though those concepts have been developed through artificial and adventitious groupings united solely for the purpose of research. As the original small group, the family will become the ultimate group in which the utility of many social psychological concepts and theories will stand or fall. Strauss' review article on the social and cultural influences of pathology (1979) contains several references to family studies, a hopeful sign that serious research is increasing. Another sign is the mushrooming of new journals which are publishing important theoretical articles, many of them by psychologists.

In Clinical Practice. The family therapy movement is undergoing an explosion akin to that of behavior modification a decade or so ago. Two American professional organizations are active in representing family therapy and its associated theory and research. The Association of Marriage and Family Therapists has as one of its major concerns accreditation of training and certification of the competency of its members. A report on those of its members who are accredited to supervise in family therapy (Everett, 1980) indicates that 26 percent, the largest proportion, are psychologists. The American Family Therapy Association is also interdisciplinary, but focuses on the more senior level. Requirements for membership are five years of clinical experience beyond the terminal clinical degree and five years of experience teaching in the field. Researchers who have made significant contributions to understanding families, and have a comparable depth of experience, are also members. Five of the 21 members of the elected Board of Directors are psychologists, as is the Executive Secretary.

Psychologists with an interest in the family have pointed out the need for more useful and valid measures of theoretical constructs (Gurman & Kniskern, 1978) and for consideration of the family context in the prediction of schizophrenia (Klorman, Strauss, & Kokes, 1977; Strauss, 1977). Unfortunately, the absence of a systems perspective in this work makes it difficult to cope with families at more than a simplistic and mechanistic level; conceptually, these approaches do not seem to have gone far beyond the reactive level of conceptualization (L'Abate, 1969; L'Abate, et al., 1978). Cromwell and Keeney (1979) have, however, used a systems theory approach to develop a training model for diagnosing marital and family system.

Conclusion

Being latecomers to a field can be a blessing rather than a curse. We can profit by mistakes of others who were there first, i.e., sociologists, anthropologists, psychiatrists, social workers, and family life educators. The major shortcoming of most of these disciplines is lack of rigorous theorizing and theory-testing through empirical or near empirical methodologies. We have a tradition of rigor in research methodology unsurpassed in the social sciences and a tradition of training that fosters bit-by-bit theory testing. This is the major professional asset that can be capitalized on in confronting the immediate and relevant "person x situation interactions" that take place within the family. While there are many reasons why we have avoided specifying the nature of such interactions, there are just as many reasons to rise to the challenge of studying the New Frontier of Psychology: The family.

References

Barker, R. C. Ecological psychology: Concepts and methods for studying the environment of human behavior. Stanford: Stanford University Press, 1968.

Bem, D. J., & Allen, A. On predicting some of the people some of the time: The search for cross-situational consistencies in behavior. Psychological Review, 1974, 81, 506-520.

Bem, D. J., & Funder, D. C. Predicting more of the people more of the time: Assessing the personality of situations. Psychological Review, 1978, 85, 485-501.

Bengston, V. L., & Black, K. D. Intergenerational relations and continuities in socialization. In P. B. Baltes & K. W. Schaie (Eds.), Life-span developmental psychology: Personality and socialization. New York: Academic Press, 1973.

Bowers, K. S. Situationism in psychology: An analysis and critique. Psychological Review, 1973, 80, 307-336.

Bronfenbrenner, U. The ecology of human development: Experiments by nature and design. Cambridge, MA: Harvard University Press, 1979.

Craik, A. H. The personality research paradigm in environmental psychology. In S. Wapner, S. B. Bohen, & B. Kaplan (Eds.), Experiencing the environment. New York: Plenum, 1976.

Cromwell, R. E., & Keeney, B. P. Diagnosing marital and family systems: A training model. The Family Coordinator, 1979, 28, 101-108.

Cronback, L. J. Beyond the two disciplines of scientific psychology. American Psychologist, 1975, 30, 116-127.

Deutsch, M., & Krauss, R. M. Theories in social psychology. New York: Basic Books, 1965.

Dunne, E. E., & L'Abate, L. The family taboo in psychology textbooks. Teaching of Psychology, 1978, 5, 115-117.

Ekehammar, B. Interactionism in personality from a historical perspective. Psychological Bulletin, 1974, 81, 1026-1048.

Endler, N. S., & Magnusson, D. Toward an interactional psychology of personality. Psychological Bulletin, 1976, 83, 956-974.

Engeln, R., Knutson, J., Laughy, L., & Garlington, W. Behavior modification techniques applied to a family unit--a case study. Journal of Child Psychology and Psychiatry and Allied Disciplines, 1968, 9, 245-252.

Everett, C. A. An analysis of AAMFT supervisors: Their identities, roles, and resources. Journal of Marital and Family Therapy, 1980, 6, 215-236.

Foa, U. G., & Foa, E. D. Societal structures of the mind. Springfield, IL: Thomas, 1974.

Foley, V. D. An introduction to family therapy. New York: Grune & Stratton, 1974.

Framo, J. L. Personal reflections of a family therapist. Journal of Marriage and Family Counseling, 1975, 1, 15-28.

Gilmore, J. V. The productive personality. San Francisco: Albion, 1974.

Glick, I. D., & Kessler, D. R. Marital and family therapy. New York: Grune & Stratton, 1974.

Goffman, E. Frame analysis: An essay on the organization of experience. New York: Harper & Row, 1974.

Gurman, A. S., & Kniskern, D. P. Research on marital and family therapy: Progress, perspective, and prospect. In S. L. Garfield & A. E. Bergin (Eds.), Handbook of psychotherapy and behavior change: An empirical analysis. New York: Wiley, 1978.

Haley, J. Why a mental health clinic should avoid family therapy. Journal of Marriage and Family Counseling, 1975, 1, 3-13.

Hartup, W. W., & Lempers, J. A problem in life span development: The interactional analysis of family attachments. In P. B. Baltes & K. W. Schaie (Eds.), Life-span developmental psychology: Personality and socialization. New York: Academic Press, 1973.

Jackson, D. D. The individual and the larger context. Family Process, 1967, 6, 139-147.

Jacobs, T. Family interaction in disturbed and normal families: Methodological and substantive review. Psychological Bulletin, 1975, 82, 33-65.

Jones, R. R., Reid, J. B., & Patterson, G. R. Naturalistic observation in clinical assessment. In P. Reynolds (Ed.), Advances in psychological assessment (Vol. 3). San Francisco: Jossey-Bass, 1975.

Kantor, D., & Lehr, W. *Inside the family.* San Francisco: Jossey-Bass, 1975.

Klorman, R., Strauss, J. S., & Kokes, R. F. Premorbid adjustment in schizophrenia...part III. The relationship of demographic and diagnostic factors to measures of premorbid adjustment in schizophrenics. *Schizophrenia Bulletin*, 1977, *3*, 214-225.

Kuhn, T. S. *The structure of scientific revolutions.* Chicago: University of Chicago Press, 1962.

L'Abate, L. (Ed.) *Models of clinical psychology.* (Georgia State College, School of Arts & Sciences, Research Paper No. 22). Atlanta: Georgia State College, 1969.

L'Abate, L. *Understanding and helping the individual in the family.* New York: Grune & Stratton, 1976.

L'Abate, L., Weeks, G. R., & Weeks, K. G. Pathology as transaction: A historical note. *International Journal of Family Counseling*, 1978, *6*, 60-65.

LeBow, M. D. Behavior modification for the family. In G. D. Erickson & T. P. Hofan (Eds.), *Family therapy: An introduction to theory and techniques.* Monterey, CA: Wadsworth, 1972.

Lynn, D. B. Curvilinear relation between cognitive functioning and distance of child from parent of the same sex. *Psychological Review*, 1969, *76*, 236-240.

McNeil, E. B. *Human socialization.* Belmont, CA: Brooks/Cole, 1969.

Moos, R. H. Assessment and impact of social climate. In P. McReynolds (Ed.), *Advances in psychological assessment* (Vol. 3). San Francisco: Jossey-Bass, 1975.

Moos, R. H. *The human context: Environmental determinants of behavior.* New York: Wiley, 1976.

Murstein, B. I. (Ed.) *Theories of attraction and love.* New York: Springer, 1971.

Murstein, B. I. *Love, sex, and marriage through the ages.* New York: Springer, 1974.

Patterson, G. R. Interventions for boys with conduct problems: Multiple settings, treatments and criteria. *Journal of Consulting and Clinical Psychology*, 1974, *42*, 471-481.

Rausch, H. L., Barry, W. A., Hertel, R. K., & Swain, M. A. *Communication, conflict, and marriage.* San Francisco: Jossey-Bass, 1974.

Shaw, M. E., & Costanzo, P. R. *Theories of social psychology.* New York: McGraw-Hill, 1970.

Spiegel, J. P. *Transactions: The interplay between individual, family, and society.* New York: Science House, 1971.

Strauss, J. S., Klorman, R., & Kokes, R. F. Premorbid adjustment in schizophrenia...part V. The implications of the findings for understanding, research and application. *Schizophrenia Bulletin*, 1977, *3*, 240-244.

Strauss, J. S. Social and cultural influences on psychopathology. *Annual Review of Psychology*, 1979, *30*, 397-415.

Watzlawick, P., Beavin, J. H., & Jackson, D. D. *Pragmatics of human communication: A study of interactional patterns, pathologies, and paradoxes*. New York: Norton, 1967.

Zajonc, R. B., & Markus, G. B. Birth order and intellectual development. *Psychological Review*, 1975, *82*, 74-88.

CHAPTER 2

The Family Taboo in Psychology Textbooks

Eugene E. Dunne and
Luciano L'Abate
Georgia State University

The frequency of family-related concepts in 60 texts is the basis for the authors' urging a greater consideration of relational factors.

Among practitioners, teachers, and researchers in the field of psychology, there is an accelerating disenchantment with traditional intrapsychic approaches to personality. This pervasive dissatisfaction with the overall predictive, diagnostic, and therapeutic value of many intrapsychic concepts points to a need for a move in new directions. Numerous recent articles (e.g., Bem & Allen, 1974; Bowers, 1973; Ekehammar, 1974) suggest that our intensive explorations of the individual *sans* his environment has inflicted us with a strong case of tunnel vision, and that we will find our way out of the tunnel not by a continued plodding toward the increasingly vague flickers of light at the end, but instead by breaking through the walls which encapsulate us, conceptually and methodologically. Recognition is growing that we must deal with the *interaction* of the person and his "situation" or "context" (Bateson, 1972; Bevan, 1968; Jenkins, 1974; L'Abate, 1969).

Unfortunately, recognition has not been accompanied frequently enough by specification of the nature of the "situation"; its definition is often vague, abstract, and difficult to comprehend. However, significant numbers of psychologists have turned attention to frames of reference which take account of the inevitability of marital and family influences on the individual. We are realizing that most traditional theoretical formulations have erred in promoting the idea that personality development occurs *in a vacuum*, away from the intimate antecedents and determinants that are the family. We are recognizing that our exclusion of this context, in which we spend two-thirds of our lifetimes (and in which our personalities and their behavioral manifestations are reinforced, repressed, distorted, or enhanced), has too often led to fragmented, arbitrary, vacuous results in the laboratory, and unnecessary frustration for both therapist and client in the clinic.

As a result, the "family" movement is undergoing an explosion of interest akin to that of behavior modification a decade ago, and the family is being systematically studied as the major determining context of the individual's development of personality and psychopathological symptomatology (Henry, 1965; L'Abate, 1975; Laing & Esterson, 1964; Lidz, 1973; and others), cognitive style (Lynn, 1969), intellectual functioning (Zajonc & Markus, 1975), health, creativity, and so on. The family therapy movement has produced not only a mushrooming supply of textbooks on these subjects (e.g., Boszormenyi-Nagy & Sparks, 1973; Foley, 1974; Kantor & Lehr, 1975) but an increasing interest in theoretical approaches that can encompass both the individual and his marital and family relationships (Foa & Foa, 1974; L'Abate, 1975; Watzlawick, Beavin & Jackson, 1967; among others).

Nonetheless, despite the fervent interest expressed in the upper echelons of academia concerning investigatory and clinical approaches to the family, and despite the more than apparent validity of such approaches, one does not have the impression that the information produced by these inquiries is being adequately disseminated to psychology students in the course of their training. Instead, it seems that a focus on the individual without his most immediate context is still the dominant focus in psychology (Framo, 1975; Haley, 1975), and that the family is still a "specialty topic" to which the student is exposed only very late in training if at all, and then only through his own devices and determination. If there continues to be a bias excluding family information, it can be objectively measured in our textbooks. This measurement is the purpose of the present investigation.

Method. To determine the extent to which the family receives consideration in textbooks, a count was made of page references to family-related terms (specifically: family; marriage; father, or father-child relationships; mother, or mother-child relationships; and birth order or ordinal position) in a representative sample of ten textbooks in each of six different areas of psychological specialization. The areas included were Child, Exceptional Child, Adolescence, Personality, Social, and Abnormal. This count for each textbook was divided by the total number of pages in that book and multiplied by 100 to yield a percentage of pages containing family-related information.

Table 1
Textbook References of Family Related Terms
(Rounded to Closest Number)

Area	n (Books)	Total Mean Pages	Family References Mean Pages	%	Range
Child	10	550	82	14.00	5.2-38
Exceptional Child	10	453	33	7.20	.4-32
Adolescence	10	525	49	9.30	4.1-18.8
Personality	10	484	4	.90	0- 2.6
Social	10	555	4	.76	0- 3.3
Abnormal	10	525	28	5.30	0- 7.9

Results. The percentages shown in Table 1 (even though inflated due to cross-referencing of family-related terms in these texts) are so small that a breakdown by type of reference will not be included here; clearly, in Social and Abnormal areas, we would be left with very small percentages indeed. As for general trends, scant attention is paid in our textbooks to the "Family" and "Marriage" topic areas. Information on parent-child relations has had little success in filtering down to the textbook level. Despite extensive and intensive study of the "Mother" role, and despite its undeniable importance to each of the specialization areas, it receives only marginal consideration in this sample of textbooks. References to the crucial "Father" role (see L'Abate, 1975) are still more limited. But the most slighted victim proved to be the area "Birth Order or Ordinal Position." In view of the abundance of ordinal position literature of the past 15 years indicating the powerful influence of that variable as a contributor to marital selection and adjustment (see Weller, Nathan & Hazi, 1974), and thus to the personality of both parents and children, we would expect it to be consistently represented in textbooks of all areas, and especially in Child, Personality, and Abnormal. This is far from the case.

It is clear from Table 1 that the more child-related the area (i.e., Child, Exeptional Child, Adolescence), the greater the mean percentage of family references. The saddening converse trend is that in Personality, Social, and Abnormal textbooks, family references are extremely scarce, and non-existent in some cases.

Another trend suggested by the data is that the more empirical an area (e.g., Social and Personality) the smaller the percentage of family-related references. Our textbooks from less empirical areas (such as Child, Adolescence, and Abnormal) reflect somewhat more attention to family factors.

Discussion. Some would argue that the survey textbooks which have served as our focus here have, as their *raison d'etre*, nothing more than a rather superficial overview of the field, and that we can therefore excuse a paucity of family-relevant information, since the family is a "special" topic. This, we think, a non-defensible viewpoint. An important part of the introductory student's interest in psychology stems from a desire to understand his own existence, and he will move farther toward that goal if his educational experience is tied to his most prevalent context. Much of our classroom training must follow the path of our textbooks, and if our textbooks promulgate a purely intrapsychic model, we might expect our teachings to be viewed as irrelevant. Would the man-on-the-street, in telling us of his problems or his joys, restrict his presentation to talk of "manifest anxiety," "ego strength," or "internal-external control"? Or would he instead speak of his family and other valued people in his life, and the way he relates with them? It should be a matter of concern, then, that our textbooks leave our students trying to believe (a) that we develop our social beings and our personalities, be they functional or abnormal, in a familial vacuum, unaffected by marriage, parenthood, divorces, births and deaths, and (b) that the family becomes entirely irrelevant after childhood and adolescence.

It might be argued that, even if introductory texts lack consideration of family-related topics, the advanced student will surely get proper exposure to this information through more specialized texts. Further informal research leads us to question this assumption. In a survey of texts on the specialized field of "socialization" within the area of "Advanced Child Psychology" (including, for example, Goslin, 1969; Clausen, 1968; Hoppe, Milton & Jimmel, 1970), we found that most discussions of the phenomenon are built around intrapsychic concepts (e.g., anxiety) rather than around interpersonal (parent-child or sibling-sibling) relationships. The percentages found were not higher but lower than those for survey textbooks. We can only wonder how much we know about socialization as it occurs in reality, since our writings describe the process as virtually devoid of relationships with external intimates. The topic of "interpersonal attraction," one of the hottest specialized topics in Social Psychology theory and research (Berscheid & Walster, 1969; Murstein, 1971; Huston, 1974), provides yet another example, with textbooks reflecting research data based on short-lived, contrived, and artificial encounter in the artificial vacuousness of the laboratory, the direct relevance of which to marital and familial happiness has not yet been adequately explored or reported. In brief, our "advanced" texts are presently doing no better job than our survey ones in providing information to today's psychologists (and parents).

The severity of the problem is made appallingly clear by the fact that 64% of the problems for which people seek help from professional psychologists are family problems—marital conflicts, parent-child or in-law relationships, deaths or illnesses of family members, etc. (Gurin, Veroff & Feld, 1960). Only 18% of the mental health caseload involves adjustment problems of the self. These data indicate that our clients do not live in a vacuum, and yet, from the earliest stages of training, we faithfully follow a psychiatric model in which the student is exposed almost solely to individual rather than familial approaches. The psychologist's early training includes exposure to a number of intrapsychic theories, with his knowledge of which he may later learn to use assessment techniques with individuals. If and when he attempts to extrapolate from the individual to the familial context, he does so through a rather magical and long chain of questionable inferences, on the basis of the patient's response to traditional intrapsychic tests (most with a proven lack of validity) or his response to the examiner himself standing in for members of a family *in absentia*. Our graduate schools continue to teach individual therapy techniques, however, as the main-stay of their training curricula, varied with some additional training in bringing individuals together in therapy groups, isolated from their family contexts. Family theory, assessment, and therapy are still taught as tangential or "special" topics. But by the time the student has mastered the mandatory individually-oriented therapy courses, he is faced with foreign language exams, dissertations, and the like, and has little time left for gaining knowledge in family research and practice. Rather than being trained to deal with the family system pathology which so often leads to ineffectiveness in treating individuals, the "fully" trained psychologist joins his colleagues in swapping humorous anecdotes about family interference in the treatment of his individual patients.

To excuse this situation by arguing that we are only

training our students for what the mental health agencies want (expertise in individual clinical or research skills) is to abdicate the university's leadership role. We submit that the professional stagnation which leads us to ignore such a potent reality as the family arises in large part from factors inside the field of psychology itself.

One such factor is the atomistic-analytic theoretical bias, through which the individual has had his environment conceptually sliced away from him as neatly as the doctor slices the umbilical cord. This is only the beginning of the operation, in the course of which the patient is surgically divided into various intrapsychic variables, traits, and characteristics, and these in turn further subdivided into smaller and more pure variables, for the sake of getting closer to man's "true essence." In our furious analytic trend, we have failed to notice that the patient has died, leaving us with a collection of divided parts, functioning neither in relation to each other nor in transaction with the immediate human and familial world. This orientation permeates our teachings from the earliest levels, and paradoxically, our frustration with its lack of results may have led us to fear unnecessarily the quantum theoretical leap which a consideration of the family entails. Nonetheless, there are conceptual frameworks available to provide guidance in our theoretical and methodological approaches to the study of the individual in transaction with his family (e.g., Barker, 1968; Goffman, 1974; Spiegel. 1971, and others). An inclusion of these more global interactional approaches in survey texts would provide students with important underpinnings for further learnings in research and clinical practice with families.

A second and related factor is the narrow empiricism which students are taught very early to accept unquestioningly. Cronbach (1975) has argued for a reversal of our priorities, suggesting that rather than blindly making experimental control and generalization the ruling concern in our research, we should shown more consideration for contextual effects, and less use of "refined" methodologies to obliterate those effects, pretending more understanding than we have. Too often our methodological and statistical "expertise" has led to experimentally elegant irrelevancies. Only by not shutting our own eyes to complexity will we be able to help our students develop vision equal to the task of exploring and helping families. Efforts toward that end (e.g., Raush, Berry, Hertel & Swain, 1974; Kantor & Lehr, 1975; Moos, 1974, 1976) deserve a place in our textbooks and our teachings.

References

Barker, R. G. *Ecological psychology: Concepts and methods for studying the environment of human behavior.* Stanford, CA: Stanford University Press, 1968.

Bateson, G. *Steps to an ecology of mind.* San Francisco, CA: Chandler, 1972.

Bem, D. J. & Allen, A. On predicting some of the people some of the time: The search for cross-situational consistencies in behavior. *Psychological Review*, 1974, *81*, 406-420.

Bersheid, E., & Walster, E. H. *Interpersonal attraction.* Reading, MA: Addison-Wesley, 1969.

Bevan, W. The contextual basis of behavior. *American Psychologist*, 1968, *23*, 701-714.

Boszormenyi-Nagy, I. E., & Sparks, G. *Invisible loyalties: Reciprocity in intergenerational family therapy.* Hagerstown, MD: Harper & Row, 1973.

Bowers, K. S. Situationism in psychology: An analysis and a critique. *Psychological Review*, 1973, *80*, 307-336.

Clausen, J. A. *Socialization and society.* Boston: Little, Brown, 1968.

Cronbach, L. J. Beyond the two disciplines of scientific psychology. *American Psychologist*, 1975, *30*, 116-127.

Ekehammar, D. Interactionism in personality from an historical perspective. *Psychological Bulletin*, 1974, *81*, 1026-1048.

Foa, U. G., & Foa, E. B. *Societal structures of the mind.* Springfield, IL: Charles Thomas, 1974.

Foley, V. D. *An introduction to family therapy.* New York: Grune & Stratton, 1974.

Framo, J. L. Personal reflections of a family therapist. *Journal of Marriage and Family Counseling*, 1975, *1*, 15-28.

Goffman, E. *Frame analysis: An essay on the organization of experience.* Cambridge, MA: Harvard University Press, 1974.

Goslin, D.A. (Ed.). *Handbook of socialization theory and research.* Chicago: Rand McNally, 1969.

Gurin, G., Veroff, J., & Feld, T. *Americans view their mental health.* New York: Basic Books, 1960.

Haley, J. Why a mental health clinic should avoid family therapy. *Journal of Marriage and Family Counseling*, 1975, *1*, 3-13.

Henry, J. *Pathways to madness.* New York: Random House, 1965.

Hoppe, R. A., Milton, G. A., & Jimmel, E. C. *Early experiences and the process of socialization.* New York: Academic Press, 1970.

Huston, T. L. (Ed.). *Foundations of interpersonal attraction.* New York: Academic Press, 1974.

Jenkins, J. J. Remember that old theory of memory? Well, forget it! *American Psychologist*, 1974, *29*, 785-795.

Kantor, D., & Lehr, W. *Inside the family: Toward a theory of family process.* San Francisco, CA: Jossey-Bass, 1975.

L'Abate, L. A communication-information model. In L. L'Abate (Ed.). *Models of clinical psychology.* Atlanta, GA: Georgia State College, 1969. Pp. 65-73.

L'Abate, L. Pathogenic role rigidity in fathers: Some observations. *Journal of Marriage and Family Counseling*, 1975, *1*, 69-79.

Laing, R. D., & Esterson, A. *Sanity, madness, and the family.* London: Tavistock Publications, 1964.

Lidz, T. *The origin and treatment of schizophrenic disorders.* New York; Basic Books, 1973.

Lynn, D. B. *Parental and sex role identification: A theoretical formulation.* Berkeley, CA: McCutchan Publishing, 1969.

Moos, R. H. Assessment and impact of social climate. In P. McReynolds (Ed.). *Advances in psychological assessment III.* San Francisco: Jossey-Bass, 1974.

Moos, R. H. *The human context: Enviromental determinants of behavior.* New York: Wiley-Interscience, 1976.

Murstein, B. I. (Ed.). *Theories of attraction and love.* New York: Springer, 1971.

Raush, H. L., Barry, W. A., Hertel, R. K., & Swain, M. A. *Communication, conflict, and marriage.* San Francisco: Jossey-Bass, 1974.

Spiegel, J. *Interactions: The interplay between individual, family, and society.* New York: Science House, 1971.

Watzlawick, P., Beavin, J., & Jackson, D. *Pragmatics of human communication: A study of interactional patterns, pathologies, and paradoxes.* New York: Norton, 1967.

Weller, L., Nathan, O., & Hazi, O. Birth order and marital bliss in Israel. *Journal of Marriage and the Family*, 1974, *36*, 794-797.

Zajonc, R. B., & Markus, G. B. Birth order and intellectual development. *Psychological Review*, 1975, *82*, 74-88.

Note

Address requests for reprints to Dr. Luciano L'Abate, Department of Psychology, Georgia State University, University Plaza, Atlanta, Georgia 30303.

SECTION I

THEORY AND METATHEORY

CHAPTER 3

A THEORY OF PERSONALITY DEVELOPMENT IN THE FAMILY*

The purpose of this chapter is to introduce a theory of personality development as it occurs within the context of the family. Following a formal approach to theory building, assumptions, and postulates, a number of models used for visual displays of the postulates will be elaborated upon and discussed as they relate to the overall formulation of the theory.

In determining how the personality of an individual is developed, many theories have tried to explain how personality formation occurs, when it develops, and what the prerequisites are for a final formation of personality. Most theories attempt to define personality growth and development as occurring in a vacuum, without any reference to the family as a significant contributor or influencer of individual personality growth and formation.

L'Abate (1976) developed a theory of personality development as it occurs over the lifespan of an individual within the family. According to Goldstein (1979), L'Abate's thesis "is that the most immediate social and cultural context of personality development is the family"; that is, the individual and the family are to be looked at together, not as separate entities. The contention is that the major matrix to be examined is the family and its transactional patterns of influence upon each member as they occur over space and time.

With psychoanalytic theories dominating the fifties and behavioral as well as humanistic theories covering the sixties, the emphasis upon the family did not increase until the seventies but has since remained a large and significant influence upon personality and therapeutic theories. L'Abate (Hansen & L'Abate, 1982) explained: "I really did it because it was an empty, free, open field, a field where no one had ventured-- there was no theory done specifically dealing with a personality theory developed within the family."

_____
*This chapter was written with the help of Joseph A. Robbins.

This personality theory could be viewed as a conceptual, theoretical model, as well as a clinical, testable model, empirically verifiable and capable of use by professionals who work with the family in a clinical setting. What counts is the relationship between the claims of a theorist and the evidence of that theory. As one would put it simply, "the ultimate proof of the pudding is in the application of the theory." This theory was developed formally, in order to formulate logical deductions as well as to test the theory empirically, both in the laboratory and in the clinic. By integrating a series of assumptions and postulates, one can arrive at several working models which are used to verify the theory as a whole and also to work with individuals within the family setting.

The framework of this theory uses assumptions as the starting point, or foundation, for theory building, which then develops into postulates, which are dependent only upon the validity of the assumptions, leading finally to a series of models used to test these postulates in the laboratory or in the clinic. The framework comprises: the two assumptions, which include the ideas of both space and time as premises upon which to build the theory; the three postulates, which include self-differentiation, priorities, and congruence; and the seven models. It is important to keep in mind that assumptions do not need demonstration or experimental proof (they are self-evident premises) to verify their validity. They are independent of one another although both can be interrelated, as we shall see later. Postulates, on the other hand, must be built upon assumptions because, by themselves, they are "neither knowable directly nor inferable, deductively or inductively" (L'Abate, 1964). Therefore, they must be totally dependent upon assumptions of both space and time in order to be justified as beliefs or truths (e.g., self-differentiation must incorporate dimensions of both space and time). Also important is that postulates must be dependent upon each other, verifiable only when one postulate contains the other postulates (e.g., the postulate of congruence must contain both postulates of self-differentiation and priorities).

Assumptions

In an earlier work, L'Abate (1964) proposed a series of assumptions and postulates by which the individual developed from the assumptions of levels and continua into the postulates of space, time, and organization.

The current theory incorporates the earlier assumptions of levels and continua into his present assumptions of space and time, thereby showing the basic, self-evident premise of space and time.

The assumption of space includes the development of movement and perception by an individual, all nonverbal aspects of communication, and will be considered here the structural aspect of the theory. The assumption of time, on the other hand, includes the development of controls and higher processes, all verbal aspects of communication, and will be considered here the functional aspect of the theory.

Space

How does one perceive and move about in his/her environement? Without an idea of space, the individual would not be able to perceive the environment in terms of distance (e.g., one's body relative to another body) and consequently would not be able to move about as a result of this loss of perception.

Five stages of spatial conceptions (L'Abate, 1964) are used in perceiving distances and in moving about. They are: (a) _action space_--a location where movements occur, (b) _body space_--the awareness of directions and distances in relation to one's own body, (c) _object space_--the relationship between objects and body space, (d) _map space_--the elaboration and unification of concrete spatial experiences into mental maps, and (e) _abstract space_--the ability to deal with abstract spatial concepts necessary to problem solving and to understanding the multidimensionality of space. With a consideration of these spatial concepts and their relevancy to the assumption of space, the concept of _approach-avoidance_ is formulated in relation to body perceptiveness and motionality at the horizontal level.

Spatially and horizontally, approach-avoidance refers to how an individual, dyad, or family meets, deals with, attacks, or withdraws nonverbally from particular situations (be it stress, a crisis, or a fistfight): approach if the situation is pleasurable and avoidance if it is painful. Hence, within the family, we are taught as children (distance-regulated) what to approach and what to avoid (e.g., approach candy but avoid a stranger with candy), and this carries over into our overall formation as individuals.

Structurally, the assumption of space is divided

vertically into four levels (two major headings) of personality. At the <u>descriptive level</u> are found the <u>self-presentational level</u>, which is appearances of the family in public (i.e., facades), and the <u>phenotypical level</u>, which is the actual functioning of individuals in the family and which includes the concept of approach-avoidance (in other words, how we as children appear to the public when we buy candy will be dependent upon how we are taught to approach candy within our families). At the <u>explanatory level</u>, the <u>genotypical level</u> includes underlying secrets, myths, etc., of the individual in the family, which influences the phenotypical and self-presentational levels. If we can understand what happens at the genotypical level, we can consequently know why individuals in a family appear as they do at the self-presentational level. The <u>historical level</u>, which temporally influences the genotypical level (as antecedent determinants) will be discussed later under the assumption of time. "The notion of levels and the degree of functioning in the family structure will depend in part on the degree of congruency between and among levels; that is, it is important how behavior manifests or presents itself at the appearance level, or facade. However, it is just as important to consider how this level is consistent or inconsistent with the other levels, i.e., phenotypical, genotypical, and historical" (L'Abate, 1976).

Therefore, the use of all levels is important in understanding how an individual in a family functions as s/he does. When we negotiate with our "selfs," we are communicating at the genotypical level; when we negotiate with our loved ones, or "intimate others," we are transacting at the phenotypical level; consequently, when we negotiate with the public, we are expressing ourselves at the presentational level.

In summary, then, the assumption of space is structured, both horizontally and vertically; since space is a characteristic of behavior, an understanding of approach-avoidance and of the four vertical levels will provide explanations for why individuals in families act as they do and for the inconsistencies that occur as a result of incongruencies between levels.

<u>Time</u>

The assumption of time refers to the amount of time for any particular action to take place within a given context. Movements in space take time. Therefore, although both assumptions are independent of each other, their interrelatedness suggests compatibility and conformity toward developing an understanding of personality formation within the family, as will be shown in the postulates of this theory.

The assumption of space pertains to nonverbal actions and motions, i.e., facial and body expressions. The assumption of time, however, deals with thought and verbal processes.

Time in so many ways controls our lives every day (e.g., What time is it? How long did it take you to do this?), so much so that three dimensions have been conceptualized in order to understand the pervasiveness of time. They are: (a) <u>historical development</u>, (b) <u>speed</u>, and (c) <u>perspective</u>. Historical development refers to past, antecedent determinants that might affect and influence present and future actions. Speed deals mainly with reaction time and how long a particular action will take for completion. Finally, the concept of perspective takes place when we view past, present, or future actions as they relate to ourselves or to other family members.

Basic to the assumption of time is the concept of <u>discharge-delay</u>, which refers to the time it takes to complete an action (e.g., thinking quickly vs. slowly). Discharge-delay can also be related to other concepts of similar temporal meaning (i.e., extraversion-intraversion, excitation-inhibition, impulsivity-reflectivity).

If the child within the family learns how to approach or avoid certain objects or persons, that same child can also be taught how to express him/herself in thought and deed in relation to the time it takes for expression. The child "learns when to delay and when to discharge. He gradually becomes aware that he must achieve greater control over his impulses if he wants to achieve the kind of gratification he seeks (praise, reward, etc.). The polarities of discharge and delay, therefore, subsume a continuum of control. A balance in controls brings about an even greater balance in spatial movements" (L'Abate, 1964, pp. 87-88).

Within the family, the assumption of time occurs through the use of <u>information processing</u> (Fig. 1), a systems concept (sociological) which explains patterns

of communication according to a circular model of
interactions between different subsystems. Information
processing is composed basically of five components:
input (space and emotionality); mediation (thinking and
planning functions, processing of thoughts into
actions), output (actions), and feedback (awareness of
the consequences of one's actions), all within a cultural context.

When these five components are placed together in a
circular model, a process will occur, whether within an
individual or a family. Any variation in the time it
takes for this process to occur will produce different
types of output, according to the speed of processing,
as it occurs within an individual and the family. An
example of information processing can be explained as
follows: the family as a system will receive information through the mediational channel and will finally
take action upon the received information through the
output level and back to where it came from (the environment). The family will usually be aware of its
actions through the process of feedback. Consequently,
this feedback will be used either to change the
family (variety feedback) or to keep it steady (constancy feedback).

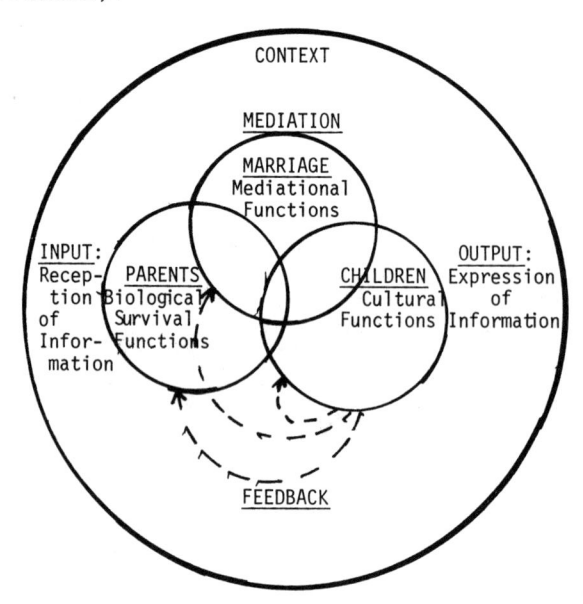

Figure 1. An Information-Processing Model of Personality Development in the Family

When the concept of information processing is combined with discharge-delay, we can understand how a different output might be produced, depending upon how slow or how fast information is processed. Of primary importance is the mediational subsystem, as it mediates input with output through the time it takes to receive and process information and put this information to use through action. This time sequence can be very short (discharge) or very long (delay), producing completely different behavioral outcomes in individuals and families.

The subsystem of mediation could be apprehended as "self, . . .implying that the unique way each individual links reception of information to its expression represents what that individual is: its self" (L'Abate, 1976, p. 64). It is here that feelings and emotions must be distinguished and differentiated so that a healthy awareness of oneself develops. If thinking, feeling, and action are congruent with each other, that individual will develop with a healthy attitude toward him/herself and others. If they are not congruent (i.e., if feeling is disturbed), the other subsystems will also be disturbed.

Space and Time

The assumptions of space and time play an important role in determining how individuals will act, react, interact, and transact with their families and environments, in relation to how they are structured (approach-avoidance/levels of behavior) and how they function (discharge-delay/information processing). We are now ready to proceed to the postulates of this theory, remembering that the postulates must rely entirely on the sturdiness of the assumptions. If the assumptions of space and time are sturdy and solid, we have a good chance that our postulates, which are built upon the assumptions, will also remain sturdy and thus will be able to withstand the strong winds and high tides of critical analysis and clinical applicability.

Postulates

In talking about the postulates of this theory, the assumptions of space and time must be included in each postulate if the theory is to remain strong and free of discrepancies. Also, all three postulates must include each other for the affirmation of a viable theory of personality development in the family. The postulates include <u>self-differentiation</u> (family formation), <u>priorities</u> (family functioning), and <u>congruence</u> (family transactions). A discussion of each will follow.

Self-Differentiation

Rather than defining the "self" with oneself (in a vacuum), the self in the family implies the definition of self by intimate others in a reciprocal, ongoing process, the self as defined by self plus the definition of others. In other words, I as an individual cannot define myself adequately until I look at the family I have grown up with over time.

To understand the concept of self-differentiation, one might best review other concepts that imply nearly the same meaning as self-differentiation. To have good <u>interpersonal relationships</u>, we as individuals must be able to be aware of our selves (thoughts, feelings, actions) in a positive, or congruent, way before we can attempt to understand and be aware of other persons with whom we interact (in other words, we are able to differentiate between ourselves and others). To be <u>responsible</u> to others, we must be able to be responsible to ourselves (e.g., basic needs established); therefore, we must be able to differentiate between our own responsibilities and others'. Finally, to <u>respect</u> others' needs, feelings, prejudices, we must be able to respect ourselves, our wants, feelings, prejudices, which mainly occurs through the process of awareness, by which we differentiate between our needs and feelings, and those of other persons. It can be seen, then, that for one to self-differentiate, one must set clear boundaries on one's own feelings, roles, responsibilities, in order to function as an independent "self," of a self-differentiated individual.

> Self-differentiation applies to how an individual learns and becomes able to be clear about oneself: (a) to distinguish various emotional states within onself,. . .sadness from joy, etc.; (b) to distinguish what is part of oneself and what is not in terms of responsibilities, role allocation, perceptions, ideas, opinions; (c) to reject what does not pertain to oneself and to agree and to disagree congruently, that is, with all of one's being and assert one's self-importance and status relevant to the situation; (d) to maintain charge and control of one's feelings, . . .etc.; (e) to assert oneself helpfully and hurtlessly in a positive,

nonjudgmental fashion (L'Abate, 1976, p. 73).

How then does self-differentiation become a postulate, in relation to the assumptions of this theory? Referring to the assumption of space, self-differentiation occurs at the genotypical level, usually at inaccessible depths of awareness, where the individual might not be congruent with the presentational or phenotypical levels of functioning. Therefore, functionality occurs when expressions at the self-presentational, phenotypical, and genotypical levels are congruent with each other, whereas incongruencies between the levels produce dysfunctionalities as a result of the inability to express, adequately and appropriately, at the proper place, time, or in the proper fashion, one's vulnerability, i.e., hurts, fears of being hurt (L'Abate, 1973).

Temporally, how we interact with our families over time will determine how we are able to differentiate ourselves from our families and from others. Systems concepts of biological, psychological, and cultural systems are used to develop an understanding of how we develop as self-differentiated individuals over a period of time. In this view, we as biological systems are born into the cultural system (the family) and we immediately begin to transact (reciprocal relationship) together as one; in other words, the biological system is dependent solely upon the family for its needs (physical, emotional). Later (around the age of 2), we begin to develop into psychological systems, able to differentiate between ourselves and our families. Therefore, the more we are able to develop into our psychological selves over time, within and away from our families, the more differentiated we become as individuals or independent "selfs" (L'Abate, 1969).

To test the postulate of self-differentiation, the concept of the symbiotic-autistic continuum was borrowed from Margaret Mahler. With this continuum, a continuum of likeness was used to understand further the concept of self-differentiation. According to this curvilinear model, the individual moves along a continuum from symbiosis ("I am you"), sameness ("I am like you, most of the time"), and similarity to differentness ("I am me"), oppositeness ("I am the opposite of you"), and autism ("I am not"). That is, the more differentiated the person, the nearer the center of the continuum will the individual be found. If s/he is undifferentiated, that person will be found at either extreme of the continuum.

Self-differentiation is not stage- or age-specific but is an ongoing and continuous process of growth and development into our "selfs." Referring again to the concepts of biological, psychological, and cultural systems, if the individual remained at the biological level of functioning (instead of growing into the psychological system), s/he would be symbiotic in behavior, totally dependent upon the cultural system. Symbiosis is a term used to describe families who are as one, totally dependent upon each other, without any individual "selfs" at all. It must be stressed that we all begin at this level of development, and it is only when we develop into our "psychological systems" that differentiation takes place: thus do we establish who we are over time, in relation to where we came from.

On the other hand, if we develop too quickly into our "psychological systems," as a result of rebellious or conflictual attitudes within the family, we then develop more autistically, alienated from ourselves as well as others. To define ourselves, we must include the definitions of others (our intimates or significant others).

Referring to our assumptions of space and time, spatially, the continuum of likeness implies an approach-avoidance relationship, in terms of distance between ourselves and others. At the levels of functioning, there must be a congruency between levels, which only occurs according to how well we are aware of ourselves to ourselves and to others, being consistent privately (at home) and publicly. Temporally, the continuum of likeness takes on a discharge-delay relationship, whereas the more symbiotic we are, the more we delay our processes, actions; vice-versa, the more we discharge, the more we become autistic (e.g., get angrier quickly). For the undifferentiated person, time will also be undifferentiated and, consequently, meaningless to the individual: that is, for the extremes of symbiosis-autism, time will be of no meaning; in the sameness-oppositeness categories, time will be focused upon abnormally, either upon the past or the future; for the similarity-differentness individual, the present is focused upon with a healthful (relativistic) perspective of the past and the future.

Our increase in self-differentiation needs conflict, a necessary component toward helpful change and differentiation, useful in that the dialectic between thesis and antithesis produces necessary changes that lead to a more differentiated person or family. In this <u>dialectical</u> view of differentiation, symbiosis-autism, sameness-oppositeness, and similarity-differentness could conflict with each other (i.e., two idea types could clash) to produce changes that result in a possible shift along the continuum of likeness.

Out of this dialectical viewpoint, the "A-R-C" model, the letters of which stand for <u>apathy</u>, <u>reactivity</u>, and <u>conductivity</u>, has been developed (Hansen & L'Abate, 1982). <u>A</u>pathy refers to the conflict within the symbiotic-autistic range of behavior, in which abuse, atrophy, or a lack or feeling, or emotion, is present. <u>R</u>eactivity, which occurs at the sameness-oppositeness levels of behavior, is characterized by repetitive husband-wife, parent-child conflicts resulting from strained relationships that occur because of the rigidity inherent at this level of conflict. <u>C</u>onductivity refers to the "helpful" conflict, which results in the similarity-differentness categories of functioning, helpful in that communication that is transacted here is the result of differentiated individuals being congruent with each other, responding to each other intimately and affectively. These three types of dialectical conflict vary in manner and in results--"hurtful" if no change occurs and "helpful" if positive change occurs.

Finally, most self-differentiation occurs at the cognitive and affective levels, i.e., the verbal and cognitive levels (time) and the nonverbal and affective levels (space). For self-differentiation to occur, congruency between both cognitive and affective levels must exist and must be consistent within the individual and the family. A recent study by Bryson (1978) found that the less differentiated individual tends to communicate bipolarly, i.e., either quite rigidly (digital) or so loosely as to be meaningless. Those persons who are classified within the sameness-oppositeness categories "are characterized as cognitively, affectively, and psychologically simple" (p. 30). In other words, the individual would either conform to or react against others within his/her scope of sensitivity. Those who are in the similarity-differentness categories, however, are characterized as

> cognitively, affectively, and psychologically complex individuals who are neither complete conformists nor non-conformists. Instead they are

> guided by their own internally-generated standards reflecting high levels of autonomy in thought and action. (p. 33)

How does the self-differentiated person contrast with the extremes of the continuum of likeness? Those who are differentiated and found toward the middle of the continuum are most likely to compare with Maslow's "self-actualized" person, autonomous and independent, able to appreciate how others are similar to or different from themselves, and includes those who are able to relate creatively to others on an interpersonal level. For those toward the extremes (sameness-oppositeness), digital thinking and alternating behavior are the norms, usually resulting in dysfunctional communication patterns (e.g., dictator, activist, passivist). The behavior of those who are found at the very extreme patterns of behaviors (symbiosis-autism) ranges through extreme dependency upon primary persons (mother-child), denial of reality, withdrawal, and destructiveness toward themselves and others.

Therefore, as we move along the continuum of likeness from the center toward symbiosis, we find that (according to approach-avoidance, discharge-delay), one becomes more passive and will delay in thought processing as one approaches and depends upon another. As one moves from the center toward autism, activity is increased, and the person will discharge rapidly as the person avoids others and, eventually, him/herself.

In closing this discussion on the postulate of self-differentiation, we might want to review briefly how differentiation occurs over a lifetime, not at particular stages in our development. From birth in our families until death, we are always going to be increasing or decreasing our differentiating capabilities, regardless of whether we are single or married, living with our families or away from them. In talking about how the family influences the child, L'Abate and L'Abate (1977) focused upon transactions that occur which possibly hinder needed differentiated growth within the child.

> If parents demand of their child conformity to their wishes and commands and in so doing take all self-determination away from the child, the only choices for the child are either to obey and conform and lose self-determination, or oppose, rebel, disobey, and learn to determine oneself through

opposition. Therefore, if we have learned to
define ourselves in opposition to our parents, it
is very likely that we will carry over such a pattern into our marriages. (p. 50)

The same process is reported in Chapters 5, 6, and 7,
as related to a similar concept called the "scripting"
process, in which parents tell the children, "Be the
same; be like us!" "A script is an ongoing program,
developed in early childhood under parental influences,
which directs the individual's behavior in the most
important aspects of his life" (p. 72).

If this is the case, this early formalization will
then continue throughout life, with these same precon-
ceived notions of oneself, and will consequently
affect other relationships, especially mating and marriage. If a couple should decide to get married and if
they have not been able to differentiate themselves
before entering into marriage, there is a low probability that increased self-differentiation will occur
unless they redefine themselves according to the present, not to the past where most of their patterns of
behavior have occurred. "To be helpful and to be different, one needs to extricate oneself from one's past
and to be able to assert oneself according to the present demands, which are inevitably different from those
of the past. If the same hurtful, unclear ways are
perpetuated, dysfunction becomes inevitable" (p. 111).

As we have seen, self-differentiation plays an
important role in how we as individuals develop
throughout our lives into what we are or could become.
As we continue to our next postulate, priorities, it is
best to keep in mind the concept of self-differentiation
and how it might play an important role in how we determine the priorities in our lives.

Priorities

In the first postulate, self-differentiation, we
reviewed how the individual and the family are formed
over the life cycle and the factors that contribute to
the development of differentiation. In the second
postulate, we will deal with how individuals in a family structure themselves according to priorities that
are established and stressed. If there is a relative,
flexible balance of priorities over the entire life
cycle, we can assume that the individuals within the
family are differentiated healthfully and are somewhat
consistent in establishing priorities for themselves

and their families.

Other concepts that are related to priorities might include: (a) <u>solidarity</u> (association and consensus within the family), (b) <u>roles</u> (implicit vs. explicit), (c) <u>loyalties</u> (invisible and transgenerational), (d) <u>myths</u>, and (e) <u>resources</u>. We can see that most of these concepts will be at the genotypical level of functioning, that is, below the level of self-awareness, and present only when they are manifested at the phenotypical/presentational levels. It is the last concept that one needs to focus on, for it relates directly to the postulate of priorities in how individuals in a family function and structure themselves. These priorities will be elaborated in Chapters 4, 6, 8, and 9. Therefore, here we shall attempt to link the postulate of priorities to the assumptions of space and time.

Spatially and at the horizontal level, the priorities of one's life will be determined by how often a certain priority is approached or avoided in terms of frequency. Vertically, one's priorities must be congruent at all levels of functioning (that is, do our priorities at the self-presentational level match our phenotypic/genotypic priorities?), appearing and actually functioning consistently at the same time.

Temporally, within the continuum of discharge-delay, the amount of time one spends with certain activities, or priorities, will depend upon how one selectively discharges or delays the time spent in those priorities. When this relates to information processing, our perceptions of different priorities will be used to process these priorities, act upon them, and on the basis of feedback, reassess, change, or maintain these priorities, according to how much time is spent in the process. Also, how priorities change over the entire family life cycle (marriage, parenthood, retirement) will determine at the historical level (space) how one will determine his/her priorities at the genotypic, phenotypic, and self-presentational levels of functioning.

In relation to the postulate of self-differentiation, if priorities are not properly differentiated, they will be used dysfunctionally and will result, because of the lack of differentiation over the family life cycle, in abnormal or insufficient formation of future priorities. For example, if the parents focus upon the children rather than themselves during the early part of the family life cycle, the parents will have a hard time dealing with themselves in old age and thus will have to formulate a new set of priorities on which to base their existence, a suddenness that can cause problems (i.e., divorce, separation, suicide).

Finally, how do priorities relate to actual functioning within the family? Who gets top priority within the family? As will be discussed later (models), two models of priorities are used to determine how priorities are ranked and stressed. One model deals with intra- and extrafamilial priorities (i.e., self, marriage, children, nuclear family vs. the extended family, friends at work, leisure activities), and the other concerns the relationship between the parents, marriage, and the children--who gets top priority within the family?

We have seen so far how the family is formed according to self-differentiation (how each member contributes to family differentiation) and how self-differentiation influences what priorities will be established within the family. Our last postulate, congruence, will take into consideration assumptions of both space and time, and the postulates of self-differentiation and priorities.

Congruence

The last postulate, congruence, deals with communication patterns within the family, which is called "helpful" communication and which Virginia Satir calls "leveling." It is from Satir's work in family therapy that some concepts have been borrowed to complete the last postulate of personality development within the family.

How is congruence defined? According to Goldstein (1979), "congruence is defined as the avoidance of dysfunctional patterns and the use of the self in a way that allows congruence between awareness and behavior as well as between words and deeds" (p. 322).

What, then, are these dysfunctional patterns of communication which make up the incongruent types of personalities? As a way to understand and to relate the postulate of congruence with a visual display of behavior, an <u>orthogonal paradigm</u> (Fig. 2) is used to understand and to identify initially certain types of dysfunctional patterns that develop from incongruencies within the individual and the family. These four patterns of incongruent behaviors (evolving from the assumptions of space and time) are <u>blaming</u> (avoidance), <u>placating</u> (approach), <u>distracting</u> (discharge), and <u>computing</u> (delay).

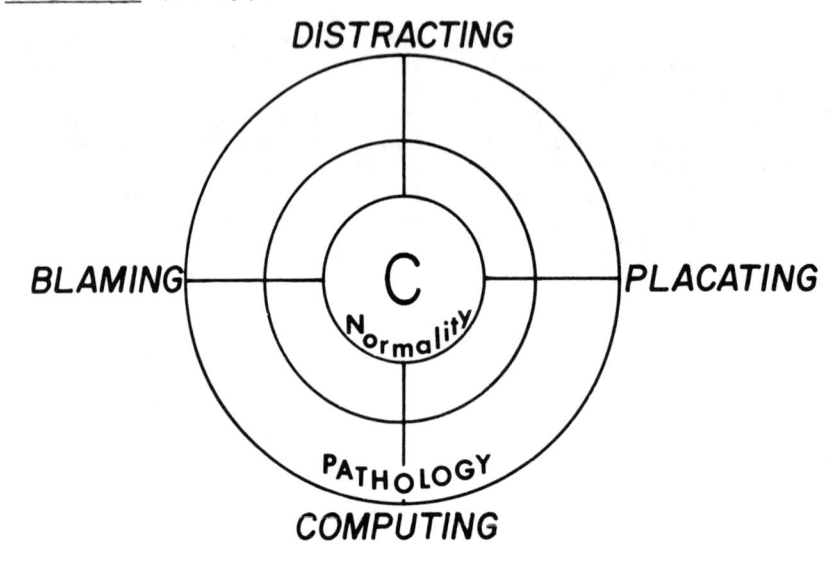

```
                    DISTRACTING

         BLAMING ─────── C ─────── PLACATING
                    Normality
                    PATHOLOGY
                    COMPUTING

                  C = Congruency
```

Figure 2. The Third Postulate of Congruency of Personality Development in the Family (L'Abate, 1976)

The blamer is one who expresses anger and blame toward others, represents disagreeable faultfinding, externalization, and displacement onto others, and is usually depicted as saying, "I am OK; you are not OK." The placater, on the opposite end of the continuum, represents one who is overindulgent in passive behaviors (e.g., agreement, denial of one's self-worth), is martyr-like, and usually depicted as saying, "I am not OK; you are OK." The computer is one who distances him/herself from others or emphasizes cold facts and logic at the expense of any feelings, and is usually depicted as saying, "I am not OK, you are not OK; only the content, i.e., facts, is OK." Finally, the distractor is one who expresses him/herself irrelevantly, being hyperactive and impulsive most of the time, and is usually depicted as saying, "Nothing is OK--who cares!"

The preceding incongruent patterns of transactional behaviors occur at the presentational/phenotypical levels of functioning and are usually the result of the inability to integrate most levels of functioning (at the descriptive and the explanatory levels), the failure to differentiate oneself in space and time, and the dysfunctional sequencing of one's life priorities over the life span.*

Congruence between space and time will lead to healthy self-esteem and functional, transactive levels of communication within the family. Congruency, then, will be located in the center of the orthonal model, halfway between approach-avoidance and discharge-delay (see Figure 2). To communicate healthfully and congruently with others, however, we must also be able to deal with ourselves at the genotypic level of functioning.

Hurtful behaviors occur within the family when our inability to negotiate (thoughts and feelings) with ourselves at a genotypical level of awareness results in dysfunctional patterns of negotiating with "intimate others" at the phenotypical level, consequently resulting in insufficient negotiating with "public others" at the self-presentational level of behavior. When this occurs, the four types of incongruent behaviors (blaming, placating, computing, distracting), will manifest themselves, depending, of course, upon the amount of negotiating or time spent with these dysfunctional patterns of behavior. If we are not able to deal responsibly with our hurt feelings, we then produce dysfunctional, non-negotiative behaviors with our loved ones and those outside the family.

On the other hand, if we are able to deal with ourselves, with our own feelings and hurts, in a helpful and positive way, and are able to share these feelings with intimate others as well as with public, or significant, others outside the family (e.g., counselors, therapists), we shall be congruent with our thoughts and feelings at all levels of negotiating: this consistency could thus be viewed as "helpful."

---

*Although it can be shown that antecedent concepts, personality, family correlates, and typologies led to the development of the current postulate of congruence, space does not permit such an extensive elaboration here; therefore, the reader is referred to the original source (L'Abate, 1976, pp. 154-172).

How then does congruency relate to the assumptions and postulates of this theory? Spatially, at the horizontal level, we are able to balance approach-avoidance tendencies with an imbalance, suggesting incongruence. Vertically, the levels of functioning (or negotiating) must be congruent and relatively free from any discrepancies that might produce too many facades, or "masks." Temporally, we must also be able to establish a balance in our discharge-delay inclinations, as it relates to how fast or how slow we process information, by way of our expressions of thoughts, feelings, and actions.

In relation to self-differentiation, the self must be congruent within the individual and with others (negotiation of feelings) as this occurs in relation to how differentiated one is; as for priorities, the more congruent they are, the more congruent our behaviors will be and vice versa. "The three postulates are necessary because they represent different aspects of development in the family. The process of self-differentiation is especially important in mate selection and family formation. The problem of priorities in the family will develop naturally from how the parents choose to assert their own individual selves. In the course of family formation (self-differentiation) and in family functioning (priorities), a certain amount of incongruency may occur; inevitably, it will be shown in how the family transacts affectively (congruence)" (L'Abate, 1976, p. 175).

Models

The use of models in this theory is just as important as the validity of the assumptions, for without a visual description of qualitative speculations, there would be no way to test the postulates empirically in order to verify the viability and usefulness of the theory.

Although an infinite number of models can be used, seven models, representative of the postulates, are used to provide the necessary link between the postulates and the empirical variables, which are formulated into useful data to be used clinically in understanding and helping the individual in the family.

Therefore, the role of models in this theory of personality development will be to: (a) translate qualitative data (postulates) into quantitative data (empirical variables), (b) provide a visual display for such theoretical speculations, and (c) provide order and structure in formulating the necessary links between the postulates and the theory (the theory, as defined here, would help the models to compete with other models from other theories and to convince others of the applicability of the model's usefulness).

Models for Self-Differentiation

The models for self-differentiation include the basic triangle, the bell-shaped curve, and the circle.

The triangle basically refers to the relationship between members within the family, usually the father, mother, and children. Whatever affects one will consequently affect the others. The "Karpman triangle" (to be elaborated in chaps. 5, 7, & 9) is used here to denote symbolically the relationships between the persecutor, rescuer, and victim. Since this triangle is dialectic in nature, members of a family often interchange roles in different situations (see Figure 3).

The Triangles of Life Roles

① Father / Mother / Child
② Adult / Parent / Child
③ I / You / We
④ Victim / Persecutor / Rescuer
⑤ Mate / Self / Parent
⑥ Home / Leisure / Work

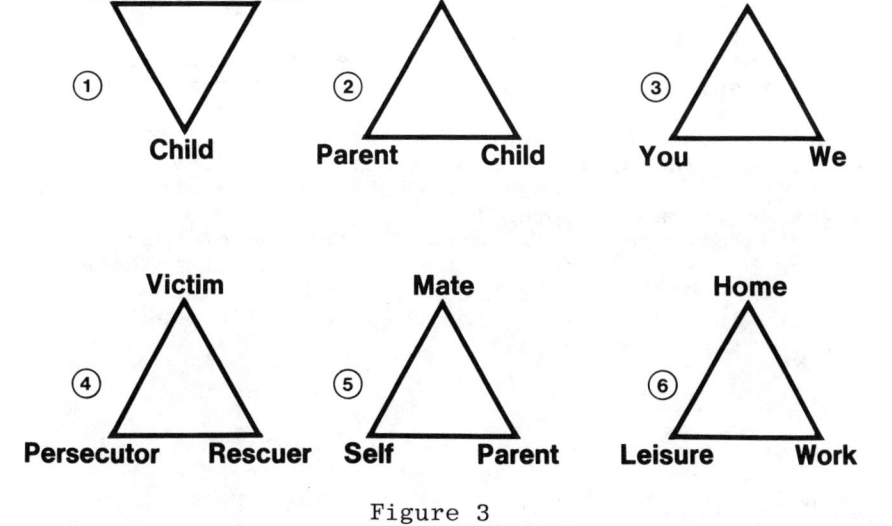

Figure 3

For example, sometimes the father will assume the persecutor role, the mother the rescuer, and the child the victim. Within an undifferentiated family, victims usually get blamed if something goes wrong with the family. The father will blame and the mother will passively rescue the child, who is victimized because of his/her vulnerability to blame and accusation. The triangle can also be used in understanding family priorities, with emphasis upon role and resource priorities. Role priorities are similar to the triangle model used for self-differentiation, in that certain roles are used in understanding priority relationships (i.e., father-mother-child, parent-marriage-children). Resource priorities refer to the composition of the "triangle of life" as being, having, and doing (to be discussed in the next chapter). In many ways, the triangle serves to maintain the family in its present state of dysfunctionality, which occurs out of the transactions between the persecutor, rescuer, and victim.

The bell-shaped curve refers to the continuum of likeness, which has already been considered. An algebraic model is used to show results of interactions between dyads, triads, etc., in algebraic form. Pathology is usually a quagmire of negatives. This is essentially the view according to an algebraic model of self-differentiation. Four possible combinations exist according to a reward/cost viewpoint: (a) both are positive (helpful relationships), (b) one is positive and the other is negative (dialectic, in that both partners can assume either a positive or a negative position), and (c) both are negative (hurtful relationships). If both are positive (at the similarity-differentness level), growth occurs as a result of the enhancement each person brings into the marriage. The slogan "We both win" could be applied here (+ + = x). If one is positive and the other is negative (sameness-oppositeness), no growth occurs because of the cancellation and, in a sense, both partners lose: if one of them loses, the other cannot win (+ - = 0). If both are negative, a division will result, leading to a breakdown in the relationship, e.g., divorce (- - = ÷).

Models for Priorities

Three models are used to show visually how families rank and order their priorities. They are the <u>overlapping circles</u>, <u>wheel</u>, and <u>concentric circles</u>.

The overlapping circles model refers to the information-processing model used earlier (see Figure 1), and it relates to how priorities are formed in relation to the reception, mediational, output, and feedback modes. The questions here are: Which mode is focused upon within this family? How does this manifest itself?

The wheel model, similar to a wagon wheel (in appearance), is used to understand intrafamily priorities composed of the parents, marriage, and the children. Referring to Figure 4, many combinations can be derived from the model, for example:

```
        Parents  = Marriage = Children
        Parents  > Marriage > Children
        Parents  > Marriage = Children
       Children  > Marriage > Parents
       Children  = Parents  > Marriage
```

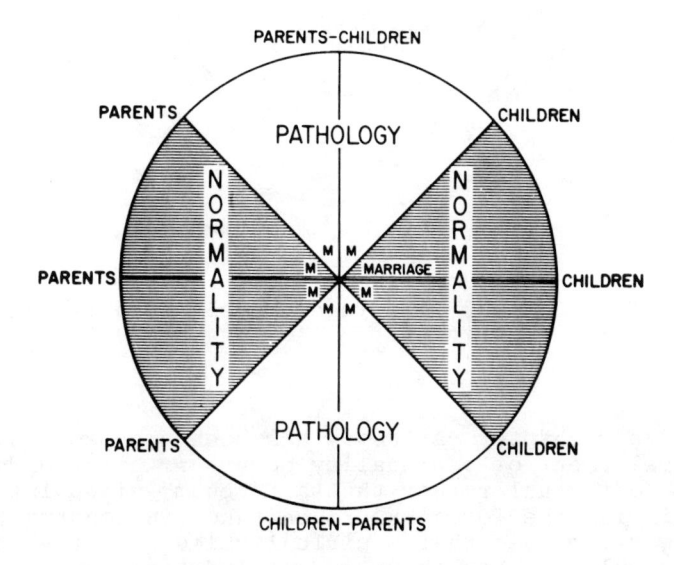

Figure 4. A Wheel Model of Intrafamilial Priorities

It is important to keep in mind what is normality and what is pathology.

The concentric circles model is used to understand both intra- and extrafamilial priorities, usually beginning in the center with the self as most important, following with the marriage, children, the nuclear family, and continuing with extrafamilial priorities (see Figure 5).

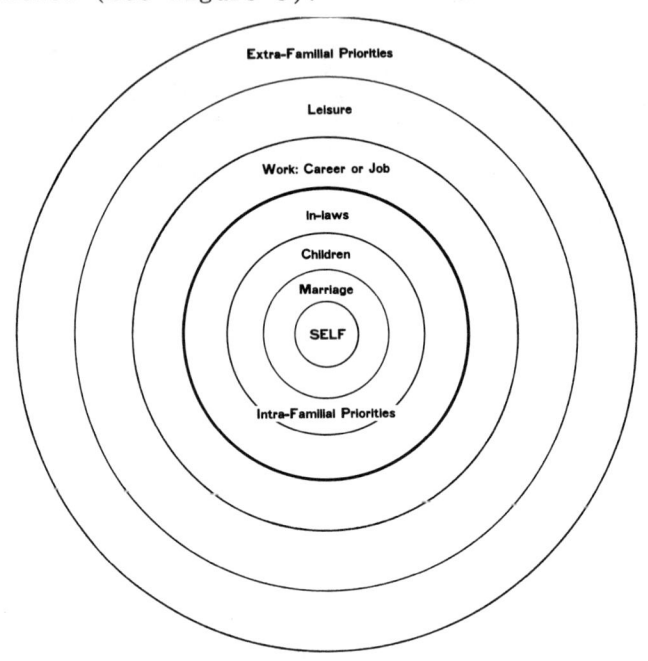

Figure 5. A Concentric Circles Model of Intra- and Extrafamilial Priorities

Conclusion

In this chapter, a theory has been proposed that the development of personality occurs within the family, a contextual rather than a "vacuum" viewpoint. By reviewing the formal approach taken in constructing the theory, we see that empirical validity rather than mere speculative hypothesizing will determine whether this theory is applicable to understanding and helping the individual in the family.

References

Bryson, C. H. Personality differentiation and communication. Unpublished doctoral dissertation, Georgia State University, 1978.

Goldstein, M. Review of: Understanding and helping the individual in the family, by L'Abate, L. (1976). *Journal of Personality Assessment*, 1979, 43, 322-323.

Hansen, J. C., & L'Abate, L. *Approaches to family therapy*. New York: Macmillan, 1982.

L'Abate, L. *Principles of clinical psychology*. New York: Grune & Stratton, 1964.

L'Abate, L. A communication-information model. In L. L'Abate (Ed.), *Models of clinical psychology*. Atlanta: Georgia State University, 1969.

L'Abate, L. Psychodynamic interventions: A personal statement. In R. H. Woody & J. D. Woody (Eds.), *Sexual, marital, and familial relations: Therapeutic interventions for professional helping*. Springfield, IL: Thomas Books, 1973.

L'Abate, L. *Understanding and helping the individual in the family*. New York: Grune & Stratton, 1976.

L'Abate, L. *Setting priorities in relating work activities and family life*. Paper read at Conference on Work and Family Life in the Seventies, Georgia State University, June 3, 1978.

L'Abate, L., & L'Abate, B. L. *How to avoid divorce*. Atlanta: John Knox Press, 1977.

L'Abate, L., & L'Abate, B. L. The paradoxes of intimacy. *Family Therapy*, 1979, 6, 175-184.

CHAPTER 4

THE DIFFERENTIATION OF RESOURCES

Luciano L'Abate, Sadell Sloan, Victor Wagner and Kareen Malone

As Lewin long ago (Hall and Lindzey, 1978) demonstrated, differentiation can take in many components and develop along many paths. It is the purpose of this paper to show how differentiation can take place along three major resources, i.e., *Being, Doing,* and *Having*. These resources are illustrated in the Triangle of Living found in Figure 1.

Figure 1

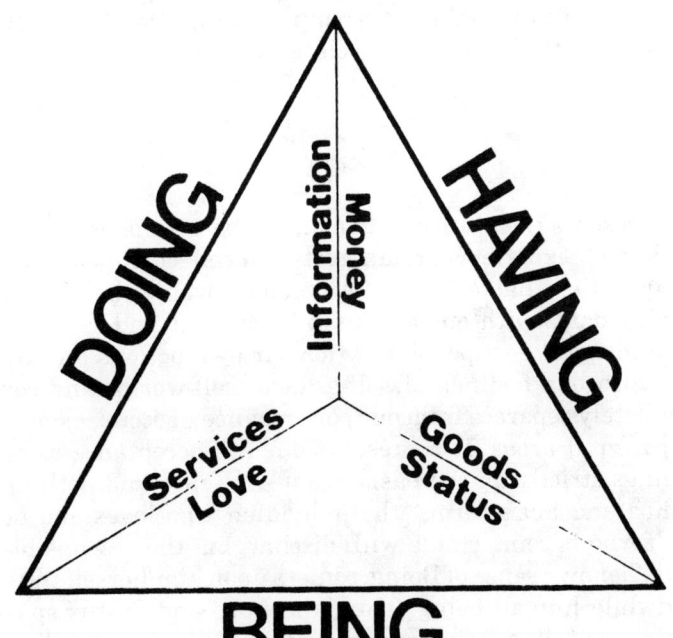

The Triangle of Living*

*Adapted from Foa and Foa (1974)

Reprint requests to Luciano L'Abate, Director, Family Studies Center, Georgia State University, University Plaza, Atlanta, Georgia 30303

This triangle is derived from and is a condensation of Foa and Foa's six resource classes (1974, 1976) of Love, Status, Information, Services, Money, and Goods. Love is defined as affectionate regard, warmth, and comfort, and status as self-worth, regard, and esteem. Doing is defined by (a) information (advice, opinions, instruction, and enlightenment), and (b) service (labor for another). Having consists of (a) money (coins, currency, and tokens), (b) goods (tangible products, objects, and materials).

We see the triangle as a useful model for portraying the relationships between Being, Doing, and Having throughout the family life cycle. The manner in which individual family members negotiate tasks at each stage of the life cycle may be characterized by varying degrees of balance among three major resources: Being, Doing, and Having. While different stages of life may demand an emphasis on one or two of the three sides of the Triangle of Living (e.g., such that the individual gives more attention to the tasks of Being and Doing), one would argue that, over time, the individual who performs his family roles in a functional manner gives comparable attention to each of the three resources, so that no one resource is given primacy over any other. Thus, we see the functional relationship of Being, Doing, and Having over the span of the entire life cycle as an equilateral Triangle of Living.

BEING

Being represents the ability to live and to be with oneself—to meditate, think, feel, experience, relax, rest, and reflect. It deals with the receptive qualities that allow us to become lovable, helpful human beings. Being deals with our ability to be content and satisfied with ourselves and to take responsibility for our own actions and lives. It represents also our feelings of self-esteem, self-worth, and contentment, completely separate from our performance in occupational, marital, and parental areas. It represents our self-acceptance as worthy human beings strictly on the basis of our existence and nothing else. Thus, in Foa and Foa's terms, the individual who loves and accepts him/herself who is comfortable with discharging the responsibility of creating his/her own sense of Being, confers upon him/herself the status of a worthwhile human being. Thus, the Love and Status spoken of here as intrinsic to the Being resource emanate from the individual's sense of his/her own personhood and are to be distinguished from the Love and Status derived from the external validation one receives following, for example, professional performance.

Similarly, Sartre (1956) developed the concept of Being as a creative receptivity to one's existential meaning. In his existential view, Being is considered to be man's most fundamental, original project, encapsulating past, present, and future. Being represents the continual resolution and renewal of the individual's identity as the self-originating creator of meaning. Such a basis for identity implies that at the core of Being lies responsibility—the ability to respond and be receptive to the self-originating powers of others, and hence, the possibility of being creatively influenced by another human being. However, while Being in its authentic fullness encompasses an interpersonal dimension, Sartre points out that Being requires a non-dominating relation to one's environment. Being, according to Sartre, requires astute and non-categorical attentiveness to ourselves and the world. Likewise, Rosen (1975) considered "in Being" as personal and individual thought, free of bias and preconception, aimed at universals, in a creative, detached, and intuitive sense that is informed by personal knowledge. Being is a focus of personal discovery free of judgments and demands, both of oneself and of others. It may be that this nonjudgmental aspect of Being allows the individual greater accessibility to the creative center of Being of those around him. In this vein, Daniels and Horowitz (1976) discussed Being as essential to authentic caring and sharing. Being, of course, is basic to the establishment and maintenance of intimacy (L'Abate and L'Abate, 1979).

DOING

Doing encompasses our performance in familial, occupational, and recreational areas. Doing is essential for the maintenance and development of human relationships, especially partnerships based on the reciprocal exchange of services and goods. The marital relationship may be viewed as the prototype for such a partnership. Within the context of the marital relationship, partners may affirm their individual Being through Doing with (sharing) and Doing for (caring). Partners who let go of and express their emotions and ideas discover a spontaneous aspect of Being, while those who hold onto their emotions constrict their possibilities for sharing and caring, thus negating their Being.

Singer (1955) pointed out how meaningful activity (Doing) is essential for psychological health. Singer differentiated between genuine activity (characterized by the capacity to be attentive, surprised, absorbed, and the ability to bear uncertainty courageously) and pseudoactivity. Pseudoactivity, in contrast to authentic Doing, is behavior which masquerades as a genuine effort and which is characterized by doing in an uninvolved, detached fashion, acting either mechanically, without interest, or with a furious, driven tension. Thus, Doing in the service of Being (i.e., those activities through which the individual expresses and extends his/herself or inner core) enhances one's sense of Being. The poet writing a poem, the husband supporting his wife, and a parent nurturing the child are examples of adaptive, creative Doing. The constructive aspect of Doing takes place when it is balanced within Being and Having. Appropriate and balanced Doing means being aware of one's priorities *vis-a-vis* self, marriage, and children between intra- and extra-familial priorities (L'Abate, 1976).

On the other hand, one may be involved in actions whose existential meaning has not yet been defined. This sort of pseudoactivity or "doing for the sake of doing" hinders, rather than facilitates, the development of a deeper sense of Being. Workaholics, who seem to be driven to work without giving consideration to the existential meaning of their activity, are good examples of individuals whose doing for the sake of doing is dysfunctional. Their frenzied activity does not allow them to derive inner satisfaction from their performance, but permits them to use Doing to avoid the responsibilities of Being. Overemphasis on Doing without the reflective corrective of Being may lead to excesses and extremes.

HAVING

Having involves the acquisition of goods and money. To assess whether Having is adjusting or not, one must consider the degree of balance between Having and the two other modes, Being and Doing. To function adaptively, the healthy personality must secure an acceptable level of personal physical comfort. The individual who is willing to own up to a need for Having, by investing in Doing activities that lead to comfortable standards of living, is attesting to valuing oneself enough to satisfy material needs. Once these needs are met, one can engage in Doing activities which allow one to fulfill potentials in the areas of intrapersonal and interpersonal development that contribute to the ongoing development of existential meaning.

If, however, the individual stresses Having by downplaying or even excluding Being, so that Doing is directed toward the acquisition of material goods without attaining a deeper level of self acceptance, then Having becomes dysfunctional. The tycoon who amasses vast amounts of goods and money but who is unable to enjoy the fruits of his/her labor may serve as the case in point. Such an individual is so invested in Having that the amassing of a fortune becomes an end in itself.

He/she does not acquire goods so that he/she can enjoy them. Rather, the idea of acquisition itself is the prime motivator. He/she never ceases to need, and therefore persists in the Having orientation. In this regard, Fromm (1976) related the Having mode to the craving for immortality, since Having is characterized by the acquisition and possession of property well beyond the limits of the necessary or the luxurious. In the Having mode, even human beings become objects of one's needs. Such an exaggerated emphasis on Doing and Having are characteristic of the dysfunctional individual, couple, or family.

DISCUSSION

While Doing and Having are intimately related, there is a major difference between the two. While Having is activity for the sake of acquisition, Doing is activity for activity's sake—the sheer appreciation of performance. Doing can be, and oftentimes is, independent of Having. The activities of missionaries and workaholics (those obsessed with Doing) are often almost independent of acquisitory desires. Thus, the present formulation, by its inclusion of the Having mode as distinct from Doing, represents an extension and elaboration of the ideas of both Fromm (1976) and Spiegel (1971). Fromm differentiated only between "having and being [as] two fundamental modes of experience, the respective strengths of which determine the differences between the characters of individuals and various types of social character." Spiegel, on the other hand, distinguished Being and Being-in-Becoming from Doing, which he considered a predominant activity orientation in self expression.

Relationship of Being to Doing and Having
Implied in Sartre's formulation of a central interactive component in the modality of Being is that while Being itself requires a nonjudgmental, receptive posture, the full development and experience of Being is derived through the expressive modalities of Doing and Having. Existential Being is not an abstract condition. Rather, Being exists within the context of one's world. Authentic Being demands that one be-in-the-world, e.g., in this room, and with this person. The expressions of man's being-in-the-world are the ontological moments, Doing and Having. We do not come into Being (in its broadest sense) without creating a world-at-hand-before-us, what Heidegger (1962) called *Zuhanden*. Transforming the world-at-large into the world-at-hand-before-us through Doing and Having is the major developmental and existential project of life. Doing and Having are the means and context

of expressing our Being to others. If Being is meaning, then Doing and Having become the creation of meaning. In the healthy individual, couple, or family, Doing and Having are in the service of Being. This idea is reflected in Fromm's (1976) assertion that:

> The mode of being has as its prerequisites independence, freedom, and the presence of critical reason. Its fundamental characteristic is that of being active, not in the sense of outward activity, of busyness, but of inner activity, the productive use of our human powers .... In the structure of being, the alive and inexpressible experience rules.

Pathology surfaces in symptoms, which may be thought of as reflections of Doing and/or Having estranged from the ultimate goal of Being. The individual who loses sight of Being will seek external validation through Doing (justifying his/her being in terms of his/her functions, i.e., "I am a doctor") or through Having (justifying oneself on the basis of possessions, e.g., cars, jewels, clothes, and becoming a compulsive consumer).

All behavior is a reflection of our Being. However, if we place all our energy of Being into Doing and Having, we become what we do and what we have. Being implies possibility. When we focus our Being only through Doing and Having, we limit the possibilities available to us. This can be seen in part as the "sickness of Western society," where we consume ourselves and our resources by Doing more to Have more—spiraling on, forgetting who and what we really are in the process.

An equilateral triangle implies an ecological perspective, where there is a balance between Being, Doing, and Having. We need to Do in order to Have, but if in the process we don't allow ourselves to Be, we defeat the purpose of Doing and Having. When an individual mistakes Having or Doing for Being, one loses sight of Being and is then prevented from experiencing full satisfaction in encounters with others. If we do not know how to care and share on the basis of Being (Daniels & Horowitz, 1976), we then turn to Doing or Having as substitutes.

The ability to Be is directly related to the ability to feel, to be aware of, and be in touch with one's feelings. How else can one feel and express love and status? If Status is achieved through Doing, and love is achieved through Having, two of the most common forms of short-circuiting feelings, the triangle becomes very weak at the base of Being. Both Doing and Having, when overemphasized, represent then, an inadequacy in the ability to feel love and status (i.e., self worth). One needs to love oneself and to feel important independent of work or possessions. When feelings are blunted, atrophied, repressed, suppressed, minimized, belittled, and put down, we lose the ability to love, to Be loved and to Be important. When importance is achieved through either Doing or Having, it becomes fused with these activities to the point that when either one of them ceases, through age or misfortune, the self has nowhere to go to find sustenance and support. The more differentiated the feelings, the greater the possibility of balancing all of the resources in this triangle.

The parent Does for his child as proof of love, while spouses give gifts, objects or money as proofs of their love. It is very difficult to base relationships on Being in an acquisitive, consumer-oriented society where most people tend to own more than they need and need more than they can own. If there is a deficit in loving and status, if we cannot love ourselves and give ourselves status and love on the basis strictly of our existence rather than our performance or our possessions, we tend to substitute the latter for the former and essentially lose sight of our Being. By losing sight of our Being, we lose ourselves.

How can we learn to appreciate Being when most of our values and pressures are directed toward our job performance and acquisition, if not indeed hoarding of goods? How can we enhance Being without downplaying or at least putting in their proper perspective Doing and Having? Without this perspective of Being, both Doing and Having will be overemphasized unduly to the point of breakdown. Mates cannot let each other Be. Parents and children do not know how to let each other Be. In any relationship there is the explicit or implicit demand of either Doing or Having or both. "True" friends and lovers are those who appreciate each other for what they are and not for what they Do or Have. Why, then, do we select friends and lovers on the basis of similarities in values and exclude them on the basis of differences? Clearly, learning how to appreciate Being is a difficult goal to reach, but a crucial one, nevertheless.

Developmental Stages

The modes of Being, Doing, and Having may be viewed as the central issues or tasks of various points in the life cycle. The individual must first negotiate the issues of identity or Being in order to progress and define the activities through which s/he will work out and fully express his/her Being. It is through the Doing of meaningful work that one may then attain a measure of satisfaction from labors. Thus, each stage of life must be successfully negotiated if one is to progress to the next, since the task of each stage is based on the preceding one.

While the individual may have dealt successfully with the issues of Being early in the life cycle, it is typically necessary to renegotiate Being later in life after the issues of Doing and Having have been encountered and issues of non-Being need confrontation. Erikson's (1950) concept of an identity crisis in adolescence followed later by the task of achieving generativity (a broader sense of self including a sense of well being and dignity derived from a respect for one's lifestyle as life draws closer to death) reflects the centrality of Being in personality development. Furby (1978) has shown how possessions are relevant to various stages of the life cycle.

If Being has not been negotiated by middle age, it must be dealt with when the individual retires and reaches the final stage of his life. If one's occupational role (Doing) has been central to one's identity, retirement and cessation of Doing may bring about a crisis that many retirees cannot handle, hence the large increase of deaths and suicides within the first year of retirement. Since Doing is curtailed and the decrease in one's income at retirement does not allow for the accumulation of new goods (Having), Being becomes especially important at this stage in the life cycle. Being is also crucial in facing death. What one has done, what occupational roles and titles one has had and what goods one has accrued during a lifetime have little to do with the acceptance of one's death. If one has not faced one's own Being and found meaning in Being devoid of roles and possessions, then one will be unable to face death.

Mental Health and Psychopathology

The present formulation also has implications for criteria of mental health. Strupp and Hadley (1977), for instance, presented a tripartite model of mental health based on societal, individual, and therapeutic criteria, with a certain amount of overlap among all three of them. Society stresses Having and Doing; individuals may stress Being and Doing, while therapists, depending on their theoretical persuasion, may emphasize any one of these three sides. Humanists would stress Being; psychodynamists would stress Doing, while behaviorists would stress Having (Havens, 1973). The present formulation, as well as transactional and ecological viewpoints (L'Abate, 1976), would stress the importance of all three sides, or the relative importance and balance of each side at different stages of the family life cycle.

Within our culture, the nature of a family's or couple's functionality varies with socioeconomic status. People in lower socioeconomic strata will be caught up in Having, which will be central to their problems. This is in line with Maslow's hierarchy of needs (1968) since survival needs such as food, clothing, shelter, etc., must be met before one can move upward, toward self-actualization (Being). When one's day-to-day existence is a struggle to fulfill one's needs for survival, getting beyond the resource of Having is extremely difficult. One could say that community psychology and social welfare agencies are resources to help individuals who are experiencing difficulty on the Having plane. Occupational therapy, vocational counseling and testing may be viewed as some ways to help individuals who are experiencing difficulty in Doing.

Most middle-class dysfunctional systems have defects in Being, not in Having (material possessions) or Doing (steady jobs and careers). Emotional problems derive from the inability to attain a clear sense of oneself. Therapy has the function of filling a void that no other institution, except perhaps, religion can fill. Thus, therapy essentially offers the opportunity for learning how to Be. Once Being is given as much importance as Having and Doing, one can live within a context of harmony with self and others. Facing the responsibilities of Being thus enables the individual to negotiate successively the developmental priorities of Personhood (Being?), Partnership (Doing?), and Parenthood (Having?).

THERAPEUTIC IMPLICATIONS

How can we teach others how to Be if we do not? Clearly an understanding of Being in relationship to the other two resources gives us a diagnostic framework from which we can derive interventional strategies, i.e., we need to help individuals in families to love each other and to give value to themselves and each other. Thus, the ultimate implication of this framework consists in defining the goals of therapeutic intervention in terms of Being rather than anything else.

Hence, we therapists need to come to terms with our Being as individuals, partners, and parents. If we do not, how can we teach others? The framework presented here defines very clearly what constitutes Being in contrast to what may seem vague and evanescent concepts from existential writers (Heidegger, 1962; Sartre, 1956). In fact, Foa and Foa's (1974, 1976) work is of such an empirical nature that the tests they developed can now de used to measure the outcome of our interventions. If this revision of their work is in any way valid it could be empirically tested, i.e., couples and families in trouble would tend to show greater deficits in Love and Status (Being) than in any other of the six resource classes proposed by Foa and Foa. The major issue here would be whether a therapeutic approach would need to be oriented toward Being in order to achieve changes in this area, or would changes in any resource class produce changes in other resources?

This framework raises more questions than we can answer. However, it does provide a useful classification for dealing with resources, diagnostically and therapeutically.

CONCLUSION

The present formulation of six resource classes into a triangle of living made up of Being, Doing, and Having relates to resource allocation throughout the human life cycle. Most interpersonal problems we see are related to our inability to Be and an overemphasis on Doing and/or Having. Functional living, therefore, is based on a clear differentiation of all three resources. Emphasis on one or two resources at the expense of one or another side of the triangle would result in personal, marital, and familial dysfunctions or at least in imbalances in living.

REFERENCES

Daniels, B., & Horowitz, L. J. *Being and Caring.* Palamato, Ca.: Mayfield, 1976.

Erikson, E. H. *Childhood in Society.* New York: W. W. Norton, 1950.

Foa, U.G., & Foa, E.D. *Societal Structures of the Mind.* Springfield, Il.: C. C. Thomas, 1974.

Foa, E. D., & Foa, U. G. "Resource Theory of Social Exchange," in J. W. Thibaut, J. T. Spence, and R. C. Carson (Eds.), *Contemporary Topics in Psychology.* Munster, N.J.: General Learning Press, 1976, Pp. 99-113.

Fogarty, T. F. "System Concepts in the Dimensions of Self," in P. J. Guerin, Jr. (Ed.), *Family Therapy, Theory and Practice.* New York: Gardner Press, 1976. Pp. 144-153.

Fromm, E. *To Have or to Be?* New York: Harper & Row, 1976.

Furby, L. "Possession in Humans: An Exploratory Study of its Meaning and Motivation," *Social Behavior and Personality,* 1978, *6,* 49-65.

Hall, C. S., & Lindzey, G. *Theories of Personality.* New York: John Wiley, 1978.

Havens, L. L. *Approaches to the Mind: Movements of the Psychiatrics Schools from Sects toward Science.* Boston, Ma.: Little, Brown, and Co., 1973.

Heidegger, M. *Being and time.* New York: Harper & Row, 1962.

L'Abate, L., & L'Abate, B. S. "The Paradoxes of Intimacy," *Family Therapy,* 1979, *6,* 175-184.

Maslow, A. H. *A Psychology of Being.* Princeton, N.J.: D. Van Nostrand Co., 1968.

Rosen, R. H. *In Being.* Ph.D. dissertation, University of Tennessee, 1975.

Sartre, J. P. *Being and Nothingness.* New York: Philosophical Library, 1956.

Singer, J. L. "Delayed Gratification and Ego Development: Implications for Clinical and Experimental Research," *Journal of Consulting Psychology,* 1955, *19,* 259-266.

Spiegel, J. *Transactions: The Interplay between the Individual, Family, and Society.* New York: Science House, 1971.

Strupp, H. H., & Hadley, S. W. "A Tripartite Model of Mental Health and Therapeutic Outcome: With Specific Reference to Negative Effects in Psychotherapy," *American Psychologist,* 1977, *32,* 187-196.

CHAPTER 5

PSYCHOPATHOLOGY AS TRANSACTION: A HISTORICAL NOTE

LUCIANO L'ABATE, GERALD R. WEEKS,
and KATHLEEN G. WEEKS
Georgia State University, Atlanta, Georgia

The purpose of this paper is to present a brief historical-developmental overview of prior conceptions of psychopathology and to offer a new way of looking at psychopathology by extending the framework used in this review. The scheme employed here for conceptualizing psychopathology closely follows the three levels of organization proposed by Dewey and Bentley (1949). This evolutionary scheme consists of three major phases: 1. action; 2. interaction; and 3. transaction. Dewey and Bentley (1949) summarized these phases as follows:

Self-action: where things are viewed as acting under their own powers.

Interaction: where thing is balanced against thing in causal connection.

Transaction: where systems of description and naming are employed to deal with aspects and phases of action, without final attribution to "elements" or other presumptively detachable or independent "entities," "essences," or "realities," and without isolation of presumptively detachable "relations" from such detachable "elements."

Relating this scheme then to views of psychopathology, pathology was viewed first historically to be mythically determined; that is, its "cause" was attributed to abstract origins like the gods or supernatural phenomena. In other words, the pathological behavior erupted entirely on its own, without any apparent external provocation. It appeared by its own power. Next, pathology was seen to be related to some definite contextual factors such as the physical or social environment. An external element of causation was called into play. This conception gave rise to such well-known terms as "psychobiological" and "social" in the area of abnormal psychology. While pathological behavior was thought to occur in relation to other systems, each system was considered independently, and the causes of behavior were believed to be *unidirectional*. Finally, a conception of psychopathology arose which depicted behavior to be the functional outcome of historical, intentional, and contextual exchanges which must be considered within the context of their being observed and evaluated by an "outsider." That is, the observer's biases, interests, and psychodynamics must be considered as part of the system of causation of behavior and as part of the explanation of the behavior of others. All parts of this system are interdependent; one behavior affects and is affected by all other parts of the system. This final conception is transactional because it does not describe unidirectional behavior, but *multi-directional* behavior.

Each of these conceptions of psychopathology is related not only to the notions of action, interaction, and transaction, but also to three additional psychological ideas: innateness, inability, and protectiveness. Each of these ideas and their elations to the conception of psychopathology we have discussed will now be drawn out in greater detail, bearing in mind the fact that, although there is considerable overlap among the ideas presented here, history is a continuous rather than a discrete process. Older ideas become incorporated into newer ideas. However, each phase represents a paradigmatic change in viewing psychopathology.

The study of the family falls primarily within the third phase of development—the transactional phase. The idea that the family should be studied within a transactional framework has been thoroughly examined by Spiegel (1971). Our thesis is that when the family is viewed transactionally the basis of much of its pathology is protectiveness; that is, the protection of itself as an ongoing unity or system.

ACTION—PATHOLOGY AS INNATENESS

The most primitive conceptions of pathology included two causes—spiritual causes and inner causes. The spiritual origins of pathological behavior derived from demons, goblins, gods, goddesses, supernatural influences, etc. Inner causes were either psychological or physiological and included such etiological factors as pride, jealousy, shame, body humors, and the brain (Clark, 1973). The most primitive of these two concepts might be termed magico-religious, or supernatural. In this view, pathology was explained by abstract, undefinable, and unspecified origins. This view pre-dates written history. It stemmed from primitive man's animistic view of the universe—a view which held that natural events, both in nature and man, had human motivations. Thus, if a primitive man became ill (mentally or physically) he would attribute the cause to one of his enemies or some malevolent, invisible god. Inner causes were later recognized as causes of mental illness. One of the earliest accounts of this notion is from Egypt around 1900 B.C. It was held that the displacement or "starvation" of the uterus caused morbid states in women.

The turning point in the history of psychopathology was the Classical era. For the first time, mental illness was conceived without the causes being attributed to demons. This period gave rise to primitive organic and psychological conceptions of pathology, some of which have carried over into modern psychiatry.

Much of modern psychiatry also falls within the framework of "action." The objective-descriptive school of psychiatry emphasizes symptoms and treats mental illness as a physical illness with the natural course of a disease. Psychoanalysis emphasizes the importance of conflict and dissociations, unconscious motivation, wishes and fantasies, and a detailed relevance of childhood elements (Havens, 1973). Hence, psychopathology is intrinsic to the individual, either biologically or psychologically.

The modes of therapy for the conceptions of pathology presented above confirm and reflect the idea of pathology as innateness. The earliest forms of treatment for madness included techniques ranging over a wide spectrum. These techniques included trephining, incantations, therapy by amulet, even numbers, charms, herbs, leeches, laying-on-of-hands, faith healing, exorcism, and all forms of physical punishment. The "therapist" was usually a medicine man, magician, or priest who was believed to possess supernatural powers. Therapy in a later phase—the Greek period—took the form of incantations which Plato described as "beautiful logic" and also included proper diet and rest. In the latest part of this phase, modern psychiatry developed procedures such as drug therapy, psychosurgery, electroshock, and psychoanalysis.

In summary, the action model, or innateness model, attributes pathology to abstract, imagined, or hypothesized internal states that essentially cause the individual to act crazy. When viewed within the action or innateness model, the dysfunctional behavior of a family member is seen as a strictly individual problem. No relationship is seen between the individual and his family. The family is assumed to be in no way responsible for the behavior of its symptom-bearer. The classic case of this situation appears when a family is confronted with a child's behaving unusually. The parents' first move may be to take the child to a medical doctor and then to a neurologist. They may avoid family therapy for as long as possible because they realize they are in some way responsible for their child's behavior. Unfortunately, the medical model often provides one way for families to define their pathology within the innateness model.

INTERACTION—PATHOLOGY AS INTERACTIONAL INABILITY

The next major view of pathology grew from an emerging humanism and advances in psychological theory. In the previous view, pathology was equated to "sickness" or "possession," which meant the individual was not responsible for his behavior. He simply could not act otherwise. The current view—the interactional—has an underlying assumption that the idea of "free will," personal responsibility, or at the very least that people can act otherwise under certain conditions, exists. Pathological behavior is conceived as the inability to behave in a "better" or "healthier" way as a result of historical and contextual factors. To be more specific, this view is commonly referred to in four major ways—the moral model, the behavioral model, the existential model, and the social schools of psychiatry.

According to Maher (1966) the moral model questions labeling a person as mentally ill. The act of labeling a person turns him into an impersonal "thing" and diverts attention away from his needs and values. This model robs the person of his sense of personal responsibility. In the moral model, pathology is represented as problems in living. The main proponent of this model is Szasz.

This behavioral model holds that pathology is the result of a learning process. One is unable to act in a healthier way because one has been conditioned not to do so by other people. This model is based on a large body of experimental literature and is not specific to any one psychologist. The definition of behavior in this model is usually based on some statistical norm.

The existential school of psychiatry emphasizes the role of feelings and emotions resulting from man's lived experience in the world. It emphasizes man's feeling of meaninglessness, isolation, loneliness, and aloneness in an absurd world. It also emphasizes how the "other" may rob us of our freedom.

Finally, social psychiatry focuses on the role of societal factors in the individual's life history. It focuses on both the individual and society. Pathology lies in both individual and social processes.

While these models and schools make different assumptions about the nature of man, it is clear they all view pathology at the interactional level. This is to say that two independent systems come into contact—one affecting the other. The direction of influence is generally seen as unidirectional; e.g., a mother influences her child to act in crazy ways, or social processes influence an individual to behave in deviant ways.

The treatment procedures following from these models and schools are well known and include individual and group therapy. The modal therapeutic situation is one in which the patient is treated in a one-to-one encounter or with persons who are strangers or persons less significant than those he has lived with and been affected by the most, his family. In short, the "patient" is treated in a vacuum.

In terms of the family, the interactional approach to treating marital and familial problems has still focused on the individual in individual therapy. The patient is encouraged to deal with other members of the family symbolically. He is encouraged to talk about his feelings about other members of the family and in some cases might be taught maneuvers to help change their behavior, as in behavior therapy. In recent years, it has become more and more popular for individually oriented therapists to see couples and families. However, even though the unit of behavior the therapist is dealing with has changed, the therapist often continues working with the same set of assumptions and techniques—assumptions and techniques derived from the interactional model. These therapists proceed by working with each member of the family separately. They assume that by sharing in each other's therapeutic experience the relationships will grow just as the individual selves do.

TRANSACTIONAL—PATHOLOGY AS PROTECTIVENESS

The final and most recent view of pathology sees the individual bound to a life script. This view has been championed by Berne (1964, 1972), Steiner (1974), and many others. Steiner (1974) defines a script as "an on-going program, developed in early childhood under parental influences, which directs the individual's behavior in the most important aspects of his life" (p. 418). This simply means the child is programmed by his parents early in life, usually before the age of six. There are many different life scripts, but almost all have one common characteristic: they limit the variety and adaptability of behavior. Scripts bind one to the past. As long as one adheres to his script, he stays the same; he does not change. The essential element of the script bestowed by the parents is: Be the same; be like us! As one can see, living a script which may or may not have been appropriate in the past is dysfunctional. Life requires that our behavior change to fit the present circumstances. Some scripts are extremely destructive, and others simply make life "mindless" or "joyless." Whatever the case, T.A. implies that scripting is at best mildly pathological and at worst a crazy way to live.

Because scripting occurs in the context of a family system, it may be viewed as transactional. The script matrix involves the father, mother, and the child. It is usually the parent of the opposite sex who tells the child what to be and the parent of the same sex who tells the child how to be it. In the scripting process, the whole system is involved. Each member influences the others, and feedback is a necessary part of the scripting process. For example, if the child does not follow the script the parents have in mind, they may punish the child and repeat the injunctions. After this process takes place several times the child becomes scripted.

A major element of T.A. is the enactment of three roles: parent, adult, and child. In the family system, these roles are enacted by the father, mother, and child with the parent and adult roles being exchanged and counter exchanged primarily between the father and the mother. T.A. discusses the "games" which result when these roles are assumed; however, they fail to explain why the enactment of the games occurs, and furthermore, why it is almost necessary that they occur, especially in a family system. For this reason we have chosen Karpman's (1968) drama triangle as one model for family pathology and for explaining the functional value of scripting. Usually the father is the Persecutor; the mother, the

Rescuer; and the child, the Victim. However, these roles may shift rapidly for either short or long periods of time. For purposes of this paper, the role of Victim is given special attention, because this role gives us the most insight into the underlying reason for the development of the drama triangle or family pathology.

The role of Victim may be identified as that of scapegoat. Scapegoating is a concept commonly found in texts on family theory and therapy. It has been argued that by assuming the role of "sick," "crazy," or scapegoat, the identified patient is protecting the family system from having to deal with itself (Vogel and Bell, 1961; Haley, 1963; Ackerman, 1968). For example, rather than the parents dealing with their own mutually destructive tendencies, they project all their problems or hostilities onto the child. Moreover, it follows that by labeling the identified patient "sick," the family protects the scapegoat from social embarrassment because he cannot act otherwise, and the family can ask for help for the scapegoated individual although they may actually be asking for help indirectly for themselves. The scapegoating process allows everyone concerned to externalize personal responsibility. The parents do not accept responsibility for their problems, because they have projected all their problems onto the child, and the child cannot accept responsibility for his behavior because he is "sick." Since everyone in the drama triangle is programmed for certain roles, no one is responsible. They are programmed; they cannot act otherwise.

In contrast to the previous mostly negative explanations of pathology (action and interaction), we propose that pathology within a transactional framework should also be considered on the basis of a positive antecedent (i.e., *protectiveness*). At the most general level of explanation, pathology as protectiveness has the function of helping the family avoid change. The family is forever ensnared or bound to the three basic roles of Persecutor, Rescuer, and Victim. Change involves doing something different, but there is a great deal of safety and security in sameness. Additionally, the need to protect oneself and members of one's family is a survival reaction: "If I protect myself and those who love me, I will be OK: I shall survive. To do so, I shall lie, cheat, act crazy, and hurt myself, or them, as long as I can keep the family system alive." The entrenchment of this position is so strong that, depending on the biases of the observer, it may be called "resistance homeostasis." Messer (1971) suggested that when families attempt to maintain a homeostatic balance, among the various devices they use to do so are the scapegoating of a member and seeking a "family healer" (Rescuer) from either inside or outside the family.

It is interesting to note that when such a system is operating, the components of the system do not consider the ways in which they have produced pathology within the system. This is because pathology is attributed to only one component of the system. Thus, family systems use explanations at the actional and interactional level (innateness and inability) to rationalize and externalize their personal responsibility. They avoid "seeing" the interrelatedness of their behavior.

The transactional approach to families and family therapy has been aptly described by Minuchin (1974). However, protectiveness as the basis of family pathology has essentially been overlooked. Haley (1976) is one of the few family therapists who noted that "underlying most marital problems is a protectiveness that keeps the problem going" (p. 157). Members may protect each other from their own feelings of hurt, etc., or they may protect themselves. At any rate, the family is willing to settle for its dysfunctionality rather than face the isolation, failure, hurt, and helplessness resulting from its dissolution. The survival of the self is equated with the survival of the family.

CONCLUSION

Conceptions of psychopathology have become increasingly complex and more encompassing. The causes of psychopathology have shown a historical progression from unidirectionality, to bi-directionality, and finally to multi-directionality. The future of psychopathology will be in the formulation and elaboration of a transactional view. This paper attempts to present only one aspect of such a formulation. Moreover, the time has arrived when we can no longer avoid recognizing the dialectics of psychopathology; namely, pathology may have positive as well as negative antecedents.

REFERENCES

ACKERMAN, N. Prejudicial scapegoating and neutralizing forces in the family group, with special reference to the role of "Family Healer." In J. Howells (Ed.), *Theory and Practice of Family Psychiatry*. New York: Brunner/Mazel, 1968.
BERNE, E. *Games People Play*. New York: Grove Press, 1964.
BERNE, E. *What Do You Say After You Say Hello?* New York: Grove Press, 1972.
CLARK, R. *Mental Illness in Perspective: History and Schools of Thought*. Pacific Grove, California: Boxwood Press, 1973.
DEWEY, J. and BENTLEY, A. *Knowing and the Known*. Boston: Beacon Press, 1949.
HALEY, J. *Strategies of Psychotherapy*. New York: Grune & Stratton, 1963.
HALEY, J. *Problem-solving Therapy*. San Francisco: Jossey-Bass, 1976.
HAVENS, L. *Approaches to the Mind: Movement of the Psychiatric Schools from Sects toward Science*. Boston: Little, Brown, 1973.
KARPMAN, S. Script drama analysis. *Transactional Analysis Bulletin*, 1968, 26, 39-43.
MAHER, B. *Principles of Psychopathology*. New York: McGraw-Hill, 1966.
MESSER, A. Mechanisms of family homeostasis. *Comprehensive Psychiatry*, 1971, 12, 380-388.
MINUCHIN, S. *Families and Family Therapy*. Cambridge, Massachusetts: Harvard University Press, 1974.
SPIEGEL, J. *Transactions: The Interplay between Individual, Family, and Society*. New York: Science House, 1971.
STEINER, C. *Scripts People Live*. New York: Bantam, 1974.
VOGEL, E. F. and BELL, N. W. The emotionally disturbed child as the family scapegoat. In: *A Modern Introduction to the Family*. Glencoe, Illinois: Free Press, 1961.

CHAPTER 6

Pathogenic Role Rigidity in Fathers: Some Observations

A great deal has been written about the pathogenicity of mothers and mother-child relationships in the last two decades. As Walters and Stinnett (1971) concluded in their review of research on parent-child relationships:

> The era of viewing children as solely products of their parents' influence is past, for it is recognized that children, themselves, exert powerful influences upon parent-child relationships. (p. 101).

They concluded their interview by stating:

> The vast proportion of the literature on parent-child relationships is concerned with mother-child relationships. However, the literature of the Sixties has indicated very clearly that the impact of fathers is of considerable significance . . . because we have believed that the impact of mothers upon the development of children is greater than the impact of fathers, we have investigated maternal impact to a far greater extent than we have examined the impact of fathers. Yet, much of the evidence of the last decade suggests that the variability of children's behavior is more closely associated with the type of father one has than the type of mother. (p. 101).

The family therapy literature (Bozormenyi-Nagy & Spark, 1973; Spiegel, 1972) shows how in the family system the relationship between parents and the marriage itself may be an important determinant of dysfunctional patterns in children. The role of the father since the seminal review by Nash (1965) has received increasing attention in the last few years. The reviews of Barry on marriage (1969) and the work of Robins on delinquents (1966) point to the father as being the major determinant of functional or dysfunctional patterns in the family.

As Barry's (1969) recent review indicated, the father is more relevant to the happiness and "mental health of the family than he has been given credit heretofore. The mother-child relationship has taken away the spotlight from him." These conclusions indicate that the father is acquiring an increasingly important position in the limelight of research. Various theories about his passivity, inadequacy, dominance, and so forth, have been advanced to relate him to his son's deviancy. These theories are too important to evaluate comparatively in regard to the thesis advanced here.

Consequently, relative to the mother-child interaction, which has been the focus of the last decade of research, the father has received relatively little attention. Our knowledge of the father is still minimal. We especially lack clinical information on the role of the father in the overall family interrelatedness. Even though some research on the family and on the father's role in it has been conducted, especially in extreme psychopathology, (Henry, 1971; Lidz, 1973) we still do not understand the specific role of the father in the child's psychopathology. As Pederson and Robson (1969) concluded in their research on the father's participation in infancy, "father-infant relationships are of greater significance than previous research attention would suggest."

It is a widely accepted idea that the father's role in the family is primarily instrumental and the mother's expressive; that is, the father deals with tasks and realities external to the family that are necessary for its ongoing functioning and provides the children with a model of coping with the environment along task-oriented lines. The mother is primarily in charge of fostering interpersonal relationships and adjustments within the family and teaches the children about emotional expressiveness and interpersonal competency. However, it is clear that these are not distinct and separate functions and that many problems can result when the parents are not also able to assume reverse roles with the mother routinely coping with many external demands as well as at times becoming a chief bread-winner, and the father having importance in fostering the emotional growth of his children.

Although the marital interaction, from a systems viewpoint, may be the actual basis for familial dysfunctions, it may be relevant to focus on the father's role in the inception, if not the aggravation, of dysfunctional patterns in children and in the family. It is the thesis of this paper that a great deal of dysfunctionality in the family, whether in the marriage or in the children, is determined by the father's inability to shift from one role to another. This inability to shift from one to another role follows a distinct process that can be described in separate sequences. This inability to shift may be present at all levels of occupational status. However, examples from professional roles will be used here, since those are the ones that the author is most familiar with because of his clinical involvement with white-collar workers rather than blue-collar workers. Perhaps, the same processes described in one occupational group should apply to other occupational groups in terms of using such a role to justify inadequacies in the demands of new roles as husband and father.

Father's Occupational Role

Aldous (1969) in reviewing the literature linking men's occupational activities to their performance in marital and parental roles found that the usual dichotomization of occupational and family role demands should be brought into question, concluding that the man's participation in the family initially appears to depend upon his holding some sort of a job. Characteristics such as job salience, synchronization of job demands with those of the family, and overlap between family and work settings affect intrafamily dynamics. The relevance of the occupational role of the father, which influences directly the amount of time available for the family and the compatibility of the demands by the job and in the house, has been emphasized also by Rossi (1968).

Many therapists have experienced patterns of problems in families that appear related in general ways to the father's occupation (Rubinstein & Levitt, 1957). For example, fathers whose occupation is engineering, medicine, and armed service officers may be most difficult to work with in family therapy centering around the child's problems. Such fathers have certain professional characteristics in common. They are in occupations that both require and supply successful ways of ordering the environment. In their occupational role they are expected to be in authority and are given tools and positions that make this authority possible. They are accustomed to organization and to subservance either from objects or people. When these professional characteristics are combined with authoritarian, intellectualism, and success on the job it is difficult to convince these men that they may have failed in their familial roles as husbands and fathers! It would appear, therefore, that some men in those professions transfer to the home the techniques that have been successful vocationally, attempting to rear children as if they were bridges, or machines, patients, or privates.

It is our thesis that the father who fails his child perpetuates in the home his professional role and cannot shift from one role to another, that is—from the professional role to the fatherly role. This inability to shift is especially indicated in many maneuvers and experiences that are evident on the basis of our clinical experience. In the first place, by keeping and retaining an authoritarian role, which may be in keeping with his professional orientation, the father sets himself up as model and compares his successes to the child's failure, maintaining a one-way communication, telling the child what to do and expecting from him unquestionable obedience. This father sees the child as somebody that he can order around. If the son does what he is supposed to do he will be all right. Consequently, he simplifies many of the child's problems: "If he followed what I tell him, he would be all right." The fatherly role and father-child relationship is essentially reduced to patterns of communication in terms of "I command, and he obeys," as a subordinate or an underling.

In many of the fathers that we have seen, who work mainly at a professional level, there is a great deal of emphasis on objectivity and sincerity. They are unable to deal with the child's feelings and present instead another side which is more "objective," bypassing completely the importance and relevance of a child's feelings. They are much more interested in facts, so to speak, than they are interested in feelings. This emphasis puts an inordinate responsibility and burden on the child because it is on him that the responsibility for improvement is laid rather than on the parents or on the father. He is to change. There is a one-sided way of communication as essentially represented on the father's inability to see himself as being connected in any way, shape, or form with the child's behavior. The child way becomes a "scapegoat" for the parents' tensions or better he becomes a "strawman," beaten to the point of becoming a "scarecrow" and consequently rejected and avoided.

In many cases we found that the father is not only unable to shift from the primary, occupational role but sometimes he uses additionally a secondary role in his relationship with the child. If the primary role fails, then the secondary role is brought about. Two clear examples of this shift were evident in a physician-businessman who "made deals with his child" as soon as or whenever the child failed to obey his commands as a physician. Here the child's educational achievement became intensely tied up to his getting something from daddy. It was inevitable that eventually the child's educational achievement deteriorated. In another instance the father, an engineer, after he found that his primary role was not working, shifted to a "Sunday school-peer role" of preaching to the child and trying intellectually to get to his "conscience" using religious concepts and cliches. In some instances the shift was back-and-forth between two non-working methods in the relationship to the child. In both instances there was an inability to deal with feelings between the fathers and their children.

Another general aspect of the father's relationship with his child is intellectualization and avoidance of feelings. The father becomes unable to feel the impact of the child's pleas and symptoms as a way of asking for help. He intellectualizes the role of father. Instead of becoming a father, he assumes the role of "corrector." The fatherly role is seen essentially as finding faults in the child's behavior and essentially correcting them, assuming that: if the child *knows*, rather than feels, what his misbehavior is, he will be able to change it.

The father keeps emphasizing to the child his intellectual superiority by keeping a dominant position over the wife as well as over the child. This superiority is maintained in terms of his professional specialization, or in terms of the claimed importance of his work and of his professional position. In one case, for instance, a father, who was incidentally both an engineer and a salesman, and whose child was probably one of the most difficult we have seen, related to the family and especially to the son as if they were employees. In fact, in a slip of tongue, this is exactly the terms he used ("my employees" instead of "my family").

The father's inability to shift from his occupational role to that of a fatherly role means that he is either unable or unwilling to change and shift from the habits he has established in his own professional world to those required by the family situation. To elaborate on the case of the physician-businessman, his child was an 11-year-old boy of above average intellectual functioning. He was two years behind in his academic achievement, with a clear learning block in reading and other problems of psychosexual identification. The two major relationships established with the child were essentially an extension of the father's main roles outside the home. He would perpetuate his two roles with the child in two ways. As a physician, he essentially treated the child as a patient: "He does not do what I tell him;" "I tell him what to do and he doesn't do it," "If he did what I told him, he would be all right." Many of these attitudes were expressed by his view that everything would be all right if the child would follow his advice and his orders. Another way in which his father related to his son was a businessman, through bribery. He made deals with his child: "If you get a B in your reading, I will buy you this particular toy," "If you achieve in school, I will let you have this object of interest to you." The whole relationship was based on a bargaining position and "making deals." After the initial interviews it was agreed by both parents that the child would need treatment together with them. The father's reaction was that perhaps the boy should pay for treatment out of his own trust fund rather than out of his father's income.

In another case, a child of above average intelligence was underachieving in his class and was a behavior problem. The father maintained a rigid atmosphere in the home. Every cent that the wife spent had to be accounted for and every way of controlling the child's behavior had to become a matter of record, such as money. The father would have liked to run the home like a nice, clearcut type of office. The professional background of the father in this case was engineering, especially concerned with filing systems and retrieval of information in a very large corporation. He was unable to achieve his professional aspirations in life. Twenty years after college he was still in the middle of the managerial scale rather than at the top. Yet, he was the source of all knowledge, science, and wisdom in his home. He assumed a role of corrector and a source of encyclopedic information.

Another father (another engineer) on the way to therapy pointed out to his own son (who was in trouble and possibly ready to be kicked out of school and sent to juvenile court) that a loose thread was hanging from his pants. This father emphasized table manners, combing hair, and good manners, bypassing completely any feelings of the members of his family. He would be the kind of father whose child on the way to state hospital would have been told: "Comb your hair," with no emphasis on the relevant aspects of a child's happiness.

Another father, another engineer, admitted failing after trying all the possible solutions, punishment, chastisement, verbal abuse, and presenting oneself as a model of perfection. Perfection is certainly one of the strong characteristics of the individual who, even though he has not achieved as he probably might or should have, considers himself as a law-abiding, church-going, fairly satisfied individual who externalizes his responsibility by finding faults in selected family members.

Some of these observations on fathers can be predicted from sex differences in the management of anxiety. As research with college students has shown, girls are much more willing to admit to weaknesses and inadequacies. In fact, this admission may well be an expected aspect of the feminine role focusing on submission, conformity, and responsibility. Men, on the other hand, may find it very difficult to admit to personal inadequacies. Low-anxiety college men, those who are supposed to have a low degree of anxiety, turn out to be the worst subjects from an experimental viewpoint; they are difficult to obtain as volunteers and would not keep their appointments once we were able to enlist their help.

Hence, the patterns we describe here may represent the failure, on the father's part, to assume responsibility for himself and to consider critically his role vis-a-vis his wife and his child. It is a predictable pattern from the way we raise our children. Boys are allowed a much greater degree of irresponsibility than girls. They tend to externalize their anxieties in physical and motoric discharge. Consequently boys have ready-made, culturally acceptable defenses that will allow them not to become affectively involved in the family problem-solving and when needed, as many child guidance clinics will attest (Rubinstein and Levitt, 1957), will not accept the therapeutic focus.

In fulfilling the primary occupational role as provider, the father may feel that no additional roles need as much fulfillment in the family. Consequently, by emphasizing his primary occupational role, he may consider as secondary and perhaps minor his roles as husband and father. In other words, his priorities favor work first and family second. Even though he may verbalize an inverse relationship, family first and job second, his primary commitment and loyalty in terms of energy expenditure, time, and emotional depletion is to his work. Consequently, there may be little left to give to the family.

This assumption of occupational primacy has dysfunctional effects on the whole family atmosphere, because work, then, becomes an excuse, or more popularly, a "cop-out," for the father's inability or unwillingness to fulfill his marital and paternal roles. Furthermore, priority on work demands sets the tone for a skew in family priorities and loyalties that usually has dysfunctional results on the whole family.

On the basis of these observations, therefore, it may be helpful to trace developmentally how such role rigidity may influence negatively the family and how it may be dealt with therapeutically and in research.

From individual to marital living

The inability to shift from living by one's self or with one's family of origin to peers in college to living with a woman may be a sufficient shock to prevent further improvement in the marriage shortly after the wedding.

This inability may show itself in not giving up one's past playmates or decreasing work habits or leisure patterns to accommodate the wife. The wife may be given all of the responsibilities the husband had previously allocated to his mother without the privileges of being a wife. In this case, the wife becomes a mother-substitute rather than a partner or a companion. Under these circumstances, the wife may wish to become pregnant right away in order to start achieving gratifications in the maternal role, since few if any gratifications, thus far, have been found in being a wife. The coming of a child produces another role change that the man needs to cope with and adjust to if further functioning in the family is to be preserved.

From marital to parental role

This shift may not be necessary if all of the responsibilities of nurturing have been left to the wife. In this case, the father can continue his role as breadwinner and his involvement in raising the child can be casual, superficial, and often irrelevant (Rapoport, 1967). In other words, he can choose not to change and to maintain his original role without adding any new responsibilities. Eventually, however, the child and the wife may start to make more demands on him in his role as father. He needs to decide whether to bend and satisfy such demands or whether he can keep the status quo in himself, producing some adjustments outside of himself; that is, in his wife and child in relation to him rather than in himself in relation to them. If he is unable (or unwilling) to shift, he may need to preserve the status quo by increasing the importance of his occupational role as breadwinner. He may not want to decrease his working habits or leisure activities, and by increasing the importance of his occupational role, use some attributes of such a role in relating to his child.

The Collusion of the Wife

Joining rather than fighting

As long as the wife is willing to accept no changes on the part of the husband, she is in collusion with him to keep him unchanged. By keeping the husband's role unchanged, she is also keeping the relationship with him unchanged. In some instances, to keep the husband as he is, unchanged, she may accept his primary role as breadwinner as given and make no additional demands on him that may require changes in work habits and priorities. In other words, she may join her husband in keeping him without relevant responsibilities in the parental role.

Fighting rather than joining

Instead of accepting the husband's role as defined by him without negotiations, give and take, and eventual change, as would be the norm, the wife may take another dysfunctional stance; that is, she may ineptly try to change him through nagging, withdrawal of sexual favors, or concentrating on making the child a problem. In other words, instead of making changes in the marital relationships, she keeps sameness in the marriage by not making herself heard appropriately and using dysfunctional modes of communication, either blackmail (sexual and emotional) or bribery.

Maintaining a "sick" role

In view of the increased responsibilities of motherhood, she may develop dysfunctional patterns of receiving attention. If joining or fighting do not work, becoming "sick," either physically or otherwise, may become an alternative. Being "sick" or irresponsible may decrease her effectiveness as a wife and mother according to acceptable social standards.

Of course, these courses of action, joining, fighting, or assuming a "sick" role can be functional. Consequently, her energies may be directed toward making the child enough of a problem to get the husband's attention indirectly.

Displacement on the child

Her personal unhappiness may be transferred to the child through an inept use of child-rearing practices, harsh disciplinary action, and inconsistent use of rewards and punishments. She may favor the rise of a sibling rivalry or may concentrate on making one particular child the scapegoat. Since she is essentially alone in raising children, she trains them to divide and conquer and to come between herself and the husband. Since the husband does not support her emotionally in the raising of children, her being alone is not sufficient to produce consistent and coherent methods of child raising. The child, then, is able to exploit such a weakness through a variety of maneuvers that will further increase the ineffectiveness of the family system.

The Collusion of Children

In a dysfunctional system, the children become as involved in keeping sameness as the parents. Sameness in the system can be maintained through a variety of negative maneuvers designed to neutralize the effectiveness of each parent. Uproar, sibling rivalry, hyperactivity, temper tantrums, and a many other symptoms may be developed to receive attention and to maintain sameness. Consequently, having learned to maintain sameness, the child may be the one who is more entrenched in keeping the status quo.

The child as a scapegoat

Under conditions requiring sameness, a condition that is essentially elicited originally by the father's inability or unwillingness to make changes in himself, eventually someone in the family will assume the "sick" role through the use of repetitive patterns of self-defeating behavior, either acting out, withdrawal, or neurotic patterns of inhibition (learning disorders, and so forth). If the mother has not assumed a sick role already, one child is eventually selected, or he may select himself to assume the role of scapegoat in the family system. As a scapegoat, most of the family tensions and conflicts are canalized into the child's behavior and his symptoms. One clear example of this process was found in a child, who at nine years of age, was still sucking his thumb after his parents had tried to discourage him through: (a) shame and punishment; (b) tying his thumb to his belt; and (c) having a dentist build a metal mouth trap that would not allow the child to introduce his thumb into his mouth. The child's sucking had received such attention from anybody in the family that anytime anybody was upset or mad, attention was given to his thumb. Consequently, the child was receiving so much attention from everybody in the family, including his siblings, that it was impossible for him or his family to give this symptom up. When the whole family was faced by the alternative that if the thumb was no longer a problem they would need to look at themselves, such an alternative was strenuously resisted on being completely alien to their way of thinking and acting among themselves.

The role of the "well" child
The well sibling has just as much an investment in keeping the scapegoat or the system the same as anyone else in the family. In fact, as Borzomenyi-Nagy and Spark (1973) and Lidz (1973) argued, the notion of the "well sibling" loses its validity when the families of scapegoated children (or individual parents, for that matter), are observed carefully. The well child is as much a part of the family collusion not to change as anyone else in the family. Among the cases that come to mind, the clearest one was the "well" brother of a drug-oriented youngster who brought drugs to his brother while he was in jail, after the brother was arrested for possession. He gains by any negative comparison of the scapegoated sibling and by avoiding looking at himself and eternalizing on the scapegoat achieves the aims of the whole family to keep the system unchanged.

Externalization on the school
The child's dysfunctionality may become more apparent in the school than it is at home. In fact, it is in the school that the family system is seen through the behavior of the children representing that family. However, if the patterns of externalization and rejection of personal responsibility that are part of keeping one's self unchanged as set by the father are pronounced enough, the school becomes the scapegoat or the teachers are culprits who dare demand change in the child and its supporting system, his family. In the confrontation, either the family changes or the child eventually will be unable to cope with the demands of school (Grunebaum et al., 1962).

Therapeutic Implications
It should be apparent by now that if the father refuses to change in his marital and paternal roles, he will resist any attempts at changing him. His absence from child guidance clinics is, by now, an accepted aspect of therapeutic interventions. Family therapy, more than any other method of intervention, may be the only alternative available, because any attempt to accept family collusions would only allow the family to remain unchanged.

Do these observations mean that the father should be "blamed" for his child's problems? Clearly and contrarily to what the reader may think, the answer must be completely negative. He is no more to blame than any other member of the family. We know by now that one child in the family can be a source of stress to the mother and to marital and familial relationships. Putting the responsibilities on the parents or specifically on the father would attest to our failure to understand how each family operates as a system. It would be very easy to make the parents culprits for their child's problems. It is much more difficult to keep an open mind (as well as open eyes and ears) and to try to understand the self-defeating patterns that the family has developed to cope with stress, hurt, pain, and inevitably, anger. These observations only emphasize the paramount importance of the father in the mother-child relation (L'Abate, 1973).

In terms of clinical interventions and research needs, after suggesting "a more effective union between family researchers and clinicians," Walters and Stinnett (1971) recommended that future efforts:

> could be designed to assist parents and children in learning more positive, satisfying ways of relating to each other as well as to others. Goals of this type of research might be to help parents and children learn more effective and satisfying ways of

communicating with each other, as well as promoting the ability of both parents and children to express respect, warmth, and high regard for each other.

These goals have been fully met by various structured Family Enrichment Programs (L'Abate, 1974), developed to strengthen families on a variety of cognitive, affective, and experiential dimensions, with special purpose programs for specific parental and filial needs.

Difficulty of the problem

If the father has considerable investment in keeping himself unchanged, naturally he will resist any external attempts at intervention. He may use, as indeed he does, his primary role as a breadwinner and his work responsibilities as reality factors in his inability to join in any intervention designed to change the family system. Yet, if he is unwilling or unable to change, little hope can exist that change in the system will occur. No wonder efforts to deal with symptoms individually, as in play-therapy with children or psychotherapy with mothers, are usually frustrating and oftentimes futile. If the father is the major determinant of familial transactions, efforts to change the system without him being present can be indeed useless! This realization, of course, has been at the bottom of many family therapists' refusal to help unless the father is willing and able to participate.

Waiting until the breakdown occurs

Oftentimes in the face of the father's unwillingness to accept help, there is little that professional helpers do except to wait and see until pressures and stresses from the "identified patient" become so extreme that involvement on his part will become inevitable.

Before letting the family reach extremes, there are a variety of techniques that the professional helper can use to help the father become involved in interventional efforts: In the first place, the father needs to be *reassured of his importance:* "I doubt whether this family could get along without you;" "It is clear to me that you are the most important member of this family."

In the second place, he needs to be made part of any helpful effort: "How can this family change if you are not part of this change?" "How can you expect X to change if the rest of the family is unable or unwilling to change." "I am aware that you are a very busy man, but unless you are willing to help us, I doubt whether anything can be done to help *anybody* in this family." Patterns of appointments, appointment times, fees, and other arrangements need to be made with his explicit agreement and approval.

In the third place, his potential role as *saboteur* needs to be brought out from the outset: "You are a very powerful man and if you want to defeat us you have that power. The question is: do you want that power to defeat us and your family or do you want to use that power to help yourself and your family?"

In the fourth place, other choices need to be available to him: "If you don't want to participate, I can recommend many other very competent professionals who will be glad to take your money to help individually whoever in this family hurts the most;" "You can spend the same amount of money to see that one gets help and the rest do not;" "You can choose what to do with your time and your money." In other words, he needs to be given choices to maintain that whatever choice he makes is his own and noone's else in the family. If no choices are given he may prefer not to make one.

In the fifth place, responsibility for changes have to be put squarely and directly on his shoulder: "If you think that I can take care of this family without your help you are mistaken;" "I need your cooperation, just like I need the cooperation of anyone else in the family;" "However, your cooperation is more important than anyone else except perhaps your wife."

A realignment of priorities can be started by asking two questions of the father: "How many jobs can you get in which you are half the man you say you are?" and "How many families do you want?" Usually these two questions and their implications are sufficient to start the father in rethinking about his priorities, commitments, and a more family-committed perspective of his energy expenditures. In addition, the helper could add: "You may be a good provider, but if you cannot be a husband and a father, how good is all the money you can make for this family?" Essentially, at this point, the importance of personal presence and availability needs to be evaluated in contrast with material goods. The choice of one over the other and the relative costs and rewards of one over the other priority need to be considered by the whole family. The father can then choose which course of action he prefers over other options.

Research Implications

As Walters and Stinnett (1971) concluded in regard to research on parent-child relationships, "More imaginative and innovative ways of conducting research need to be more widely explored" (p. 103). Some of these ways may be found in new Marital Evaluation Battery and Family Evaluation Battery developed by L'Abate and his students (L'Abate, 1972, 1973a, 1973b).

In one attempt to verify the hypothesis about fathers' occupational role we selected two groups of children from the files of our laboratory divided according to the occupation of the father. One group included occupations typical of an intellectualizing, internalizing pattern (engineers, physicians, and CPA's). The other group included occupations representative of an acting out or externalizing pattern (salesmen, lawyers, foremen, business executives). Impressionistically it appeared that as a whole, children from the first group were more inhibited than the second group, who as a whole was characterized by conduct problems and acting-out. Of course this is the very beginning of what we hope will be a long series of studies.

Conclusion

Quite a few years ago, in a meeting with a famous investigator of mother-child relationships in apes, I pointed out to him how I considered his research incomplete because he was not including the father-mother relationship as an independent variable. After I made my point, we paused, he hesitated then said: "Damn it, I'll have to change my whole laboratory!" That's probably what we will need to do in the clinic.

REFERENCES

Aldous, Joan. Occupational characteristics and male's role performance in the family. *Journal of Marriage and the Family,* 1969, *31,* 707-713.

Barry, W. A. Marriage, research and conflict: An integrative review. *Psychological Bulletin,* 1969, *73,* 41-54.

Boszormenyi-Nagy, I., & Spark, Geraldine M. *Invisible Loyalties.* New York: Harper & Row, 1973.

Grunebaum, M. G., Hurwitz, I., Prentice, N. M., & Sperry, B. M. Fathers of sons with primary neurotic learning inhibition. *American Journal of Orthopsychiatry,* 1962, *32,* 426-473.

Henry, J. *Pathways to madness.* New York: Random House, 1971.

L'Abate, L. Family enrichment programs. *Journal of Family Counseling,* 1974, *2.*

L'Abate, L. Psychodynamic interventions: A personal statement. In R. H. Woody and Jane D. Woody. *Sexual, marital, and familial relations: therapeutic interventions for professional helping.* Springfield, Ill.: C. C. Thomas, 1973. 122-180. (a)

L'Abate, L. The laboratory method in clinical child psychology: Three applications. *Journal of Clinical Child Psychology,* 1973, *2,* 8-10.

L'Abate, L. The laboratory evaluation of families. Paper read at a symposium on approaches to group testing. American Psychological Association, Hawaii, September, 1972.

Lidz, T. *The origin and treatment of schizophrenic disorders.* New York: Basic Books, 1973.

Nash, T. The father in contemporary culture and current psychological literature. *Child Development,* 1965, *36,* 261-297.

Pederson, F. A., & Robson, K. S. Father participation in infancy. *American Journal of Orthopsychiatry,* 1969, *39,* 466-472.

Rapoport, Rohna. The study of marriage as a critical transition for personality and family development. In P. Lomas (Ed.), *The predicament of the family: A psychoanalytical symposium.* New York: International Universities Press, 1967, 169-205.

Robins, Lee N. *Deviant children grown up.* Baltimore, Md.: Williams & Wilkins, 1966.

Rossi, A. S. Transition to parenthood. *Journal of Marriage and the Family,* 1968, *30,* 26-39.

Rubenstein, B. O., & Levitt, M. Some observations regarding the role of fathers in child psychotherapy. *Bulletin of the Menninger Clinic,* 1957, *21,* 16-27.

Speigel, J. *Transactions.* New York: Science Books, 1972.

Walters, J., & Stinnett, N. Parent-child relationships: A decade review of research. *Journal of Marriage and the Family,* 1971, *20,* 70-111.

CHAPTER 7

PROTECTIVENESS, PERSECUTION, AND POWERLESSNESS

LUCIANO L'ABATE, GERALD R. WEEKS, and KATHLEEN G. WEEKS
Georgia State University, Atlanta

The purpose of this paper is to examine the functional value of scripts within a transactional framework. In transactional analysis, pathology has been viewed as one's being bound to a life script—a view developed by Berne (1964, 1972), Steiner (1974), and many others. Steiner (1974) defined a script as "an on-going program, developed in early childhood under parental influences, which directs the individual's behavior in the most important aspects of his life" (p. 418). There are many different life scripts, but almost all have one common characteristic: they limit the variety and adaptability of behavior. Scripts bind one to the past. As long as one adheres to his script, he stays the same. The essential element of the script bestowed by the parent is: "Be like us; be the same" (L'Abate, 1976).

Scripting occurs in the context of a family system where all the parts are interlocking. Thus, scripting is a transactional process because it occurs in relation to all the members of the system. The script matrix involves the father, mother, and child. As Steiner (1974) pointed out, it is usually the parent of the opposite sex who tells the child *what* to be and the parent of the same sex who tells the child *how* to be it.

Our thesis is that pathology within a transactional framework should be considered on the basis of a positive antecedent—protectiveness. At the most general level of explanation, pathology resulting from protectiveness has the function of helping the family to avoid change and thereby remain intact. In order to achieve a stable system of transactions, the family becomes forever ensnared or bound to the three pathogenic roles of persecutor, rescuer, and victim. These three roles form an interlocking system which Karpman (1968) has called the drama triangle. For this reason, the drama triangle has been chosen as an example for family pathology and for explaining the functional value of scripting. In this triangle the father is usually persecutor, the mother is rescuer, and the child is victim. However, these roles may shift rapidly for either short or long periods of time, i.e., the victim can become either a rescuer or persecutor.

Rescuer

The role of rescuer is a particularly feminine role; however, it is not limited strictly to that sex. In this role selflessness, generosity, and cooperation are emphasized. The rescuer is one who helps others at his own physical and/or emotional expense. The process of rescuing may be injurious not only to one's self but to the person rescued as well. For example, a father may continually save his son from conflicts with the law. This will only serve to reinforce his son's behavior by keeping him in the role of victim. The son's payoff may be that this is the only way he can obtain attention from his parents. Thus, rescuing serves to keep one in a "one-up, I'm O.K." position and places the person rescued in a "one-down, I'm not O.K." position.

Persecutor

According to Steiner (1974), the role of persecutor emerges from a rescuer-victim transaction. The new roles are those of persecutor-victim. This change in roles may occur as a result of two processes. First, a person (rescuer) may attempt to help someone (victim) who is not helping himself. This usually results in the rescuer's failure to give help (rescue) which in turn produces anger over his frustration. This anger will manifest itself toward the victim in a persecuting stance. Secondly, each time a victim is rescued by a rescuer, he is being placed in a one-down, powerless position. Over time, being forced into this kind of position may result in anger, thus leading the victim to take a persecutor position with regard to his would-be rescuer.

The training ground for the persecutor role is the nuclear family. In the nuclear family, it is the father who commonly displays this role and transmits it to his children through modeling. He determines what is "right" and "wrong," "good" and "bad," and "correct" and "incorrect," then exercises his power as judge by deciding what punishment is appropriate when his "law" is violated. Silverman (1975) discussed a particular personality type, the victimizer, whose persecuting stance is determined by a need for control, and also a need for constant justification of his own actions so that he can represent his actions to be "good" and "correct."

Victim

The role of victim is played by a person who cooperates or colludes with a persecutor and/or rescuer. By refusing or failing to overcome his own situation, he chooses a one-down position. This selection may occur because the victim is relatively powerless as compared to the persecutor or rescuer. Oftentimes the victim in a family is the child. Victimization may also occur because it is sometimes easy and inviting to let others take control over us. One does not have to make decisions or accept personal responsibility when he is controlled externally.

The victim is not as powerless as one might imagine. There may be a great deal of power in powerlessness. The victim may acquire the attention, effort, and even the money of many rescuers. He may manipulate the system in ways that bring all these payoffs and may eventually gain enough power to assume the role of persecutor.

Most research on the victim role has focused on the scapegoat. This research may be used to support our thesis that pathology from a transactional viewpoint is a means of protection, survival, and sameness. Specifically, pathology as protectiveness serves to maintain the nuclear family intact, either actually or in the eyes of the family.

The Scapegoat as Family Protector

Scapegoating is a concept commonly found in texts on family theory and therapy. It has been argued that by assuming the role of "sick," "crazy," or scapegoat, the identified patient is protecting the family system from having to deal with itself (Ackerman, 1968; Haley, 1963; Vogel & Bell, 1967). Furthermore, Vogel and Bell (1967) asserted that the role of the scapegoat is to stabilize tensions in the family and to help it to maintain its solidarity.

First, scapegoating may mask marital discord. Secondly, the scapegoat may be used by the parents for their acting-out of stored hostility and covert dependence. On a deeper level, scapegoating may interlock with the unresolved conflicts of separation and maturation the parents experienced in their families or origin. Finally, the cooperative scapegoat may have the covert approval of the family as a "good" and loyal family member. In any event, scapegoating is an attempt to "balance" the system.

Haley (1963) also discussed the protective functions of scapegoating between the mates. He maintained that scapegoating between mates was the primary obstacle standing in the way of a couple's changing, and that the couple scapegoated in such a way to protect one another. Although each partner might make wild attacks on the other, it is understood that some issues are not to be used in scapegoating. His example is illustrative:

> A wife who was the manager in a marriage would insult her husband for his drinking, lack of consideration, bad behavior, and general boorishness. Alone with the therapist one day she said the real problem was the fact that her husband was just a "big baby" and she was tired of mothering him. When the therapist asked why she had not brought this up in a session with her husband present, the woman was shocked at the idea of hurting his feelings in that way. (p. 133)

Ackerman (1968) conceptualized the triangle in the family even before Karpman's formulation. He stated, "We observe certain constellations of family interactions which we have epitomized as a pattern of family interdependence roles, those of destroyer or persecutor, the victim of the scapegoating attack, and the 'family healer' or the 'family doctor' (p. 628)." He also recognized a pattern of attack, defense, and counterattack, a shifting in roles. Vogel and Bell (1967) elaborated on the reasons for the change in roles. They held that role reversals may be a way to rationalize scapegoating. For example, mothers of bed wetters saw themselves as victims because of the inconvenience involved.

In summary, the clinical or theoretical literature supports the thesis that the victim or scapegoat protects the family; the victim is the rescuer!

POWERLESSNESS

According to Steiner (1974), scripting robs one of his autonomy; it makes the person powerless. Thus, becoming scripted to a family triangle (rescue triangle) makes one powerless. As long as the victim is kept powerless and dependent, the family will remain the same or the victim will remain under the family's control. This is consistent with our thesis that scapegoating occurs in order to protect the family's survival.

Another way to conceptualize powerlessness is through the social learning construct of external control. Goodstadt and Hjelle (1973), for instance, found that externally controlled subjects (high powerless) used more coercive power with people than internally controlled subjects. Thus, this finding suggests that externally controlled people are more likely to scapegoat. Scapegoating parents may in fact be just as powerless as the scapegoat in terms of how they experience themselves.

The question which now arises is why does the family accept powerlessness? From what are they trying to protect themselves and others? What are the feelings that underly these three roles? We suggest that these feelings are in part related to the experience, management, and expression of *hurt*. Hurt is a painful feeling of loss, helplessness, abandonment, inadequacy, or any feeling that nonphysical injury has been done to oneself. Unfortunately, many of us are not able to get in touch or deal with our feelings of hurt or fears of being hurt. The result of not being able to identify properly or express our hurt feelings is externalization. Thus, in an interlocking system such as a family, each member is in some sense protecting the others from their hurt by assuming a "target" role for them. It seems easier to externalize our hurts than to share them. Recall also the example from Haley. The wife was protecting her husband from hurt. She felt he could not deal with the fact that he was just a "big baby."

According to Andrews (1974), unexpressed hurt leads to distance and then detachment. He presents the case of a family which illustrates well the above sequence and our present thesis. This case involved a couple who implicitly agreed never to express their hurt openly and directly. The husband in this case had a despotic father who had crushed his autonomy. Because of this, he had come to feel weak and powerless, but attempted to disguise it through "power bluffs." His wife likewise felt powerless, and so he used her helplessness to bolster his despotism. She initially dealt with his despotism by vicariously identifying with his power, but she eventually came to resent him bitterly. However, she accepted their relationship with passive compliance. The relationship became a perpetual serial transaction of despotism-compliance-frustration-resentment-despotism. When children were added to this family, they expressed their resentment (hurt) by becoming involved in gangs; they became delinquent. This served to turn the family away from the transaction described earlier. Andrews also mentions in a number of other places how hurt is at the base of a great deal of family pathology.

IMPLICATIONS FOR THERAPY

As stated earlier, therapy at the transactional level should include all members of a system. Hence, therapy modes would include groups, couples, and families, and treatment by two or more therapists in conjunction. The ultimate goal of transactional therapy should be teaching the system how to get in touch with and express its hurt. In working toward that goal, the system could be shown how it uses the archetypal roles of the family (mother, father, child) in the form of victim, persecutor, and rescuer roles. This process would entail dealing therapeutically with the issues of protection, persecution, and powerlessness. Protection must be shown to be a way to keep a (family) system intact and unchanged. It should be shown how the persecutor projects onto others his own emotional situation, thus denying personal responsibility and his own hurt. Rescuing can be shown to be a position used to keep others one-down. It is a way to control others and at the same time fulfill one's script of being good and generous while avoiding guilt over having needs, desires, and personal wishes. It is also a way to save others from the hurt that they cannot deal with themselves. Finally, powerlessness or victimization can be shown to be a means of resisting change. It too involves rejection of responsibility for oneself and one's hurts. In short, therapy should involve the realization that we are the only ones who can change ourselves, that we must accept personal responsibility, and that we must learn to accept and express our hurt.

Earlier it was mentioned that at least two therapists should be involved in transactional therapy. We feel this is a crucial practical issue. The reason for having two therapists is that this therapeutic situation would duplicate the triangle found in one's family. It would have the added benefit of reducing the possibility of becoming entangled in a rescue game.

Slack (1972, 1976) has formulated a triad theory of therapy which closely follows our thinking. He proposed that therapy occur within the context of three people. These people would include someone who has never had a problem (e.g., a therapist), someone who has a problem (e.g., an alcoholic), and someone who has overcome the problem (e.g., an ex-alcoholic). He views change in therapy as a result of change in roles. Ideally, the person with the problem will acquire the role behavior of the person who has overcome the problem, and perhaps eventually the role behavior of the person who never had the problem. It is interesting to note that in this kind of therapeutic triangle, it would be easy for the person who never had the problem to become a rescuer; the person who had overcome the problem to be a persecutor; the person who has the problem to be the victim. It then appears that the one way to "break" the scripting which occurs in the family triangle is to become energed in a similar triangle which allows for counterscripting.

CONCLUSION

The purpose of this paper has been to show that family pathology may have a positive antecedent, namely, protectiveness. Because pathology is related to scripting and because scripting occurs in the family matrix of father, mother, and child, the Karpman triangle was chosen as an illustration of family pathology. It was proposed that the functional value of the Karpman triangle is to protect the family system. By assuming the roles in the triangle, the family's survival is insured. The family is protected from disintegration because the individual members are locked into roles which enable them to avoid changing.

The underlying reason for protectiveness in the family system is the inability to deal with hurt. The result of not being able to get in touch with the feeling of hurt is externalization. In a family, each member assumes a "target role" for the other to externalize his hurt. Externalization may take three basic forms as represented by the roles in the Karpman triangle.

REFERENCES

ACKERMAN, N. Prejudicial scapegoating and neutralizing forces in the family group, with special reference to the role of "family healer," in J. Howells (Ed.), *Theory and practice of family psychiatry*. New York: Brunner Imazel, 1968.

ANDREWS, E. *The emotionally disturbed family*. New York: Aronson, 1974, 16, 35, 146.

BERNE, E. *Games people play*. New York: Grove Press, 1964.

BERNE, E. *What do you say after you say hello?* New York: Grove Press, 1972.

GOODSTADT, B., & HJELLE, L. Power to the powerless: Locus of control and the use of power, *Journal of Personality and Social Psychology*, 1973, 27, 190-196.

HALEY, J. *Strategies of psychotherapy*. New York: Grune & Stratton, 1963.

KARPMAN, S. Script drama analysis, *Transactional Analysis Bulletin*, 1968, 26, 39-43.

L'ABATE, L. *Understanding and helping in the family*. New York: Grune & Stratton, 1976.

SILVERMAN, S. The victimizer: Recognition and character, *American Journal of Psychotherapy*, 1975, 29, 14-25.

SLACK, L. The theory of triads, *Educational Technology*, 1972, 12, 23-29.

SLACK, C., & SLACK, E. Triad therapy: It takes three to break a habit, *Psychology Today*, 1976, 9, 46-50, 93.

SPIEGEL, J. *Transactions: The interplay between the individual, family, and society*. New York: Science House, 1971.

STEINER, C. *Scripts people live*. New York: Bantam, 1974.

VOGEL, E., & BELL, N. The emotionally disturbed child as the family scapegoat. In G. Handel (Ed.), *The psychosocial interior of the family: A sourcebook for the study of whole families*. Chicago: Aldine, 1967.

CHAPTER 8

Marriage: The Dream and the Reality

LUCIANO L'ABATE AND BESS L. L'ABATE*

One of the major polarizations in marriages of workaholic husbands is their pursuing of "The Great American Dream," while their wives are left to pursue the "Petty Realities of Life." This polarization is related to other polarities in these marriages with husbands presenting nice, reasonable, pleasant facades, while their wives present bitchy, angry and/or depressed pictures. Diagnosis and therapeutic issues of this polarization are discussed.

The purpose of this paper is to review one of the major areas of polarization in marriage that does not seem to have received the attention it deserves. This polarization, more often than not, takes place along a continuum in which the husband pursues his "Dream(s)" of success, i.e., money, achievement, power, while the wife is left home to deal with the "Realities" of life, i.e., children, house, chores, etc. The result of this polarization is an inability to be or become intimate (L'Abate & L'Abate, 1979). Trollope put it well a long time ago:

A burden that will crush a single pair of shoulders will, when equally divided—when shared by two, each of whom is willing to take the heavier part—become light as a feather. Is not that sharing of the mind's burdens one of the chief purposes for which a man wants a wife? For there is no folly so great as keeping one's sorrow hidden.

Levinson, Darrow, Dean, Levinson, and McKee (1978) have addressed themselves to the topic of the function of "The Dream" in the formative development of man's evolution in personality. Originally this Dream has a "vague sense of self-adult-world... At the start it is poorly articulated and only tenuously connected to reality" (p. 35). Eventually, this Dream becomes articulated within the channel of maximal exposure taken by the man, i.e., his occupational choice. He dreams of winning the Nobel prize if he is a physicist or biologist, becoming a renowned writer, winning the Pulitzer prize, becoming a great athlete, artist, businessman, etc. Levinson et al. poignantly described the functions of "The Dream" in the lives of the forty men they studied.

Part of the marital contract for such men, explicit or implicit, is that the wife will help the husband achieve his Dream, whatever it may be. Thus, in this arrangement the marital relationship is initially one-sided. The agreement is for the wife to "help" the husband, as in the cases of nurse-doctor marriages, but there is no clear or explicit agreement that there will be reciprocity in this relationship. The woman initially may agree to help in exchange for material goods or vicarious rewards that may derive from the husband's success. But Levinson et al. (1978, p. 109) note:

If in supporting his dream she loses her own, then her development will suffer and both will later pay the price. Dynamics of this kind often surface in transitional periods such as the Age Thirty Transition or the Mid-life Transition.

---

*Luciano L'Abate is Professor of Psychology and Director, Family Study Center, Georgia State University, University Plaza, Atlanta, Georgia 30303. Bess L. L'Abate is in part-time private practice.

Key Concepts: family, intimacy, marital interaction, marital intervention, marital polarization, marital psychopathology, marital therapy, marital workshops, marriage.

The foregoing quote speaks to the very point of this paper. There are many marriages of hard-driving, competitive, and ambitious executives, managers, achievement- and success-oriented professionals who, through their workaholic investment in their jobs, hope, attempt, want, and oftentimes succeed in fulfilling their Dream. But, this fulfillment may be achieved at a great cost and sacrifice to the marriage and to the family. Failure to actualize the Dream may lead to feelings of inadequacy and failure that may be externalized in the marriage in the form of affairs, blaming wife for lack of support, among others.

Components of this Dream are enacted by the decision that to achieve this goal he will need courage, strength, and determination, as shown through the following characteristics: (a) reason and logic as the means through which the Dream is achieved; (b) strength, courage, determination are demonstrated by keeping his feelings to himself, and repressing, denying, and avoiding any expression of feelings that may possibly suggest vulnerability, weakness, or even worse, inadequacy!

A previous paper (L'Abate, 1975) explained part of family dysfunctionality in terms of the man's rigid inability to switch from a managerial role at work to a nurturant role at home. Further elaboration is needed about the roles of *both* men and women in coming to grips with issues of intimacy in marriage (L'Abate & L'Abate, 1979). The major dysfunction-producing aspects of this Dream seem to be: (a) drive and intensity of purpose, as shown by excessive and exclusive absorption in the occupational role; (b) inability to shift, differentiate, and integrate demands from work and from home; and (c) inability to experience feelings, to improve dialogue, and achieve intimacy in marriage.

The Polarities of Marriage

Considerable effort is made by the husband to promote proper appearances. A good first impression is sought through clothing, car, and house. Thus, a great deal of his functioning is directed at presenting the self in as good a light as possible. The wife, on the other hand, is involved with more practical issues; those issues that exist below, or underneath, the flow of self-presentation and go beyond the first blush facade of appearance (L'Abate, 1976). The husband either neglects chores and responsibilities, or is apparently unaware of the trivia that occupy his wife's attention. The more she brings these "Realities" to his attention, the more he resists dealing with them.

One way wives demonstrate their initial involvement and collusion with The Dream is that most of them have no careers of their own. All of their selves have been given to the pursuit and sharing of The Dream without demands of reciprocity. Eventually, when the futility or irrelevance of the collusion hits them, the emotional toll and cost that this Dream has extracted from them usually provokes a depression. If the wives are not depressed at the beginning of therapy, usually they are still angry and frustrated. Eventually they will be able to become depressed, a sign that therapy is working. The husbands, of course, find it much more difficult to get in touch with their underlying feelings of depression. But if therapy is effective, they may be able to get in touch with the emptiness that determined part of the pursuit in the first place. The husbands' selves were given up for professional roles or titles to the extent that little self remains. In fact, many of these men and some of their wives have a hard time understanding the concepts of *being*, which will be discussed later on in this paper. Some of these existential issues have been considered by Crosby (1976).

Further polarities of the "Dream" role are a *nice-nasty* quality that covers the man's attempt to achieve success on the outside by being a "nice guy," and by putting forth a self-presentational facade (L'Abate, 1976) of a "hail-fellow-well-met" glad-hander, with all of the qualities that accompany such a role. This stance, of course, polarizes the wife toward the opposite extreme of nastiness. Her increasing frustration and loneliness are expressed in "bitchy," angry outbursts and blaming statements that are surprising and incomprehensible to the husband. How could a "nice guy" like him be considered such a lowdown creature? Why does she continue bugging him about small, irrelevant details like plumbing, yardwork, and the infinite little occurrences that take place in the household every day? Why should he be concerned with diapers and diaper rash? He is in pursuit of the far greater Dream that cannot in any way be detoured, sidestepped, or interfered with by such petty irrelevancies. One husband, a worldwide traveler tycoon, became enraged when his wife asked him to deal with the gardening contractor, who for $350.00 a month was not getting the job done. Imagine him having to bother with such trifles! He was involved in multimillion dollar projects all over the USA and in foreign countries! How could she dare bother him with a chore which clearly belonged with the realm of her responsibilities and not his?

The wife's reactions oftentimes are so alien to the picture that the man has of himself and of his role that the discrepancy between the Dream picture and the Reality presented by the wife becomes unacceptable. He becomes unwilling to come to terms with it and begins acting out by becoming even more immersed in his job, picking up a mistress on the side, drinking more, etc. If and when the wife is successful in bringing him into the therapy office, he feels ganged up on by the therapist, if the therapist in any way, subtle or otherwise, sides with the wife's Reality.

These couples may display other polarities:

1. *Intimacy and isolation* - it is clear that many of these couples never dealt in their marriages with the issues of intimacy. Consequently, they are destined to be isolated from each other in what could seem an "arrangement" rather than a marriage.

2. *Enmeshment with families of origin* - many of these couples, even after more than ten years of marriage and thousands of miles from their families of origin, remain enmeshed to the point of still spending vacation time with them and fighting with each other over them.

3. *Delegation from parents and loyalty binding* - Very often these couples present some of the aspects of delegation discussed by Stierlin (1974), to the point that their success is bound to the "failures" of their parents. Their parents' failures (either economic or interpersonal or both) need to be remedied by them.

4. *Anniversary reaction or separation phase* - oftentimes the major precipitating reason for therapy is ostensibly fear of loss (i.e., finding husband has had an affair) or the children's reaching grade school age and leaving the wife.

5. Another dimension of the dream-reality continuum is the *expressive-inexpressive* (rational-irrational) distinction (L'Abate, 1980) emphasized for many years by Balswick (1980).

The wife's increasing worry about realistic details of everyday, routine household life (chores) points to another polarization between mates, i.e., *pessimism-optimism* whereby the wife begins to look at the dark side of family happenings, including the behavior of the identified patient (IP), usually one of their children, while the husband is bound to deny it, by belittling its severity or seriousness, thereby delaying, until the breaking point, any possible intervention (L'Abate, 1975). The IP, whether the wife or child, will need to escalate to the maximum level of noise (attempted suicide, being kicked out of school, flunking, etc.) to obtain the husband's attention and acknowledgement that something may need to be done. At this point professional help may be sought.

Discussion

Some of these conclusions about the woman's role in a "workaholic" husband's life are supported by the research of Macke, Bohrnstedt and Bernstein (1979), who examined the cornerstone of traditional views of marriage that housewives experience their husbands' successes vicariously. Macke et al. maintained that the specific role requirements of traditional marriage may reduce a woman's self-esteem and render her more vulnerable to stress. To obtain some verification of this hypothesis, Macke et al. obtained relevant information from 121 mostly upper middle class women, who are roughly similar to the couples we see in our clinical practice. They found that a husband's success affects a housewife's self-esteem positively, *but* only indirectly, through its effect on perceived marital success. Only the husband's income by itself had a positive effect on self-esteem. Apparently a housewife, according to Macke et al., can translate money into consumer products or other material means of increasing her status among peers, and thus indirectly her self-esteem. Macke et al. also found that other successes of the husband seem to work against the self-esteem of those wives who were not working. This finding, which parallels our findings with clinical couples, is enhanced by the finding that none of the above outcomes were present in working wives.

Boss, McCubbin, and Lester (1979) reviewed how the wives of corporate executives cope with their husbands' frequent absences and long work hours. Their major coping strategies, which we find absent in the wives we have observed in our clinical practice and on which we base our generalizations are: (a) fitting into the corporate lifestyle (frequent entertaining and social group activities); (b) developing self (as independent from the husband); and (c) establishing independence (emotionally as well as socially).

Diagnostic Implications

Diagnostically, one important way of checking on the couple's overinvolvement with work, for the husband, or with children, for the wife (L'Abate, 1975), is to ask them about their priorities. What is more important to each of them in order of preference? Most men will reply: "My family and my work." Most women will say: "My husband and my children." Neither one of them usually mentions the self as an important aspect of priorities (L'Abate, 1976). If and when the concept of self is mentioned, the notion seems to be strange and questionable. However, when the problem is rephrased: "How can a bridge stand on weak pillars?", the point is driven home that the establishment of a functional self is just as important for the marriage as any other priority. When the question is raised: "How can parenthood be achieved without a partnership?", or "How can a partnership be achieved without personhood?", it becomes even clearer that all of these issues have not been considered by the couple. In both mates the self is ill-defined, unclear, and essentially weak.

The woman may show signs of inadequacy, if not hatred, whereas the husband attempts to hold on to the occupational self to achieve a certain degree of selfhood. When the woman who defined herself as "housewife" is asked to find any definition of self that precedes "housewife," developmentally and in importance, she may have a great deal of trouble in coming up with a definition of self that includes concepts of womanhood, personhood, or individuality. The weaker she is in individuation, the more she relies on her husband and her children to define herself. Her self-concept is essentially reactive and external to both sources of satisfaction. The husband will show just as much trouble in understanding the concept of manhood separate from occupational, marital, or tertiarily, familial functions (manager, lawyer, husband, father). It is crucial at this point to assert the importance of a self-concept on which to base the marriage (Crosby, 1976). This assertion is sometimes met with questioning glances. Oftentimes, it is then best to congratulate the couple for losing their selves for the love of the other: "You must have had a self if you lost it!"

The best empirical framework within which some of the above conclusions can be evaluated, and eventually tested, is that of Foá and Foá (1974). They not only have developed an exchange theory that can encompass some of the above, but have also developed tools to assess it. Briefly, this theory assumes six classes of resources: Love, Status, Money, Goods, Services, and Information. A revision of this theory (L'Abate, Sloan, Wagner, & Malone, in press) groups Love and Status as components of *being*, Information and Services as components of *doing*, and Money and Goods as components of *having*. Within this framework we can see that many of these couples function very effectively in the *doing* and *having* areas, but are quite defective or ineffective in the *being* area. They do not know how to *be*, as experienced by: (a) expression of deep or soft feelings, (b) relaxation and letting go in leisure time, whereas for them business and pleasure many times are mixed, (c) inadequate definition of self as separate from an occupational (manager, lawyer, etc., rather than "woman" or "person"). As noted previously (L'Abate, 1976), these priorities in resource exchange are mixed up, diffused, fused, or confused. Their whole orientation to *doing* and *having* is so uncritically ingrained that understanding the implications of a *being* orientation is as difficult as experiencing feelings or assuming an "I" position.

Therapeutic Implications

What is the goal of therapy under these conditions? Obviously one goal is for the couple to learn to negotiate realistic and functional objectives for themselves, and for the husband to learn to give reciprocally while the wife learns to expect, request, and demand this reciprocity from her husband. Ultimately, the goal will be for them to learn to share their pain and depression. Previously the marriage has been on a reactive see-saw or rollercoaster. When one partner is up, the other is down. Eventually, in the course of therapeutic intervention, the couple is able to avoid such examples of affective polarization and learn to share more emphatically their hurts and pains (L'Abate, 1977; Frey, Holloy, & L'Abate, 1979). At this point, the marriage may become a *real* marriage and not an arrangement. To reach this point usually both partners have to learn to negotiate important issues without incongruent affect or avoidance of the issues involved. Berkowitz (1977) has essentially developed a position that is very similar to the present one. He stated that:

A central developmental task of the family is to help its members develop the capacity to cope with the grief attendant on separation and loss... to work through such feelings, each member must be able to acknowledge the affect as present, internal, and belonging to the self... family members may avoid awareness of such feelings within themselves. The disclaimed emotions remain powerful unconscious motivators of behavior, exerting their influence despite their denial.

The wife in many ways, at least in the beginning of married life, has colluded with the husband by agreeing with him that, explicitly or implicitly, she would share "The Dream" with him and do whatever would be necessary to help achieve it. How could she now betray him? The sheer force of the Reality brought about by household and childrearing responsibility that can only increase with married life eventually forces the wife to take a second look at herself and the nature of the marriage. If she does not become aware of her collusion, she does become aware of her giving up of her own self to allow the husband's self to prevail unilaterally. Depression, and all of its concomitants (feelings of low self-worth, rejection, fear of abandonment, etc.) come to the forefront, forcing the husband to become involved whether he likes it or not.

Oftentimes, the wife will see individual therapists who unwittingly would enter into a collusion with the husband by accepting the wife as a "sick," dependent woman, the IP (L'Abate, Weeks, & Weeks, 1979). Under these conditions, the husband is now free, and treatment becomes a long-drawn affair between the woman and her therapist, where eventually she may get over her depression, but may be unwilling to accept her husband as he is and as he has remained, since no intervention has taken place to change his involvement and love affair with The Dream!

The hard-driving, success-pursuing, reasonable and logic-oriented husband is not only preoccupied by his Dream at the expense of performing his husbandly and fatherly chores, but he also cannot speak about it even though, as therapy unfolds, he comes to realize that his Dream serves to cover up a great deal of hurt and emptiness.

In treatment, the foregoing patterns persist and become, in fact, highlighted. The husband typically smiles a great deal and presents most of the aspects mentioned above. When the wife cries, he becomes embarrassed and either takes it as a personal affront or becomes angry, or avoids dealing with it, because he is unable to empathize with her tears. He sees the wife's increased dependency and helplessness as a yoke around his neck that is slowing down the process of attainment of his Dream and interferes with his work and his ever-present job commitments. Some of these men (Supermen) are so convinced of their inherent power and attributes that it may take very extreme behavior on the IP's part to convince the husband to join and share the realities of everyday life.

The most difficult part in therapy of these couples is not to side with the wife, but to see her behavior as equally contributing to the overall trouble as the husband's. She needs to be supported without injury to the husband's feelings of inadequacy, or he may feel that both therapist and wife have colluded and "ganged up" on him.

Conclusion

We have presented a major polarization of marriage that allows us to put together into one conceptual framework diverse strands of clinical experience and empirical evidence about marriage, its successes and its failures.

REFERENCES

Balswick, J. Explaining inexpressive males: A reply to L'Abate *Family Relations*, 1980, 29, 233-234.

Berkowitz, D. A. On the reclaiming of denied affects in family therapy. *Family Process*, 1977, 16, 495-502.

Boss, P. G., McCubbin, H. I., & Lester, G. The corporate executive's wife's coping patterns in response to routine husband-father absence. *Family Process*, 1979, 18, 79-86.

Crosby, J. E. *Illusion and disillusion: The self in love and marriage*. Belmont, CA: Wadsworth, 1976.

Foá, V., & Foá, E. *Societal structures of the mind*. Springfield, IL: C. C. Thomas, 1974.

Frey, J., Holley, J., & L'Abate, L. Intimacy is sharing hurt: A comparison of three conflict resolution methods. *Journal of Marriage and Family Therapy*, 1979, 5, 35-41.

L'Abate, L. Inexpressive males or overexpressive females? A reply to Balswick. *Family Relations*, 1980, 29, 231-232.

L'Abate, L. Intimacy is sharing hurt feelings: A reply to David Mace. *Journal of Marriage and Family Counseling*, 1977, 3, 13-16.

L'Abate L. *Understanding and helping the individual in the family*. New York: Grune & Stratton, 1976.

L'Abate, L. Pathogenic role rigidity in fathers: Some observations. *Journal of Marriage and Family Counseling*, 1975, 1, 69-79.

L'Abate, L., & L'Abate, B. L. The paradoxes of intimacy. *Family Therapy*, 1979, 6, 175-184.

L'Abate, L., Sloan, S. Z., Wagner, V., & Malone, K. The differentiation of resources. *Family Therapy*, (in press).

L'Abate, L., Weeks, G., & Weeks, K. Of scapegoats, strawmen, and scarecrows. *International Journal of Family Therapy*, 1979, 1, 86-96.

Levinson, D. J., Darrow, C. N., Dean, E. B., Levinson, M. H., & McKee, B. *The seasons of a man's life*. New York: Alfred Knopf, 1978.

Macke, A. S., Bohrnstedt, G. W., & Bernstein, I. N. Housewives' self-esteem and their husbands' success: The myth of vicarious involvement. *Journal of Marriage and the Family*, 1979, 41, 51-57.

Stierlin, H. *Separating parents and adolescents: A perspective on running away, schizophrenia, and waywardness*. New York: Quadrangle/The New York Times Book Co., 1974.

APPENDIX
Instructions for Workshop Format

In conjunction with this paper, which in various formats has been given to a variety of organizations, we have found it useful to translate the above abstractions into a direct workshop format. Here are the instructions used *with couples* (real or simulated). We hope they will help any reader who may want to apply them in a workshop or enrichment format.

How many are here with their spouses?

Those who are not will have to role play with one another.

Now I (We) hope everyone is more or less partnered.

1. For the next 5 - 10 minutes we want each couple to talk to each other about your dreams or life goals. This should be your personal, individual dreams—not goals as a couple. Possible and impossible.
2. Now talk about where you want to be 5 years from now, 10 years, 20 years. (5-10 minutes)
3. Now talk about the similarities or discrepancies of your dreams. (5-10 minutes)
4. Now discuss the realities that are interfering with your dreams. (5-10 minutes)
5. How much of your past or present life are you giving up or sacrificing for dreams to be realized in the future? Has your marriage paid a price for the dream? Have your children? Discuss whether it is or has been worth it. (5-10 minutes)
6. Discuss ways you can integrate your dreams and realities so that you both win in the present and the future. How many of you will continue these dreams at home?
7. Now it is feedback time. Would any one couple like to share with us anything they have learned about themselves or their marriage in these discussions? (Take as much time as it seems feasible.)

SECTION II
FEELINGS AND INTIMACY

CHAPTER 9

Of Scapegoats, Strawmen, and Scarecrows

Luciano L'Abate
Gerald Weeks
Kathy Weeks

ABSTRACT: The thesis of this paper is that much pathology derives from our inability to deal with our feelings of hurt. The inability to deal with hurt results in the externalization of responsibility which in turn creates victims and dysfunctional behavior. The drama of the externalization of responsibility involves the same individual, the victim, or "identified patient," playing three successive dysfunctional roles: the scapegoat, the strawman, and the scarecrow. This view of pathology is basically transactional because the process occurs in a familial context where all the parts of the system are intrinsically related in producing a victim.

This paper attempts to describe the process through which we drive ourselves and others "crazy." We submit that such a process, either within husband-wife or parent-child relations, stems from externalization of personal responsibility which reflects our inability to deal with hurt feelings. The process follows three distinct steps: (a) the first step is scapegoating; (b) the second step is strawmanning; and (c) the third step is scarecrowing.

SCAPEGOATING

The process of externalization can occur in a variety of ways called by different names and by different theorists, but all referring to the same general process: "thinking" by Bach and Wyden (1969); "mystification" by Laing (1965); "double-bind" by Bateson (1972); "contradictory communication" or "blaming" by Satir (1972). Regardless of the names we might use to describe this process, the result is the same: an external target, either a spouse, child, or parent is chosen by members of a system to assume responsibility for whatever is "wrong" in the relationship. The scapegoat not only assumes and accepts this role, but oftentimes becomes so entrenched in it that he is unable to behave otherwise. The scapegoater supposedly remains free from stigma and symptoms, although both the scapegoat and the scapegoater have externalized responsibility for their personal behavior.

The Rationale for Scapegoating

To summarize the research of Bermann (1973), scapegoating is a means of group defense. When tensions in the family become so intense that individual intrapsychic defenses are inadequate, and the stress is close to the surface, scapegoating is used to compensate. In addition, the scapegoat offers the family the greatest gain at the least cost.

The choice of an insider or a family member as the scapegoat occurs for a number of reasons. First, each family has its unique problems. Since other families in the community are not having the same sorts of problems, there is no common basis on which to cultivate a common external target. Secondly, because the scapegoat is immediately present, the family can experience its control and effectiveness in scapegoating directly, thereby serving to elevate its self-esteem. Third, scapegoating is economical. Thus, it becomes clear that a scapegoat is the beginning of the last resort for the family. It occurs when the family cannot deal with its tension, and once the process is started, the cost-profit ratio for the family is so high, it is difficult to stop the process.

Subjective vs. Objective Awareness

The work of Duval and Wicklund (1972) shows there are two major kinds of self-awareness—objective vs. subjective. According to these authors, subjective self-awareness consists of the inability to evaluate oneself, forcing attention outward toward other people, tasks, and external forces. On the other hand, objective self-awareness allows an individual to look at himself as an object and permits rational assumption of personal responsibility and internal change.

We view the inability or unwillingness to look at oneself— the major characteristic of the subjectively self-aware individual —as the inability to get in touch with one's feelings of hurt and the inability to express hurt feelings in a helpful manner to one's intimates. Specifically, subjectively self-aware individuals would tend to project harmful intentions and hurtful behavior toward their physical and social environment. Furthermore, their inability to deal with their own feelings of hurt implies that it is difficult for them to deal with hurt feelings expressed by intimate others.

In a previous paper (L'Abate, 1975), it was suggested that the inability on a male's part to assume the roles of husband and father as opposed to those of businessman or executive, for example, may produce hurt in his wife and/or children. The male's pathogenic role rigidity may well stem from the repeated observation that men in our culture are trained to avoid the hurt feelings of others and fail to express their own feelings of hurt. If this is the case, it would follow that they would be more pathogenic in their hurtful behavior than women. Of course, this generalization is strictly a normative one; that is, there are many possible exceptions, such that some women are also unable to get in touch with their hurt feelings and to express them in a helpful or constructive fashion. It may well be that most males' inability to deal with hurt may be externalized to their wives who may then further externalize these feelings to the children, very much according to the principles of displacement.

Externalization and Scapegoating

The process of externalization has been empirically validated by hundreds of studies on Rotter's (Rotter et al., 1972) internal-external dimension. It is clear from all these studies that a great many people (externals) do feel themselves to be the helpless victims of external circumstances and find it easier to blame external targets for how they act and feel. Moreover, this process is so embedded in our culture that it appears socially acceptable until it reaches dysfunctional proportions.

Another name for the same process of externalization is "responsibility attribution" (Jones et al., 1971; Miller & Ross, 1975). This important social psychological concept proposes that attributions are based on the assumptions, expectations, and personal needs of the attributers. Thus, the kind of attributions made to others are frequently erroneous.

These authors propose that what lies at the base of external control and responsibility attribution is the inability to deal with feelings of hurt.

STRAWMANNING

As we stated earlier, the "strawman" is a person who accepts the label of being "sick" and who is used by others in the family to avoid dealing with their own dysfunctionality. The first aspect of "strawmanning," namely the acceptance by the scapegoat of the label being forced upon him, is crucial to the ultimate success of his intimates' efforts. They succeed in diverting the responsibility for the dysfunctionality of the family system only if the scapegoat makes no effort to throw off the full responsibility for the emotional situation present within the system. Even if the scapegoat is able to comprehend the role into which he is being cast early in the process of externalization, Ackerman (1966) pointed out:

> If, on occasion, a member tries to avoid being sucked into the family conflict and for his own safety seeks to remain unaligned, he achieves, at best, merely a temporary and precarious protection. Over a stretch of time, such an attempt at non-involvement is shortlived and must fail. (p. 85)

Thus, in terms of his self-awareness, the strawman is subjectively self-aware; that is, since his psychological state of being has been decided for him, and he apparently is unable to overcome involvement in the process, then there is no reason for him to look at himself or to himself for answers to his dilemma. In terms of locus of control, the strawman has lost control over what his role in the family is and will be. At this point, it might even be speculated that the strawman is somewhat relieved that the "battle" is over. Now, he too may relinquish the responsibility he has to himself for pulling himself up out of the trap in which he finds himself. He is able to rationalize this position to himself because maybe he really is "sick." Once the strawman makes this admission, he has become fully entrenched in the externalization drama.

The second aspect of strawmanning is the family's use of the strawman to avoid dealing with their own dysfunctionality. A strawman is used as a "red herring" by a system. It is his behavior that the family uses as an irrelevant issue in order to avoid looking at itself or changing. If the family is not functioning properly, they point to the strawman and say, "There's our problem," and the strawman points to himself and says, "I'm sick." There is no question as far as the family is concerned about what the "relevant" issue is with regard to the failings of their system.

SCARECROWING

Again, the scarecrow is one who is separated from his familial context because he is "crazy" and can only relate to others in seemingly "crazy" ways. The scarecrow is avoided and isolated.

The family, correspondingly, by isolating the scarecrow, perpetuates the debilitation he suffers and adds to the stigma attached to him. Their alienation of him reinforces further his own belief that his is indeed "sick." In addition, the more he believes in his "craziness," the fewer are the chances that he will be able to deny that he is fully responsible for the dysfunctionality of the family.

An example of this process was seen in a recent rape case interviewed by the senior author in a hospital emergency room: A 19-year old salesgirl in a 5-10¢ store was brutally attacked, both vaginally and anally, by two men who had followed her from her place of work from where she drove away at night. She had been recently rejected by her boyfriend for another girl after losing her virginity to him. Her family history essentially presented the victimized Cinderella's Syndrome: an invalid martyr-like mother, alcoholic father, and a younger brother she had to care for, in addition to the parents. She also reported feeling abused at work by her fellow employees and her boss.

She seemed to have been carefully selected by the two men who attacked her because her pattern of being a victim was not only present in the past but present at the time of the rape, i.e., in relationship also to her boyfriend's rejection, who rejected her once again, when she went to seek his help after the rape. Incidentally, she had left all four doors of her car unlocked even though she was driving away from the store parking lot at night.

HURT AS A DETERMINANT

As we have stated, the family is the social matrix within which dysfunctional behavior is formed. It is also within the family that one learns how to deal with his feelings of hurt. Since the inability to deal with hurt results in the externalization of responsibility which creates dysfunctional behavior, the concept of hurt becomes one of those genotypical concepts (L'Abate, 1964, 1976) that could be considered explanatory of a great deal of dysfunctionality inside and outside the family.

A great deal of seemingly normal behavior can be viewed as an avoidance of dealing with one's hurt feelings. We may change jobs, locations, and even our mates to achieve such an avoidance. We may use our mates or our children as "foils," driving them "crazy" and then use their craziness as reason to abandon them through divorce, separation or hospitalization. In some instances, we have sanctioned or institutionalized ways to deal with hurt feelings by creating sex stereotypes; i.e., women can cry, but "strong" men do not. To admit to hurt feelings is equated with being weak. Consequently, we do drive ourselves apart from each other—males from females, parents from children—because we differ essentially on how we deal, admit to, become aware of, and express our feelings of hurt.

Of course, hurt is an inevitable component of living. How can we live and not be hurt? Furthermore, if we were not hurt, how could we deal with hurt if and when we hurt ourselves by hurting others? Thus, sooner or later we are destined to be hurt, especially by ourselves. Yet, we are so unprepared to deal with these feelings that we may produce even greater hurt in ourselves and those we love most.

From the viewpoint of hurt, then, behaviors can be divided into two major classes—"hurtful" or "helpful." The former can be considered to be any form of defensive, negative, or destructive behavior of a noncongruent type (mystification, thinging, invalidation, etc.). The latter is the kind of behavior that supports, enhances, and congruently makes us and others feel good, proud, excited and, positive. Hurtful behavior makes us feel "shitty," helpless, ashamed, bad, sad, etc. (L'Abate, 1973).

In terms of motivation for therapy, individuals, couples, parents and families ask for help if and when they hurt. They want help because they care and do not want to hurt or see those they love hurt, including themselves (L'Abate, 1973).

The Concept of Hurt in Past and Present Literature

The concept of hurt has been present since Freud talked about "psychic pain." However, few writers, except perhaps Szasz (1959), Ginott (1965), and Bakan (1968) have fully used it in their conceptualizations. This term is notably absent in the writings of many psychological theorists and is totally lacking in the research literature. This absence in the literature in no way implies its absence as an important component of behavior.

Jourard (1974) reviewed some theories of what he calls "psychological suffering." Nevertheless, he, as well as many other sources reviewed by these authors, failed to find evidence that this concept of "hurt" has received the attention it deserves on the basis of our clinical experience. Janov (1971), Satir (1972), and L'Abate (1973) have used similar concepts in trying to get at the motivation for dysfunctional as well as functional behavior. Furthermore, L'Abate (1973) maintained that unless therapists are able to deal with these feelings in themselves, they will experience great difficulty dealing with them in the people they mean to help. Unless these feelings of hurt are dealt with properly, it is doubtful whether the outcome of psychotherapy can be considered successful.

Ginott (1965) recognized the importance of dealing with hurt feelings by recommending that parents react more to their children's behavior by letting them know how they feel ("it hurts me that . . ."). In spite of his insistence that they talk about their feelings of hurt, he did not feel that awareness of these feelings needed to be a prerequisite for talking about them. Apparently, he felt that by talking about them in a congruent fashion, parents would eventually become more aware of them—a real switch from the schools of therapy that would advocate a completely opposite approach; that is, become aware and then talk.

Andrews (1974) also recognized the importance of dealing with hurt feelings. In his analyses of "games" that couples and families play, he saw that the inability to deal with hurt underlies many games. His games offer one of the best descriptive analyses of what happens when hurt is not dealt with directly; e.g., the game, "Might Makes Right."

Finally, Kopp (1969) considered hurt from the point of view of refusing to mourn. He pointed out that if we do not accept our pain or hurt we create unfinished business. This unfinished business keeps us stuck in trying to "redeem the past" through other people. For example, a person may demand that others compensate him for his pain as in the case of a child who loses its parents and demands sympathy and love from others.

The Intrinsic (Paradoxical?) Link Between Hurt and Care

Care and hurt are intrinsically interwoven. We are hurt by and, in turn, we hurt people who care for us and whom we care for. Hurt is the proof of caring. That is: we do not care for another person unless we share his hurt. There simply cannot be one feeling without the other.

Strangers, people we are distant from, do not have the power to hurt us. We may be temporarily upset by an accident happening to someone we do not know because it makes us aware of the possibility that we may be vulnerable to the same hurt. However, the reaction is temporary and quickly forgotten. Only if the same accident happened to anyone we cared for would we be hurt. As Szasz (1959) stated:

> in all close human relationships which are characterized by a high degree of *mutual interdependence,* the suffering and unhappiness of one member assumes a *signal-function* for his partner.

This burden is usually assumed whenever our self-esteem is low and dependent on our partner's or our children's happiness.

Grief and Bereavement

Another aspect of hurt feelings is grief and bereavement for the loss of a loved one. The fear of death and the management of approaching death in ourselves as we grow older or in loved ones is another component of hurt feelings as Schoenberg et al. have illustrated (1970). In addition, Pincus (1974) has shown that when the pattern of interaction in the marriages was strongly characterized by identification, projection, or projective identification, the mourning process is much more difficult. In fact, the mourners may die soon themselves or become ill. Grief, of course, can be internalized into somatic symptoms or can be externalized through anger, hostility, and acting-out.

As Freund (1974) pointed out, grief is also present in divorce. Whether such a grief was present before the divorce and was one of the determinants of the divorce remains to be seen. The loss of a close person, even hated or those used as a foil for one's projections and externalization, also causes grief.

Marris (1974) extended the concept of bereavement to any experience involving loss or change such as the loss of one's job, house, business, or graduation into the educated elite. He maintains that continuity gives life meaning; it makes life intelligible. As he stated:

> Grief, then, is the expression of a profound conflict between contradictory impulses to consolidate all that is still valuable and important in the past, and preserve it from loss; and at the same time, to re-establish a meaningful pattern of relationships, in which loss is accepted. (p. 31)

IMPLICATIONS FOR THE CLINICAL SETTING

Collusion

Anytime we accept an individual as "sick" or "crazy" and separate him or her from his family, the therapist becomes part of a collusion with the rest of the family or a mate, who is actually driving the indentified patient crazy. The therapist legitimatizes the "crazy" label the strawman was forced to assume. The strawman as bewildered, mystified, invalidated, and scapegoated is further invalidated by the therapist's acceptance of his condition as patient. It is a further blow by the therapist in collusion with the scapegoaters. It is an additional binder put on him to accept his condition as being "sick" or "crazy."

Consequently, for every patient we accept into our hospitals and clinics, we let go those who really need to be looked at (and locked in). For example, whenever we accept a child as emotionally disturbed, we avoid looking at the "emotionally disturbed" marriage that may have produced the disturbance in the child. A strawman is simply part of a dysfunctional system.

The Future of Individual Psychotherapy

To the extent that we become scapegoats and eventually scarecrows, we need to affirm that psychopathology occurs in the context of relationships to mostly intimate others. The consequence of such a realization is that the first task of the therapist is to consider psychopathology as a familial problem. To do otherwise is oftentimes to collude unwittingly with the family in its scapegoating of the "identified patient" it presents. Thus, family therapy rather than individual therapy would be advised. Indeed, Langsley and Kaplan's (1968) study supports our view in showing that better outcome results when there is a refusal to admit an individual as "patient" without involving his family. It is this context that drove that "patient" to our office or clinic. It is that context that needs changing. The question of the usefulness of treating individuals without their context must be answered on both ethical and professional grounds. Dealing with the scapegoaters as well as the scapegoats may help us avoid strawmen and scarecrows.

REFERENCES

Ackerman, N. *Treating the troubled family.* New York: Basic Books, Inc., 1966.
Andrews, E. *The emotionally disturbed family.* New York: Aronson, 1974.
Bach, G.R., and Wyden, P. *The intimate enemy: How to fight fair in love and marriage.* New York: William Morris & Co., 1969.
Bakan, D. *Disease, pain and sacrifice: Toward a psychology of suffering.* Chicago: University of Chicago Press, 1968.
Bateson, G. *Steps to an ecology of mind.* New York: Ballantine Books, 1972.
Bermann, E. *Scapegoat: The impact of death-fear on an American family.* Ann Arbor: The University of Michigan Press, 1973.
Duval, S., & Wicklund, R.A. *A theory of objective self-awareness.* New York: Academic Press, 1972.
Freund, J. Divorce and grief. *Journal of Family Counseling.* 1974, 2, 40-43.
Ginott, H. *Between parent and child.* Toronto, Canada: Collier-Macmillan, 1965.
Janov, A. *The primal scream: The anatomy of mental illness.* New York: G. P. Putman's Sons, 1971.

Jones, E.E., et al. *Attribution: Perceiving the causes of behavior.* Morristown, N.J.: General Learning Press, 1971.

Jourard, S.M. *Healthy personality: An approach from the viewpoint of humanistic psychology.* New York: Macmillan, 1974.

Kopp, S. The refusal to mourn. *Voices,* 1969, 28-32.

L'Abate, L. Pathogenic role rigidities in fathers: Some observations. *Journal of Marriage and Family Counseling,* 1975, 1, 77-87.

L'Abate, L. *Understanding and helping the individual in the family.* New York: Grune and Stratton, 1976.

L'Abate, L. Psychodynamic interventions: A personal statement. In R. H. Woody & J. D. Woody (Eds.) *Sexual, marital, and family relations: Therapeutic intervention for professional helping.* Springfield, Ill.: C. C. Thomas, 1973, 122-180.

L'Abate, L. *Principles of clinical psychology.* New York: Grune & Stratton, 1964.

Laing, R. Mystification, confusion, and conflict. In I. Bosormenyi-Nagy and J. Framo (Eds.) *Intensive family therapy.* New York: Harper & Row, 1965.

Langsley, Donald G., & Kaplan, Daniel M. *The treatment of families in crisis.* New York: Grune & Stratton, 1968.

Marris, P. *Loss and change.* New York: Pantheon, 1974.

Miller, D.T., and Ross, M. Self-serving bias in the attribution of causality: Fact or fiction? *Psychological Bulletin,* 1975, 82, 213-225.

Pincus, L. *Death and the family: The importance of mourning.* New York: Pantheon, 1974.

Rotter, J.B., Chance, June E., and Phares, E.J. (Eds.) *Applications of a social learning theory of personality.* New York: Holt, Rinehart, & Winston, 1972.

Satir, Virginia. *Peoplemaking.* Palo Alto, California: Science and Behavior Books, 1972.

Schoenberg, B., Carr, A.C., Peretz, D. & Kutscher, A.H. (Eds.) *Loss and grief: Psychological management in clinical practice.* New York: Columbia University Press, 1970.

Szasz, T.S. The communication of distress between child and parent. *British Journal of Medical Psychology,* 1959, 32, 161-170.

CHAPTER 10

Intimacy Is Sharing Hurt Feelings: A Reply to David Mace

Luciano L'Abate

Mace's arguments concerning the love-anger cycle in marriage are criticized on philosophical (theoretical) and technical (clinical) grounds. Underneath the smoke-screen of anger there is the fire of hurt feelings. Dealing with these feelings decreases the expression of anger and helps the couple reach "real" intimacy: the sharing of hurt feelings. Victories we can share with anybody. Anybody is willing to share victories with us. Hurt feelings, on the other hand, belong within the marriage.

Dear Dave:

I am delighted to comment on your article (Mace, 1976) concerning marital intimacy and the deadly love-anger cycle. In the same issue of the Journal there is also another article (Dayringer, 1976) concerning fair-fight training that is a different view that addresses itself to the same issue—the expression and management of anger (Bach and Goldberg, 1974). I, for one, beg to differ with both formulations on theoretical and therapeutic grounds. I happen to believe that *anger is the result of hurt feelings and fear and that underneath anger there is a great deal of unresolved and unexpressed pain and fear of further hurt.* Intimacy is sharing these hurt and hurtful feelings and fears, not anger. What I fail to see in both your formulations as well as in that of Bach and his followers (and I do have tremendous respect and admiration and love for both of you, because I have experienced both of you either as therapist or as theorists) is the failure to consider and to emphasize the presence and repetitive cycles of these unresolved feelings of hurt and fear. Once these feelings are dealt with and we are able to conceptualize ourselves as hurt human beings, we can then come to terms with our anger and avoid projecting it on others.

Most of us, especially men, are unable to get in touch with, become aware of, and express properly these feelings of hurt and fear of pain, as I have discussed in previous formulations (L'Abate, 1973, 1975). For men especially, it is easier to get mad than to be sad. Anger is smoke and underneath that smoke there is the smoldering fire of hurt feelings. Women, to be sure, have an easier time of it and get in touch with these feelings. However, their experience is usually no more constructively expressed than in men.

These hurt feelings and fears that underlie anger may be related to unresolved grief, past frustrations and failures, feelings of inadequacy, present loneliness, or poor self-esteem. It derives from this proposition that just dealing with anger *is not enough.* To me, it is equivalent to dealing with smoke without dealing with the fire. If we deal with the fire directly the smoke may dissipate. Thus, I consider any attempt to deal directly with anger alone, as another well-intentioned and rationalized (as Daryinger does as well as you do) but incomplete and insufficient effort to resolve conflicts and confrontations between mates. Dealing with anger may dissipate the smoke and perhaps lower the intensity of the fire. However, to me, intimacy between marital partners means *sharing of all those hurt feelings and fears* and not fighting. To put it another way, you may alleviate the symptom (anger) but you may not have dealt with the underlying causes (hurt feelings). You may have given the couple new techniques of negotiation and confrontation. However, I respectfully submit that unless we deal with these underlying hurt feelings within ourselves and we are then able and willing to share them with our partner, no complete resolution can be found.

There is another troublesome aspect of your formulation (as well as that by Bach as represented in Dayringer), that is: what I would call a mechanistic engineering approach to anger, that is dealing with anger as something to be changed technically, as if we were dealing with robots rather than relationships. I, for one, prefer to deal with human relationships, not at their face value, that is, taking anger as something to be manipulated and changed at its own level, but with an appreciation that everytime I deal with anger in myself, my mate, my children, my clients, my friends, and my students, in other words, the totality of my human experience, if and when I probe into how and why that anger came into being, I usually find a hurt individual, a hurting relationship, and a hurt marriage.

Another argument against your proposal can be leveled against the failure to deal with the *context* of anger. That is, anger comes out of a context of hurt. Failing to deal with this context may adjust our marriage as an engineer would fix our car. However, I would seriously question whether you can increase intimacy by dealing directly and strictly with anger alone. I would not doubt, however, that by helping couples deal with their anger better, you (and Bach) may make it easier for them to share their hurts and fears as well. You may decrease the fighting but have you increased intimacy?

Since many of us are unable to break through the smoke-screen of anger and resentment, we cannot deal with the raw fire of hurt or so-called depression. I am afraid that most of us do not know how to cope with these feelings except to use panaceas and circumlocutions. We become as helpless as the very individuals we want to help. This helplessness is very likely related to our inability to deal with our own hurts and depressions. Once the breakthrough occurs and the underlying depressive core is finally reached it is very important to deal with it *positively* (L'Abate, 1975); that is: to assert that this is probably the first time in his or her life that the individual has been giving a congruent message. Getting in touch with our hurts, crying, and grieving are all manifestations of this final congruence of both verbal and nonverbal aspects of our selves coming together and merging. It is at this time of grieving that we are at our best, that we have finally reached our humanness and vulnerability. We are healed through the redeeming congruence of our awareness and congruent expression of our hurts. This hurt confirms and enhances us. It takes us away from robot-like control of our emotions into humanity. It is our ticket of entry into the human race. It is our admission and declaration of our finality and relativity. Why block it by dealing with anger and keeping the smoke to hide the fire?

If the experience of crying is devalued, bypassed, ignored, or mishandled, the crying will persist and no healing will take place. Consequently, the smoke of anger is destined to stay on between us. It is in the marriage that these hurts need to be shared. What is love and intimacy but the sharing of our hurts and trusting our mate enough to share them with him or her? Most of us as male therapists do not know how to cope with crying because crying has been equated with weakness and femininity. We are the victims of the great American stereotype. Hollywood has prevailed. We have allowed ourselves to be robbed of the experience of hurt and crying. Crying, the experience of our level of hurt, makes us whole. It confirms us. We need to assert its importance to couples as strongly and as positively as we can and show how our inability to share it in the marriage is the major liability that threatens marriage—not anger.

Again and again I meet professional counselors, therapists in training, both males and females, who look at me with incredulity and puzzlement: "What is he talking about?" I am more concerned about our profession as a collection of humans than as a profession of technocrats and technicians who follow single 1, 2, 3 rules *a la* Bach or *a la* Mace and "fix" the love-anger cycle! Let us deal with our humanity first and then worry about techniques. Let us clear how to cope with hurts in ourselves and our marriages. If we are males, let us learn from our mates. Especially if they are *not* professionals, they have a great deal to teach us. Most of them, the non-professional everyday housewives, know more how to get in touch with hurt than we will ever be able to do. Hurt may not be expressed properly and it may be used to divide us rather than to unite us. If we can use this hurt to unite our marriages *maybe* (I say *maybe* advisedly) we may be able to help couples in their marriages. Otherwise, we may be able to "fix" marriages but we may not be able to heal them. I personally prefer to heal rather than to fix, even though I recognize how hard this job is.

Now that the theoretical assumption is clarified, what does it mean in therapeutic translation? It means that the therapeutic push and effort is for partners to become aware of these unresolved, unexpressed feelings of hurt and fear. Allow these feelings to prove our humanity, our vulnerability, and our fallibility and our need to share these feelings with someone we can trust, usually our mate. Since the anger is recognized in its pervasiveness, we need to ask ourselves where does it come from? From our mates? If we accept such an external determination, we are taking away from ourselves the fact that humanly we *alone* are responsible for our feelings, whatever they may be, and *we* are responsible for how we are aware of them and how *we* express them. If we allow ourselves to externalize or project them onto our partners, this becomes an easy way to avoid personal change in ourselves. As long as our partners need to change, we do not have to.

Thus, my approach as a helpful healer is to deal from the very beginning of the therapeutic relationship with these hurt feelings, acknowledge their presence, and indicate their powerful effects on the marital relationship.

To test our own different assumptions and procedures, we could set up a variety of situations (as I have attempted to do experimentally) by asking undergraduates to write down what experiences make them angry. Most of the experiences they listed were of hurtful nature! A therapeutic analogue or simulated role-playing situation of anger could be separated experimentally into three groups: one group receives your training; a second group receives fair-fighting training; a third group is helped to deal with the hurt feelings underlying the anger. In fact, most of these techniques (except yours) have already been written up in our enrichment programs for couples (L'Abate, 1975). It would make for creative and meaningful research. Let me see what my students and I can do to resolve this issue.

Dave, you may have repaired many angry couples and taught them how to clear the air between themselves; however, a) once we are able to deal with our depressive core positively and b) are able to take responsibility for it, i.e., we are responsible for how we hurt ourselves, how we allow hurt to ourselves, and how we express it; c) then, the issue of anger becomes irrelevant and secondary. It fades in the background of culturally sanctioned myths that we counselors have helped maintain to avoid dealing with *our* hurts.

If we are not able to deal with our hurts, how can we help others?

Therapeutically, I would substitute different steps for your steps:
1. Where there is anger, recognize there is hurt.

2. Deal with these hurt feelings and help these feelings be expressed in terms of "I" or impersonally, "It hurts me . . ."

3. Avoid projecting these feelings onto your mate and assume responsibility for our own hurt.

4. Forgive ourselves for trying to be perfect and invulnerable by denying hurt feelings in ourselves.

5. Redefine the self in terms of our errors and weaknesses, as being human and not "crazy" or demanding to be invulnerable "perfect" supermen and superwomen.

Thus, I feel that the cycle of marital intimacy at first blush may seem one of love-anger. However, underneath that level there is a cycle of love-hurt. To me and to my wife that level is much more meaningful, helpful, and constructive than the one you submit. Care to check it out?

Lovingly,
Luciano L'Abate

REFERENCES

Bach, G. F., and Goldberg, H. *Creative aggression*. New York: Doubleday, 1974.

Dayringer, R. Fair-fight for change: a therapeutic use of aggressiveness in couples counseling. *Journal of Marriage and Family Counseling*, 1976, 2, 115-130.

L'Abate, L. A positive approach to marital and familial intervention. In L. R. Wolber and M. L. Aronson (Eds.) *Group therapy, 1975: an overview*. New York: Stratton Intercontinental Medical Books Corp. 1975, pp. 63-75.

L'Abate & Collaborators. *Manual: marital enrichment programs for the family life cycle*. Atlanta, Georgia: Social Research Laboratorie, 1975a.

L'Abate, L. Pathogenic role rigidity in fathers: some observations. *Journal of Marriage and Family Counseling*, 1975, 1, 63-78b.

L'Abate, L. Psychodynamic interventions: a personal statement. In R. H. Woody & J. H. Woody (Eds.) *Sexual, marital and familial relations: therapeutic interventions for professional helping*. Springfield, Illinois: C. C. Thomas, 1973, pp. 122-180.

Mace, D. R. Marital intimacy and the deadly love-anger cycle. *Journal of Marriage and Family Counseling*, 1976, 2, 131-137.

CHAPTER 11

Intimacy Is Sharing Hurt Feelings: A Comparison of Three Conflict Resolution Models

Joseph Frey III[*]
Judy Holley[**]
Luciano L'Abate[***]

To check on the validity of three different methods of dealing with anger, 1) calm, rational discussion, 2) "fair fighting," and 3) sharing of hurt and of fear of hurt, two different studies were performed. In the first study a video-taped procedure was presented to 36 undergraduates. Their preferences indicated no support for the hypothesis of sex differences in dealing with conflict and some support to differential preferences for each of three methods. In the second study, three structured programs directly derived from the three theoretical positions were administered at random to 11 couples. Their reactions suggested some support for the position that intimacy may be found in sharing of hurt feelings. Theoretical issues and directions for future research are considered.

The purpose of our research was to investigate and compare three methods of achieving emotional intimacy. The methods we studied were the calm, rational approach advocated by Ellis (1976), the fair-fighting approach advocated by Bach and his followers (Bach and Goldberg, 1974), and another approach based on sharing hurt feelings advocated by L'Abate (1977). Historically, intimacy has been a slippery concept. In the laboratory it has been equated with self-disclosure, while more experiential approaches have emphasized the complex nature of intimate relationships. Definitions and descriptions of intimacy are legion and the interested investigator can become quickly overwhelmed by this abundance. Whatever intimacy may be, we must address how it is achieved and maintained.

The three approaches investigated in this study are typical of a "conflict resolution" approach. Basically, they assert that intimacy is achieved in resolving conflicts, so that it's not conflict *per se* that affects relationships, but how that conflict is processed (Strong, 1975). Within this framework, the three approaches studied here propose different methods of processing conflict in order to achieve intimacy. Each method is different and each is based on its own conceptualization of intimacy. Bach advocates "fair-fighting" (Bach & Wyden, 1968) as a method that views intimacy as "two people openly expressing their unique needs" (1968, p. 283). To achieve intimacy, couples must openly conflict and

---

[*]Joseph Frey III is a PhD candidate in the Family Studies Program at Georgia State University.
[**]Judy Holley, MA, is a graduate of the Social Psychology Program at Georgia State University.
[***]Luciano L'Abate, PhD, is Professor of Psychology and Director of the Family Studies Program at Georgia State University, Atlanta, Georgia.

105

appropriately display their anger towards each other. However, this approach has been soundly criticized on theoretical grounds by Straus (1976) and Feshbach (1971). These authors assert that Bach's basic assumption, that couples display their aggressive tendencies "creatively," is based on unsupported hypotheses and may be destructive to relationships.

Ellis' approach to intimacy in the marital relationship is based on his rational-emotive therapy. He endorses an approach by Mace (1976) that unresolved anger destroys relationships and must be dissipated. For Mace, intimacy involves two people moving closer to each other and in this process becoming vulnerable. This vulnerability can be destroyed by sudden outbursts of anger. Consequently, both Mace and Ellis advocate techniques for allaying and/or dissipating anger, such as acknowledging it, renouncing it as inappropriate, asking one's spouse for help, counting to ten, going for a drive, or even sex. Mace bases his approach on the frustration-aggression hypothesis. He states: "Our civilized society reduces danger but increases frustration. So for most of us, anger is triggered off when we don't get what we want and need" (1976, p. 136). On the other hand, anger for Ellis is a result of a person's irrational beliefs. Ellis deals with these beliefs by dissipating the anger they cause. So achieving intimacy, for both Mace and Ellis, involves treating anger as an emotional and irrational hindrance which must be allayed.

L'Abate (1977), however, insists that dealing only with anger is an "incomplete and insufficient effort to resolve conflicts and confrontations between mates." Instead, L'Abate states that "anger is the result of hurt feelings and fear and that underneath anger there is a great deal of unresolved and unexpressed pain and fear of further hurt." So anger is the "smoke" and hurt is the "fire." To deal directly with anger as Bach, Mace, and Ellis advocate is to ignore the real issue of hurt feelings and fear. For L'Abate, intimacy is sharing these hurt feelings.

In comparing these three approaches we hypothesized that females would react more favorably to the sharing hurt approach and consider it to be more intimate, while men would react more favorably to the calm, rational approach of Ellis and Mace or the fair-fighting approach of Bach. Two studies were done to test this hypothesis; the first used video-taped scenarios, the second an enrichment approach (cf. Wright & L'Abate, 1977).

Study I[1]

In this study the independent variables were video-taped scenarios of a couple resolving the same conflict using the three different approaches. Each scenario consisted of three parts: the actual conflict resolution, a tape of the actress saying her lines, and a tape of the actor saying his lines. The dependent variables were the subjects' ratings of the scenarios on a questionnaire and preferences for each of the three approaches in response to various questions.

Method

Description. We used a modified role-playing technique developed just for this study. Role playing in social psychology experiments is a relatively recent methodology which is usually traced to a critique of deception experiments by Kelman (1967). Since then, there has been a steady stream of studies using a variety of role-playing methodologies (Mixon, 1972; Smith, 1975), and an increasingly acrimonious debate pitting role playing and deception techniques against each other (Miller, 1972; Forward, Canter, & Kirsch, 1976; Cooper, 1976). To bypass the usual problems associated with role playing we combined it with the theatrical techniques of acting and directing, that is, subjects were told what was expected of them and then coached in playing the roles we presented to them. While acting is not a substitute for real life, we reasoned that it would elicit intrapersonal reactions similar to, but not the same in magnitude as, those reactions subjects experience in real life. As a manipulation check on this hypothesis, we included an item in our first questionnaire asking subjects to rate their degree of involvement. Furthermore, to minimize the infinite number of variables present when two people interact, we decided to use a constant stimulus as one of our "subjects," that is, we essentially eliminated one person and substituted a video-tape recording of a confederate couple. The couple was taped resolving a conflict situation in three different ways: Bach's "fair fighting" approach, Ellis and Mace's calm, rational approach, and L'Abate's sharing hurt feelings approach. After each scene we then taped each member of the couple individually saying their own lines, leaving space where the other member's lines would be. As they were taped individually, they conveyed a "newsroom" effect of talking to the viewers. So a female subject would view the first conflict scene and then interact with the actor; essentially taking the role of the actress. The situation was reversed for male subjects.

Subjects. Subjects were 18 males and 18 females enrolled in an introductory psychology class at Georgia State University. They were all single and were required to participate in experiments to complete course requirements.

Dependent Measures. Two questionnaires were used for evaluating the Ss' reactions to their interactions with the stimulus tapes.[2]

Stimulus-Tapes. Subjects read their lines from cue cards right below the television monitor, but had mimeographed dialogues available to them when answering questionnaires. Subjects rarely made use of the mimeographs. The actress and actor were student volunteers from an introductory drama course at Georgia State University. Their reason for participation was to gain experience in front of a television camera. We rated them of medium attractiveness. We thought that using an average attractive couple would eliminate positive and negative biases caused by extremes in attractiveness. Nevertheless, as precaution, subjects were directed to fill out questionnaires on the basis of their reactions to dialogue, not to the actor and actress themselves.

Each conflict resolution sequence and individual interaction sequence was from three to four minutes long. Subjects were required to do each individual interaction three times. Preliminary practice trials indicated that three was the optimal number of repetitions. More trials produced a reported loss of interest and boredom. Less trials produced a reported feeling of not being involved enough to fill out the questionnaire truthfully.

Apparatus. A black-and-white video-tape monitor and playback deck were used to show the stimulus-tape.

Procedure. Subjects were run one at a time. After being seated in front of the monitor they were given instructions concerning their responsiveness to the three different role playings by actors of the opposite sex.

Immediately prior to being shown each script, subjects were briefed on how they should act in the scene. Instructions were as follows: *Fair-fighting:* "This script involves the appropriate display of anger. Don't be afraid to raise your voice or to show your anger at the situation." *Calm, rational discussion:* "This approach involves maintaining a calm and reasonable manner toward the conflict. You should resist any temptation to show your feelings except where called for by the script." *Sharing hurt feelings:* "This script involves not just anger, but also feelings that have been hurt. Don't be afraid to express those hurt feelings through your tone of voice or facial expression." Although vague, these directions were necessary to cue the subjects as to how to act out each script. Subjects who were resistant to putting any emotions into a script were lightly prompted. Immediately after interacting with each individual script, subjects filled out questionnaire 1. After viewing all three scripts, subjects were given questionnaire 2 to fill out. They were then de-briefed and dismissed.

Results

Data from questionnaire 1 were analyzed using a multivariate analysis of variance, enabling us to treat each question as a separate dependent variable. No significant differences were found for any question as a function of the three conflict-resolution methods. Subjects did answer all questions favorably, between 3 and 4 on a scale of 1 to 5. This was important for question 3, which checked involvement with the dialogue.

Data from questionnaire 2 are shown in Table 2 (along with data from Study II). A chi-square analysis was used to analyze the data in two ways: 1) including the "none" response in the statistical equation, and 2) dropping subjects who responded "none" from the analysis. We feel the latter method is a stronger test of significance.

The results do not support our hypotheses concerning sex differences. However, there are marked differences among each of the three approaches in terms of preference. Subjects liked Bach's fair fighting approach significantly more (16 out of 36) than the

Table 1. Chi-Squares and Levels of Significance for Studies I and II Using Questionnaire 2

Questionnaire 2	Study I (N=36)		Study II (N=23)
	Method 1*	Method 2**	
1. Method liked most	Fair-fighting $x^2=12.66$; p. .01	n.s.	Fair-fighting $x^2=16.74$; p. .001
2. Method would rather use to resolve conflicts	Calm, rational discussion $x^2=16.21$; p. .005	n.s.	n.s.
3. Most intimate method	Sharing hurt feelings $x^2=28.64$; p. .001	Sharing hurt feelings $x^2=21.88$; p. .001	Sharing hurt feelings $x^2=19.00$; p. .001
4. Method most suited to interpersonal style	n.s.	n.s.	Calm, rational discussion
5. Method would rather learn	Calm, rational discussion $x^2=13.44$; p. .001	Calm, rational discussion $=9.66$; p. .01	$x^2=9.24$; p. .01 Fair-fighting $x^2=9.24$; p. .01
6. Method became most involved in	n.s.	n.s.	Fair-fighting $x^2=6.24$; p. .01

*Includes "none" responses in statistical equation (see "Results" section, Study I).
**"None" responses not included in statistical equation (see "Results" section, Study I).

other three choices (including "none"); this difference is not significant when compared directly with the other two methods. Subjects stated they would rather use the calm, rational approach in resolving conflicts (18 out of 36), but this also lost significance when compared directly with the other two methods. In deciding which script was most intimate, subjects (24 out of 36) strongly agreed that sharing hurt feelings was the most intimate, even when compared directly with the other two methods. In asking subjects which script they would rather learn in a training program they chose the calm, rational discussion approach (20 out of 36).

Study II[3]

Method

Subjects

Subjects were 22 married couples. One spouse of each couple was enrolled in an introductory psychology course at Georgia State University and received course credit for the couple's participation in the experiment.

Procedure

The 22 couples who signed up for the experiment were randomly assigned to the treatment (12 couples) and control (10 couples) conditions. Each experimental couple individually attended a total of four sessions with the experimenter, the last being for follow-up and de-briefing.

Treatment subjects were told they would have three marital enrichment sessions on conflict resolution, each session ending with each spouse independently completing two checklists indicating current feelings. During the fourth session, each subject completed three additional questionnares prior to de-briefing. To control for order effects, two couples were randomly assigned to each of six possible sequences for the three conflict resolution models. Control subjects were told that their sessions would consist of independently completing two checklists indicating current feelings. During the fourth session, they completed two additional questionnaires prior to de-briefing.

An enrichment approach was used in the three treatment sessions. This is a structured intervention approach "based on pre-arranged, often written down instructions that individuals specifically trained for the purpose present for a couple to follow" (Wright & L'Abate, 1977). Instructions for the sharing of hurt and fair-fighting sessions are in the respective manuals for enrichment programs prepared by the junior author and his associates (L'Abate, 1975a, 1975b). Instructions for the calm, rational approach, written especially for this study, were based on the concepts presented by Ellis and Harper (1975). To minimize variability of the treatments across couples, the enrichment instructions for the three methods were pre-recorded on a cassette tape and played during the sessions.

Dependent Measures

Experimental sessions: The Multiple Affect Adjective Check List (Zuckerman & Lubin, 1965) and the Profile of Mood States (McNair, Lorr, & Droppleman, 1971) were independently completed in randomly varied sequence by subjects during the treatment and control sessions. Both measures assess by means of self-report the psychological aspects of emotion as a current state rather than an underlying personality trait.

Follow-up sessions. Subjects in the treatment group independently completed questionnaire #2 from Study I.

Results

Affects and Mood Checklist. Three affect states (anxiety, depression, and hostility) and six mood states (tension, depression, anger, vigor, fatigue, and confusion) were analyzed using a repeated measures ANOVA. No significant differences were found for any affect or mood as a function of treatment or conflict resolution method.

Conflict Resolution Methods. This data was analyzed in the same manner as the data from Study I, that is, using chi-square (without the "none" response in the statistical equation). As can be seen from Table 1, the fair-fighting method was most liked, the method subjects would rather learn, and the one they became most involved in. Calm, rational discussion was picked as being most suited to interpersonal style, and sharing hurt feelings was chosen as the most intimate. As in Study I, sex differences were not significant.

Discussion

As is the case with most laboratory research, our results must be interpreted with caution when applied to the "real world." Despite our use of unmarried college sophomores in Study I, our use of married couples in Study II affords us the luxury of making some generalizations to the "outside" world as regards internal validity. We looked at reactions to methods of conflict resolution which supposedly facilitate intimacy—we did not study intimacy *per se*. The nature of the phenomenon by definition precludes its experimental manipulation. But given such limitations, we feel some important issues about an elusive concept have been raised.

Clearly L'Abate's sharing hurt feelings approach was perceived by subjects in both studies as the most intimate method of conflict resolution. But the other two approaches equally impressed subjects in other ways. We believe these differences are understandable when the functional significance of each approach is examined.

Our subjects may have liked the fair-fighting approach because of its "tough guy/gal" approach which deals with conflicts through self-assertion. This approach enables the person to mobilize his anger in a way that enhances feelings of competence. Calm, rational discussion may have been the most preferred in Study I and most suited to styles of behavior in Study II because of its effectiveness at dissipating anger, that is, it goes beneath the conflict so the couple can neutralize the irrationality which lies at the root of the anger. Sharing hurt feelings may be perceived as most intimate—and probably as the most threatening—since it deals with conflict at a causal level. It goes beneath the anger to the hurt which may smolder at even deeper levels. The finding that subjects prefer to learn calm, rational discussion (Study I) or fair-fighting (Study II) also suggests that sharing hurt feelings is risky and threatening.

These results suggest that intimacy should be viewed as a vertical rather than a horizontal concept. The latter approach proposes a variety of "intimacies" to account for a myriad of situations. Clinebell and Clinebell (1968) describe 10 varieties of intimacy as well as marital intimacy. However, viewing intimacy vertically with self-presentational, phenotypic, and genotypic levels (L'Abate, 1976) may make it a more relevant and meaningful concept. Self-presentational intimacy refers to superficial efforts at being intimate—efforts which enhance how someone comes across to another. Phenotypic intimacy is related to efforts aimed at resolving conflicts and dealing with anger. And genotypic intimacy involves the risk and vulnerability of sharing our hurts and fears. Therapy aimed only at self-presentational or phenotypic intimacy is incomplete. Fair-fighting and rational discussion may help systematize couples whose conflicts are destructive and chaotic, but they miss the most accessible avenue to deepening a couple's relationship. To facilitate our clients' intimacy with each other, we must teach them to be vulnerable—to share their hurts and fears, not just their anger.

REFERENCES

Bach, G. & Goldberg, H. *Creative aggression.* New York: Doubleday, 1974.
Bach, G. & Wyden, P. *The intimate enemy.* New York: Avon Books, 1968.
Clinebell, H. J. & Clinebell, C. H. *The intimate marriage.* New York: Harper & Row, 1970.
Cooper, J. Deception and role-playing: On telling the good guys from the bad guys. *American Psychologist,* 1976, *31,* 605-610.
Ellis, A. Techniques of handling anger in marriage. *Journal of Marriage and Family Counseling,* 1976, *2,* 305-315.
Ellis, A. & Harper, R. A. *A new guide to rational living.* Englewood Cliffs, N. J.: Prentice-Hall, 1975.
Feshbach, S. Dynamics and morality of violence and aggression. *American Psychologist,* 1971, *26,* 281-292.
Forward, J., Canter, R. & Kirsch, N. Role-enactment and deception methodologies. *American Psychologist,* 1976, *31,* 595-604.
Kelman, H. C. Human use of human subjects: The problems of deception in social psychological research. *Psychological Bulletin,* 1967, *67,* 1-11.
L'Abate, L. & collaborators. *Manual: Family enrichment programs.* Atlanta, GA: Social Research Laboratories, 1975(a).
L'Abate, L. & collaborators. *Manual: Enrichment programs for the family life cycle.* Atlanta, GA: Social Research Laboratories, 1975(b).
L'Abate, L. *Understanding and helping the individual in the family.* New York: Grune & Stratton, 1976.
L'Abate, L. Intimacy is sharing hurt feelings: A reply to David Mace. *Journal of Marriage and Family Counseling,* 1977, *3,* 13-16.
Mace, D. R. Marital intimacy and the deadly love-anger cycle. *Journal of Marriage and Family Counseling,* 1976, *2,* 131-137.
McNair, D. M., Lorr, M. & Droppleman, L. F. *EITS manual for the profile of mood states.* San Diego: Educational and Industrial Testing Service, 1971.
Miller, A. G. Role-playing: An alternative to deception? A review of the evidence. *American Psychologist,* 1972, *27,* 623-636.
Mixon, D. Instead of deception. *Journal for the Theory of Social Behavior,* 1972, *2,* 145-177.
Smith, J. L. A games analysis for attitude change: Use of role-enactment situations for model development. *Journal for the Theory of Social Behavior,* 1975, *5,* 63-79.
Straus, M. A. Leveling, civility, and violence in the family. *Journal of Marriage and the Family,* 1974, *36,* 13-29.
Strong, J. R. A marital conflict resolution model: Redefining conflict to achieve intimacy. *Journal of Marriage and Family Counseling,* 1975, *1,* 269-276.
Wright, L. & L'Abate, L. Four approaches to family facilitation: Some issues and implications. *Family Coordinator,* 1977, *26,* 176-181.
Zuckerman, M. & Lubin, B. *Manual for the multiple adjective checklist.* San Diego: Educational and Industrial Testing Service, 1965.

NOTES

[1] This study was carried out by Joseph Frey under the direction of Luciano L'Abate.
[2] Copies of the questionnaire and dialogues of the stimulus tapes are available upon request from the junior author (LL).
[3] This study was carried out by Judy Holley under the direction of Luciano L'Abate.

CHAPTER 12

THE PARADOXES OF INTIMACY

Luciano L'Abate and Bess L. L'Abate

ABSTRACT

The importance of intimacy in dyadic relationships makes this concept a critical and crucial one to review and to explore in its therapeutic and human implications. Three paradoxes, derived from a definition of *intimacy as sharing of hurt and of fears of being hurt*, are considered in this paper: (a) we need to be separate in order to be close; (b) we hurt and are hurt by those we love the most; and (c) we need to comfort and be comforted by those we have hurt or who have hurt us. Circular and linear solutions and resolutions for these paradoxes are suggested.

The purpose of this paper is to reassert the importance of intimacy in dyadic relationships and to present a definition that leads us into at least three paradoxes which, we feel, have profound human and therapeutic implications. To support our contention that intimacy is an important aspect that deserves scholarly and professional attention, we need to review some of the different positions that we have found in the literature. Derlega and Chaikin (1975), for instance, reviewed some of the issues of intimacy in marriage from the viewpoint of "self-revelation." However, at no time was there a consideration of paradoxes or even more specifically of intimacy as sharing of feelings. Dahms (1974) defined intimacy as a developmental process rather than a static entity. He suggested a three-tiered hierarchy: Level 1. *Intellectual,* based on superficial selling of one's self-ideal rather than the real self; Level 2. *Physical,* which includes touching and sexuality; and Level 3. *Emotional,* is characterized by (a) *mutual accessibility;* (b) *naturalness;* (c) *nonpossessiveness;* (d) *processed over time.* Jackson and Bodin (1968) considered the paradoxes of marriage.

Davis (1973) provided one of the most detailed analyses of intimate relationships from a sociological viewpoint. He defined an intimate relationship as an ongoing social interaction between relatively equal pairs who reciprocate numerous intimate behaviors. The four pairs who typically achieve some degree of intimacy are: (a) friends, (b) lovers, (c) spouses, and (d) siblings. Hence, intimacy becomes an important aspect of social interactions to the point that Davis would like to develop a science of intimate relations called "philemics." Although he admittedly failed to offer a theory of intimacy *per se,* Davis presented a detailed discussion of most cultural and empirical factors that enter into intimate relationships, i.e., (a) ways in which strangers lay groundwork for a potentially close relationship by making each other's acquaintance; (b) ways in which acquaintances who are becoming intimates set up cycles of corporeal copresence; (c) ways in which intimate couples escalate intimacy indicating communications; (d) ways in which they reciprocate increasing quantities of public and confidential information; (e) ways in which they exchange greater and greater amounts of environment-alleviating aid; (f) ways in which they integrate more and more of their basic beings; (g) techniques indicating use of reintegrating their ever-disintegrating relationship; and (h) causes that may ultimately wreck an intimate relationship and consequences that this collapse will have on those who built it.

Davis criticized psychologists ("from classical Freudian to ultramodern T-group") for viewing intimacy as (a) essentially biological; (b) not teaching its harm because it is biological; (c) whatever harm one experiences is imaginary and/or self-induced; (d) "fear of getting hurt" is irrational and ought to be overcome; and (e) no one should be afraid to become intimate because intimacy is ultimately beneficial. Davis differed from the above formulations he attributed to "psychologists" in general, and made intimacy: (a) a social and historical condition; (b) where parts of a self fuse with parts of another self; (c) this fusion can be seen as potentially harmful; (d) consequently whatever pains one may experience in intimate relationships are as real as any biological pain (some would argue as being more painful than biological ones!); (e) therefore, "fear of getting hurt" is an important aspect of self that should be acknowledged and enhanced so that each individual can (f) select those intimates who can reciprocate intimacy for mutual growth against those whose use of intimacy is ultimately destructive to themselves and others!

As detailed and important as Davis' analysis is, including his suggestions for research in this field, his presentation suffers from a sociological bias that determines a certain degree of attributions concerning what "psychologists" do feel about intimacy. If there is a field of science to study intimacy, i.e., philemics, then psychotherapy of marriages and couples becomes *applied philemics,* because it is in this very field that one can study in depth how couples build, or fail to build, intimacy to the point that the goal of therapy in general and of marriage therapy in particular is to help individuals become more constructively intimate with each other.

Among other sociologists, (Lowenthal & Haven, 1968) intimacy is defined as the presence of a confidant: "The presence of an intimate relationship serves as a buffer both against gradual social losses in role and interaction and against the more traumatic losses accompanying widowhood and retirement." In his review of love and intimacy, Coutts considered three types of intimacy: (a) intellectual, (b) emotional, and (c) physical. Most of what he says about emotional intimacy (pp. 15-17) is relevant to the present context:

> Most of us are so unaccustomed to exploring and identifying our feelings that we leave them unnamed or have difficulty distinguishing them from our thoughts....Two people are emotionally intimate when both have similar feelings at the same time....The more completely there is a mutual sharing of feelings, the greater the emotional intimacy....The most important prerequisite for emotional intimacy is that we do not have to apologize for, or defend our feelings.

Feldman (1979) suggested a model of intimacy that included implicitly a paradoxical position, i.e.: "existing side by side with the wish for intimacy is fear of intimacy, derived from one or more unconscious fantasies and conflicts." He conceptualized five major types of fear of intimacy: (a) fear of merger; (b) fear of exposure; (c) fear of attack; (d) fear of abandonment; and (e) fear of one's own destructive impulses. Instead of so many variations, we prefer to condense all of Feldman's fears into one major fear, which seems to be the underlying dimension, i.e., the sharing of (past) hurts and fear of being hurt (in the future: L'Abate, 1975, 1976, 1977; Frey, Holley, & L'Abate, 1979). In this work we have defined "intimacy" as "the sharing of hurt feelings and of fears of being hurt." From this definition derive three other paradoxical conditions that make difficult the goal of reaching intimacy in most dyadic relationships, and that make it even more difficult for an intimate relationship to survive, unless a certain degree of intimacy is achieved.

Instead of an eclectic approach preferred and suggested by Feldman, (1979), we prefer a specifically paradoxical approach because we find it more congenial to our clinical *modus operandi*, more in keeping with our theoretical biases (L'Abate, 1976) and actually simpler and more economical in terms of outcome. When one subscribes to a paradoxical view of reality (L'Abate, 1975; Selvini-Palazzoli et al., 1978) it is difficult not to overinterpret or not to see paradoxes lurking in every corner. Whether one needs to view reality as a paradox in order to practice paradoxical therapy (Soper & L'Abate, 1977; Weeks & L'Abate, 1977) remains to be seen. We do not necessarily equate *intimacy* to marriage, even though that is where intimacy ideally "should" be found. Intimacy is still difficult to reach outside or inside of marriage.

Intimacy, defined as the sharing of hurt and of fears of being hurt (L'Abate, 1976, 1977; Frey, Holley, & L'Abate, 1979), presents at least three paradoxical conditions that make its attainment very difficult. These three "conditions" are: (a) one needs to be separate in order to be close; (b) the ones we love have the greatest power to hurt us; and (c) we must seek comfort and be comforted by those we hurt and who hurt us. Our conception is illustrated by Levinson (1978, p. 30):

> The recognition of vulnerability in myself becomes a source of wisdom, empathy and compassion for others. I can truly understand the suffering of others only if I can identify with them through an awareness of my own weakness and destructiveness. Without this self-awareness, I am capable only of the kind of sympathy, pity and altruism that reduces the other's hardship but leaves him still a victim.

Self-awareness, therefore, is a prerequisite for disclosing and expressing these feelings for them to be shared. This position, then, makes self-awareness an extremely important area to relate to intimacy.[1]

In considering issues of intimacy in marriage it may be necessary to specify further the functions that marriage may perform in the area of emotional needs. In other words, we need to specify the nature of the "emotional" aspects of marriage, reconceptualizing marital functions in a different fashion than has been the case heretofore.[2] Briefly, in the emotional sphere marriage performs at least four distinct functions: (a) *self-survival,* i.e., married folks live longer and better than non-married, divorced, and single individuals[3]; (b) *self-confrontation,* to the point that many people who divorce do so to avoid coming to terms with their selves; (c) *reconciliation of differences,* to the point that differences could unite as well as break up a marriage. It is how these differences are used that matters. They can bridge or break a marriage, and (d) *sharing of hurt feelings,* one of the constant themes of emphasis in our work (L'Abate, 1977; Frey, Holley, & L'Abate, 1979; L'Abate & L'Abate, 1977). These functions are essentially dependent on the degree of closeness-togetherness and separation-individuation of each couple, how well or how poorly differentiated each couple is (L'Abate, 1976).

It is within the context of these functions that it is important to consider: (a) issues of intimacy, what we mean specifically by it; (b) the paradox of being separate in order to be intimate; and (c) the three paradoxes that derive from (a) and (b), the definition of intimacy and its paradoxes. Ultimately, (d) we may give some suggestions on how to increase intimacy in couples and dyads.

This paradox has been repeated in different form by Haley (1963), and more recently by Boss and Whitaker (1979), i.e., togetherness versus separateness. As one of the students present in the class (Boss & Whitaker, 1979) commented (p. 387):

> Perhaps if we could accept the dialectical nature of separation-togetherness rather than viewing them as either/or situations, we could live life more easily and view more acute forms of separation as natural and less traumatic.

This paradox is part of what Heller (1979) calls "a social support paradox: are close ties to others sources of strength or of stress?" Hence, the major, basic issue of intimate relationships is one of how can this closeness be fostered and used creatively to decrease conflict and enhance self and other?

It is important to consider, however, that many theorists and therapists eschew feelings and emotions (a) as being irrelevant to the process of therapeutic change, and (b) other aspects of psychological functioning like cognition and/or behavior being more important and relevant to the process of change. Our position, in contrast to cognitive and behavioral emphases, is that (a) emotions are as important as cognitions or actions; (b) emotions in couples and families need to be expressed constructively and separated sharply from thinking or actions. What we feel is one thing, what we do about our feelings is another. Dysfunctional relations and inadequate intimacy is obtained when feelings and especially feelings of hurt and fears of being hurt are not expressed properly; (c) hence, feelings need to be acknowledged and expressed reciprocally, while actions need to be negotiated through reasoning. Theoretical and therapeutic implications from this Emotions-Reasoning-Action (E-R-A) model can be found elsewhere (L'Abate & Frey, 1981.[4,5] In this section we shall concentrate on the difficulties that are found in trying to find and enhance intimacy between spouses, one of the most critical aspects of marital therapy.

We Only Hurt the Ones We Love

As trite and corny as such a statement may be, hurt and caring are intrinsically interwoven. We oftentimes give those we love a license to hurt. Functionally speaking, we are rarely if seldom hurt by strangers. The degree of hurt increases as the degree of closeness and caring increases. Hurt and fears of being hurt only result from the intensity of close relationships and not from superficial or transient relationships. Hence, there are feelings that relate to our vulnerability in a caring relationship. We can all be let down, betrayed, deceived, rejected and abandoned. This is a real possibility more than ever before in view of divorce rates, mobility (leaving), and death. We all are vulnerable to losses (L'Abate et al., 1979).

Vulnerability and Impotence. There is nothing we can do if and when those who love us hurt us, whether they do it intentionally or unintentionally. ("The road to hell is paved with good intentions.") Thus, we are helpless to avoid hurt even though we can and should try to minimize the possibility of its occurrence. Yet, there are losses that are inevitable.

The Inevitability of Hurt. We cannot live and not be hurt. Even if those we love were never to deceive, betray, or let us down, like our parents, eventually they are bound to die and to leave us. Hence, there is nothing we can do about it. Hurt, therefore, is just as inevitable as joy and pleasure. The polarities of human existence, i.e., pleasure-pain, are as difficult to handle as life and death. However, we can derive more enjoyment from our pleasures if we can handle our hurts better.

Vulnerability, Trust, and Fallibility. We trust those we love not to hurt us, yet they, as well as we, are fallible human beings, and as such we cannot expect them not to hurt us at times. Hence, vulnerability and acknowledgment of such a condition needs to be related to trust and to fallibility.

Separateness and Closeness

One needs to be separate enough from one's partner to avoid "fusion," "enmeshment," "loss of self," "getting hooked," "symbiosis," etc. This separate sense of self, based mostly on Being rather than Having and/or Doing[6] allows us to be and remain close without any demands for solution. To be separate and to be together at the same time one needs to possess a sufficient feeling of a differentiated self (L'Abate, 1976) so that one will be able to *stay* with someone else's hurt without fusion, entanglement, or "hook-up." It means being able to BE with that someone without having to DO anything, or to get or give material things (HAVING) as a substitute for feeling.

Hence, to BE with someone who hurts there is no requirement of performance. Availability and presence is all that is required to share the feelings of hurt together. To obtain such a goal (an ideal for many) one needs to be aware of the reciprocity of human existence (*"Do ut des"*). We want those we love to be available to us when we need them. Hence, we need to keep in mind the prerequisites for being separate and close at the same time: (a) *Being* rather than Doing or Having; (b) *Feelings* rather than Thoughts or Actions; (c) *Sharing* rather than Negotiating (Thoughts are negotiated, Actions exist!); and (d) *Presence* rather than Performance.

Comfort From Those Who Hurt Us

Marriage is that strange relationship where we need to seek comfort from the very person who hurt us! In fact, if we do not do it, the relationship is imperiled! No wonder intimacy is so difficult to achieve.

How is comfort for our hurt to be obtained? Strangers do not care. Professionals only care if and when they are paid. Thus, we are faced by the inevitability of having to seek comfort for our feelings and fears from those we have hurt and who have hurt us, because only through this comfort can we hope to achieve a resolution for our pain.

Comfort is achieved through the ways we have outlined previously. Comfort for the grief of death is achieved through sharing our pain with those who care for us and who also cared for the deceased as much as we did. Hurt among the living is different. If no comfort is obtained from those who hurt us, there may be no confrontation of vulnerability and of reciprocity.

SOLUTIONS AND RESOLUTIONS OF PARADOXES

Among the many ways of dealing helpfully with these paradoxes we need to distinguish between two major classes of interventions: (a) circular, or indirect, paradoxical, unexpected, as described by Selvini-Palazzoli et al. (1978), and (b) linear, or direct, gradual, step-by-step confrontation of the paradoxes. *Both* approaches are necessary to help bring about changes in intimacy or improvement in the intimacy level of couples and families. Among the many that we have tried out the following produce a greater chance of success.

Circular Resolutions

A paradox can be solved (a) by posing another paradox, or (b) where an impasse is present, the recognition of the presence of a paradox may help; (c) by prescribing the impasse itself, or, more linearly, by following any or all of the five steps outlined as resolution. How can these paradoxes be solved or resolved? Supposedly, paradoxes, by definition, are unsolvable. Yet, the following possibilities present themselves to move out of the impasse.

Recognition of Paradoxes. Just recognizing the nature of these three paradoxes may be sufficient, at times, to help couples get out of their impasse. The fact that they can face and see them either as part of the general contradictory nature of human nature may help solve and resolve them. The coexistence of contrasting states, feelings, attitudes, etc. as *normative* rather than *deviant* is part of a dialectic recognition where *being human means being contradictory*! This point may need further development.

Presentation of Another Paradox. Instead of commenting on the paradoxes of human life, presentation and consideration of *all three* paradoxes presented here may be helpful. Sometimes, it is helpful to present a completely different paradox.

Prescription of Paradox. A more direct way suggested by the work of the Palo Alto and Milano groups (Selvini-Palazzoli et al., 1978) is the prescription of the paradox as a homework assignment in a very concrete and ritualized fashion ("Make sure you fight, to become intimate, at least for 10 minutes after supper every Monday, Wednesday, and Friday for four weeks, or until we see you next time.")

Linear Solutions

Admittedly there are many linear ways of dealing with these paradoxes and their implications. Among these we suggest the following focuses:

Intrinsic Overlap of Caring and Hurt. It is important to realize this connection and its existential implications for intimacy. Once this connection is made, the paradoxical nature of the foregoing impasses may be resolved.

Separation of Feelings from Actions. Feelings are to be shared. Actions are to be negotiated through reasoning in a way that gives importance to the feelings of the parties involved. Resolution of hurt is based on the other partner sharing the hurt, staying with it for as long as is necessary, and reassuring the hurting partner of his or her importance and worth in the presence of a caring relationship. No courses of action, no negotiation of problem-solving need to be considered at this point. What is needed is the *presence and sharing* with one's partner. If and when a partner is not able to share this hurt, then it remains unresolved like a sour, festering wound.

Separation of Personality and Performance. It helps to recognize that one can care for somebody and hurt them at the same time and that what one does does not necessarily mean that one is as one does. It is necessary to relate this separation to child-rearing patterns and to consider the destructiveness of equating personality and performance.

Admission of Vulnerability. We all are vulnerable to being hurt and feeling afraid of being hurt. Once such a vulnerability is acknowledged and accepted, it allows us to protect ourselves from potential hurts and in spite of such protectiveness to realize that no matter how careful we may be, we remain vulnerable to hurt as part of our living (and dying). In fact, we are vulnerable especially to those whom we care for and who care for us.

Admission of vulnerability means forgiving ourselves and others for not being perfect supermen and superwomen (L'Abate, 1975) and giving up the equation that being perfect means being "good" and being imperfect (and vulnerable) means to be "bad"! To be human means to be imperfect! To be perfect means to be heavenly and not of this earth!

Balance of Digital and Analogic Modes. Awareness of these two modes of thinking (Wilden, 1972) and the danger implicit in the use of one at the expense of the other helps put getting hurt and feeling hurt in a more relativistic perspective. Digital means either/or dichotomies. Analogic means both/and continuities. Both digital and analogic modes of thinking are necessary to differentiate personality from performance and feelings from reasoning and from actions.

Awareness of these contradictions and paradoxical positions may help us solve and resolve inevitable injuries present in intimate relationships as they are usually found in marital and family therapy.

CONCLUSION

From a definition of intimacy as sharing hurt feelings we derive three additional paradoxes that need *both* circular and linear therapeutic approaches.

REFERENCE NOTES

[1] L'Abate, L. The role of awareness in therapy reconsidered (submitted for publication).
[2] L'Abate, L., & Blossman, C. B. Introduction to marriage and the family (unpublished manuscript, 1979).
[3] A review of the literature to support these functions is found in 2.
[4] L'Abate, L., Wagner, V., & Frey, J. Further implications of the ERA model (submitted for publication).
[5] L'Abate, L., Ulrici, D., & Wagner, V. Implications of the ERA model for a classification of skill training programs for couples and families (submitted for publication).
[6] L'Abate, L., Sloan, S., & Wagner, V. The triangle of life: Differentiation of resources (unpublished manuscript).

REFERENCES

Boss, P. G., & Whitaker, C. "Dialogue on Separation: Clinicians as Educators," *The Family Coordinator,* 1979, *28,* 394-398.

Coutts, R. L. *Love and Intimacy: A Psychological Inquiry.* San Ramon, Ca.: Consensus Publishers, 1973.

Dahms, A. H. "Intimate Hierarchy," in E. A. Powers & M. W. Lees (Eds.), *Process in Relationship: Marriage and Family.* St. Paul, Mn.: West Publishing House, 1974, pp. 73-92.

Davis, M. S. *Intimate Relations.* New York: The Free Press, 1973.

Derlega, V. J., & Chaikin, A. L. *Sharing Intimacy: What We Reveal to Others and Why.* Englewood Cliffs, N.J.: Prentice-Hall, 1975.

Feldman, L. B.. "Marital Conflict and Marital Intimacy: An Integrative Psychodynamic-Behavioral-Systemic Model," *Family Process,* 1979, *18,* 69-78.

Frey, J., Holley, J., & L'Abate, L. "Intimacy Is Sharing Hurt Feelings: A Comparison of Three Conflict Resolution Models," *Journal of Marriage and Family Therapy,* 1979, *5,* 35-41.

Heller, K. the Effect of Social Support: Prevention and Treatment Implications," in A. P. Goldstein & F. H. Kaufer (Eds.), *Maximizing Treatment Gains: Transfer Enhancement in Psychotherapy.* New York: Academic Press, 1979, pp. 353-382.

Jackson, D. D., & Bodin, A. "Paradoxical Communication and the Marital Paradox," in S. Rosenbaum & I. Alger (Eds.), *The Marriage Relationship.* New York: Basic Books, 1968.

L'Abate, L. "A Positive Approach to Marital and Familial Intervention," in L. R. Wolberg & M. L. Aronson (Eds.), *Group Therapy 1975: An Overview.* New York: Stratton Intercontinental Medical Book Corp., 1975, pp. 36-75.

L'Abate, L. *Understanding and Helping the Individual in the Family.* New York: Grune & Stratton, 1976.

L'Abate, L. "Intimacy Is Sharing Hurt Feelings: A Reply to David Mace," *Journal of Marriage and Family Counseling,* 1977, *3,* 13-16.

L'Abate, L., & Frey, J. "The ERA Model: The Role of Feelings in Family Therapy Reconsidered: Implications for a Classification of Theories of Family Therapy," *Journal of Marriage and Family Therapy,* 1981, *6,* (in press).

L'Abate, L., & L'Abate, B. L. *How to Avoid Divorce: Help for Troubled Marriages.* Atlanta: John Knox Press, 1977.

L'Abate, L., Weeks, G., & Weeks, K. "Of Scapegoats, Strawmen, and Scarecrows," *International Journal of Family Therapy,* 1979, *1,* 86-96.

Levinson, D. J. et al. *The Seasons of a Man's Life.* New York: A. A. Knopf, 1978.

Lowenthal, M. F., & Haven, C. "Interaction-Adaptation: Intimacy as a Critical Variable," *American Sociological Review,* 1968, *33,* 20-30.

Selvini-Palazzoli, M., Boscolo, L., Checchin, G., & Prata, G. *Paradox and Counterparadox.* New York: Brunner/Mazel, 1978.

Soper, P. H., & L'Abate, L. "Paradox as a Therapeutic Technique: A Review," *International Journal of Family Counseling,* 1977, *5,* 10-21.

Weeks, G. R., & L'Abate, L. "A Bibliography of Paradoxical Methods in Psychotherapy of Family Systems," *Family Process,* 1978, *17,* 95-98.

Wilden A. *System and Structure: Essays in Communication and Exchange.* London: Tavistock, 1972.

Luciano L'Abate is Professor of Psychology and Director, Family Studies Program, Georgia State University, Atlanta, Georgia 30303; Bess L. L'Abate is in part-time private practice of marriage and family therapy with her husband. Requests for reprints should be addressed to Dr. LAbate.

SECTION III

THE ROLE OF FEELINGS IN THERAPY

CHAPTER 13

The E-R-A Model: The Role of Feelings in Family Therapy Reconsidered: Implications for a Classification of Theories of Family Therapy

Luciano L'Abate*
Joseph Frey III**

The importance of considering a continuum of Emotionality (E) separately from Rationality (R) or Activity (A) is emphasized. A model showing equally all three aspects is presented that allows a clearer classification of family therapy theorists than has been possible heretofore. Diagnostic, therapeutic, and research implications are hinted at, but will be part of future work.

This paper presents a model of therapy which attempts to account for the roles of Emotionality, Rationality, and Activity (E-R-A) in therapeutic change and suggests a scheme of classification of family therapies based on this model. Essentially, we argue that Emotionality is an important aspect of relationships, therapy, and change—an aspect that has been neglected and denigrated by some individual and family therapists and theoreticians. We bring out the following points: (a) conceptual considerations which accord Emotionality (E) equal footing to cognitive (R) and behavioral (A) aspects within a person; (b) developmental considerations of Emotionality which we feel extend the typical approach to emotions within individuals to emotions within relationships; (c) criticism of approaches that belittle the role of Emotionality in life; (d) support for our E-R-A model which we think provides a balanced view of Emotionality, Rationality, and Activity—giving each equal importance and value, regardless of theoretical orientation; and (e) a classification of family therapies based on this model.

Conceptual Considerations
First, Emotionality has been "mistreated" in how it has been applied to "everyday psychology," probably owing to misconceptions stemming from a cognitive–rationalistic perspective in both psychology (clinical and experimental) and western philosophy. In the first place, Emotionality has been confounded with actions. That is, if one feels sad, he/she should cry; or if one feels angry, he/she should aggress. Schafer (1976), for example, maintained that thoughts, wishes, and emotions are all actions and should be designated as such in verbal forms denoting action. He did not separate the definition of a situation

---

*Luciano L'Abate, PhD, is Professor and Director, Family Studies Program, Department of Psychology, Georgia State University, Atlanta, GA 30303.
**Joseph Frey III, PhD, is Assistant Professor, Department of Pediatrics, University Medical Center, University of Alabama, Birmingham, AL 35294.
Request for reprints should be addressed to Dr. L'Abate.

from the definition of the reaction to it because they are both "correlative." We think an equation of Emotionality = Activity represents a "short-circuiting" of the emotional system. In fact, we believe the fusion of any two aspects of Emotionality, Rationality, or Activity obfuscates the major issue: all three processes are equally important and relevant (on paper and in real life.)

Secondly, Emotionality has been classified into positive–negative categories. Usually painful emotions are called negative, while pleasurable emotions are called positive. We consider such a classification mystifying and confusing. Emotions are! They represent our human, biological, organismic reactions to life events. They *per se* are neither positive nor negative, neither creative nor destructive. How and when these emotions are processed into Activity is where judgments of positivity or negativity can be made.

Thirdly, a conceptual shortcoming deriving from the previous shortcoming pertains to grouping together as "negative" emotions some that differ in topological structure and developmental sequence. For instance, hurt and anger are put together as "negative" without considering that each of these emotions occurs at different developmental stages and performs different functions, that is, hurt is a more difficult, complex emotion to reach and to express, especially for men, while anger is relatively easier to experience and to express for men than it is for women.

Fourth, another shortcoming in conceptualizations of Emotionality is the rational-irrational dichotomy. Instead of a continuum of Emotionality, we often view emotions digitally (either-or) as being either rational or irrational rather than accepting them dialectically and analogically, as being *both* rational *and* irrational (Wilden, 1972). The use of this dichotomy, then, leads us to use an even more destructive equation, such as rationality is "good" (acceptable, necessary, important) and irrationality is "bad" (unacceptable, unnecessary, unimportant). This irrationality is relevant to the polarization between sexes, that is, women are said to use or express emotions "irrationally," while men, on the other hand, are "rational," superior human beings in control and in charge of their lives. Emotionality then becomes something to avoid, shy away from, suppress, repress, deny and negate. Both dichotomies, incidentally, govern and are the basis of many views and theories on emotions and feelings (Arnold, 1960). *We seriously question these dichotomies* as being humanly and scientifically untenable.

A mechanistic view of man (behavior as computer) may emphasize rationality at the expense of irrationality. Both views are essentially emphatic of one aspect of behavior over another. Behavioral and systems positions would avoid dealing with the issue because of its assumed irrelevance or of secondary and tertiary relevance to Activity. A good example of the equation of Emotionality with "irrationality" in therapy is illustrated by Jurjevich (1978), who "emotionally" criticized at length the obsessive emphasis on emotions that characterizes mental health professionals. Furthermore, he equated Emotionality and emphasis on the importance of emotions to "doing your own thing" at the expense of everybody else, that is, emotionality with hedonism. Consequently, he took to task theorists, like Moreno, Perls and Rogers, who he felt "contributed to irrationalizing therapeutic procedures." We believe Jurjevich's equations are unwarranted, especially when we specify that Emotionality needs to be considered with and in relationship to Rationality and Activity. His attack, nonetheless, illustrates the danger of any one-sided viewpoint that is enhanced by putting down what is seen as another competing and antagonistic viewpoint. Instead, we view these three major viewpoints as *different* and each as conbituting in its own particular way to the process of change.

Emotionality can and should be conceptualized on a continuum. Instead of being contradictory and mutually exclusive, opposite emotional states such as love-hate and hurt-joy may be normatively present and may be coexisting. This is why human beings are different from computers. The coexistence of contrasting emotional states separates human beings from machines. When emotions are not fully felt, expressed, and shared, they tend to fuse, mix-up, and influence behavior by "merging" destructively with either over-Rationality (compulsivity) or excessive Activity (impulsivity) and to push one to behave more digitially (either-or) than analogically (both/and). Our position is that Emotionality, Rationality, and Activity need a balance of both digital and analogic processes rather than one process exclusively at the expense of the other two. Families and theorists alike suffer from this condition.

Relationship/Systems Considerations

From a relational point of view, Emotionality plays an important role in the development of one's relationships. The infant uses emotions as signals to express to the outer world what is happening internally. These "signals," or emotional expressions, are very likely the primal forces of the mother-infant bond.

As the child grows older, R and A became increasingly more refined and relevant to the mediation of E. The major issue, here, is *differentiation* of E from R and A so that all three processes are separate and viable. It is only in the clear separation of these processes that all three can function interdependently, providing human beings with the resources to deal effectively with the environment. This specificity of resources prevents any of these processes from being fused to another, avoiding the dangerous short-circuiting of E, R, and A.

It is in the differentiation of E that adults also find a basis for intimate relationships. Hurt feelings, their awareness, expression, and sharing are at the basis of a great deal of our inability to extend ourselves as individuals to others in intimate relationships (L'Abate, 1977). We posit that *H*urt, *E*mptiness, *L*oneliness, and *P*ain (HELP)[1] not only are individual experiences, but can provide one with the opportunities to reach out and connect with others. To experience H-E-L-P is to experience oneself as *alone and separate*. It is in this separateness that two people can finally come together as individuals. The more one can stand alone in one's helplessness, the more able one is to establish togetherness (L'Abate and L'Abate, 1979). The deeper two people can share their feelings with each other, the stronger, more intimate, and more solid is their relationship. Thus, emotions, being individual phenomena, which establish one's separateness as a human being, also afford the opportunity to bridge the chasm of H-E-L-P and establish relationships by sharing one's deepest feelings with another. Although this seems true for all emotions, it is the complex experience of H-E-L-P which facilitates intimacy the most. Other emotions, especially anger, while being statements of separateness, often become ways of avoiding the deeper aspects of one's individuality within a relationship. Anger may so completely take over the inability to express hurt, short-circuiting it, that it may be expressed destructively, even in violence.

The theoretical "leap" is that E governs distance in relationships. The majority of theories subsumed under the heading of family/systems theories hypothesize that individuals in relationships experience both a movement toward others to maintain the relationship system, and a movement away from the relationship to maintain the self. A sampling of such theories and their terms for this process include: Bowen (1978): differentiation and fusion; Minuchin (1974): enmeshment and disengagement; and L'Abate (1976): symbiosis and autism. Our position is that individuals in systems use E as centripetal or centrifugal forces (Stierlin, 1977) to express both their separateness and togetherness. The family is the proving ground for this process, and in order to function maximally, must allow individuals the opportunity to negotiate the helpful expression of E. The major task for the family in this regard is to allow each individual access to his/her emotions as an experience of separateness and differentness, while maintaining access across emotional boundaries for contact, support, and togetherness.

The E-R-A Model

Our model postulates that E, R, and A are all equally important parts of the "self." No one aspect or component is primary over the others. All three aspects are needed for any individual and/or relationship system to function at its optimal potential. We view effective interpersonal functioning as the ability to use all three aspects as resources; the implication is that emphasis on one aspect, or neglect of one, inhibits the utilization of personal resources, making it more difficult to deal with the vicissitudes of daily living. For example, a person who bypasses the cognitive R aspect will likely act on his/her E without thinking—probably engaging in excessive emotionality and/or impulsivity. At the opposite extreme would be an individual frozen in a sort of behavioral paralysis. This is the person who has bypassed A so that E and R lead only to anxiety and/or depression. The individual who shortcircuits E will appear very logical and reasonable; at the extreme s/he may engage in ritualistic, obsessive behavior designed to ward off emotions (especially anxiety).

Therapeutic Implications

Therapeutically this model is eclectic. It implies that any form of therapy which focuses on any one, or combination of aspect(s), can be effective. Basically, the E-R-A model is systemic. Causal attributions of change based on any one aspect are avoided; and arguments about which aspect is primary for therapeutic change to occur are irrelevant. Since we are operating within a systems framework, it is not important where change occurs first. A change in any of the aspects is important; but we do not think it will last unless it also affects the other two aspects.

The relevance of an eclectic approach to therapy is obvious. A therapist who can facilitate his clients' access to all three aspects would be more effective than a therapist who operates only on one. We are not saying that the theoretical or therapeutic "purist" is ineffective. (S)he will be effective because sooner or later clients who change, change across all three aspects—no matter where the initial therapeutic focus is. This approach sidesteps the sanctimonious attitude of righteousness that proponents of different therapies have sometimes taken. In fact, we are, in a sense, taking the coward's way out. Nevertheless, we feel safe on empirical and theoretical grounds. Biofeedback research (Jencks, 1977) has demonstrated that interrelatedness of E, R, and A, indicating that a change in the behavioral aspect at the neuromuscular level effects concomitant changes in E and in R. Social psychological research on emotions reveals that one's cognitive appraisal of a situation can elicit an emotion with subsequent behavioral changes (Schachter & Singer, 1962).

From an eclectic viewpoint, the therapist needs to be aware and cognizant of the different aspects. The application of all three aspects can be a way of safeguarding oneself from exclusive dogmatism and rigid smugness about the superiority of one approach over the other two. All three aspects are relevant to behavior and have something worthwhile to say about relationships. Intellectual insight alone (R) without actions (A) is not enough; feelings (E) alone without proper processing (R) are not enough either. Actions (A) without proper cognitive processing (R) and feelings (E) are also not enough. All three are needed to survive. An eclectic approach cannot avoid being a transactional or systems approach that includes all aspects *plus* the therapist's personality, that is, his/her emotional maturity, intellectual and cognitive competence, and actions. Most models of supervision could be classified according to these three aspects (Liddle & Halpin, 1978). Also clinical applications flow directly from this model. Fulmer (1977), in describing a treatment approach with families of schizophrenic men, admonishes therapists to avoid dealing with feelings ("Don't elicit affect") because:

> These families usually do not respond well to attempts to elicit and clarify their feelings

toward each other. The parents usually defend against therapeutic attempts to elicit affect by denial, disinterest, or intellectualization.

Consequently, Fulmer recommended setting "concrete tasks" for the family in much the same way as that recommended by Haley (1976) and Selvini-Palazzoli, Boscolo, Cecchin, & Prata (1978). In our clinical experience, the major problem in communication between mates and parent-child dyads is the proper and constructive expression of E. This is the area where many social skills training programs seem to be quite appropriate (L'Abate, 1980).

Typology of Therapies

Therapies can be categorized as to their focus on E, R, and A., and according to their preferred or claimed emphasis (*see* Table 1).

Table 1

Classification of Family Therapy Theories for an E-R-A Model

Characteristic Modalities	Emotionality	Rationality	Activity
Historical Background Schools of Thought	Humanism, Existential, Gestalt, Experiential	Psychoanalytic-Cognitive	Behavioral-Systems
Temporal Perspective	Present	Past	Future
Representative Theorists	Satir, Bandler & Grinder, Napier & Whitaker	Boszormenyi-Nagy & Sparks, Stierlin, Bowen & Associates, Framo	Adlerians Palo Alto Group Milano Group Behaviorism Minuchin Haley
Preferred Therapeutic Interventions	Sculpture, Nonverbal role-playing	History, Genograms	Task Assignment Prescriptions
Locus of Change	Family feelings and immediacy	Family of origin Inside individuals	Family Relationships and problem solving
Predicted Length of Therapy	Variable, Intermediate	Long	Short-Fixed
Activity Level	Mostly inside office	Least active	Mostly outside office

Any classification is subjective. There are exceptions for each case, for example, cognitive behavior modification that may not fit one category, may fit two or even all three aspects of this proposed classification. The importance of at least taking a step toward preparing a classification is to obtain further clarification of the issues derived from an E-R-A model. The E-R-A should be more correctly an E-R-A-Feedback that acknowledges the presence and importance of the feedback derived from A back to E and processed through R. The illusion of classification may seem more desirable than the uncertainty of confusion (L'Abate, 1981).

Ritterman (1977) proposed a paradigmatic classification of family therapy theories that essentially differentiated between mechanistic and organismic theories but failed to specify which of the many models fit in which category. The mechanistic-organismic distinction seems too abstract, vague, and general to specify differences among most therapy models. The E-R-A model, on the other hand, could handle the task of specification in greater detail, especially in terms of emphasis on any of the three aspects of the E-R-A triangle. As Weakland (1977) commented on Ritterman's paper:

> Judgments about theories should, at the least, have an empirical basis as well as an ideal basis—what sort of practice is actually associated with the theory and what observable outcomes result.

Guerin (1976) proposed another scheme, starting with Beels and Ferber's (1969) classification and ending by differentiating among four general systems orientations: (a) general systems; (b) structured family therapy (Minuchin); (c) strategic family therapy; and (d) Bowenian family systems theory and therapy. Our classification differs from Guerin's. We place Bowen and his school with its emphasis on the past and the family of origin, which in a crucial way distinguishes this school from other sytems orientations, in a different category.

The emphatic E school (Satir, Stachowiak, & Taschman, 1975) gives a great deal of attention to how feelings are felt, expressed, and translated within family transactions. Sculpting, role-playing, and attention to awareness and delivery of emotional messages is given (Papp, 1976).

The emphatic R school (Mace, 1977; Ellis, 1977) tends to deal with cognitive representations, rational discussions, controls, ignoring of feelings and concentrating on how a family solves or fails to solve problems cognitively as a function of past (cognitive) experience. More will be needed to support each position. Bowen (1978) emphasizes talking about "emotional adjustment." Yet, most of the procedures he and his followers use are rational, they do not use awareness exercises for role-playing as Satir and her followers do.

The A-oriented schools (Selvini-Palazzoli et al., 1978) emphasize active change outside the office therapy by prescribed rituals, changes in relationships, and dual schedules. Behavioral and systems theorists may not like being lumped under the same roof (Haley, 1978), yet both stress observable actions. Another important viewpoint to be included within the A aspect is the Adlerian (Fischer et al., 1978; McDonough, 1978). Systems therapists (Structural and Strategic) point to essential differences between a linear behavioral perspective and an essentially circular and/or paradoxical perspective held by most systems theorists. Differences, of course, could be used to divide and separate different subgroups within each category of classification, for example, Bowen's school vesus the intergenerational invisible loyalties group; and between Satir's followers and the Boston group (Constantine, 1978). Pointing out these differences would add to this classification because it would make it more complex, once the basic E-R-A triad and temporal orientation are accepted as a basic of this classification (L'Abate, 1981).

Hence, given any orientation, various subgroups could derive within each, including overlapping groups between two of the three E-R-A aspects. It takes two parties to pigeonhole. If a party does not feel comfortable in accepting the primacy of one aspect over the others, it needs to declare itself so that its position *vis-a-vis* others can become clear to everyone concerned. Each theory (theorist) should classify its historical roots, its preferred and most prolonged mode of intervention, and what it considers the primary, secondary, and tertiary aspects of behavior. For instance, within each aspect the humanistic school could be subdivided into (a) the *phenomenological,* (b) *existential,* and (c) *experiential* schools. The first would relate to Rogers' *nondirective* approach, the second to Napier and Whitaker's (1978) approach, while the third would relate to Satır's and the Gestalt schools. By the same token, within the cognitive school, another subdivision could be made between *cognitive-past* (Bowen, 1978; Boszormenyi-Nagy, & Spark, 1973; Stierlin, 1977) and *cognitive-present* schools like reality therapy, the rational-emotive school, or transactional analysis.

Thus, this classification scheme could account for most of the family therapy theories presently available. A still unexplored area is the classification of methods (L'Abate, 1981) which relates to each of the three aspects. This area needs to be explored systematically and the present framework could be used as a base (Ulrici, L'Abate, and Wagner, 1981).

Feldman (1976) proposed four basic models or paradigms of the process of change which show some similarity to the present classification; (a) insight/working through;

(b) conditioning/reinforcement; (c) modeling (social learning); and (d) paradox. Our scheme essentially lumps together the last three paradigms and adds the humanistic approach to it. A critic would object to our lumping together behavioral approaches under the rubric of "systems" since many behaviorists either reject such a notion outright or are somewhat ignorant of it. These orientations, however, are put together (with the Adlerian school) in terms of concrete orientation toward observables and immediacy in symptom relief, and, most of all, in terms of both systems and behavior therapists being *conductors* (Beels & Ferber, 1969) rather than reactors. Even though we question the use of such a dichotomy for therapists, most systems, behavioral, and Adlerian therapists are definite in the task assignments and specific instructions given to the family to be carried out away from the therapy room, a procedure not usually followed by "pure" representatives of the other two approaches.

Any classification scheme is based on "pure" representatives of other classes. We doubt whether such a purity is either present or desirable. Clearly, to reach a classification one needs to assume a purity (nonoverlap) that may be humanly or theoretically impossible. Specification of procedures on the part of the proponents of each viewpoint could help in determining which procedures produced which outcomes at what cost. For instance, advocates of sculpting as promoting awareness of unspoken feelings within the family find it useful as a diagnostic and therapeutic technique. Proponents of a problem-solving approach (Haley, 1976) question adamantly its role and stress active changes outside of the office. Any classificatory system is bound to produce therapists who emphasize at least two of the three major aspects, such as *cognitive* behavior modifiers or Gestalt and experiential therapists giving homework assignments. In spite of these wider eclectic practices, the major point of emphasis on either of the three aspects still remains.

Finally, the simiiarity of our scheme to the one presented by Havens (1973) is acknowledged. We plan to test this model through a content analysis of the indices in references of representative texts from the various schools. If our position is valid, we would expect that, relative to any other comparable topic, references to E should be more frequent in representative texts of this school than in texts of the other two schools, which would emphasize, by the same token, R or A. As naive and simple as it may appear, such analysis would help us validate the present model and its derivative classification of family therapy theories. A differentiation of methods according to this model has already been accomplished (Ulrici et al., 1981).

Conclusion

We have argued for the relevance and inclusion of Emotionality in an overall Emotionality-Rationality-Activity model on developmental, theoretical and practical therapeutic grounds. This model lends itself to a classification of family therapy theories in a more specific fashion than can be achieved otherwise.

REFERENCES

Arnold, M. B. *Emotion and personality*. Vol. I. *Psychological aspects*. New York: Columbia University Press, 1960.

Beels, C. C., & Ferber, A. Family therapy: A view. *Family Process*, 1969, *8*, 280–318.

Boszormenyi-Nagy, I., & Spark. G. M. *Invisible loyalties: Reciprocity in intergenerational family therapy*. New York: Harper & Row, 1973.

Bowen, M. *Family therapy in clinical practice*. New York: Jason Aronson, 1978.

Constantine, L. L. Family sculpting and relationship mapping techniques. *Journal of Marriage and Family Counseling*, 1978, *4*, 13–24.

Ellis, A. Techniques of handling anger in marriage. *Journal of Marriage and Family Counseling*, 1976, *2*, 305-315.

Feldman, L. B. Processes of change in family therapy. *Journal of Family Counseling*, 1976, *4*, 14-22.

Fischer, J., Anderson, J. M., Arveson, E., & Brown, S. Adlerian family counseling: An evaluation. *International Journal of Family Counseling*, 1978, *6*, 42-44.

Framo, J. L. Family of origin as a therapeutic resource for adults in marital and family therapy: You can and should go home again. *Family Process*, 1976, *15*, 193-210.

Fulmer, R. H. Families with schizophrenic sons: A description of family characteristics and strategy for family therapy. *Family Therapy*, 1977, *4*, 101-111.

Guerin, P. J. Jr. Family therapy: The first twenty-five years. In P. J. Guerin, Jr. (Ed.), *Family therapy: Theory and practice*. New York: Gardner Press, 1976, 2-22.

Haley, J. *Problem-solving therapy*. San Francisco: Jossey-Bass, 1976.

Havens, L. L. *Approaches to the mind: Movement of the psychiatric schools from sects toward science*. Boston: Little, Brown & Co., 1973.

Jencks, B. *Your body: Biofeedback at its best*. Chicago: Nelson/Hall, 1977.

Jurjuvich, R. M. Emotionality and irrationality in psychotherapeutic fads. *Psychotherapy: Theory, Research and Practice*, 1978, *15*, 168-179.

L'Abate, L. *Understanding and helping the individual in the family*. New York: Grune & Stratton, 1976.

L'Abate, L. Intimacy is sharing hurt feelings: A reply to David Mace. *Journal of Marriage and Family Counseling*, 1977, *3*, 13-16.

L'Abate, L. Skill training programs for couples and families: Clinical and non-clinical approaches. In A. S. Gurman & D. Kniskern (Eds.), *Handbook of family therapy*. New York: Brunner/Mazel, 1980.

L'Abate, L., & L'Abate, B. The paradoxes of intimacy. *Family Therapy*, 1979, *6*, 175-184.

L'Abate, L. Classification of counseling and therapy theorists, methods, processes, and goals: The E-R-A model. *The Personal and Guidance Journal*, 1981, in press.

Liddle, H. H., & Halpin, R. J. Family therapy training and supervision literature: A comparative review. *Journal of Marriage and Family Counseling*, 1978, *4*, 77-98.

Mace, D. R. Marital intimacy and the deadly love-anger cycle. *Journal of Marriage and Family Counseling*, 1976, *2*, 131-137.

McDonough, J. J. Jr. Sibling ordinal position and family education. *International Journal of Family Counseling*, 1978, *6*, 62-69.

Minuchin, S. *Families and family therapy*. Cambridge: Harvard University Press, 1974.

Napier, A. Y., & Whitaker, C. A. *The family crucible*. New York: Harper & Row, 1978.

Papp, P. Family choreography. In P. Guerin (Ed.), *Family therapy: Theory and practice*. New York: Gardner, 1976.

Ritterman, M. K. Paradigmatic classification of family therapy. *Family Process*, 1977, *16*, 29-46.

Satir, V., Stachowiak, J., & Taschman, H. A. *Helping familes to change*. New York: Jason Aronson, 1975.

Schachter, S., & Singer, J. E. Cognitive, social and physiological determinants of emotional states. *Psychological Review*, 1962, *69*, 379-399.

Schafer, R. *Action: A new language for psychoanalysis*. New Haven: Yale University Press, 1976.

Selvini-Palazzoli, M., Boscolo, L., Cecchin, G. F., & Prata, G. *Paradox and counterparadox*. New York: Brunner/Mazel, 1978.

Stierlin, H. *Psychoanalysis and family therapy*. New York: Jason Aronson, 1977.

Ulrici, D., L'Abate, L., and Wagner, V. The E-R-A model: A heuristic framework for classification of social skills training programs for couples and familes. *Family Relations*, 1981, in press.

Weakland, J. H. Comments on Ritterman's article. *Family Process*, 1977, *16*, 46-48.

Wilden H. *Systems and structure: Essays in communication and exchange*. London: Tavistock, 1972.

NOTES

[1] We are indebted to Victor Wagner for conveying this acronym, given to him by a pair of clients, to us.

CHAPTER 14

The E-R-A Model: A Heuristic Framework for Classification of Skill Training Programs for Couples and Families

DONNA ULRICI, LUCIANO L'ABATE, AND VICTOR WAGNER*

The purpose of this paper is to provide a model for categorizing marital and family skill training programs according to their theoretical orientation. Our concerns are both empirical and clinical. The former is to provide researchers with a framework for more explicit investigation of program outcomes. The latter is to alert counselors and clinicians to the significant psychological dimensions operating within various skill training programs and to the effect that these variables may have on program clientele.

Structured skill training programs designed to enhance marriage and family life cover a wide range of interests and concerns, including (a) communication skills, (b) couples encounters, (c) couples enrichment, (d) fair fighting, (e) problem solving training, (f) parenting skills, and (g) family enrichment. These diverse programs vary on dimensions of content area, target populations, methods of instruction, length of training, therapeutic objectives, and psychological rationales. However, classification of these programs

---

*Donna Ulrici is a Ph.D. candidate in the Family Psychology Program at Georgia State University and Psychologist, Developmental Services of Cobb/Douglas Counties, GA. Luciano L'Abate is Director, Family Study Center, Psychology Department, Georgia State University, University Plaza, Atlanta, GA 30303. Victor Wagner is a Post-Doctoral Fellow in the Division of Family Studies, Department of Psychiatry, University of Rochester, School of Medicine, Rochester, NY.

Key concepts: classifications, couples, enrichment, families, interventions, psychotherapy, structured social skills, training programs, theory.

(Family Relations, 1981, 30, 307-315.)

has primarily focused on two areas, *what* the program teaches, i.e., content, and *who* the program addresses, i.e., target population (Miller, 1975; Otto, 1976; L'Abate, 1977, 1980).

Structural skill training programs have recently gained prominence as a viable means for preventive and quasi-therapeutic intervention within family systems (Gurman & Kniskern, 1977; L'Abate, 1980). Therefore, classification in terms of *how* each program deals with interventions, i.e., theoretical orientation and methodological emphasis, has become more relevant vis-a-vis the issue of attempting a greater specificity of matching problems with programs.

Major research on family and marital programs has examined the efficacy of a particular program content to improve the skill of a target sample. Findings report the degree of change between pretest and posttest evaluations of a designated program (Gurman & Kniskern, 1977). Few studies have compared the relative effectiveness of one approach to training a skill to that of another approach (L'Abate, 1980; L'Abate & Rupp, Note 1). Categorization and investigation of skill training programs which do not examine how programs operate to effect change appear contrary to the prevailing needs of family facilitators who strive to implement the most beneficial approach to intervention.

L'Abate and Frey (in press, 1981) have suggested a classification framework for therapeutic approaches to intervention based on their orientation to change. They proposed *Emotions, Reasons,* and *Actions* are the three

Table 1
Classification of Intervention Methods According to the E-R-A Model

Emotions	Reasons	Behavioral	Systemic
		Actions	
Methods focus on experiential exercises which differentiate feeling states of solitude and solidarity.	Methods focus on the development of conscious understanding which supports rational control of emotions and behavior.	Methods focus on the application of scientific principles to shape and control behavior.	Methods focus on adjusting dimensions of cohesion and adaptability which maintain family functioning.
1. Developing intrapersonal awareness through individual exercises of meditation, fantasy trips, imaginary dialogues, here and now awareness.	1. Teaching new facts, concepts and theories through lectures, readings and discussions.	1. Solving behavioral problems through experimental analysis—quantifying behavior, determining controls, implementing interventions and evaluating.	1. Restructuring operations in response to situational stress or developmental changes through: (a) Reorganization of family interactions within the session (e.g., enact ment, increasing intensity, reframing) (b) Liner task assignments to directly change operations (e.g., rescheduling family duties, assigning age appropriate task) (c) Paradoxical task assignments that emphasize operational problems and points out complementary relationships (e.g. role reversals, behavioral extremes).
2. Developing awareness of interpersonal relationships through interactional task of role play, sculpting, etc.	2. Relating past influence to present functioning through cognitive recreation of past events, (e.g., psychoanalytic dialogues, genograms, rational reevaluations.)	2. Teaching and increasing desired behavior and extinguishing unappropriate techniques of operant conditioning, (e.g., negative and positive reinforcement, extinction, punishment, differential reinforcement.)	Establishing appropriate boundaries for cohesion and autonomy through a) Directives given within the session e.g., spatial rearrangement, demanding interactions, blocking interactions, unbalancing the social network). b) Liner and paradoxical assignments for daily context. (e.g., rituals, activities to support coalitions or limit enmeshment.)
3. Developing bodily awareness through physical exercises of creative movement and interpersonal body contacts.	3. Developing insight to differentiate feelings from actions through analysis of one's present and past relationships, (e.g., working through transference, understanding defense operations and ego controls)	3. Regulation of overt behavior through symbolic mediational processes (e.g., observational learning), and cognitive mediational processes (e.g., modification of set interpretations.)	
4. Teaching skills of interpersonal sensitivity and communication through lectures, readings,	4. Teaching skills of rational thinking and ego control through lectures, discussions, and practice at rational	4. Extinguishing unappropriate or undesirable behavior through deconditioning (e.g., flooding;	

Table 1 (Cont'd)
Classification of Intervention Methods According to the E-R-A Model

Emotions	Reasons	Actions	
		Behavioral	Systemic
demonstrations and practice exercises.	problem solving and decision making.	desensitization techniques) and adverse conditioning procedures. 5. Practice application of learned behavior through behavioral rehearsal (e.g., role play, simulation exercises) 6. Implementing desired behavior or its approximation through behavioral task performed in daily context. 7. Teaching behavioral principles through lectures, models and practice exercises.	

major modalities or aspects involved in therapeutic change. The model explains that there is a separate yet interdependent relationship among these modalities of Experiencing, Reasoning, and Acting: "Our emotions (E), reasoning (R), and actions (A) systems are all the major resources we have for dealing with our internal and external environments" (L'Abate & Frey, in press, 1981). None of these three aspects is more important or takes primacy over the other two, but rather, we need access to all three aspects to reach our potential as human beings. This classification system can be used diagnostically to differentiate qualities of persons as well as taxonomically to categorize therapeutic approaches to intervention and their methodological techniques. Although this model may have important implications for most methods of marital and family interventions, the focus of this paper is on the application of this model to skill training programs for couples and families. We want to demonstrate the applicability of this model for a classification of these programs.

The following section provides a description of Emotional, Reasoning, and Action approaches to intervention. Table 1 presents a specific classification used by the three approaches. Based on the criteria of content, method of instruction, and psychological rationale, family and marital skill training programs are delineated and categorized according to the E-R-A model.

Classification of Marital and Family Skill Training Programs

According to the E-R-A model, family interventions with an emotional orientation focus on content that is concerned with the immediate here and now, with consideration being given to how feelings are expressed and translated within couples, families, or group transactions. Humanistic schools of existential, experiential, and phenomenological psychology have provided rationales that are congruent with an emotional, empathic orientation. Intervention methods within the emotional orientation usually take place within the structured program context. They often are directed toward increasing sensitivity to emotional messages and developing skills

Table 2
Emotionally Oriented Skill Training Program

Program	Content Focus	Methods of Training	Theoretical Rationale
1. Catholic Encounter (Bosco, 1976)	Couples, spiritual feelings, interpersonal commitment.	Interactional task to develop interpersonal awareness.	Need periodically to experience rebirth of communications, feelings and commitment.
2. Marriage Enrichment Program-Reformed Church (Vander Haar & Vander Haar, 1976; VanEck & VanEck, 1976)	Couples-Search for meaning in life and marriage	*Phase I*-Task and exercises developing interpersonal awareness. *Phase II*-Exercise of interpersonal awareness and bodily contact. Teaching skills of sensitivity and communication.	Couples can express intimacy and meaning in life through marriage.
3. Christian Marriage Enrichment Retreat (Green, 1976)	Couples-Defining priorities, values and the meaning of love. Improving intimacy and communication.	Interactional exercises, bodily awareness techniques and written exercise of intrapersonal awareness.	A retreat can provide opportunity to integrate religious values and married life and to foster growth.
4. Marriage Rebirth Retreat (Schmitt & Schmitt, 1976)	Couples-the experience of separation and reunion	Group Task developing individual awareness and couples task of inter-personal communication.	Rankian concepts of experience and meaning in life through a marriage relationship.
5. Gestalt Marriage Enrichment (Zinker & Leon, 1976)	Couples-Creative use of conflict in a relationship	Exercises of interpersonal and bodily awareness. Task to develop awareness of interpersonal transactions. Teaching communication process skills.	Gestalt concepts of experiencing reconstruction of relationships and using conflict for growth.
6. Conjugal Relationship Enhancement (CRE) (Rappaport, 1972, 1976)	Couples, increasing intimacy and improving communications	Teaching skills of interpersonal sensitivity and effective communication	Although behavioral principles are used in teaching, the primary focus is on Rogerian concepts of positive regard and empathic listening.
7. Filial Therapy and PARD (Guerney, 1969)	Parent/child improving communications	(Same as CRE)	(Same as CRE)
8. Second Chance Family (Malamud, 1975)	Family-Accepting one's human fallability and conflict with others	Exercise of intrapersonal awareness and interactional task for interpersonal awareness	Experiential encounters can build understanding of self and others.

Table 3
Reason Oriented Skill Training Programs

Programs	Content Focus	Method of Training	Theoretical Rationale
1. Preventive maintenance model (Sherwood & Sherer, 1975)	Couples-How relationships are established, maintained and changed.	Teaching a theoretical model to understand marriage interactions. Giving rational labels to feeling states and teaching how rational language can be used for decision making.	Rational-emotive theory—Developing new concepts to understand relationships and the use of reasoning to guide behavior.
2. Family Evening Home-Mormon Church (Cowly & Adams, 1976)	Family and extended family—Psychological and theological concepts.	Preplanned programs teaching psychological and theological concepts through family discussions.	Marriage and parenthood are a sacred obligation. Religious concepts can be used to solve family problems.
3. Jewish Marriage Encounter (Kligfield, 1976)	Couples-meaning marriage and Jewish family life in terms of "cosmic" significance and the techniques of an "I-Thou" dialogue.	Teaching a communication and unification theory as a foundation for a marriage relationship. Differentiating love as a feeling from love as an act of will. Formulating a decision to love. Engaging in couples' dialogue.	Buber's concept of marriage as a state of communication, i.e., I-Thou dialogue and a unification where eternal "Thou" is always present. Unification through communication is a sacred goal.
4. Institute for Transactional Analysis (Capers & Capers, 1976)	Couples-Understanding various ego states and their controls. Achieving intimacy through ego control.	Teaching a transactional theory of behavior. Using verbal and nonverbal exercises to differentiate different ego states.	Transactional theory of parent, child, and adult ego states within each person. Awareness of different states can help one control their ego and renegotiate marriage on adult terms.
5. Jealousy Program (Constantine, 1976)	Couples-Defining types of jealous behavior and the process of jealous behavior.	Teaching new concepts of jealousy, and teaching ways to apply these concepts to jealousy problems.	An understanding of jealousy processes can control jealous behavior.

involved in making positive contact with others. Table 2 presents skill training programs which focus on an emotional orientation. These programs strive to support marriage relationships or family life by improving how individuals experience and express intimate feelings. Programs 6 and 7 focus directly on teaching effective skills of interpersonal sensitivity and communication. Programs 1, 3, and 8 use exercises that develop a sense of self and others and provide experiences of separation and sharing as a means for facilitating intimate relationships. Programs 2, 4, and 5 have incorporated touch and awareness exercises and direct training of communication skills to reach their goals.

Reasoning schools tend to focus on content and deal with knowledge of and reasons about the family's or couple's intrapsychic and interpersonal processes. Their methodology focuses on cognitive representations of reality—the past as well as the immediate is considered. There are hypothetical and rational discussions of specific problems and emotional issues. Calm, logical approaches to behavior and feelings are emphasized. The reasoning approach to intervention is based on theories presented by psychoanalytic and cognitive schools of psychology. Table 3 presents the reason oriented skill training programs. Although the content focus of their programs is diverse, all are based on the idea that a better theoretical understanding of interpersonal interaction and family transaction will help to solve daily problems and improve relationships. Programs 1, 2, and 5 are primarily educational, while programs 3 and 4 have included exercises to provide an experiential understanding of new concepts presented.

Action oriented programs focus on defining and solving specific family and/or marriage problems. They aim at preventing future problems. These methods include behavioral techniques and principles, practice tasks to be performed during the structured program, and task assignments to be implemented in daily life. Action approaches have emerged from distinctly different psychological positions of behaviorism, family systems, and Adlerian theories. Although these theories disagree on many of the processes that operate to control interaction, all three agree that change is best effected through active behavioral tasks directed at changing one's everyday observable interactions. Programs 1 through 5 use behavioral principles to teach couples new and more effective courses of action. Programs 6, 7, and 8 develop new structures of family transactions through behavioral tasks that engage families in a new system of communication and involvement with each other or with members of their social network.

From an examination of Tables 2, 3, and 4, it is apparent that the training programs presented here are more or less representative of one of the three modalities, and programs with a more eclectic approach are not included. One should note that the classification of a program in one of the three modalities does not demand purity in focus but rather is based on evaluation of the major assumed or alleged emphasis of the program. Therefore, this classification of skill training programs involves interpretation of the major theoretical emphasis as well as an evaluation of specific areas of emphasis. As long as interpretation and evaluation by their nature are subjective processes, we are aware that our designation and weighting of criteria for classification may not be absolute. These limitations withstanding, this classification system is offered as a viable structure to determine dimensions of skill training programs that may significantly affect program outcome.

Discussion and Conclusions

Logically, one may surmise that to provide the most effective outcome for program participants, program selection should be based on a match that goes beyond content concerns and population specifications. It should also consider what psychological orientation to programming best fits the needs and characteristics of the family, couple, or groups of clients. For example, recognition of the strengths and the weaknesses on Emotional, Reasoning, and Action modalities could enable one to choose a preexisting skill training program which emphasized aspects more relevant to existing characteristics and needs of a couple or a family. Presently, investigators are only beginning to consider the

Table 4
Action Skill Training Program

Program	Content Focus	Method of Training	Theoretical Rationale
1. Behavioral Exchange Negotiations A. Liberman Program (Liberman, 1970, 1976) B. Stuart Program (Stuart, 1976)	Couples-Communication. Skills tracking of positive and negative interpersonal behavior, conflict negotiations and contingency contracting.	Teaching behavioral principles for interpersonal communications. Reinforcement of positive interactions. Instruction, practice exercises and task assignments for negotiation skills.	Couples can use behavioral principles to improve communications and solve problems.
2. Communication Skill Training CST (Miller, Nunnally, 1974, Miller, 1975)	Couples-(Training can be used separately or as a part of other programs) Sending and receiving clear direct communications.	Teaching communication skills through lectures, models, practice exercises and evaluative feedback.	Communication problems can occur due to skill deficit couples can benefit from learning new behavioral skill.
3. Assertiveness Training (Fensterheim and Baer, 1975, Baer, 1976)	Couples-Self enhancing behavior that does not deny rights of others.	Teaching assertive behavior through instructions, modeling, role play, task assignments, and evaluative feedback.	Aggressive and nonassertive behavior is learned and more appropriate assertive behavior can be learned and used to benefit couples interaction.
4. Problem solving A. Blechman & Olsen (1976); B. Kieren et al. (1975)	Couples-Effective means of problem solving through specific steps of deductive reasoning and outcome evaluations.	Teaching problem solving steps. Simulated practice exercises with positive reinforcement for following steps.	Behavioral concept that empirical principles can be used to solve daily problems.
5. Behavioral programs for Parents (Patterson & Gullion, 1971)	Parents-Behavioral management principles of conditioning and social learning.	Teaching of behavioral principles or programmed self instruction to learn principles.	Behavioral principles of learning can be used to manage child behavior.
6. Adlerian Parent-Child Programs (Dreikurs & Sultz, 1967)	Family-Birth orders, family constellations, rules, consequences of positive and negative transaction.	Discussions, family conferences for problem solving and task assignments.	Adlerian concepts that family life education can prevent future problems.
7. Family Growth Group (Anderson, 1976)	Families—Making families more adaptable systems. Developing awareness of family growth, potential. Developing cohesion between families that share a larger community.	Directing exchange of information within and between families. Task assignments that build support systems within and between families.	Systematic concept of families as a system—family potential can grow from transactions with other family systems.
8. Family Communication Systems Program (Benson et al., 1975)	Parents-Presenting families as an enmeshed system, clarifying needs and problems of families in terms of systems relationships.	Using objective directives to develop family goals and teach listening skills. Behavioral task of active involvement to teach parents ways to effectively intervene in their family relationships.	Systematic concepts that families should clarify problems and needs in terms of their family relationship systems.

significance of matching specific characteristics of the clientele with complementary treatment modalities (L'Abate & Frey, in press; Frey, L'Abate, & Wagner, Note 2). The question of whether program selection should be based on a matching of strengths, that is, choosing a program orientation which emphasizes the clientele's strong resources, or on a matching of weaknesses, that is, choosing a program orientation which concentrates on the clientele's least effective domain, remains open for theoretical debate. However, classification of skill training programs according to *Emotions, Reasons,* and *Actions* provides a framework within which researchers and clinicians can examine the interplay between the clientele's characteristics and intervention approaches.

Research on the relative effectiveness of different program approaches for specific clientele could not only benefit selection of skill training programs but also provide insight into how different psychological approaches operate to effect change. It follows that empirical and clinical application of this model could extend to most methods of marital and family interventions. However, we must conclude that the formulation of this classification framework is just the beginning. The value of this model remains heuristic, and the therapeutic significance is still dependent upon the effective outcome of its application. Therefore, we welcome clinical and empirical evidence in support or consideration of this classification system.

REFERENCE NOTES

1. L'Abate, L., & Rupp, G. Enrichment: *Skill training for family life.* (Manuscript submitted for publication).
2. Frey J., L'Abate, L., & Wagner V. Further implications and elaborations of the E-R-A model for family therapy (Manuscript submitted for publication).

REFERENCES

Anderson, D. A. The family growth group: Guidelines for an emerging means of strengthening families. In H. A. Otto (Ed.) *Marriage and family enrichment: New perspectives and programs,* Nashville: Abington, 1976.

Baer, J. *How to be an assertive not an aggressive woman in life, love and on the job.* New York: Signet, 1976.

Benson, L., Berger, M., & Mease, W. Family communication systems. In S. Miller (Ed.), *Marriage and family enrichment through communications.* Beverly Hills: Sage Publications, 1975.

Blechman, E. A., & Olson, D. H. L. The family game: Description and effectiveness. In D. H. L. Olson (Ed.), *Treating relationships.* Lake Mills, IA: Graphic Publications, 1976.

Bosco, A. Marriage encounter: An eciemenical enrichment program. In H. A. Otto (Ed.), *Marriage and family enrichment: New perspectives and programs.* Nashville: Abington, 1976.

Capers, H., & Capers, B. Transactional analysis tools for use in marriage enrichment programs. In H. A. Otto (Ed.), *Marriage and family enrichment: New perspectives and programs.* Nashville: Abington, 1976.

Constantine, L. L. Jealousy: From theory to intervention. In D. H. L. Olson (Ed.), *Treating relationships.* Lake Mills, IA: Graphic Publishing Co., 1976.

Cowly, A. J., & Adams, R. S. The family home evening: A national ongoing enrichment program. In H. A. Otto (Ed.), *Marriage and family enrichment: New perspective and programs,* Nashville: Abington, 1976.

Dreikers, R., & Sultz, V. *Children: The challenge.* Chicago: Adlerian Institute, 1976.

Fensterheim, H. & Baer, J. *Don't say yes when you want to say no.* New York: Dell Publishers, 1975.

Green, H., A Christian marriage enrichment retreat. In H. A. Otto (Ed.), *Marriage and family enrichment: New perspectives and programs.* Nashville: Abington, 1976.

Guerney, B. G. (Ed.) *Psychotherapeutic Agents: New roles for nonprofessional parents and teachers.* New York: Holt, Rinehart & Winston, 1969.

Gunman, A. S., & Kniskern, D. P. Enriching research on marital enrichment programs. *Journal of Marriage and Family Counseling,* 1977, **3**, 3-9.

Kieren, D., Henton, J. & Marotz, R. *Her and his: The problem solving approach to marriage.* Hinsdale, IL: Dryden Press, 1975.

Kligfeld, B. The Jewish marriage encounter. In H. A. Otto (ed.), *Marriage and family enrichment: New perspectives and programs.* Nashville: Abington, 1976.

L'Abate, L. ENRICHMENT: *Structured interventions with couples, families and groups.* Washington, D.C.: University Press of America, 1977.

L'Abate, L. Skill training programs for couples and families: Clinical and non clinical applications. In A. S. Garmant & D. Kriskern (Eds.), *Handbook of Family Therapy,* New York: Brunner/Mazel, 1980.

L'Abate, L. Toward a theory and technology of social skills training: Suggestions for curriculum development. *Academic Psychology Bulletin,* 1980, **2**, 207-228.

L'Abate, L., & Frey, J. The E-R-A Model: The role of feeling in family therapy reconsidered: Implications for theories of family therapy, *Journal of Marriage and Family Therapy,* in press, 1981.

Liberman, R. P. Behavioral approaches to family and couple therapy. *American Journal of Orthopsychiatry*, 1970, 40, 106-118.

Liberman, R. P., Wheeler, E., & Sanders, N. Behavior therapy for marital disharmony: An educational approach, *Journal of Marriage and Family Counseling*, 1976, 2, 383-396.

Malamud, D. I. Communication training in the second chance family. In S. Miller (Ed.), *Marriage and families: Enrichment through communication*. Beverly Hills: Sage Publications, 1975.

Miller, S. (Ed.) *Marriage and families: Enrichment through communication*. Beverly Hills: Sage Publications, 1975.

Miller, S., Nunnally, E., Wackman, D., & Brazman, R. *Alive and aware, improving communication in relationships*. Minneapolis: International Communications Programs, Inc., 1974.

Otto, H. A. (Ed.). *Marriage and family enrichment: New perspectives and programs*. Nashville: Abington, 1976.

Patterson, G. R. & Gullion, E. M. *Living with children: New methods for parents and teachers*. Champaign, IL: Research Press, 1971.

Rappaport, A. F. The effects of an intensive conjugal relationship modification, *Dissertation Abstracts International*, 1972, 32, 6571-6572A.

Rappaport, A. I. Conjugal relationship enhancement program. In Olson (Ed.), *Treating relationships*, Lake Mills, IA: Graphic Publishing Co., 1976.

Schmitt, A., & Schmitt, D. Marriage renewal retreats. In H. A. Otto (Ed.), *Marriage and family enrichment: New perspectives and programs*. Nashville: Abington, 1976.

Sherwood, J. J., & Scherer, J. J. A model for couples: How two can grow together. In S. Miller (Ed.), *Marriage and families enrichment through communication*, Beverly Hills: Sage Publications, 1975.

Stuart, R. B. An operant interpersonal program for couples. In D. H. Olson (Ed.), *Treating relationships*. Lake Mills, IA: Graphic Publishing Co., 1976.

Vander Haar, D. and Vander Haar, T. The marriage enrichment program, phase I. In H. A. Otto (Ed.), *Marriage and family enrichment: New perspectives and programs*. Nashville: Abington, 1976.

VanEck, B. & VanEck, B. The Phase II marriage enrichment lab. In H. A. Otto (Ed.), *Marriage and family enrichment: New perspectives and programs*. Nashville: Abington, 1976.

Zinker, J. C., & Leon, J. P. The besalt persective: A marriage enrichment program. In H. A. Otto (Ed.)., *Marriage and family enrichment: New perspectives and programs*. Nashville: Abington, 1976.

CHAPTER 15

TOWARD A CLASSIFICATION OF FAMILY THERAPY THEORIES:

FURTHER ELABORATIONS AND IMPLICATIONS

OF THE E-R-A-Aw-C MODEL

Luciano L'Abate, Atlanta, GA
Joseph Frey III, Birmingham, AL
Victor Wagner, New Orleans, LA

Abstract

Implications of a classification of family therapy theories based on a fivefold model of Emotionality-Rationality-Activity-Awareness and Context are discussed. Comparisons with other classificatory suggestions are critically reviewed. Therapeutic and training implications are also presented.

In previously published papers (L'Abate, 1981; L'Abate & Frey, 1981; Ulrici, L'Abate & Wagner, 1981), we have presented an Emotionality-Rationality-Activity (E-R-A) model that allowed us to classify family therapy theories, as well as various psychotherapy theorists, methods, processes, and goals (Hansen & L'Abate, 1982). The purpose here is to expand this model by adding two more categories, Awareness and Context (Aw and C).

Briefly, this model includes humanistic approaches (phenomenology, experientialism, and existentialism) under the rubric of Emotionality. Under Rationality are included most cognitively-oriented therapeutic approaches (psychodynamic, object relations, transactional, reality, and rational-emotive). Under the rubric of Activity are included various behavioral approaches. Approaches such as Adlerian, structural, strategic, and systems therapy fall within the rubric of Context. A list of theorists to include under the rubric of Awareness is still in the making (L'Abate, Note 1). The validity of this classification was tested empirically (L'Abate, Note 2) through a beginning, tentative content analysis of representative books for three E-R-A schools: Satir, Stachowiak, and Taschman (1975) and Napier and Whitaker (1978) for the humanistic (E) approach; Boszormenyi-Nagy and Spark (1973) for the rational approach, and Haley (1976) for the context approach. This content-analysis tended to support the hypothesis that therapists from the humanistic schools tend to use more Emotionally tinged words than either Rational or Activity-oriented terms. The therapist from the context school (Haley) tended to use Activity terms more often than Emotionality- or Rationality-oriented terms. Of course, this was a very gross and tentative analysis, its major shortcoming being the lack of agreement among coders on what constitutes a term related to each of the three categories. Russell and Stiles (1979), on the other hand, in their review of the literature on classifying language in psychotherapy, came up with the first three categories of the E-R-A-Aw-C model.

Since these early proposals, further work has appeared that tends to support, in the eyes of these writers, the validity of an E-R-A-Aw-C model. This chapter's purpose is to review such work from the viewpoint of the original model and consider its various treatment and training implications.

Recently, Williamson (1979) reviewed some of the most important issues of family therapy. First among these issues was an integrated world view that would encompass children's sexuality, marriage, and family within the context of our society. The second issue was a need for a conceptual model of treatment that is related to techniques. The third issue was how to measure family therapy outcomes. The fourth issue was the professionalization of the discipline and the core-identity of a separate profession of family therapies. The fifth issue represented a variety of individual responses that are difficult to catalog. The purpose of this paper is to elaborate on and explicate Williamson's second issue, i.e., a conceptual model related to techniques.

Recent Contributions

Various theorists have, since submission of the original model, contributed possible classifications of family therapy theorists, which bear on the E-R-A-Aw-C. Their pros and cons, similarities to, and differences from this model will be considered in this section.

Olson and Sprenkle (1976) covered conceptual and programmatic trends in treating relatonships that are relevant to the classification presented in the previous paper since in some ways they were following an

<u>implicit</u> rather than an <u>explicit</u> classification similar to the present one. They identified three theoretical influences on the current family therapy scene. The first is social learning theory (G. R. Patterson, J. Alexander, and R. Stuart). The second is general systems theory, in which they included a hodgepodge of theorists whom we would categorize instead into completely different frameworks. For instance, they put Bowen with Haley, Boszormenyi-Nagy with Minuchin, missing essential differences between these theorists, a differentiation that the classification based on E-R-A-Aw-C takes into consideration. Just because a theorist conceives of the family as a "system" is not sufficient to consider him/her a general systems theorist. One needs to consider many other modalities of treatment (i.e., temporal perspective, preferred foci of intervention, method of intervention) before classifying someone as "general systems." In this respect, Olson and Sprenkle put together theorists who differ on a variety of modalities, as acknowledged in the present classification. We consider a general systems theorist someone (a) who acknowledges the theoretical debt and uses concepts consistent with the work of von Bertalanffy and Bateson and (b) who uses procedures that are consistent with theoretical assumptions. Satir, for instance, is put by Olson and Sprenkle in the same category, general systems theorists, as those already cited. Yet, her method of intervention, which is mostly linear and nonverbal, differs considerably from those used by strategic and structural therapists, who are considered under the rubric of general systems theories and who, in our classification, are closer to social learning theorists than Olson and Sprenkle can consider in their review. Their third conceptual trend--Rogerian, client-centered approaches--fits much more closely within the humanistic school than any other identifiable trend. Of course, Olson and Sprenkle's intention was more expository than classificatory. In spite of their intentions, they ended up with a classification system that we find incomplete and inadequate, for the reasons we have outlined.

Buckley (1968) classified schools of family therapy according to (a) psychodynamic, (b) communication, and (c) structural. In the psychodynamic school, he considered Nathan Ackerman, Norman Paul, and Ivan Boszormenyi-Nagy; in the communication school, Don Jackson, Jay Haley, and Virginia Satir; in the structural school, Salvador Minuchin. Thus, Buckley's classification, when compared with ours, shows some

some overlap with it. We differ mainly in classifying Virginia Satir with Jackson and Haley. The latter (Haley, 1976), with emphasis on short-term, problem solving, prescriptions, and paradoxical reframing, is quite critical of psychodynamic, "growth"-oriented approaches, especially any use of sculpting and nonverbal exercises. Satir, on the other hand, uses these "growth" techniques extensively and in our classification would fit into the humanistic school, which emphasizes feelings and emotions.

As Zuk (1976) maintained, "those that claim an integrated theory and technique have an obligation to set it out in simple, straightforward terms which invite rigorous evaluation" (p. 299). We believe that our E-R-A-Aw-C model and a classification of family therapy theories derived from it will allow such a rigorous evaluation, in a more detailed fashion than has been possible heretofore.

In trying to differentiate theoretical assumptions, techniques, or therapeutic roles and styles, and personality characteristics of family therapists, Kolevson and Green (Note 3) used a classification similar to ours even though they applied different terms to the various family therapy theorists. In the Communication Model, which would be equivalent to a humanistic perspective, they considered Satir, Bandler, and Grinder. In the Systems Model, they put Bowen, whom we consider in the psychodynamic school, and essentially equated Haley's Strategic and Minuchin's Structural Modes, which we placed in the Context category.

The preliminary results of their research, which consisted of asking a very large number of family therapists (N = 630) to answer items (on a 6-point scale) about theoretical orientation, therapeutic roles or styles, and personality characteristics, suggest that, as would be expected, there are convergences and divergences among the three orientations. The communication approach seems to be closer to systems than to the structural/strategic. Both communication and systems value growth in the therapist and/or family members rather than resolution of specific conflicts, advocate the use of co-therapists, and view improvement as resulting from the interaction with the therapists. Structural/strategic therapists, on the other hand, emphasize active involvement and the direct responsibility of the therapist to direct the course of therapy. Communication and systems therapists value taking a family history and sharing with the family the therapist's perceptions, "believing that change can be facilitated by helping family members deal with their feelings about themselves and each other." Structural/strategic therapists tend to emphasize present factors and how the family will react in the future to active manipulations (task assignments, homework prescriptions, etc.) rather than to past events or present feelings. Their therapeutic styles tended to correlate somewhat with their theoretical assumptions. Communicators showed highest correlations (p < .001), with their theoretical orientations on supporting, reflecting, reacting, modeling, participating, and reality testing. Systems therapists showed highest correlations on reflecting, observing, and reality testing, while structural/strategic therapists showed the highest correlation on provoking, reacting, and participating.

In terms of personality factors as measured by Cattell's 16 PF, four different correlations with theoretical orientation (p < .05 or better) were found for communicators (emotionally stable, venturesome, imaginative, self-sufficient) and two for systems therapists (emotionally stable and venturesome). No correlations were found for structural/strategic therapists (a pattern that closely parallels their theoretical beliefs about the personality of the therapist).

In their analysis of nearly 400 controlled studies of psychotherapy, counseling, and behavioral approaches, Smith and Glass (1977) were able to scale and classify multidimensionally 10 different kinds of therapeutic approaches. They obtained 4 different clusters of therapies: (a) ego, transactional analysis, and rational-emotive; (b) psychodynamic (Adlerian, Freudian, and psychoanalytic); (c) behavioral (implosive, systematic desensitization, and behavior modification); and (d) humanistic (Gestalt and Rogerian). Although this classification is somewhat similar to the one presented here, it differs in the placement of Adlerian therapy within the Freudian psychodynamic fold. The picture (p. 757) showing these therapies together and apart does show the Adlerian approach as actually closer to the rational-emotive and transactional therapies than to the other two psychodynamic ones. The major difference between these two groups would be the emphasis on the present versus emphasis on the past.

Levant (1980) proposed a classification of family

therapy theories based on Ritterman's (1977) original suggestion. He used two orthogonal dimensions of external group versus individual behavior: internal-subjective on the horizontal axis; holistic versus elementaristic analytic polarity on the vertical axis. This scheme produces four quadrants that subsume: I, existential-phenomenological and experiential approaches in the individual-holistic quadrant; II, psychodynamic in the individual elementaristic-analytic quadrant; III, structural school in the holistic-group quadrant; and IV, communication interaction systems schools in the group-elementaristic-analytic quadrant.

Levant (1980) also noted that the differences between communications systems (Haley, Watzlawick, Selvini-Palazzoli et al.) and structural (Minuchin) family therapy are not so great as Ritterman's scheme would lead one to believe. Levant noted other flaws in Ritterman's scheme, especially its difficulty in classifying Bowen's as well as Boszormenyi-Nagy and Spark's multigenerational theories.

The major disagreement between Levant's placement and the one derived from an E-R-A-Aw-C model lies in his placing Satir, Bandler, and Grinder with the structural/process groups instead of putting her and her associates in the experiential paradigm, where she rightfully belongs in her present-oriented temporality, the here and now of a humanistic perspective, and the use of experiential exercises to include changes in awareness and in feelings, mostly directed toward changing families' subjective experiences. Levant's conclusion parallels closely those arrived at by the E-R-A-Aw-C model on completely different bases, that is, the use of feelings and emotionality.

Levant concluded his paradigmatic model by proposing three "mutually exclusive" therapeutic paradigms: (a) the experiential; (b) the historical; (c) the structural process, a classification that parallels very closely the one proposed by the E-R-A-Aw-C model.

As Levant noted:

What is needed in the social sciences [and in the field of family therapy?] now is less emphasis on the promotion of particular theoretical orientations and more emphasis on the empirical determination of the actual range of application of particular theories [italics ours]. With regard to theories of family therapy we need to know which approach rendered by whom is most effective for <u>this</u> <u>family</u> with <u>that</u> special dysfunction in <u>this</u> context and under <u>these</u> circumstances. (Levant, 1980, p. 12)

Zuk (1979) divided the field of family pathology according to: (a) intergenerational emphasis, which usually employs concepts and language of psychoanalysis; (b) communication, which employs paradoxical prescriptions in the here and now, with a de-emphasis of historical factors; and (c) scapegoating, which examines a conscious awareness of victims and victimizers, the existence of cliques, coalitions, and collusions in the family. Zuk, furthermore, contrasted theories of family pathology with theories of family therapy, which he divided into (a) go-between process, (b) strategic, and (c) structural.

As interesting as this classification may be, with some parallels with the present one (scapegoating would fit into the humanistic fold), Zuk failed to support it with either relevant references or evidence of its validity. He commented:

The future of classificatory systems or taxonomies of family pathology is not bright because of the failure of the existent systems to have applicability to the clinical case. No doubt such systems will continue to be of research and scholarly interest. Systems are needed which have clear and direct application to the clinical case and which are clearly related to the presence in the family of a member with disturbed behavior. The systems must not be so general that they fail to have definite predictive value for the psychiatric symptoms shown by family members/individual. (Zuk, 1979, p. 360)

To conclude this section, various strands of evidence tend to support an E-R-A-Aw-C model for a classification of family therapy theories as well as other theories of psychotherapy.

What are the implications of this model for actual therapeutic interventions?

Treatment Implications

The E-R-A-Aw-C model suggests that therapeutic interventions can be made in five basically separate yet interrelated areas, namely in the domains of Emotionality, Reasonability, Activity, Awareness, and Context. According to L'Abate (1976), what is more available needs to be worked on first, before the least available and more difficult levels of behavior.

The E-R-A-Aw-C model assumes that in general there is a developmental sequence in deficits in Emotionality, Rationality, Activity, Awareness, and Context, which leads to a specific sequence of therapeutic interventions. On the other hand, emphasis on feelings alone, without paying attention to reasoning and action, can be just as therapeutically defeating as any one-sided emphasis. Howard, Krause, and Orlinsky (1969), for instance, took the position that:

> The feelings that patients and therapist experience during a psychotherapeutic session are events of central importance in the treatment process. Exploration of affect is a prime task of the patient and affective cues are used by the therapist in understanding and relating to the patient.

On the basis of their study of affective reactions in both therapists and clients, Howard et al. suggested various alternatives that therapists could use in dealing with "negative" feelings in themselves or their clients. What was not suggested was an exploration and exploitation of such feelings for mutual therapeutic benefit.

Following the same sequence, Activities are more readily available than Rationality, which is usually more available than Emotionality. Therefore, a therapist can manipulate Activity through prescriptions and/or homework assignments (L'Abate, 1973, 1977) before s/he can deal with Rationality and/or Emotionality. As Activities are changed, as in brief therapy (Selvini-Palazzoli, Boscolo, Cecchin & Prata, 1978; Watzlawick, Weakland & Fisch, 1974), there is the eventual possibility of dealing with Rationality. Ultimately, successful treatment means that clients are able to Act appropriately, Reason adequately, and express Emotions both appropriately and adequately, in a helpful and constructive fashion (self-awareness), to self and others within the Context of each specific situation (Satir, 1972).

Hence, the E-R-A-Aw-C model suggests that Activities are usually the relative assets more readily available for therapeutic interventions. Once Activities have been dealt with initially, allowing treatment to continue, Rationality is engaged enough to allow the ultimate step of successful therapy, that is, dealing with Emotionality, which governs our closeness and distance from each other, i.e., intimacy. Although most therapeutic interventions with Activities may stop there, changing Activities may change Rationality and/or Emotionality. By working on Rationality, one could help change Activities and/or Emotionality. By changing how Emotionality is considered, one may change either Rationality or Activities, or both. Awareness is closely related to Emotionality.

A somewhat different approach to intervention, but one which is certainly compatible with the E-R-A-Aw-C model, is outlined by English (1971). English, writing from a transactional analysis framework, discussed the developmental sequence whereby real feelings get suppressed and supplanted by racket feelings, and outlined the techniques to uncover these real feelings and to help the client get in touch with them.

According to English, some parents, upon recognition of particular feelings in their child, will train the child not to feel them or not to be aware of certain perceptions. This training can occur through several methods, including ignoring the child when s/he evidences a particular kind of feeling, directly telling the child that s/he is not feeling what s/he claims to be feeling, or relabeling the child's feeling as something else. In all these cases, the parent makes no distinction between feeling and action and implicitly communicates that danger lies with the feeling itself. The lack of differentiation between thinking and feeling results in an individual's developing in an emotionally constricted way, and has direct implications for the E-R-A-Aw-C model.

The model suggests that intervention should be made where it can be most readily assimilated. Obviously, if an individual has been reared in a way that discourages the expression, even the feeling, of anger, dealing with the individual in an experiential way to emote a catharsis of anger will be, at least initially, useless. As English suggested, these individuals who invest in a particular racket to cover up another feeling often have never really experienced the buried feeling and practically need to learn it. Hence, in the service of emotions, reasoning can be the appropriate channel to develop the resources to allow experience of the emotion. Along similar lines, English noted how a client may need to be taught through the use of the adult ego state (i.e., reasoning) how to distinguish awareness of feeling, identifying or naming the feeling, showing it, and acting on it. Orlinsky and Howard (1978, p. 307), in reviewing the cognitive structure implicit in therapists' messages and therapeutic outcome, found two studies with a negative relationship to outcome and "rationality" of therapists' messages. The reviewers concluded that "therapists are better advised to pursue the logic of feeling than the logic of fact."

Case Illustration #1

A 16-year-old girl was referred for sexual promiscuity, truancy, and drug abuse (i.e., impulsive behavior). The interview of mother-stepfather, three other siblings (one older brother and two younger sisters) from the mother's previous marriage and the "baby" from the present marriage produced a figure of extreme emotional deprivation. Mother was too busy (she worked in addition to taking care of the house) to pay attention to the children. She did not remember when she last hugged them or said something positive to any of them. She "nagged" a lot about their not completing their chores, and most of her reactions to them were either critical or punitive. The stepfather found it difficult to intervene except to support the mother's punitive maneuvers. When the use of positive words and deeds (actions) was introduced, the family initially had a great deal of trouble talking about feelings and expressing them congruently. Eventually, as therapy progressed, they were able to speak about and express feelings more congruently.

Case Illustration #2

The typical polarization in most marriages was found (L'Abate, 1976) in a housewife, 35, and a husband, 40, a mid-level manager. Reason for referral was excessive quarreling, a great deal of distance, and the wife's depression and unhappiness about her husband's overinvolvement in work and his inability to handle the leadership role as partner and as parent of two prepubertal children. The polarization was found in the emotional sphere. The wife was regarded as "irrational, flighty, volatile," while the husband was "reasonable, logical, superrational, and distant"

(L'Abate, Note 2). The first endeavor is to decrease frequency and intensity of fighting through prescription of the symptom ("Fight more") and ritualization ("Fight on alternate days and alternate who is going to take the initiative of starting the fight"; Selvini-Palazzoli et al., 1978). Hence, our emphasis is on Action. Oftentimes, sexual issues may be dealt with through linear prescriptions of sensate focusing, use of Seemans' technique, etc. Again, emphasis is on doing and acting. As the level of tension is reduced, work begins on issues of self-definition, priorities, and congruence (L'Abate, 1976). Most of this work is done at the Reasoning levels since at this point in the process, the couple is not yet able to assume the "I" position or to talk about or express individual emotions, especially hurt. As most common Reasoning issues are dealt with, challenged, clarified, and, usually, changed, we are able to enter the third and last area--the area of intimacy and sharing of joyful, rageful, mournful, or hurtful emotions. We know we are able to reach this point when both partners are <u>both</u> emotionally at the same level and the seesaw, roller coaster oneupmanship-onedownmanship is no longer evident. When both partners achieve a balance in all three modalities of functioning and feel adequate to be on their own, they no longer need professional help.

Prescriptions and homework assignments thus work well at the beginning; genograms and history taking, including trips back into the family of origin, work well in the second stage; sensitivity and role-playing techniques work well in the third and final phase of the therapeutic process. Such a process may not be the same with couples as with families. In families with school-age children, in addition to homework assignments, we may indulge in a great deal of sculpting because this is a very pleasurable activity that most children enjoy and that gives a great deal of information about the family and its structure. Aspects of Rationality that may be intertwined as Activities and Emotionality are dealt with. We are not about to suggest that E-R-A-Aw-C is the normative therapeutic sequence since a great many blind alleys, false starts, detours, and regressions are part and parcel of the change process. Yet, the model allows us to determine which modalities are the most used by each family and give them as strengths (i.e., activity-oriented versus intellectualizing families). Different modalities are used as sources of entry into the ultimate and most well-defended modality--Emotions!

Robertsen (1979), in working with individuals, favored a sequence that is exactly the reverse of the one presented here. He favored the use of a humanistic approach (client-centered and Gestalt) at the beginning, proceeding then to behavioral, rational-emotive, and transactional approaches. He tended to rationalize this sequence in terms of first establishing rapport, trust, and intimacy before moving on to more systematic relief. The issue is whether a sequence that seems to work for individuals can work for couples and families in which symptomatic relief (Action) seems to be the first order of business (Haley, 1976). Clearly, this sequence, whether A-R-E or E-R-A, is an important issue that will need further empirical consideration in the future.

Implications for Training

In its integrative eclecticism, the E-R-A-Aw-C model implies an eclectic approach not just to theory, but also to training. In the training of family therapists, emphasis on any one approach may be a pitfall. For example, a Milan model of paradoxical suggestions and homework assignments may not work on a family that is polarized on a cognitive-emotional continuum and lacks behavioral resources. Such a family may benefit more from a behavioral skill training approach focusing on learning negotiation skills. We believe that family therapists should have a wide variety of tools at their disposal to provide families access to their resources. Thus, a paradoxical reframing technique (cognitive relabeling) typically makes accessible the emotion system even when an "emotionally"-oriented therapist may have failed to get a family to express itself.

Conclusion

The usefulness of an E-R-A-Aw-C model to classify family therapy theories is upheld further from a review of more recent contributions to classification. Treatment and training implications also derive from the model.

Reference Notes

1. L'Abate, L. Personality and adjustment: An interpersonal perspective. Manuscript in preparation, 1982.

2. L'Abate, L. Beginning verifications of the

E-R-A-Aw-C model. Unpublished manuscript ditto. Family Study Center, Georgia State University, undated.

3. Kolevson, M. A., & Green, R. B. The paradox of therapeutic intervention: A comparative study of the theoretical frameworks and personalities of family therapists. Paper presented at the 37th Annual Conference of American Association of Marriage and Family Therapists, Washington, DC, October, 1979.

References

Boszormenyi-Nagy, I., & Spark, G. M. Invisible loyalties: Reciprocity in intergenerational family therapy. New York: Harper & Row, 1973.

Buckley, W. (Ed.). Modern systems research for the behavioral scientist: A source book. Chicago: Aldine Pub. Co., 1968.

English, F. The substitution factor: Rackets and real feelings. Transactional Analysis Journal, 1971, 4, 27-32.

Haley, J. Problem-solving therapy: New strategies for effective family therapy. San Francisco: Jossey-Bass, 1976.

Hansen, J. C., & L'Abate, L. Approaches to family therapy. New York: Macmillan, 1982.

Howard, K. I., Krause, M. S., & Orlinsky, D. E. Direction of affective influence in psychotherapy. Journal of Consulting and Clinical Psychology, 1969, 33, 614-620.

L'Abate, L. Psychodynamic interventions: A personal statement. In R. H. Woody & J. W. Woody (Eds.), Sexual, marital, and familial relations: Therapeutic interventions for professional helping. Springfield, IL: C. C. Thomas, 1973.

L'Abate, L. Understanding and helping the individual in the family. New York: Grune & Stratton, 1976.

L'Abate, L. Toward a systematic classification of counseling and therapists, theorists, methods, processes, and goals: The E-R-A- model. The Personnel and Guidance Journal, 1981, 59, 263-265.

L'Abate, L., & Frey, J. The E-R-A model: The role of feelings in family therapy reconsidered: Implications for a classification of theories of family therapy. Journal of Marriage and Family Therapy, 1981, 7, 143-150.

Levant, R. F. A classification of the field of family therapy: A review of prior attempts and a new paradigmatic model. *American Journal of Family Therapy*, 1980, 8, 3-16.

Napier, A. Y., & Whitaker, C. A. *The family crucible*. New York: Harper & Row, 1978.

Olson, D. H. L., & Sprenkle, D. H. Emerging trends in treating relationships. *Journal of Marriage and Family Counseling*, 1976, 4, 317-329.

Orlinsky, D. E., & Howard, K. I. The relation of process to outcome in psychotherapy. In S. L. Garfield & A. E. Bergin (Eds.), *Handbook of psychotherapy and behavior change: An empirical analysis*. New York: Wiley & Sons, 1978.

Ritterman, M. K. Paradigmatic classification of family therapy. *Family Process*, 1977, 16, 29-46.

Robertsen, M. Some observations from an eclectic therapist. *Psychotherapy: Theory, Research, and Practice*, 1979, 16, 18-21.

Russell, R. L., & Stiles, W. B. Categories for classifying language in psychotherapy. *Psychological Bulletin*, 1979, 86, 404-419.

Satir, V. *Peoplemaking*. Palo Alto, CA: Science & Behavior Books, 1972.

Satir, V., Bandler, R., & Grinder, J. *Changing with families*. Palo Alto, CA: Science & Behavior Books, 1976.

Satir, V., Stachowiak, J., & Taschman, H. A. *Helping families to change*. New York: Jason Aronson, 1975.

Selvini-Palazzoli, M., Boscolo, L., Cecchin, G. F., & Prata, G. *Paradox and counterparadox*. New York: Brunner/Mazel, 1978.

Smith, M. L., & Glass, G. V. Metaanalysis of psychotherapy outcome studies. *American Psychologist*, 1977, 32, 752-760.

Tomm, K. M., & Wright, L. M. Training in family therapy: Perceptual, conceptual, and executive skills. *Family Process*, 1979, 18, 227-250.

Ulrici, D., L'Abate, L., & Wagner, V. The E-R-A model: A heuristic framework for classification of skill training programs for couples and families. *Family Relations*, 1981, 30, 307-315.

Watzlawick, P., Weakland, J., & Fisch, R. *Change: Principles of problem formation and problem resolution*. New York: W. W. Norton, 1974.

Williamson, B. S. The number one issue in family therapy today. *AMFT Newsletter*, 1979, 10, 1-5.

Zuk, G. H. Family therapy: Clinical hodgepodge or clinical science? *Journal of Marriage and Family Counseling*, 1976, 4, 299-303.

Zuk, G. H. Theories of family pathology: In what direction? *International Journal of Family Therapy*, 1979, 5, 356-361.

SECTION IV

LINEAR METHODS IN FAMILY THERAPY

CHAPTER 16

THE LABORATORY EVALUATION OF FAMILIES*

Luciano L'Abate

The family is coming of age. I am speaking now from the viewpoint of a psychologist. Psychology as a whole has neglected the study of the family. It is only more recently, with the advances in clinical applications, that we psychologists have started to look at the family. If one picks up textbooks on personality development, and I happen to have picked up a few, and check how many references there are to the family, the usual count is from a casual mention to, at the most, one or two pages. Most personality theories talk about the cultural context of the personality, but, as a whole, theoretical emphasis on the influence of the family on personality development has been minimal. If one takes the field of social psychology, one also finds that although there are many concepts and techniques that are very relevant to the study of the family, American experimental social psychology as a whole has left out of the picture the family as a small group. It is time that clinical psychologists become concerned and interested in this particular area.

We at Georgia State hope to have and to be the first clinical department of psychology to offer a Ph.D. in family psychology. According to NIH, no psychology department in the United States has a doctoral program in family psychology, which is just another way of supporting what I was saying about the lack of references to the family in the personality and social psychology fields.

There have been many changes that have produced great concern about the family. There have been

---

*Paper read at a symposium on group testing approaches at the Annual Convention of the American Psychological Association, Honolulu, Hawaii, September 2, 1972.

political concerns, especially in relation to population control. There has also been an increase in the theoretical interest, especially as a derivative form, in the family therapy area. When one reviews, then, the whole area of family therapy, one sees a very interesting datum occurring: only 3% of all family therapists are interested in researching the family. This datum is even worse than the 5% for psychotherapists!

The major aspect that seems to be one of the dominant methodological problems in family research is family assessment, an area in great need of innovation. I shall review briefly various techniques of family assessment that have been traditionally used, using these techniques as a straw man to talk about techniques we have developed that we hope are better than the ones already existing.

The primary problem of family assessment has been that a great deal of the research has been sociological in nature, using field methods; that is, most people have interviewed mothers. Most recently, children have been interviewed about their parents. When one reviews the field of what has been called "family assessment," 66% of the studies have usually been done with only one member of the family alone: either the mother or one child. Studies in which the whole family--the complete family--has been studied, are probably--I will not say a handful--but they can be counted on both hands.

Another approach, of course, has been the case history. This is the time-honored psychiatric technique of case history, which has some advantages: the material is readily available; it does generate a great deal of data; and, sometimes, if administered well, avoids unreliable, subjective inferences of clinical impression. That is, one has the information and supposedly objective data. It does have the disadvantage of being selective in the emphasis of the interviewer. Furthermore, many studies have demonstrated that retrospective recollection is not exactly one of the more reliable techniques of gathering information. So much for case histories.

Interviews certainly still are and will be the most common form of data gathering. There are four different types of interviews done with families. One is structured, which is similar to questionnaires; semistructured, which allows for a good combination

of breadth and depth; and focused, which is the kind
of interview in which one can very specifically put all
one's emphasis on a particular area. Problems of time-
consuming content analysis are specific to the interview.

After the interview, we go into an area which is
dear to our clinical hearts, the use of tests--objective
and projective tests. One of the major objective techniques has been Leary's Interpersonal Checklist, which
is an adjective checklist, followed by the PARI, which
is a parent attitude research inventory, and MMPI, used
mostly with the parents. There are very few objective
techniques that could be given to the whole family.
Why? Well, most of the techniques require a certain
degree of education. In many cases, the child is left
out. The only way to get the child has been to use
projective techniques which, by the very nature of the
stimulus material, limited their administration to
adults and children. In the last years, we have had
the consensus Rorschach, the administration of
Rorschach cards to the whole family. Essentially,
each member of the family looks at each card and gives
his/her response to see if all members can reach a consensus. The same thing has been done with TAT cards.
There have been family drawings, a marble test, which
is a test of how the family divides all the goods
("marbles") that have been put together, and there have
been many other variations, such as drawings of the
whole family.

All this is nice and good. The only trouble is
that: (a) these techniques were developed specifically
for individuals, not specifically to study the family;
and (b) they are terribly, terribly expensive. What I
mean by expensive is that they take a hell of a long
time to administer. If you think how long it would
take to administer the Rorschach to an individual,
score it, and interpret it, it is a luxurious test. It
is the Rolls Royce of psychological testing because it
is very expensive. We have to decide whether the cost
is worth the returns we get from it. Some psychologists
have been very critical of techniques of this kind and
have rejected them wholesale. My point about these
techniques, particularly projective techniques, is that
they are not relevant to the family. We are essentially
asking the family to respond to stimuli that in some
cases have nothing to do with the family. I think that
we could find better ways--we should be able to find
better ways--of assessing families, which would be more

relevant to the time and age in which we are today. I shall come back to this point because one of our tests derives essentially from the Rorschach, and I shall show you how we have gone about making it a "cheaper" test.

Another area, besides projective techniques, personality tests, and objective tests, interviews, questionnaires, and case histories, has been the observation and control of experimental studies, in which some very ingenious techniques have been used. In fact, this is the most interesting aspect of family research. This area has yielded techniques such as Strodbeck's revealed differences technique, in which the husband and the wife take a test. After they have answered True or False, the interviewer looks at their answers and has them reach a decision about items on which they have different answers. Others have developed problem-solving tasks that the whole family must work on; e.g., Westman and Miller have developed a problem-solving task that can be monitored from the outside. Again, it was not the whole family, only the parents and the identified patient, who were actually part of the research. Many of these tasks could only be used with adolescents. If many of these techniques were used, they were usually used with a portion of the family--the identified patient and the parents.

There have also been very ingenious process measures of family interaction: the most useful have been Chottle's Interaction Chronograph and Bales' Interaction Technique. The chronograph is strictly a measurement of the pauses and length of speech. It is a content-free analysis of what is said during the interviews or therapy hours. These have been the kinds of process measures used most frequently, in fact, in some cases, the only ones. The other kind of controlled experimental situation has been simulation driving, in which, in a toy-like situation, the husband and wife drive cars to different gates and through different routes. They can cooperate or they can compete with each other. It is a very imaginative thing; the only trouble is that it can only be used with Mommy and Daddy, and the children are left out.

I want to spell out a few of the problems of family assessment, which I have indicated so far, summarizing briefly. First of all, there has been a failure to study the family as a whole. As I said, there are few studies that we can find in the literature in which all of the family has been studied. There is no question that this is a problem, especially if you have a 1- or 2-year-old child who is screaming and crying and kicking around. It is difficult to include him in a family study. There has been a concentration of attention to one or two members of the family, primarily, as we have said, to mother-child. Father, in the early years, had been mostly left out of the picture. He is only coming in through the back door of family therapy. Second, there has been an inadequate use of available methods. That is, what has been used has essentially been methods developed for individuals, adopted for the family. Third, there is a dearth of techniques to study families. Fourth, one of the major bug-a-boos of family research is, of course, the classification of families. That has been a really difficult problem. It is not unsurmountable, but on the whole what has happened in the classification of families is that the identified patient has been used to generalize to the family, which is to say that if an individual lies a few times, he is a liar. The same kind of generalization that we do at the personality level, we have done to the family. In many cases, of course, this has been an unwarranted overgeneralization. A fifth area of concern has been the failure to differentiate between manifest and overt levels of behavior in the family. There are various levels of functioning in behavior, and these levels need to be differentiated operationally, theoretically, and conceptually, as well as in therapeutic operations. Sixth, there have been attempts to differentiate, let's say, the existence of family myths, of the family ego mass (as Bowen's talk about the undifferentiated ego mass), but, as a whole, one of the major shortcoming of family assessment has been the lack of theory to guide assessment. All of the techniques that I have mentioned before are techniques created ad hoc. That is, they were there already. There has not been the creation of theory that would guide the creation of instruments that would then be tests for the theory itself. I think this is one of the great deficiencies of family assessment. When we look specifically at psychological techniques (and I will clearly focus on these because they are of major interest to me), these techniques (objective and projective) have been used with individuals rather than with families. These methods limit the age range and the literacy level at which they can be used. The second practical limitation has been cost and time. The assessment of a family with the existing instruments may last a day. This kind of testing, with existing instruments, is very time consuming. I end this brief review, therefore, by concluding that we need to develop new techniques for family evaluation.

We have to set up some requirements for the creation of new instruments. We have to ensure that these instruments are applicable to all age levels from the beginning of school up. We have to limit these instruments to school age and up because I believe that family therapy and family study with children below 5 is probably impossible. A behavioral model, that is, helping the parents deal with the child below 6 years of age to achieve stimulus control of the child, is probably a better model. There is no sense studying a family with a 3-year-old child when the child is probably 'non-studyable," not under control. I must say very clearly that I shall limit my lower age level to 6. I also want to make sure that the tests are applicable to all levels of literacy. That means that we must avoid the written word. Furthermore, we need to develop some techniques that can be helpful in the area of cross-cultural research in the family. Also, we want them to be objective and efficient in time, cost, and, perhaps, self-scoring. We want them to be simple to score and to interpret. We need to remember that the family is a vast and most interdisciplinary area. Our techniques should be helpful to the various disciplines interested in the family. I am not interested in developing tools that have the right of control in the proprietary hands of psychologists. I want to make sure that we have tools that can be used by a variety of professions, without having to refer to esoteric terms. In fact, I want to develop tools that can be used in some cases by nonprofessionals. I am sure that some of my colleagues would not like what I am saying, but I think that I shall stand firm on the point that the techniques I want to create would be used by a variety of people. No discipline can set itself to be the watchdog or guardian of any aspect of the family, certainly not psychology, especially in view of its own lateness in becoming involved with the family. The other requirement that I want to set is that, naturally, these instruments have to be relevant and related to the study of the self in the family.

Ideally, we need to coordinate theory, testing, and therapy. Let's see whether this can be done because this is a pretty big order and it takes a lot of guts or presumption, or both, to do this. In the course of our work, we have developed what we believe are three statements, which we call the three postulates of personality development in the family. These postulates, in order to have value, must account for the positive aspects of family functioning as well as the pathological, or dysfunctional, aspects. These statements have helped us coordinate theory and testing at the same time (already introduced in chap. 3).

The first postulate is that the family is healthy whenever it allows its individual members to assert their own values positively. This is what I call the postulate of self-differentiation. We have the family that will help the child or its members to assert themselves positively, and we have a family that will help its members assert themselves negatively. From this viewpoint, I put myself clearly in the field of self-theorists. I never really thought of myself as a self-theorist or as supporting a self-theory. The more I worked with families, however, the more I became enamored of the self. Until this time, even through individual aspects, the self had been a very generic and vague term which, of course, escaped operational definition. The more I worked with families, the more I felt I had to use this concept of the self and the concept of differentiation. The first statement can lend itself to a theoretical and methodological model: a bell-shaped curve over a continuum of likeness. The pathology here lies in extremes of symbiosis and sameness, oppositeness and autism. In the middle is the healthy aspect of functioning, the fact that the family allows some degree of similarity and some degree of difference. Briefly, the major way in which I think the family produces pathology as part of self-differentiation is the demand for sameness-oppositeness; in other words, "I am good; I want you to be like me" or "I am no good; I want you to be the opposite." This is in the sense that if you are really hooked on sameness, you will get oppositeness; if you get differentness, to the individual who thinks in dichotomies (black and white), differentness seems oppositeness. Differentness will be considered oppositeness. I am saying that the family fails to assert the worth of its individual members through at least three different ways: demand for self-differentiation through sameness; self-differentiation for oppositeness, and self-differentiation for differentness.

The second postulate deals with how the family fails to understand, set up, and be clear about priorities. It lends itself to another model that, instead of being a curvilinear model, yields what I call a spokes model. It is something like a wheel, with the marriage in the pivot and the parents and the children at the opposite extremities of the spokes. This model allows me to see how the three parts of the family--parents, marriage, and children--are coordinated to let the marriage and the family function or dysfunction. This model illustrates that if there is enough flexibility of movement, with the marriage strictly in the center between the parents and the children, we are going to have normality. When we have the parents very much on top, with the marriage in the middle and the children somewhere in the bottom, or vice versa, the parents on the bottom and the marriage and children in the middle, we are going to have pathology. This is strictly a descriptive model.

The third postulate is strictly lifted and copied from Virginia Satir. I translated it into what I call an orthogonal model, which basically says that when there is pathology in a family, the pathology will come out along four different directions: blaming-placating as extremities on the horizontal axis, and distracting-computing as extremities on the vertical axis. Given the three statements, we must see how we can create instruments that would allow testing of the three models generated from the theoretical statements. The first model, as you remember, dealt with self-differentiation. This statement requires the creation of instruments for the measurement of the self.

If one looks at the assessment of individuals and of personality as traditionally done, we define personality and the self by self-declaration. This is how we have traditionally gone about defining the self, with all the inevitable distortions coming from the fact that most of us will, given the choice, usually choose positive statements about ourselves. The whole area of personality testing in the United States is "bugged" by what is called response sets. That is, most people will respond in a positive direction; thus, the definition of personality is through self-definition, i.e., the individual speaks about him/herself. The way I want to define personality is personality as a process and as a dynamic aspect that requires a reciprocal definition by intimates in the family, whereby the definition is an individual participating in his/her own definition and in the definition of those who define him/her. The self is thus viewed as a total aspect of the family input. I think that this form of definition is very important. Since we have developed three techniques about self, I just want to mention briefly how the self can be measured. One way is to do it symbolically. We developed a test made up of nonsense symbols. This work is being done by one of our faculty members, Dr. Joel Fagan, and one of our graduate students, Gail Bell, for her doctoral dissertation. These very simple symbols, just nonsense symbols, do have correlations to feelings of liveliness, quietness, anger, and guilt. We plan to take these symbols, which have been tested very carefully and found to have very clear relationships to feelings, and use them in family assessment, i.e., the symbolic definition of self in the family. Everybody in the family will participate in this particular definition.[1]

The second definition is through feelings. We developed a test of the description of the feelings of the family in which we are using the Satir model. Basically, we have members of a family in four different stances and three levels of intensity: anger, distractibility, and sadness. There are six members of the family--two adolescents, father and mother, and two children; that gives us 3 x 4 x 6, 72 pictures, which we give to the members of the family, saying, "Pick up the pictures that apply to your family." From here, we take the scores themselves, the pictures they have chosen, and an answer sheet, and we can translate these into a family scoring of the total points accumulated from the individual members. This will give us one way of defining the family feeling and perhaps even of classifying families.[2]

The third definition is essentially metaphorical. By metaphorical, I mean that if you give the Rorschach to people, what will be the answers that most people give? Well, 80% or 90% of the Rorschach responses, as you know, are animals. That's a metaphor. If you want to be very psychodynamic about it, you can talk about the libidinal, or unconscious, aspects of the self, or, if you like, the animal-like aspects of the self. We have 90 of these pictures on which we have Semantic Differential ratings on their stimulus value. The family sorts them in terms of which animals

---

[1] This test is now called the Bell-Fagan Symbols Test.

[2] This test is now called Feelings in the Family.

represent various family members. That again makes individuals move to the overall family. We have a family score sheet on how everybody is seen through the pictures picked up by everybody in the family. This, then, would be a third method of defining the self in the family, which would apply to postulate #1.[3]

The third postulate can be defined also through different tests that we developed. One is hypothetical situations in which the adolescents are given hypothetical situations for which the four forced choices fit the Satir model ("What would you do?"). Since Satur does have nonverbal stances for each particular dysfunction--blaming, placating, computing, distracting--it lent itself beautifully to the creation of what we call the Family Situations Picture Test, in which we have depicted the four physical stances, reduced it to 6 members of a family (parents, 2 adolescents, and 2 children of two sexes) and worked out combinations and permutations for all, for a total of 264 pictures. We then administer them to the family. They pick up the pictures that apply to the family, score themselves on individual answer sheets, and we translate them into family scores. This test allows us another way of classifying the family and describing it in a 2 x 2 space, very much as Leary used to do with his adjective checklist. We have been able to use this test with various literacy levels and with children from 6 years up. Another test (<u>Who would say this?</u>) was developed from family therapy records by picking out statements describing Satir's fourfold model. We ask the members of the family who can read to pick up the statements that would apply to the various family members.

In conclusion, we have stated three postulates of personality development in the family and developed ways and means, models, and techniques to test these postulates. Assessing families and enriching them through intermediaries[4] can be a very rewarding experience. I hope a few psychologists will join me.

---

[3] This test is now called the Animal Concept Picture Series.

[4] This aspect of the laboratory method will be elaborated in the next chapter.

<u>Note</u>. Research on the usefulness of these pictorial and verbal test batteries to assess couples and families will be reported in forthcoming papers.

CHAPTER 17

The Laboratory Evaluation and Enrichment of Couples: Applications and Some Preliminary Results

Luciano L'Abate, R. W. Wildman II, J. B. O'Callaghan, S. J. Simon, M. Allison, G. Kahn, and N. Rainwater*

Data relating to the effects of structured versus unstructured interventions with three couples are presented and compared. Arguments are presented for the standard use of: 1) routine, pre- post-intervention assessment, 2) laboratory procedures in the assessment and treatment of couples, and 3) paraprofessionals in intervention with couples. This report is part of a systematic program of research into the appropriate use of structured and unstructured intervention and into the optimal matching of client family and intervention approach.

The purpose of this report is to illustrate applications of the laboratory method (L'Abate, 1968) to the evaluation and enrichment of couples and to present some preliminary results of this approach. This presentation is meant to be more clearly illustrative of methodology rather than of outcome. Research on outcomes on a large number of families is in progress and will be reported later.

The reviews of Olson (1970) and of Gurman (1973a) touch on many issues that are important in a laboratory approach to the evaluation and enrichment of couples. Olson (1970) emphasized the need to bridge gaps between research, theory, and clinical practice, an emphasis shared by the laboratory method. Olson also recommended "selective interdisciplinary borrowing." This practice, as will be shown later in this paper, is consistent with the use of a variety of laboratory procedures. Finally, Olson considered the need for using paraprofessional, a practice that started the laboratory approach: Because of the endless demand for professional marital and family therapy, there needs to be greater utilization of all available resources, and the use of paraprofessionals seems to be an important resource.

In his review of the effects and effectiveness of marital therapy, Gurman (1973b) noted the need for multidimensional evaluation of marital therapy outcomes and controlled comparative studies. He concluded his review by stating, "The door is wide open for the development of even more potent change processes."

More recent publications in the area of marital therapy, notably the contributions of Ard and Ard (1969), Chapman (1974), Fitzgerald (1973), Greene (1970), Nichols (1974), and Silverman (1972), as well as those of Goodman (1973) and Gurman (1973a), suggest the absence of an empirical approach in

*Luciano L'Abate, PhD, is Professor of Psychology and Director of Family Studies Program at Georgia State University, Atlanta, GA 30303. The remaining authors are post-Masters graduate students in psychology or counseling at Georgia State University, majoring or minoring in the Family Studies Program.

the field of marital counseling and therapy. Both an empirical approach and an insistence upon accountability are components of the laboratory approach.

Briefly, the main components of the laboratory method are as follows: clear separation of duties and responsibilities between professional and paraprofessional personnel. Supervision and professional responsibility lie in the hands of a director who uses unstructured, impressionistic procedures. Actual execution and service lie in the hands of paraprofessionals who use standard operating procedures of a structured nature, such as objective questionnaires, paper and pencil rating sheets, and, in intervention, structured techniques outlined in marital enrichment manuals (L'Abate, 1974a).

Enrichment manuals are booklets of written programmed instructions for usually six lessons of discussion and exercises designed to improve the marital relationship. At present, several "Marital Enrichment Programs" have been written by the senior author and his graduate students. The themes and titles of the programs include the following: Marital Assertiveness, Cohabitation, Conflict Resolution, Equality, Marital Negotiation, Reciprocity, Sexuality, and Working Through. Copies of these programs are available upon request from the senior author.

Through the use of the laboratory method, the components of service and research, evaluation and intervention, theory, and practice become intertwined and complementary to each other rather than separate or antagonistic, as in traditional procedures. The cases to be presented here illustrate how intervention can take place within the framework of the laboratory method without disservice to the rights and privileges of clients or students. In these particular cases, graduate students served as direct interveners. However, their relative lack of sophistication about marital intervention could illustrate the applicability of the same procedures in the hands of even less sophisticated paraprofessionals, an approach already used in applying this method to the evaluation and enrichment of families (L'Abate & Smith, 1975).

Method

Procedure

Two couples (One and Two) were administered the *Azrin Reciprocity Marital Counseling Program* (Wildman & L'Abate, 1974). This is a learning theory-based program adapted from a study by Azrin, Naster, and Jones (1973), who formulated a model of marital counseling based on reinforcement theory. According to this view, marital discord is the results of nonreciprocated reinforcement; therefore, the counseling procedures attempt to establish reciprocity of reinforcement. The adapted, structured program is conducted in six sessions in which the couple is taught to use the principle of reciprocity in interpersonal interactions. Specific components of the sessions are as follows:

1) "catharsis," in which the marital partners discuss their marriage from its origins to its present troubled state,
2) "old satisfactions," in which the partners list present actions that please each other (reinforcements) and are taught to let each other know they appreciate the other's efforts,
3) "new satisfactions," in which the enrichers aid the couple in discovering, agreeing upon and listing new reinforcers to improve each other's happiness,
4) "compromise," in which the couple is taught to reach mutually satisfying solutions to disagreements,
5) "happiness contracting," during which formal agreement to the informally agreed upon satisfactions (reinforcements) is obtained, and
6) "sexual communication," in which the spouses are aided in learning each other's sexual needs to develop reciprocity in this area of marital unhappiness.

These programs were administered by two male-female teams of psychology graduate students with no previous marital counseling experience.

Subjects

In Couple One, the husband, 31, had nearly completed college and had held a large number of jobs during his short working career. The wife, 28, worked as a legal secretary to help the family through its latest financial crisis. The marriage was the husband's second. The wife's mother lived with them in a small apartment with no furniture and helped care for their two young children. This couple had been interviewed by the senior author and his wife. The presenting problems at that time were general incompatibility and a persistent inability to manage the family's finances. The couple was referred to two of the senior author's students for structured intervention. The husband consulted a psychiatrist because of anxiety beginning during Week Number 6.

Couple Two had been married for ten years. They first met while they were working for the same company. Each had been married and divorced once prior to being married to each other. The husband was a 33-year-old business executive who had worked his way up from being a desk clerk to the area manager for a large business concern. He and his present family had been transferred five times during his tenure with the company. The wife was a 31-year-old housewife and mother. They had three children: two girls, eight and five years old, and a boy, age seven, who had been diagnosed as mentally retarded. Each of the spouses had a high school education. Approximately five years prior to the present intervention, the husband began seeing a psychiatrist because, as he stated, he was "almost an alcoholic." The couple, along with their children, lived in an attractive, middle-class environment. The couple started the program at the suggestion of the wife, and both brought a very favorable attitude to the sessions. Their presenting problems were a breakdown in marital communication and disagreement about how to handle the children.

One other couple was treated in a six session intervention using an approach other than the *Azrin Reciprocity Marital Counseling Program*. Couple Three was given six sessions of unstructured marital therapy based on the writings of Don Jackson (Lederer & Jackson, 1968). Therapy was conducted by one experienced female marital counselor. Couple Three was composed of a 24-year-old husband and a 23-year-old wife. They had been married six years. The couple had three sons ranging in age from 13 months to five years. They originally sought help because of difficulty in controlling the behavior of their eldest son. Much of the son's misbehavior had subsided before the beginning of therapy, but the couple elected to follow through on their request for help.

The first session focused on the behavior of their five-year-old, whom the mother described as "the neighborhood nuisance." He was rarely in his own yard and several neighbors complained to her about his activities, e.g., disturbing the garden, mistreating the cat, and so on. In addition, he was troublesome at home. The mother was instructed and encouraged to (a) set limits and (b) to find ways to help her son reestablish himself as the senior son with the appropriate responsibilities and privileges, e.g., expecting him to help with chores and allowing him to stay up later than his brothers.

During the five remaining sessions the couple shifted to their concerns about the marital relationship. Therapy consisted of making them more aware of their interactional behavior and in suggesting ways of bringing about changes.

The husband was a full-time student who also worked full-time. The wife had become unhappy with her role and resentful of the time he spent outside the home and/or studying. She was able to discuss her expectations and present disappointments about the marriage. Her husband in turn talked about the strain he was experiencing. Over the five sessions, they began to deal with each other honestly, rather than withdrawing, as was the husband's pattern, or criticizing, as the wife had begun to do. They were able to negotiate in several areas so that each could get something that he or she wanted in the relationship. He agreed to help more with the children when he was at home (particularly with discipline) and she agreed not to complain about her husband's watching television as a way of "unwinding" when he came home at night.

The primary function of the therapist with couple Three was to listen for recurrent patterns of behavior and to suggest new ways of relating which would maximize the change for a change in the interactional pattern. She also reinforced the obvious caring in the relationship and occasionally "reframed" a situation so that one or both were able to approach the conflict in a novel way.

Evaluation

Measurement is seen as an integral component of the enrichment process. Emphasis is placed upon evaluation for three reasons: 1) it helps in the selection of appropriate enrichment programs; 2) it provides a means of monitoring the efficacy of the enrichment process; and 3) it provides a basis with regard to the issue of accountability. The illustrative case studies which follow make use of the Marital Enrichment Battery (Wildman, Weiss, & L'Abate, 1973) on a pre- post-intervention basis. It is important to note, however, that most of the components of the battery have no established reliability or validity (with the possible exception of the Marital Happiness Scale; Azrin, Naster, & Jones, 1973). The sensitivity and reliability of these tests are currently being investigated. The description of the battery which follows is included here not to demonstrate outcome but to illustrate what type of instruments might be implemented in the laboratory use of the family enrichment model.

The Marital Evaluation Battery

1) *The Marital Questionnaire.* This questionnaire, based on the theories of Satir (1972) and L'Abate (1974b), attempts to measure the extent to which an individual's attitudes are consistent with being a functional and effective spouse and parent. The questionnaire consists of 260 statements with which the subject is asked to either agree or disagree. A point is given for agreement with a functional statement as well as for disagreement with a maladaptive statement. Thus, the higher the score, the greater the indication of psychologically healthy attitudes across the measured dimensions. The test consists of 13 scales: Likeness (a measure of self-differentiation); Priorities (a measure of priority structures within the family); Blaming; Placating; Computing; Distracting (based upon Satir's 1972 model); Caring; Enjoyment; Forgiveness; Protectiveness; Responsibility; Seeing-the-Good; and Sharing-of-Hurt (the latter seven scales measure a subject's relative strengths and weaknesses on L'Abate's (1975) seven tasks of marital enhancement.

2) *Likeness Grid.* This instrument is based upon the work of Kelly (1955) and involves the subject rating himself on a scale of likeness to significant persons in the subject's life. This instrument provides another measure of self-differentiation as defined by L'Abate (1974b).

3) *Transactional Analysis (TA) Test.* This test provides a measure of a person's personality according to the T.A. model of Parent, Adult, and Child. The instrument consists of a series of situations followed by three alternative responses to the situation. Each statement is consistent with one of the ego states as defined by Berne (1964). The test is scored according to the percentage of responses which are in each of the three parts of the personality.

4) *Marital Happiness Scale (MHS).* The Marital Happiness Scale (Azrin, Naster, & Jones, 1973) consists of 10 subscales (relevant to the marriage) with which spouses rate their degree of satisfaction (from one to 10).

Couple number One through Three completed the Marital Questionnaire, Likeness Grid, and Transactional Analysis Test on a pre post-basis. The Marital Happiness

Scale was completed on a nightly basis during the six weeks of enrichment or therapy and weekly during pre-testing or follow-up.

Results

This section is intended primarily as an illustration of the routine and efficient application of empiricism and accountability to the provision of service to couples. Because the Marital Happiness Scale is the only assessment instrument reported in the literature (Azrin, Naster, & Jones, 1973), the results will be reported mainly on this measure, with brief comments on the results obtained using the other measures described in the Evaluation section.

Figure 1 shows the weekly averages on the Marital Happiness Scales for couples One through Three. As can be seen, couple One experienced a pre- to post-intervention increase of approximately two points (a gain comparable to that obtained and noted as significant by Azrin, Naster, & Jones (1973). The couple attributed the depression in the scales during weeks 10 and 11 to serve financial difficulties and the wife's belief, later discovered to be unfounded, that she was seriously ill. The senior author contacted this couple six weeks following the termination of data collection. At that time, the couple reported that they were much more compatible and satisfied with their marriage. The Marital Evaluation Battery changes parallel the improvements in terms of self-differentiation (Bowen, 1966, L'Abate, 1974b). Also, and more dramatically, they appeared to become more positive and optimistic toward themselves and their marriage.

Figure 1 also shows the Marital Happiness Scale data for Couple Two. No significant overall improvement in Marital Happiness Scale scores was found for this couple, although a minor, upward trend is observable during weeks two through five. Verbal reports by the couple during the six-week follow-up indicated that what little improvement had occurred was due to their actually executing the prescribed procedures. Yet, towards the end (Session 6) and beyond, they admitted that they were remiss in practicing the procedures. These verbal reports correspond closely with the trends presented in Figure 1. The Marital Evaluation Battery pre- post-test comparisons for Couple Two suggest clinically significant improvements. Why these improvements are not also apparent on the Marital Happiness Scales is not immediatedy clear. The inconsistency between the Marital Evaluation Battery and Marital Happiness Scales raises the question of which is really the more valid indicator.

Couple Three, who received unstructured marital therapy, experienced a two point increase on the Marital Happiness Scale. This is the same magnitude of increase as was observed with couple One. While some improvement on the Marital Evaluation Battery is noted for couple Three, there is not the consistent pattern of healthy change observed in couple One.

It is hoped that the preceding outcome report accompanied by the graphic displays of "progress" exemplify one way of efficiently and routinely monitoring couple progress in enrichment or therapy. Future work in this area might concentrate on isolating the assessment procedures which most efficiently and sensitively demonstrate the effectiveness of therapeutic intervention.

Discussion

The data from couple One are entirely consistent with the findings of Azrin et al. (1973), thereby providing a systematic replication of their work. It would seem to be significant that the same program should have only a temporary effect on couple Two. The trainers who actually dealt with that couple speculated that the husband's psychotherapeutic experience was an interfering factor. That is to say, five years of insight-oriented therapy had taught him one mode of dealing with others so well that it was difficult for him to operate within the reciprocity framework. An alternate explanation suggested by the trainers is that they themselves served as cues for maintaining the reciprocal behaviors. When they stopped seeing the couple on a weekly basis, the couple was no longer prompted to keep their contracts. Clearly, more attention will have to be given in the future to *which* programs are appropriate for *which* couples or families (Gurman, 1973b; L'Abate, 1969). Perhaps, too, maintenance is an issue which needs to be addressed by the program.

One of the most interesting findings from the present study was the improvement on the Marital Happiness Scales of couple Three, the couple who had received unstructured marital therapy. This improvement on a behavioral outcome measure is intriguing. The improvement in couple Three challenges Eysenck's (1952) contention that non-learning theory-based therapy is ineffective. Non-behaviorists should, in the authors' judgement, make increased use of behavioral outcome measures. It may well prove to be that, as has been true with Rational-Emotive Therapy (e.g., Trexler & Karst, 1972), much "talk therapy" is effective, even in the sense that behaviorists define effectiveness, but that this effectiveness has not been demonstrated due to a lack of measurement devices.

It is the authors' conclusion that many of the goals of marital therapy can be accomplished within a structured framework administered by inexperienced trainers. The present study illustrates the use of the laboratory method, including the following components:

1) structured enrichment programs based on empirically validated methods,
2) inexperienced trainers supervised by one accomplished therapist,
3) ongoing evaluation of improvement from the clients' viewpoint,
4) test batteries administered both pre- and post-intervention, and
5) follow-up assessment through clients' ratings.

The laboratory approach has decided advantages over a non-empirical approach to marital counseling. Structured programs provide a basis for continual modification and improvement of procedures. The use of a large number of relatively inexperienced personnel under the supervision of a few professional therapists is one solution to the burgeoning expense of and demand for marital therapy. Additionally, therapists and researchers are provided with a context for development of assessment tools to demonstrate the effectiveness of their approaches. Considering the tremendous increase in marital schism and family crisis (Etzioni, 1974; Mowrer, 1975), the laboratory method, and specifically the enrichment model, can be considered as an additional option in the field of family intervention and research.

REFERENCES

Ard, B. N., Jr., & Ard, C. C., (Eds.). *Handbook of marriage counseling*. Palo Alto: Science and Behavior Books, 1969.

Azrin, N. H., Naster, B. J., & Jones, R. Reciprocity counseling: A rapid learning-based procedure for marital counseling. *Behaviour Research and Therapy*, 1973, *11*, 365-382.

Berne, E. *The games people play*. New York: Grove Press, 1964.

Bowen, M. The use of family therapy in clinical practice. *Comprehensive Psychiatry*, 1966, *7*, 345-374.

Chapman, A. H. *Marital brinkmanship*. New York: G. P. Putnam, 1974.

Etzioni, A. The next crisis: The end of the family. *Evaluation*, 1974, *2*, 6-7.

Eysenck, H. J. The effects of psychotherapy: An evaluation. *Journal of Consulting Psychology*, 1952, *16*, 319-324.

Fitzgerald, R. V. *Conjoint marital therapy*. New York: Aronson, 1973.

Goodman, E. S. Marriage counseling as science: Some research considerations. *The Family Coordinator*, 1973, *22*, 111-116.

Greene, B. L. *A clinical approach to marital problems: Evaluation and management.* Springfield: Thomas, 1970.

Gurman, A. S. The effects and effectiveness of marital therapy: A review of outcome research. *Family Process*, 1973, *12*, 145-170. (b)

Kelly, G. A. *The psychology of personal constructs.* New York: Norton, 1955.

L'Abate, L. The laboratory method in clinical psychology: An attempt at innovation. *The Clinical Psychologist*, 1968, *21*, 182-183.

L'Abate, L. The contiuum of rehabilitation and laboratory evaluation. In C. Franks (Ed.), *Behavior Therapy: Appraisal and Status*, New York: McGraw-Hill, 1969.

L'Abate, L. Family enrichment programs. *Journal of Family Counseling*, 1974, *2*, 32-38. (a)

L'Abate, L. Understanding and helping the individual in the family. Paper read at the Theory Construction Workshop, National Council for Family Relations, St. Louis, MO, October, 1974. (b)

L'Abate, L. A positive approach to marital and familial intervention. In Wolberg, L. R., & Aronson, M. L., (Eds.), *Group Therapy*, New York: Stratton Intercom, 1975.

L'Abate, L., & Smith, D. The laboratory evaluation and enrichment of families. Research in progress, Georgia State University, 1975.

Lederer, W. J., & Jackson, D. *The mirages of marriage.* New York: W. W. Norton, 1968.

Mowrer, O. H. New hope and help for the disintegrating American family. *Journal of Family Counseling*, 1975, *3*, 17-23.

Nichols, W. C., Jr., (Ed.). *Marriage and family therapy.* Minneapolis: National Council on Family Relations, 1974.

Olson, D. H. Marital and family therapy: Integrative review and critique. *Journal of Marriage and the Family*, 1970, *32*, 501-538.

Satir, V. *Peoplemaking.* Palo Alto: Science and Behavior Books, 1972.

Silverman, H. L., (Ed.). *Marital therapy: Moral, sociological and psychological factors.* Springfield: Thomas, 1972.

Trexler, L. D., & Karst, T. D. Rational-emotive therapy, placebo, and no-treatment effects on public-speaking anxiety. *Journal of Abnormal Psychology*, 1972, *79*, 60-67.

Wildman, R. W., II, & L'Abate, L. *The Azrin Reciprocity Marital Counseling Program.* Unpublished manuscript, Georgia State University, 1974.

Wildman, R. W., II, Weiss, D., & L'Abate, L. Marital Evaluation Battery: A pilot study. Unpublished manuscript, Georgia State University, 1973.

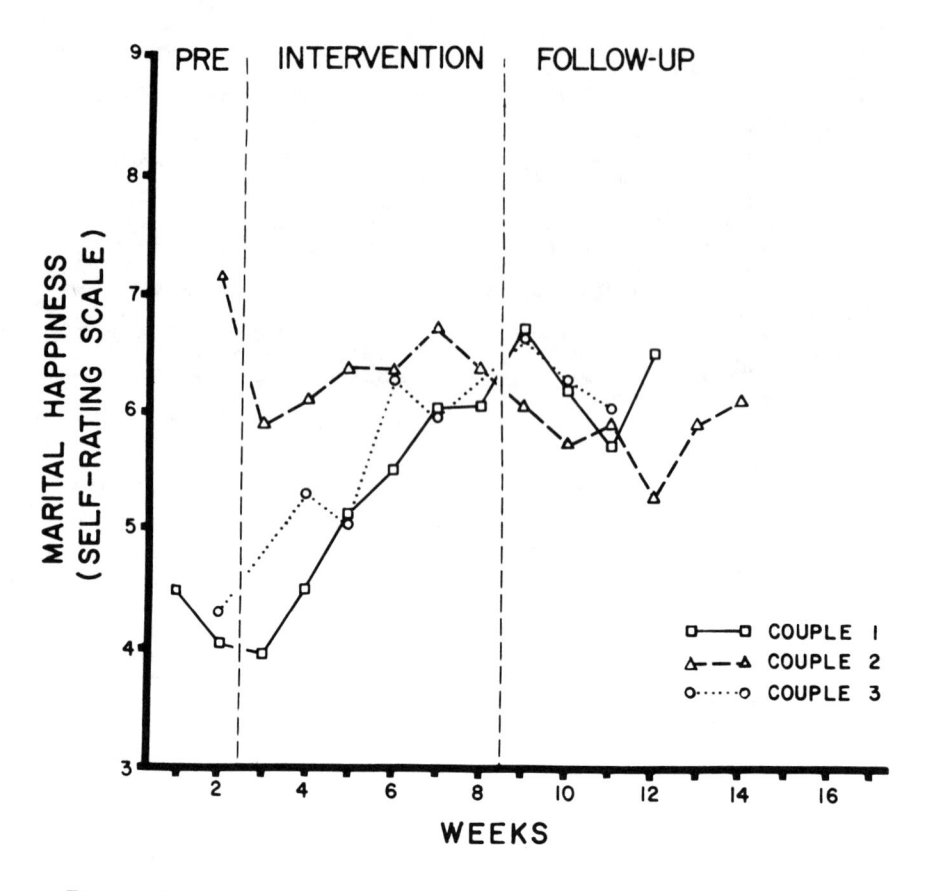

Figure 1. Average weekly scores on the 10 sub-scales of the Marital Happiness Scale for three couples.

CHAPTER 18

FORCED HOLDING: A TECHNIQUE FOR TREATING PARENTIFIED CHILDREN

Jackie Johnson, Gerald R. Weeks and L. L'Abate

The purpose of this paper is to present the "forced holding" technique as a therapeutic intervention that will help to establish a clear, intergenerational chain of command in the family between the adults and children when such a chain is missing or inadequate. The technique helps parents reestablish the control and/or authority that has been given up and directed onto one or more children, usually the symptom bearer. The technique is used to redistribute power and make generational boundaries firmer. It should be used when the therapist asks the question, "Who is the boss in the family?" and the child answers in one of the following ways: (a) "I am" or (b) reluctantly wavers between the parents, or (c) contradicts the appropriate verbal answer ("Daddy is") by laughing, making faces, rolling eyes, and by other disqualifying signals.

This technique has been found especially useful in treating single parent families when there is a power struggle between the remaining parent and one or more children. Typically, the power conflict within the single parent family assumes one of two forms. First, the remaining parent may impose a "parentified" role onto a given child thereby relinquishing parental authority that is needed by the child (Boszormenyi-Nagy and Spark, 1973). The remaining parent may look to one or more children to assume a "parentified" role by becoming either a pseudo-spouse and/or pseudo-parent, in which case the child becomes

Ms. Johnson is a doctoral student in the Family Studies Program at Georgia State University.
Gerald R. Weeks, Ph.D., Assistant Professor of Psychology, University of North Carolina at Wilmington, Wilmington, North Carolina.
Dr. L'Abate is Professor and Director of the Family Studies Program at Georgia State University.
Reprint request should be sent to: Dr. Gerald R. Weeks, University of North Carolina at Wilmington, P.O. Box 3725, Wilmington, North Carolina, 28406.

The authors would like to express their appreciation to Flo Dawson, Ed Jessee and Victor Wagner, who are graduate students in the Family Program at Georgia State University, for their contributions to this manuscript. Also, all case studies reported in this article were supervised by Dr. L. L'Abate. The contribution of Bess L. L'Abate is gratefully acknowledged. The second author would also like to thank John Schoonbeck and Jane Ferber for their help in developing this procedure.

caretaker of the needs of the parent and of the other children. Second, the single parent, by virtue of being a solo parent, is more prone to become inconsistent and overburdened by parenting duties. In both instances, the power boundary between parent and child may become blurred or non-existent in which the child believes he or she is as powerful as the parent (Haley, 1976).

The forced holding technique involves having the child sit on the parent's lap with one of the parent's legs over the child's body to entrap him/her. The parent's arm should encircle the child's torso and the child's hands should be held. With older children, the child should lie face up on the floor and the parent should straddle the stomach of the child with the hands pressing firmly down on the shoulders, wrists or hands. In both cases, the area surrounding this activity should be unencumbered, with no sharp or hard surfaces exposed. Glasses, pens, shoes, and other such objects should be removed before the process begins. With larger and stronger children it is advisable for the other parent or therapist to help the parent in maintaining control, usually by holding the legs down so that one parent, usually the mother, appears to have the most control. Once the parent and child have assumed this position, the therapist has the parent repeatedly ask the child: "Who is the boss?" until the child can *congruently* respond that his parent is the boss. By congruent, it is meant: (a) eye contact is maintained with the parent; (b) the response is in the form of a complete sentence; and (c) there are no distractions or contradictions.

There are a number of guidelines which should be followed in employing this technique. First, it should be employed early in the therapeutic process. When used later, the child may feel that he has been betrayed by the therapist(s) and it will take longer to reestablish a trusting relationship. The forced holding session may last 1-3 hours. The therapists and family should have adequate time to devote to the process and the parents should be questioned about any time limitation from the outset. In some cases we have explained the process before we began the session and in others we simply ask that the family be willing to spend the time needed. Secondly, assuming that the parent is willing to try the technique, the child may resist sitting on the parent's lap or lying on the floor. A couple of paradoxical techniques may be used to maneuver the child into position. One involves telling the child that you know he/she doesn't want to do what you have asked, but that when the parent finds out what it is about he/she will like it a lot less. The other technique is to provide a worse alternative to the child. For example, "O.K., either you sit on your father's lap or I will pick you up and put you there." The family's first reaction to this technique is that it is a game. The child will giggle and laugh. The parent will not know what to do initially and should be told to just sit on top for a few minutes to see what happens. After a short period of time the mother should be reassured that she is not hurting the child and she is to ask the child, "Who is the boss?"

As the process unfolds, the child will become angry, and should be encouraged to express this anger through struggling, screaming, crying, pounding fists on the floor, etc. The parent's anger must be carefully monitored and controlled. When the child begins to actively struggle in response to the parent's question, the therapist can make the interpretation that the child really did think he was the boss. The next phase in this process is rage—the child will curse, scream, bite, spit, make excuses, etc.—usually moving into this stage with little confrontation. However, if the child does not move into this stage, the therapist can intensify the confrontation by saying such things as "If you are the boss, why can't you get up?" or "If you are the boss, prove it." When the child enters the rage phase it is important to reassure the mother that this child's reaction is normal and indicate that the child will probably get even more angry. The first part of the rage phase is essentially non-verbal. It is pointless for the mother to talk to the child. Once the rage begins to subside the mother should again ask the question, "Who is the boss?" This phase may last from 15 minutes to 2 hours. After the child has congruently said that mother is the boss, therapist and parent should shift to a more supportive stance. The therapist should say that he/she expected the child to put up a good fight and commend the child for his/her struggle. The mother should then be instructed to tell the child that she is the boss, will remain the boss, does not need the child to take care of her, and that the child is the boss of him/herself which is a full-time job. It is essential to keep the eye contact constant between parent and child and to coax the mother in making statements and giving directions. At this point the mother should be required to set limits and make rules regarding the child's behavior. The parent is not allowed to ask the child questions. The parent gives the child directives and has the child repeat the directive. During the final phase of the forced holding session, children generally become quiet and often appear to be stunned or in a trance. The child is probably re-organizing the family structure mentally. Many children want to be held on the lap after the "forced holding" on the floor and this is encouraged. We proceed to praise the mother for her work and again congratulate the child for putting up a good fight. Intense nurturance has been observed in many cases during the period following the forced holding. It is important to remember that once the forced holding session has started, it should not be stopped prematurely; this would constitute a public victory for the child which would add to, rather than reduce the problem. Before the parent(s) leave the session the therapist should point out that the child will test the parent, perhaps asking the child how he/she will test the mother and then asking the mother what the child will do.

To facilitate the maintenance of the verbally established boundary, the family may be given a task (see Haley, 1976 and Minuchin, 1974) which should reinforce the parent's position of being in charge. We do suggest that the parent spend 15 minutes a day during the first week holding the child.

We have used the forced holding technique and found it to be very successful with families seen in therapy as well as in a structured intervention situation such as enrichment (L'Abate, 1976). We will present several cases illustrating when and how to use this technique based upon families seen in our laboratory.

Case 1: A single parent family consisting of a 38-year-old divorced mother and an 11-year-old daughter were seen in therapy. The mother presented the daughter's defiance against her as the main reason for entering therapy. The daughter's defiance was not only against her mother but also against her teachers and friends. Over the course of therapy, it was learned that the mother was inconsistent in setting limits with her daughter, gave in to her daughter's demands, e.g., buying whatever she wanted at the grocery store and cooking whatever she wanted for breakfast; looked to her daughter to be an adult; and last, the mother placated the ex-husband in front of the child whenever problems arose concerning the daughter. Moreover, the mother reported that her daughter respected her father and wanted to be with him more than with her.

It became evident that the daughter saw herself to be as powerful, if not more so, than her mother and that reestablishing the mother's authority was necessary for this family. The question, "Who is the boss?" was asked of the daughter, who quickly answered that her father was boss. Next, the question was asked again except this time, the question applied only to the relationship between the daughter and mother. The daughter answered that she was the boss of her mother. The daughter was asked to sit on her mother's lap. She refused. Then, she was asked to lie on the floor. She agreed, and the mother was instructed to straddle the daughter in accordance with the procedure described earlier.

The mother was instructed to ask repeatedly, "Who is the boss?" At first the daughter treated the event as a game. Later, she began to fight back and at times cried to be released. One of the therapists had to support the mother's hold by securing the daughter's legs. The session lasted 1 hour before the daughter unequivocally stated that her mother was the boss.

After the daughter's release, the mother was asked to recapitulate her main feelings and reactions to her daughter during the struggle. The mother, who had a history of being an intellectualizer, began to express strong emotional feelings about her daughter for the first time in therapy. Also, the various ploys used by the daughter in the struggle (e.g., crying and other manipulative behaviors) were explored. From this, the mother began to realize that her daughter also used these same ploys in their relationship in order to get her way.

During the remainder of the session and for several sessions thereafter, the daughter continued to be angry and silent toward the therapists and her mother. Several follow-up sessions were conducted for the purpose of dealing with the daughter's anger toward her mother and distrust of the therapists. Also, follow-up support was given to the mother as to how she could assert her power with her daughter and ex-husband.

In this family the forced holding technique marked a breakthrough and a new beginning. The mother began to assert her rightful power and authority so that her daughter could be free to be the child. Also, this technique served as a vehicle for opening up the mother and child to a deeper expression of their feelings toward each other.

Case 2: A single parent family comprised of a 30-year-old professional mother with two boys, one 9 and the other 8, were referred for therapy. The symptom carrier was the 8-year-old son who had a history of sporadic encopresis, constant bedwetting since birth, and general hyperactivity and rebelliousness. The forced holding technique was instituted after three evaluation sessions.

During the session, the mother picked up immediately on the instructions and demanded in a very determined and assertive manner to know who was the boss. The child, who was being held, replied laughingly but clearly to her question: "I am." The mother contradicted him, and a struggle ensued wherein the child eventually curled up on the floor with his mother pinning him down and sitting on him for about 45 minutes. The child was determined to hold out for the whole hour, because he kept asking for the time from his brother, who eventually was told to be quiet and not to answer. During the struggle the therapists helped the mother in asserting that she was the boss. The mother was told that the child had to give the straightforward and complete message—"You, mother, are the boss." Also, the boy was told that he would need to be the boss of himself and that this responsibility would require all of his efforts and energy. Eventually, he was able to give the required congruent message without hesitation, with eye contact, in a clear voice, seriously and without contradictory facial expression.

After his release, the matter of bedwetting was brought up, which up to this time had not been considered. He was given the choice of using a "buzzer pad" which would wake him up if and when he started to wet, or going to the bathroom before going to bed, with his taking responsibility for doing so. Some doubt was expressed by the therapists as to whether he would be able to assume responsibility for his body. The boy called the next morning to report that he "did not do it," indicating that this was the first time in his life in which he had awakened to a dry bed. After two weeks of dry nights (except for one relapse), he was asked whether he could wet the bed again in order to earn a reward in money. He refused. After two follow-up sessions, therapy was terminated to everyone's satisfaction.

Case 3: In this case, a six-year-old boy was referred for bullying and "fomenting" a revolution with his peers in a private school. The father was a professional man in his early thirties, and the mother was a professional mental health worker. A younger, four-year-old sister completed the family. The mother spent a great deal of time in the initial session explaining how the boy had been raised according to the latest psychodynamic practices in which she had avoided "hurting the ego" of the child. During the session, it became clear that the parents were overpermissive and did not set limits. Also, the father seemed cowed by his wife's superior knowledge of "psychodynamic practices" and seemed unable to establish his role as a father.

While the parents were talking, the boy kept distracting them by getting up, moving around the room, and speaking out of turn. The boy was quite articulate and bright, and his school grades were excellent. When he was asked: "Who is the boss in this family?" he laughed loudly and vacillated between his parents. The boy was obviously using one parent to deny the power of the other through pointing and wavering between them: "You are, no, you are." The boy continued to treat the question as if it were a game.

At this point, the father was instructed on how to hold the child. The child willingly sat on his father's lap and the father was told to ask him the question again. As predicted, the boy laughed and started wiggling to break his father's hold. When he saw that the father meant business and would not let go, he started crying, trying to get his mother to come to his rescue. She seemed too shocked to respond and said nothing even though her eyes and expression conveyed pain, fear, anxiety, and protectiveness. Eventually the boy stopped crying and was able to comply with the question by saying clearly and straightforwardly: "You, Daddy, are the boss." Next, the boy was told to acknowledge that when his father was gone, his mother would be the boss. After being released by his father, the boy sat quietly for the rest of the session.

On a second visit, the father was able to show that he was in control by clearly telling the boy, "Sit down and be quiet, please. You can talk when mother and father are finished." The mother reported being greatly relieved at relinquishing so much responsibility for the child's behavior. A six-month follow-up indicated that the child's school problems had disappeared, and everyone in the family was getting along fine.

Case 4: A single parent family consisting of a 32-year-old, divorced, professional woman with two children—a girl, age ten and a boy, age seven—applied for family enrichment. The mother stated that she was concerned about frequent bickering between the children, about her son's attitude and emotional development because of not having a father in the home, and about communication. The mother had been divorced for several years.

During the course of enrichment, we observed that the mother was overpermissive with the children and was unable to establish a firm boundary between herself and both children. The mother allowed the son privileges that infringed on the rights of the daughter. The daughter was expected to adopt an adult role and to be tolerant of her brother. The boy was observed to be hyperactive and demanding of his mother's attention, as he talked about himself continuously and was very affectionate with his mother. It became apparent that the boy had more power than anyone else and that he was usually able to manipulate his mother to get whatever he wanted. When asked, he proudly admitted that he was the boss of the family, although his mother and sister protested.

During the fifth session, the subject of who was boss in the family was explored again. The boy maintained that he was still the boss. We asked him to sit on his mother's lap, which he did. The mother held both of his wrists while he continued to say that he was the boss. We said that his mother would hold him until he told who was *really* boss in the family. The boy at first tried to kiss his mother. Later, he struggled more vigorously, although he was laughing in the process. Eventually, he began kicking, biting, pleading, and crying. The mother continued to wrestle with him and was surprised at his refusal to admit that she was boss. We continued to speak in a calm manner saying, "Go ahead and tell her, so you can get loose. She knows who is the boss. It is hard to give up being boss when you have been in charge so long. It must be a hard job to be boss. Why don't you just take a rest from it. Maybe you are afraid she won't love you if you are not boss any more." With this last statement, the boy shook his head in agreement with a deluge of tears. We also told him that he would see that his mother loved him because he was himself and not because he was smart or powerful.

In all, the struggle lasted about ninety minutes, placing us well beyond the limits we had set for the session. Finally, the boy tried to get away once more. He began hitting his mother with his fists, screaming, "You are, you are, you are!" His mother let him go. We suggested that he might enjoy being a seven-year-old again and knowing that he did not have to work so hard.

In a follow-up visit one month later, we asked each family member whether there had been any changes in the family since our last visit. The boy reported that he was no longer able to be the boss and gave several examples of how he was complying with his mother's limits. The mother substantiated the fact that her son was more cooperative and that the bickering between him and his sister had decreased. The boy also seemed very pleased to see the benefits, and the mother reported that he saw us as friends.

Case 5: In this single-parent family the forced holding was not successful. The family consisted of a mother, teen-age daughter and a twelve-year-old girl, who was the symptom bearer. The mother refused to carry out the physical struggle as instructed, although the twelve-year-old with sitting on her lap. Instead, the mother made verbal pleas rarely heeded by the daughter. The older daughter, who was the parentified child, assumed major responsibility for correcting her sister, corrections which resulted in a long series of bickering episodes that were watched helplessly by the mother. Forced holding was initiated. However, the mother refused physical involvement and confrontation with her daughter when the struggle became tough, because the mother said that she needed to behave like a "lady" and to her, a physical struggle was not "lady-like." Consequently, a time-out procedure was instituted as a solution to the problems in this family.

This case serves as an example of how important it is to assess whether or not the parent(s) wants to assume control and to be responsible as a parent. The forced holding technique will not be effective unless the parent(s) is ready and well-prepared to assume this responsibility.

DISCUSSION

The forced holding technique presented in this paper is similar to techniques used by Erickson (1962) and Zaslow and Breger (1969).

Haley (1973) has also described in detail this approach as used by Erickson. However, there are differences between our technique and the others referenced here.

For example, Erickson's case involved the rebellious behavior of an eight-year-old boy in a single-parent family (Haley, 1973). His basic technique is similar to ours except that Erickson had the mother and son perform the technique at home, whereas we feel that it is most effective when applied in the office where the therapist(s) can directly monitor the procedure. Using the technique in the office under the therapist's direction and support is especially applicable to single-parent families, since the parent may resist or waver in completing the technique. Also, the sole parent may not be able to restrain the child without the physical support of the therapist. Further, it has been our experience that this technique often results in a deep emotional experience for the parents(s) and child. It is recommended that it can be used safely only in the presence of a therapist who can facilitate this emotional experience for the benefit of the entire family.

Another added benefit to using the technique in the office is that it affords the opportunity for observing first-hand the interaction between the parent and child during their power struggle. For example, the child typically uses crying and manipulative behaviors in order to get his or her way. Exploring the reactions of the parent and child after the forced holding and exploring the child's ploys used during the struggle will increase the parent's awareness of how the child has been successful in winning past power struggles at home and in other situations.

Zaslow and Breger (1969, pp. 246-288) described a technique for working with autistic children called the "rage reduction method." The children in the cases that we have reported here are not as seriously disturbed as those described by them. In fact, some of the children discussed by these researchers had previously been defined as hopeless. Zaslow and Breger emphasized the therapist working with the child, although they later found that the technique was more effective when the parents used this technique in the session and continued treatment at home.

CONCLUSION

The forced holding technique has been presented as a method of intervention for reestablishing intergenerational boundaries between parent(s) and children where the child feels he/she is in charge or in power within the family. The method serves the function of rechanneling authority and power back to the parent(s), thus aiding the children to assume the role of children and the parents to assume the role of parents. The conditions under which this method is to be applied were described and illustrated through five case studies. Some of the conditions were that it be used (a) in the presence of a therapist; (b) when it is indicated that the parent(s) wants and is capable of assuming parental responsibilities; and (c) when therapeutic follow-up support can be provided for assisting the parent(s) in maintaining authority.

REFERENCES

Boszormenyi-Nagy, I., Spark, G. *Invisible Loyalties: Reciprocity in Intergenerational Family Therapy.* Hagerstown, Md.: Harper and Row, 1973.

Erickson, M. "The Identification of a Secure Reality," *Family Process, 1:* 294-303, 1962.

Haley, J. *Uncommon Therapy.* New York: Norton, 1973.

Haley, J. *Problem-Solving Therapy.* San Francisco: Jossey-Bass, 1976.

L'Abate, L. *Understanding and Helping the Individual in the Family,* New York: Grune and Stratton, 1976.

Minuchin, S. *Families and Family Therapy: A Structural Approach.* Boston: Harvard University Press, 1974.

Zaslow, R., Breger, L. "Theory and Treatment of Autism," in L. Breger (Ed.) *Clinical Cognitive Psychology: Models and Integrations,* Englewood Cliffs, N.J.: Prentice-Hall, 246-291, 1969.

CHAPTER 19

THE ROLE OF FAMILY CONFERENCES IN FAMILY THERAPY

Luciano L'Abate, Ph.D.

ABSTRACT

The value of the Family Conference as a vehicle for change in families is stressed. Helpful guidelines for conducting meetings are outlined. Implications for integration of the Family Conference into family therapy are discussed.

Changing families is an arduous process. Families must often learn new strategies of negotiation, decision-making, and problem-solving. How much does the learning that takes place in the therapy hour generalize outside of it? The issue is one of *transfer*. Usually this transfer is slow; at times, one wonders whether it occurs at all. However the family, as Adler recognized long ago and as recent parent education has affirmed (Abidin, 1980), still remains the most powerful agent of change.

The Family Conference is one way of training family members to avoid reactive (repetitive) methods of relating to each other and to assume a more assertive, goal-directed stance in intimate relationships. This method has been elaborated by some authors (Dreikurs, Gould and Corsini, 1974) and yet missed by others.

Surprisingly, a recent book, *Building Family Strengths* (Stinnett, Chester, & DeFrain, 1979) fails to consider the potential usefulness of the Family Conference to build family solidarity. In contrast to earlier Adlerian approaches, (Dreikurs & Soltz, 1964), a recent Adlerian publication (Dinkmeyer, Pew, & Dinkmeyer, 1979) ignores the Family Conference as a positive addition to the therapeutic armamentarium. The same omission occurs in a recent and extensive handbook for parent education and intervention (Abidin, 1980). Gurman and Kniskern's (1981) review of the family therapy literature includes no significant references about this topic. Even more surprising, no references on Family Conferences were found in a family life education book (Klemer & Smith, 1975), or a childrearing manual (Wesley, 1971). However, Kern and Wheeler (1977) do acknowledge this as an important aspect of family life and family therapy.

Reprint requests to Luciano L'Abate, Ph.D. Family Study Center, Georgia State University, University Plaza, Atlanta, Ga. 30303.

The evening meal is one of the most important settings where family members: (a) congregate, (b) face each other eyeball to eyeball, and (c) learn or fail to learn how to give and take, negotiate, share, joke, and meet essential needs for enjoyable conduct with caring people. A family meal linked with a Family Conference can be a major source of learning about self and intimate others. Primary functions of the Family Conference are to help parents become Conductors instead of Reactors or Apathetic bystanders (L'Abate, in preparation), and to help the father assume responsibility as head of the household. In addition, the ability to conduct Family Conferences is a measure of outcome for family therapy, that is, if therapy has succeeded, the family should be able to initiate Family Conferences.

Dreikurs and his associates (1974) are responsible for developing and encouraging the Family Council or Conference as a standard operating procedure to help families change. Specifications for the Family Conference include: (a) regularly scheduled meetings, (b) an open forum, (c) agreed-upon rules (Robert's Rules of Order), (d) no interruptions, (e) freedom of expression, (f) no fear of consequences, (g) equality for all members, (h) joint deliberations, (i) reciprocal responsibility, and (j) mutual decision-making and problem-solving. The purposes of this Council, as Dreikurs and his associates see them, are: (a) greater happiness, (b) efficiency in problem-solving, (c) better communication among members, and (d) less need to use punishment, coercion and various aversive or avoiding procedures.

According to the original format, the following steps must be followed: (a) set a date for the first meeting, (b) invite *all* family members, (c) include everyone who lives under the same roof, (d) choose a presiding officer, (e) give information about goals, purposes, and means, and (f) create ground rules to follow in the conduct of the conference. Ground rules cover parliamentary order; emergency decisions; situations where there are nothing but gripes; wrong decisions; making amendments and alterations; reciprocal responsibilities; pitfalls and obstacles. Usually this procedure can follow consideration of (a) household chores, (b) what has been improved, (c) what needs improvement, (d) new business. Discussion and clarification of orderly, parliamentary procedures should be done at a level that all family members can understand. To solve conflict democratically, four courses of action are pursued: (a) create mutual respect, (b) pinpoint the issue, (c) seek areas of agreement, and (d) share responsibilities.

Many other issues relating to the processes and problems arising from this format are considered in the Dreikur monograph. To encourage children's participation, parents are encouraged to (a) provide a treat at the end of the meeting, (b) include pleasant news or plans,

(c) follow through on decisions, (d) avoid scolding between sessions, (e) discuss issues calmly, (f) stand up for their ideas or opinions but not insist that anybody agree with them; (g) go along with what seem to be mistakes and after expressing an opinion clearly, let logical or natural consequences take their course, (h) in the face of persistent sabotage, table the meeting to another time, (i) avoid superficial agreement with either the spouse or the children (i.e., insist that bilateral agreements need respect and that all changes occur only with consensus).

The two major positions in a Family Conference are chairman (usually the father) and recording secretary (usually the mother). However, some reversal of roles and of responsibilities (including the children assuming them at times) would demonstrate the flexibility necessary to make fair changes. The family must agree at the beginning upon the Order of Business and allowable types of motions, such as to amend, table, postpone, reconsider, question, and adjourn. The duties of the chairman are to preside, keep calm, talk no more than necessary, conduct meetings in a business-like manner, extend courtesy to those present, and to be on time or even early to meetings. The duties of the secretary are to take notes and make permanent records of meetings with detailed minutes, names, motions and decisions.

Dinkmeyer and McKay (1976) call this conference the Family Meeting and essentially overlap in many of their points with the suggestions given by Dreikurs et al. (1974). They do add that this meeting should function to create opportunities for (a) hearing and being heard, (b) experiencing positive feelings about one another and giving encouragement, (c) distributing chores fairly among members, (d) experiencing concerns, feelings and complaints, (e) settling conflicts and recurring issues, and (f) planning family recreation.

Common mistakes made in these Conferences, according to Dinkmeyer and McKay (1976) include: (a) waiting until every member agrees to attend (instead of beginning with those who are willing), (b) starting later, (c) meeting for too long a time, (d) domination by one or more members, (e) overemphasizing or focusing on complaints and criticisms, and (f) not putting agreements into action.

An Appendix to this paper contains the guidelines given to families in therapy with the author. Family Conferences are discussed during the therapy hour to implement their use and to evaluate how the family is dealing with issues outside the office.

One of the most important aspects of giving these guidelines is *timing*—when to implement them and when not to. If the guidelines are given prematurely, the family will be unable to follow them and will fail. Some families are reluctant to take up a task when they have met previous failure. On the other hand, even a premature administration will give the therapist an indication of how dysfunctional a family is. Discussion of the reasons for this failure will give the therapist very important diagnostic information on how the family fails to function and what needs to be done to correct it. The best way of giving these guidelines to a skeptical family is to comment paradoxically, "I am not sure whether your family is ready to handle Family Conferences. Many families fail and I will be interested in whether you can do it or not."

Families that are ready to participate in Family Conferences develop important negotiation skills that will transfer to other interpersonal relationships.

APPENDIX

Guidelines for Family Conferences
Luciano L'Abate, Ph.D.

Dear Family Members:

These guidelines have been found useful in helping families conduct the business of living. Without a structure like Family Conferences, families can flounder and fail. The Family Conference helps families accomplish their goals.

The Family Conference is one major vehicle through which family members can learn to negotiate—can learn how to give and take. It assumes that the family does eat the evening meal together at least two to three times a week. It is during one of these times, preferably Fridays *after* the evening meal, that the conference should be held under the following specified conditions (unless told otherwise):

1) Announce plans for the conference at least *one week in advance* whenever everybody is present; i.e., "Next Friday we are going to have a Family Conference right after supper and all of us have to be there." If other plans have been made you can make the following changes: (a) find another evening more suitable to everybody, or (b) change the time of the meal to an earlier hour so that the meal and the conference can still take place. Plan about one hour for the meal (sometimes 1/2 hour may be sufficient) and one hour for the conference.

2) Do not conduct "business" or matters to be considered at the conference during the meal or any meal, unless it is a matter of urgency (this could happen during meals during the week but *not* during the meal prior to the conference).

3) Make sure that food and dishes are cleared from the table and that the table is free of anything but usual decorations and note paper.

4) Set a timer (clock or whatever) for one hour and make it *very clear* from the onset that the conference will last one hour and whatever

business has not been dealt with during this conference will be dealt with during the next conference. It is *imperative* and absolutely *mandatory* that the conference *does not* last longer than the stated time.

5) Set general rules of conduct during the conference if you need to, such as:
    a. Speak as long as necessary on the point being considered.
    b. Do not interrupt the person speaking.
    c. Follow Robert's Rules of Order concerning consideration, decisions, agreements, tabling of matters, and voting.

6) Give ample freedom for everyone to have their say without interruptions, ridicule or distractions. If there are distractions, become aware that distractions, as much as withdrawals, speak about how the family *as a whole* functions or fails to function.

7) Avoid and help others avoid using the YOU pronoun. As long as the YOU pronoun is used, the family will not get anywhere. Encourage the use of the personal pronoun "I", as in, I feel, I think, I am aware, I wonder, I am afraid.

8) Start by encouraging everybody to share *good* positive feelings about themselves and the family. "I feel good about . . ." I insist that each member come up with at least *one positive* comment about themselves or others. If positives cannot be found, this indicates how much your family has become immersed in a quagmire of negativity.

9) After positives, encourage everybody to voice complaints, beefs, displeasures and anger. Allow *feelings* to be expressed *as long as* these feelings are not confused with actions or with negotiations. Take notes of these complaints and of who made them. Use *I* statements and avoid You statements.

10) Once everybody has had his/her say, lead the discussion toward whatever matter should be considered first, i.e., whatever is urgent to most family members. List matters or issues in terms of priority.

11) Once a decision is reached as to what issue has first priority, discuss *freely* all of the pros and cons regarding how the matter should be solved. Include implications, ramifications, costs, rewards, and consequences for each possible choice. *Do* discuss and encourage discussion of all possibilities *no matter how* outlandish they appear at first blush. Do not allow put-downs or belittlement of any viewpoint expressed.

12) If the discussion gets out of hand to the point where no mutual give and take can take place, give the family a choice: "We either calm down and resume discussion, or we will have to end this conference today and go on next week to deal with the same matters."

13) If one or more members seem commited to sabotaging (distracting, etc.) the course of events, bring up the issue of *change:* "Does this family want to stay the same?" or "As long as we cannot conduct our

matters properly we cannot start nor end anything we do among ourselves."

14) Conduct yourselves as *leaders* and not dictators or tyrants. Remember you are part of the system and no member of a family is any better than the so-called "worst" member. Do not gang up on anybody.

15) These guidelines are only given as a beginning. Each family needs to develop its own way of conducting its business (as long as it pays off for the family to conduct it this way). Please *let me know* how you are doing in following these guidelines in the next session.

REFERENCES

Abidin, R. R. (Ed.). *Parent Education and Intervention Handbook.* Springfield, Ill.: Charles C. Thomas, 1980.

Dinkmeyer, D. & McKay, G. D. *Systematic Training for Effective Parenting: Parent's Handbook.* Circle Pines, Minn.: American Guidance Service, 1976.

Dinkmeyer, D. C., Pew, W. L., & Dinkmeyer, D. C., Jr. *Adlerian Counseling and Psychology.* Belmont, Ca.: Wadsworth Publishing Co., 1979.

Dreikurs, R., Gould, S., & Corsini, R. J. *Family Council: The Dreikurs Technique for Putting an End to War between Parents and Children.* Chicago: Henry Regnery, 1974.

Gurman, A. S., & Kniskern, D. *Handbook of Family Therapy.* New York: Brunner/Mazel, 1981.

Kern, R. M., & Wheeler, M. S. "Autocratic vs. Democratic Child Rearing Practices: An Example of Second-order Change," *Journal of Individual Psychology,* 1977, *21,* 223-231.

Klemer, R. H., & Smith, R. M. *Teaching about Family Relationships.* Minneapolis: Burgess Publishing Co., 1975.

L'Abate, L. Styles in intimate relationships: the A-R-C Model. Manuscript in preparation.

Stinnett, N., Chester, B., & DeFrain, J. (Eds.). *Building Family Strengths: Blueprints for Action.* Lincoln, Neb.: University of Nebraska Press, 1979.

Wesley, F. *Childrearing Psychology.* New York: Behavioral Publications, 1971.

SECTION V

CIRCULAR APPROACHES IN FAMILY THERAPY

CHAPTER 20

A POSITIVE APPROACH TO MARITAL AND FAMILIAL INTERVENTION

Luciano L'Abate, Ph.D.

Editors' Summary: There has been a tendency to overemphasize negative reasons for families coming into therapy (e.g., disturbed behavior of the identified patient, existing familial strife, etc.). With minimization of positive aspects, such focus results in a dislocation of the therapeutic process, with gathering resistance, early termination and other unfortunate outcomes. By stressing from the beginning of treatment positive reasons for the families' seeking help, the therapist may contribute an important dimension that will enable the members to work through major problems. It is within the power of the therapist to dissect out of a piece of behavior, even neurotic behavior, certain positive features which can help prevent reinforcement of self-defeating acts and attitudes. Examples are given of how interpretations may be made to highlight the constructive purposes of pathological conduct. The therapeutic impact of such a positive approach is discussed.

The present approach maintains that the necessary conditions for entrance and continuation of a couple or family in therapy are positives and not negatives. Many rationales for families coming into therapy have been couched in negative terms, that is, in terms of the misbehavior of the identified patient, the degree of covert or overt conflict among and between family members (sibling rivalry, parental strife, parent-child problems, etc.) or the pathology evident in the family because of acting-out problems, etc. It is the purpose of this approach to present and discuss the positive aspects of why couples and families seek help.

When couples and families enter therapy for reasons that are accepted by the therapist as being negative, the possibility of change and improvement is decreased considerably. The identified patient, if there is one, either directly or indirectly has to assume the burden of being the reason for the couple or family seeking therapy, or the overtly dysfunctional dyad (siblings, parents, parent-child) needs to focus on its misbehavior, overemphasizing it unduly and making this negative behavior the *raison d'être* and condition *sine qua non* for seeking and staying in treatment. Emphasis on negative behavior increases the chances of a couple or a family dropping out early in the treatment, either when the symptoms have decreased or when excuses for dropping out can be made (lack of money, not much time, too great a distance, etc.).

Furthermore, if self-defeating behavior is the result of negative circumstances (or reinforcements)—like severe punishment, rejection, negative labeling, inconsistent rewards, etc.—the professional helper, by keeping a negative outlook, fosters the continuation of defeating behavior. It is important for the professional helper to have and keep a positive viewpoint *because the cost of a negative attitude toward behavior is greater than the rewards of a positive attitude.*

It is the function of the family therapist, then, to bring out, from the outset, the major positive reasons for the family's coming, reasons that have been forgotten and submerged by the urgency and immediacy of the misbehavior. Before considering each of these reasons, however, we should consider our assumptions about behavior, which need to be translated into the helping process. These assumptions need to be considered within the context of paradoxical human nature and the need to affirm our existence in positive rather than negative terms.

THE PARADOX OF HUMAN NATURE

One man's strength can be another man's weakness: It is practically impossible to label or call any behavior an asset or a liability until we understand the function of that particular behavior within the context of the individual's perception and its meaning and impact on intimates and family members. Any behavior has at least two possible interpretations. It can be considered an asset or it can be considered a liability. Hence, behavior is what we interpret it to be or how *we choose* to interpret it. If our orientation is a negative one, as are most orientations based on pathology, our choice of terms will emphasize a deficit, liability-oriented view of behavior. If our orientation is a positive one, our choice of terms will emphasize a strength, asset-oriented view of behavior.

Another way of stating the same point is that each behavior can have at least two sides or aspects to it and it is up to the professional helper to point out *continuously* the positive aspect [8]. Positive attitudes are most important at the beginning of the helping process. It is at this point that *assets* need to be established and assessed. If these assets are not sought out, it is likely that a break in the therapy will occur. From the very beginning, the motivation for asking for help needs to be couched in positive terms.

Asking for Help as a Positive Act

Instead of a negative rationale for seeking help, a positive one can be substituted, *i.e., people ask for help because they care about themselves and because they want to do something about their problems.* Their asking for help, then, is a positive act arising from *strength*. Those too weak to ask for help are the people whose hurt reaches such extremes that eventually someone else will take responsibility for their behavior, usually through hospitalization or incarceration. *It takes a great deal of strength to ask for help,* since many are so weak that they deny the need for help and, therefore, do not seek it. By not asking for help, it is very likely that their destructive behavior will persist and even increase.

The point should be made routinely that asking for help represents a positive way of obtaining change, since it implies the couple's or family's assertion of their human limitations and it faces them with their basic helplessness and impotence. Facing our inherent helplessness and impotence *is* strength.

At the bottom of this helplessness and impotence, there is usually the assumption that we should be able to change those we love who are defeating themselves and us. Hence, our basic helplessness comes from the hope that we can change those who hurt. This is probably one of the most destructive assumptions made in mental health work, *that we can change others.* This is a logical and existential impossibility. We cannot change others unless we manipulate them through coersion and other hurtful ways. We, individuals and professional helpers alike, can only change ourselves. Others who came in contact with us change to the extent that they want to change. We can only change ourselves and, to the extent that *we* change, we make it easier for others to change.

It follows from this paradox that behavior has multiple functions: Power can be used to defeat or to win. Energy can be used to defeat: "It takes as much energy to build as it takes to tear down. How do you want to use your energy?" Crying, for instance, is an indication of strength, not weakness. It takes a strong person to admit to personal failures and weaknesses. It takes strength to admit and take personal responsibility. It is easier to divorce than to stay in a marriage and work for a better marriage.

Evidence for Choosing Positives

Some of the evidence to support a positive viewpoint in the personal and professional life and practice of the helper is to be gleaned from the results of Door et al. [1], who found that nonprofessional mental health workers reported more positive attitudes toward job-related concepts. Rychlack [9] found that normal high school males think more positively about the future than comparable, abnormal adolescents. Jacobs et al. [3] found that in T-groups with undergraduates "positive feedback" was rated as being more desirable and as having greater impact on the individual. In fact, greater cohesion was reported among groups where positive, rather than negative, feedback was used. Lewinson and Graf [6] studied the relationship between engaging in "pleasant" activities and mood level in normal and psychiatric groups, finding that a significant relationship existed between mood level and number of pleasant activities engaged in for all groups. Depressed patients, as a whole, engaged in fewer pleasant activities than a normal group.

THE TASKS OF POSITIVE HELPING

In the process of helping couples and families, the helper needs to face at least seven tasks. Unless these tasks are dealt with, it is doubtful that the process of helping will be successful.

The First Task: Seeing the Good Throughout

We love someone because we are able to see the good in him and accept whatever may not be good as an inevitable part of him that is greatly overshadowed by the good. Whenever the negatives overwhelm the good we see, love ceases to exist. How can we love the people we want to help, if we let them submerge us with their negatives? The process of loving needs to be instituted from the very beginning, as soon as we reject the negatives that they use initially to make themselves acceptable for therapy. We accept negatives as a *sine qua non* for acceptance into therapy. Why not stress positives? ("I may be wrong, but don't you come here because you care for each other?"). How can we help others to love each other, if we fail to show this love from the very beginning? ("I know that your [mate, child] is bugging you, but isn't it so that you care for him [her]?") ("I am sorry, but I cannot accept what you are telling me." "I beg to disagree. Aren't you here because you care?")

Pointing out and emphasizing the positives encourages the process of staying in therapy. Could it be that the high dropout rates, and what is called lack of motivation for therapy in the mental health field, may be due to our working on the negatives? If we know that honey works better than vinegar, are we not using the latter anytime we accept the family's initial and unfortunately recurrent emphasis on negatives?

It is important for the professional helper to consider alternative ways of conceptualizing behavior. For instance, the reason for referral could be turned into: "You chose to come here because you care a great deal about yourself (your child, your spouse, your marriage, your family)." It is important then to emphasize care and love for oneself and other intimates, rather than negative aspects. The same approach should be used in showing that certain supposedly negative behaviors (blaming, acting out) have positive aspects to them, i.e., care, concern, protectiveness, and even love.

The therapist needs to convey directly and forcefully all of the positive actions that have been taken to change and improve: to ask for help is a strength and not a weakness; to hurt is a sign of ability to get in touch with one's feelings; it takes a strong person to ask for help; and it takes a great deal of competence to find competent help. Assets should be stressed in terms of job persistence: "You are a good provider." "You have done a good job of taking care of yourselves and your children." "You must be competent because only competent people ask our help."

It is important for the helper to assert that each individual asking for help has sufficient resources to change himself if he hurts badly enough. In other words, the helper needs to find all of the positives, physical, intellectual, emotional and financial assets, that the individual can use, if he or she chooses to, to change himself or herself. The responsibility for change needs to be individual: "If each of us waits for others to change without changing our behavior, we can wait until the cows come home." If we care about ourselves and if we care enough to ask for help we can change ourselves.

The Second Task: Caring

If individuals do not care for themselves or others, it is very likely that they will continue in their self-defeating behavior. If they care about themselves, it is possible that they will ask for help for themselves and those they love. This caring needs to be brought out as soon as an answer, usually in negative terms, is given to the opening, "What can I do for you?" or "Why are you here?" In assessing the presence and degree of care for each other that a family has, the helper needs to ask whether it is true that care is present: "Am I wrong in concluding that you came here today because you care about yourselves and each other?" If care is not present it is very doubtful that these individuals would go to the trouble of calling a professional helper. Lawyers, courts and other institutions (jails, hospitals) are available to those who do not care [4].

Care is the assertion and affirmation of the importance of one's self and the selves of one's family. This characteristic presence of care should be pointed out at the very outset of therapy. The therapist should have the courage and the strength to assert its presence and, in so doing, contradict whatever psychopathological explanations are given for seeking therapy: "Because we are not getting along." "My husband drinks." "Jimmy is not doing well in school, etc." After listening to each person's explanation, the therapist should make his position very clear. "I beg to disagree with all of you, but aren't you here today because you care an awful lot about each other and about yourselves?"

Thus far, we have not found any couple or family that has disagreed with us in establishing firmly and solidly, that their primary reason for asking for help was not the dysfunctionality, but the functionality, of the couple or family: "After all there are a lot of couples and families that hurt as much and more than you do, but they apparently don't care enough about themselves and each other to ask for help. Is that right?"

The presence of care needs to be emphasized whenever its direct and indirect expressions emerge during the course of therapy: "You are really taking up for her." "Is it that hard for you to accept that you care for each other if you keep coming here week in and week out?" "We can't believe you don't care if you are willing to pay our bill?" "I wonder if you aren't contradicting yourselves. You may not love each other, but you certainly show an awful lot of care for each other."

Mayeroff [7] considered caring as the process of helping others to grow, so that they can care for themselves and others. Caring involves knowledge about oneself and others, patience, honesty, trust, humility, hope and courage. Through the process of caring, one actualizes his potential. Hence, caring may imply a reciprocal pattern—the carer is taken care of by the person he cares for. Caring is being with someone, as well as being with ourselves.

It is difficult to care for others unless one takes care of oneself. Caring for others cannot take place at the expense of one's self—that becomes placating. Often it is difficult to distinguish between caring as a positive, helpful act and placating, except that in the latter, the placator hurts. No hurt is present in caring.

The Third Task: Sharing Hurt

We hurt for those we love. If we care about ourselves, and we find ourselves unable to change and feel helpless to do anything about changing, we hurt. If those we love hurt, we hurt too; hence hurt is the result of caring. We find it very difficult if not impossible to hurt for those we do not care about. It is difficult, nearly impossible, for the professional helper to help others if he is unable or unwilling to deal with his own personal hurt. Denial of personal hurt implies the inability to get in touch with and be aware of the inevitable hurt that results from the very fact of existence. We cannot live and not be hurt, or if we are protected from hurt, how can we deal with it when we inevitably face it in the course of living? No wonder that in order to be "normal" some degree of conflict is necessary, since without it and the inevitable hurt that conflict brings, we would be unable to cope. Hence "adjustment" could not conceivably occur unless we are able and willing to cope with hurt. This hurt needs to be shared with those who care for us and it should be part of the focus of the initial interview.

Sharing joys and victories is a process than can occur easily with anyone. Most of the time we are willing and able to share anyone's victory. However, are we able to share hurt and pain? It is difficult to achieve awareness of personal hurt and to be aware of hurt in those we love. How can we share our personal hurt with someone else, if we deny it or are unaware of its presence in ourselves?

Sharing the hurt means being present, being available and listening. There is no requirement on the listener to remedy a situation that is beyond his power to change.

Recognition of helplessness: There is nothing one can do in the face of hurtful and self-destructive behavior, except to point it out, identifying it for what it is and understanding how little gain is achieved from it. The individual has the choice of continuing to behave destructively, or of making himself available to learning helpful behavior: "If you want to go on destroying yourself (or your marriage, or your family), you can do it without help. If you want to change and behave helpfully, you can count on us. What will it be?" "You will need to decide how you want to spend your life. We cannot and will not make that decision for you." "It costs as much to get a lawyer to destroy this marriage as it costs to help you build this marriage. However, the decision on which it will be is up to you."

It is important to recognize one's helplessness before hurt and hurtful behavior, since this behavior may have persisted to the point of acceptance as a final given: "If you think I'll accept your hopelessness to defeat yourself and us, you are mistaken. I accept your feelings of hopelessness, but that does not mean I'll allow your behavior to defeat us." "I can see how you can feel hopeless and helpless, but that does not mean that you can control and defeat everybody with those attitudes." "If you want to consider other positive ways to live with yourself, we may suggest a few." "Hopelessness and helplessness can be very self-defeating. You are welcome to accept this defeat in yourself, but that does not mean I'll accept it." "If you want to continue working with us, you may need to give up hopelessness and helplessness." "What have helplessness and hopelessness gotten you thus far? If hopelessness and helplessness have gotten you nothing but control and manipulation, perhaps it's time we try some more positive way. What do you think?" "Between now and next time you'll have to decide whether you want to control by helplessness and hopelessness or by being helpful and hopeful. The decision is yours."

Helplessness as control: The manipulatory aspects of one's claimed helplessness and inadequacy need to be brought to the fore: "You are as helpless as a ten-ton truck." "You are as weak as an army tank." We need to be convinced that people who ask for help are not as helpless as they think or feel they are. In fact, their helplessness is a strength because it is their helplessness that motivated them to ask for help and to do something about their situation. "It takes a strong person to admit to helplessness. It takes a strong man to cry; you are lucky you can cry." "I have met many weak people who unfortunately can't. I wish I could say the same thing about your mate (child, etc.). Apparently, he feels so weak that he can't."

Turning anger or guilt into hurt: Anger may well be externalized guilt or feelings of helplessness. Regardless of its possible structural or historical antecedents, a great deal of anger may derive from frustration and defeat and the hurt that accompanies any loss of self and of self-esteem. Anger may be like sand and smoke—it renders us blind to our hurt and to the hurt of those we love. It is important to help convert anger into hurt about one's failure to be helpful to one's self and others: "I can see that you are very angry with each other. Are you hurting too?" "You seem furious with her (or him), but who is your worst enemy?" "If you are your worst enemy, who should you be angry at?" "What's underneath that anger?" "If you feel guilty, does it mean you hurt for yourself?" "If you hurt, does it mean you care for yourself and those you love?"

The Fourth Task: Forgiving

Forgiving is the act of canceling demands for perfection in ourselves and in others and accepting our inherent fallibility as human beings. Forgiving also means learning from past errors to correct present behavior and then letting go of the negative past. One has to forgive oneself for being human before one can forgive others.

Canceling demands for perfection and infallibility in oneself and in others, accepting that we err and goof, but that these errors and goofs do not make us into terrible human beings and that these errors are better forgotten, is important. The past is of no help except to justify and defend wrongdoings or to blame, especially when emphasis on the past is used to ruin the present. Hence, the injunction of dealing with the present positives (and forgiving the past negatives): "I understand that you have hurt each other deeply." "Am I to understand that you want to learn how to help each other rather than to keep on hurting?" "Tell me, what does it do for you to keep bringing up the past? Apparently you seem to enjoy bringing it up, but what does it do for you, for your marriage, or for your family?"

Forgetting the past and leaving it behind is based on the following practical, theoretical, and empirical considerations:

Past hurts cannot be changed: There is nothing anyone can do about the past, but there is a great deal that can be done in the present and in preparation for the future.

Overemphasis on past hurts interferes with the present: Attention and time spent on past hurts and experiences can only take away from present joys and experiences. It delays or defeats the enjoyment and use of the present: "You can bring up the hurtful past and do nothing now but waste time, or you can leave the past behind and live in the present. Which way would you like to go?"

The past belittles us, the present enhances us: As Heuscher [2] commented: "As we commit ourselves to the future of ourselves, our experience of self-worth is enhanced." "You may have behaved like a (son of a) bitch in the past but that does not mean you have to behave like one now, does it?"

Overemphasis on the past is hurtful. Emphasis on the present and future is helpful: As Smeltzer [12] demonstrated: "Most forms of psychopathology cause the individual to cling to a dominant past orientation and to have a constricted future time perspective.... From the first part to the second part of psychotherapy [tape-recorded interviews], there was a significant decrease in past orientation, a significant increase in present orientation, and a significant increase in future orientation...." In other words, the past is related to psychopathology. The present and the future are more related to healthy functioning, as demonstrated also by the work of Vincent and Tyler [13] with adolescents and Smart [11] with alcoholics.

It follows from the above considerations that overemphasis on past hurts, although not intrinsically damaging, may unduly lengthen the process of helping. The present is changeable, the past is not.

The Fifth Task: Responsibility

At the practical level, love of one's self and others is expressed in direct terms of holding down a job, financial security, solvency, running a household, etc. In other words, all the caring and protection in the world are irrelevant and strictly verbal unless the care and protection are translated directly into practical and financial responsibility, a pattern that needs to be pointed out repeatedly as a strength: "You are a good provider, Mr. Smith." "I bet you are a good cook, Mrs. Jones." "Holding on to your job is important to you, isn't it?" This responsibility is translated into paying bills, especially those received for professional help. When this responsibility is defaulted, it is probably symptomatic of the therapist's failure to reach the caretaker and the breadwinner: "I wonder whether you are defeating yourself and your marriage or your family by not paying the bills?"

Responsibility also means being accountable for one's actions rather than finding external causes to attribute them to and blame them on—a pattern that is extremely common in marital and familial transactions. Responsibility means being in charge of one's self and being aware of and in control of one's feelings, so that helpful courses of action can be followed.

Responsibility means one's ability to make mistakes and to realize one's essential fallible humanity. Responsibility, then, means having the courage of one's imperfections, the ability to recognize one's errors and to learn from them rather than to repeat them. By error is meant any behavior that is hurtful to oneself and/or to others in one's family.

Responsibility means not giving up oneself for the sake of others. It means keeping constantly in mind the priorities that often become confused in family living: self, marriage and children. We act irresponsibly when we give ourselves up for the sake of the marriage or the children.

Responsibility, then, means the ability to reconcile what sometimes appear to be irreconcilable or antagonistic priorities. "How can you win so that everybody in the family wins?" Responsibility means being in charge of one's own happiness or unhappiness: "If you cannot make yourself happy, how can you expect to make your family happy?" "How will your family learn to be happy, if you don't teach them?" "If your family is responsible for your happiness, then, it also becomes responsible for your unhappiness, isn't that right?" "If you give yourself up for the sake of the children, how are they going to develop selves of their own?"

Lang [5] discriminated among four meanings of responsibility: (1) as duty or obligation; (2) as accountability or being held answerable for one's behavior; (3) as reliability or trustworthiness; and (4) as ability to respond to the needs of another.

Duty or obligation may be voluntarily assumed or imposed by another. Accountability may consist of the "I am aware that I did it" experience, or of the experience of being held answerable for one's behavior. Reliability or trustworthiness may consist of authenticity and integrity, or of the "other directed" role playing of one who seeks to be as he believes others wish him. When the locus of responsibility is experienced within, one's ability to respond to another's needs is expressed in genuine responses. When the locus is outside the individual, indifference replaces response.

Lang related these patterns of responsibility to four different patterns of familial authority: (1) superordinate authority, power exercised by parents; (2) subordinate authority, power exercised by children; (3) correlative authority, power shared by parents and children alike; and (4) anarchical authority, no power exercised by anybody.

It takes a certain degree of responsibility to enter and to stay in a therapeutic relationship. However, the choice of therapeutic focus, self, marriage or child as identified patient, indicates the level of responsibility taken initially. If the self and marriage are the focus, it is relatively easy to keep a therapeutic relationship. If the child is initially the patient, it may take some doing to help the parents assume their responsibilities vis-à-vis family priorities, i.e., self, marriage and then children.

The Sixth Task: Protectiveness

Protectiveness represents the ability to assert one's self-importance to the point of being willing to fight if and when it is necessary. It means setting limits about what one wants and does not want and what one is willing to put up with or not put up with in himself and others. In a way, the helper indicates what he is willing to do and not do in protecting himself professionally and personally in terms of contracts and demands made on his time, his schedule, telephone calls, weekend visits, emergencies, appointments, expectations, etc. By being clear about what he can and is willing to do and not to do, he shows how he protects himself. Eventually this issue will come up in the process of helping each individual in the marital or parental couple deal with how he or she is willing and able to assert himself or herself. How clearly or unclearly, forcefully or passively, negatively or positively are they asserting their own importance?

This characteristic of protectiveness implies the aspect of defending one's self, one's marriage and one's family against the forces that tend to break up any one of these components. The threat of danger to any of these areas brings about a protective reaction. We ask for help to protect our investments. We invest in ourselves, our marriage and our families and we will go to great lengths to protect them from threat or breakdown even to the point of asking for help and defying social pressures against being thought "crazy," or "sick." Protectiveness implies the desire to find ways and means to counteract breakdown and the unknown of malfunctioning behavior.

Self-preservation: Preserving one's self means keeping on continuous guard to make sure that the self, the marriage and the children are preserved from losing their relative positions and priorities. Giving up one's self means giving up of one's marriage and children. The self needs continuous nurturance and maintenance.

Maintenance of marriage: After establishing the priority of the self, the importance of safeguarding, maintaining and reinforcing the marriage as the second priority needs to be emphasized: "If you let yourself down, how can this help this marriage?" "If you let your mate down, how can this help the marriage?" "If you defeat your own self, how can this marriage win?" "If you lose with each other, how can your children learn to win?" "If you can't make your marriage work for you, how can your children learn to make it in life?"

Children are third: The position of the children vis-à-vis the parental selves and the marriage (as a separate, functional entity) needs to be established: "After the children are grown and gone, what will happen to this marriage?" "Children are visitors in your home." "It seems that you both have given up your own selves and the marriage for the sake of the children. What has all this giving up gotten you?" "We understand your love for the children, but isn't the cost you pay for this love too high?"

Essentially, the therapist needs to establish that if we cannot protect, nurture, take care of, preserve and maintain ourselves vigilantly, this failure boomerangs on the marriage and on the children: "If we do not look at ourselves, our marriage hurts; if we do not look at our marriage, our children hurt; and if we do not look at our children, the whole family hurts."

The Seventh Task: Enjoyment

With emphasis on negatives, the fun of life is gone—there is little enjoyment in sex, companionship and being together. To foster enjoyment, it needs to take place in a sexual and companionable context within the family and in social life with friends.

To enjoy living [10] means to be excited about what one is doing, doing it with humor and pleasure. These characteristics, (1) excitement, (2) humor, (3) pleasure, and (4) pride need to be communicated to the participants and brought into the process of intervention by the helper.

Excitement: The *joie de vivre* of therapy implies that the therapist is not only enjoying living, but that he is comfortable with himself at various levels of being—sexual, intellectual, emotional and interpersonal. He needs to be able to communicate this feeling to the couple or family. Part of his excitement is expressed in how he deals with his own sexuality, his feelings of adequacy and his personal pain. If he has not dealt with his lows, how can he deal with his highs?

Humor: Marital and familial therapy without humor would be dull and boring. The therapist needs to have a sense of the ridiculous, and to be comfortable enough to laugh, to crack a joke and to be ironic without being condescending.

Pleasure: Can pleasure be achieved without excitement? There are certain pleasures that come from contentment, calmness and submission that are of a different nature than the outcome of excitement. Perhaps pleasure may be subtle excitement on one hand, or gross, fleshly delight and sensory experience on the other. Both are needed in family living. Excitement may not lead to pleasure. It may lead to hard work, commitment and determination. Pleasure may represent letting go of controls, giving up dominance or even withdrawing. It can be sexual, sensory or perceptual. Enjoyment is a more pervasive state than pleasure. Pleasure is, among other things, the full expression of one's sexuality with one's mate.

Pride: To be proud without being arrogant means being aware of one's level of competence and helpfulness. Being proud means also being aware of one's limitations.

REFERENCES

1. Door, D., Cowen, E. L., Sandler, I., and Pratt, D. M.: Dimensionality of a test battery for nonprofessional mental health workers. J. Consult. Clin. Psychol. 41: 181-185, 1973.
2. Heuscher, J. E.: Existential psychotherapy and the temporal experience. World J. Psychosynthesis 4: 29-33, 1972.
3. Jacobs, M., Jacobs, A., Feldman, G., and Cavior, N.: Feedback II—The "credibility gap": Delivery of positive and negative and emotional and behavioral feedback in groups. J. Consult. Clin. Psychol. 41: 215-223, 1973.
4. L'Abate, L.: Psychodynamic interventions: A personal statement. *In* Woody, R. H., and Woody, J. D. (Eds.): Sexual, marital, and familial relations: Therapeutic interventions. Springfield, Ill., C. C. Thomas, 1973, pp. 122-180.
5. Lang, L. H.: Responsibility as a function of authority in family relations. Dissertation Abstracts 29: 3668-3669A, 1969.
6. Lewinsohn, P. E., and Graf, M.: Pleasant activities and depression. J. Consult. Clin. Psychol. 41: 261-268, 1973.
7. Mayeroff, M.: On caring. New York, Harper and Row, 1970.
8. McDougald, D.: Emotional maturity instruction. Atlanta, Georgia, 1972.
9. Rychlak, J. F.: Time orientation in the positive and negative phantasies of mildly abnormal versus normal high school males. J. Consult. Clin. Psychol. 41: 175-180, 1973.
10. Satir, Virginia.: Peoplemaking. Palo Alto, California, Science and Behavior Books, 1972.
11. Smart, R. G.: Future time perspectives in alcoholics and social drinkers. Proceedings, 75th Annual Convention, American Psychological Association, 1967, pp. 191-192.
12. Smeltzer, W. E.: Time orientation and time perspective in psychotherapy. Ph.D. dissertation, Michigan State University, 1968.
13. Vincent, J. W., and Tyler, L. E.: A study of adolescent time perspectives. Proceedings 73rd Annual Convention, American Psychological Association, 1965, pp. 341-342.

CHAPTER 21

PARADOX AS A THERAPEUTIC TECHNIQUE: A REVIEW

PATRICIA H. SOPER and LUCIANO L'ABATE
Georgia State University, Atlanta

Paradox has been a philosophical curiosity since Epimenedes of Megara devised the paradox of the liar and Zeno of Elea produced the paradoxes of infinity (Hughes and Brecht, 1975). Interest in paradox waned until the late nineteenth century revival of logic (Edwards, 1967). Recently, family therapists have developed an interest in pragmatic paradoxes leaving logical and semantic paradoxes to the domain of philosophers and linguists.

A paradox is defined as a "contradiction that follows correct deduction from consistent premises" (Watzlawick, Beavin, & Jackson, 1967). Watzlawick et al. (1967) viewed pragmatic paradoxes as most important in the study of human interaction because these paradoxes arise in ongoing interactions and determine behavior. Haley (1955) pointed out that a paradoxical behavior has two levels of abstraction. One level denies the assertion of the other; the second statement of the paradox is about the first but is at a different level of abstraction. Haley went on to say that this type of paradox is inevitable in the process of communication.

This paper is concerned with the nature of paradox as a therapeutic intervention from an historical and theoretical perspective. Included is a review of types of paradoxical interventions as well as a brief review of related approaches with heavy paradoxical overtones. Major emphasis is on the use of paradox in family therapy through relevant individual approaches such as paradoxical intention and hypnosis.

THE THERAPEUTIC DOUBLE BIND

The Palo Alto group (including both the Bateson project and the Mental Research Institute) is credited with the recognition of pathological aspects of paradoxical communication in their work on the double bind (Bateson et al., 1956; Bateson et al., 1963; Watzlawick, 1963). The direct outgrowth of their work is the therapeutic double bind which is a mirror image of the pathological bind (Watzlawick, et al., 1967). The therapeutic double bind presupposes an intense relationship between the therapist and client. The therapist enjoins the client to change while remaining unchanged with the implication that the injunction is the agent of change. The client is in the position either of changing and demonstrating control over his pathology or of resisting by behaving nonsymptomatically. Thus, the client is bound to change. The therapeutic setting dissuades the client from leaving the field by withdrawing or commenting on the paradox (Watzlawick et al, 1967; Feldman, 1976).

Varieties of therapeutic double binds that are closely associated with the Palo Alto group are: (1) prescribing the symptom and (2) reframing. Prescribing the symptom is quite simply instructing the client to maintain or exaggerate his symptomatic behavior. Watzlawick et al. (1967) view making the client behave as he has been behaving as applying a "be spontaneous" paradox. If the client is asked to display his symptom which is a nondeliberate, spontaneous behavior, then he cannot be spontaneous any more since the demand precludes spontaneity.

A number of practitioners report the use of this paradoxical instruction to bringing about change in clients. Farrelly (1974) frequently encourages his clients to continue with their symptoms to an absurd degree to "prove" the client's irrational contentions about himself. Montalvo and Haley (1973) report that the child therapist may even encourage a symptom as a means of bringing about change. Fischer (1974) and Prosky (1974) make reference to the usefulness of enlisting the family's oppositional feelings against the therapist. Andolfi (1974) reports that Jackson utilized prescribing the symptom with paranoid patients by teaching them to be more suspicious. In families disrupted by divorce, Peck (1974) instructs the partial family to take their incompleteness more seriously which resolves the members' ambivalence.

Feldman (1976) cites the usefulness of the technique of prescribing the symptom in dealing with a depressed client. The therapist may *implicitly* encourage the client to remain depressed by commenting, "It's a wonder you aren't more depressed." The client can respond by remaining depressed, and thus acknowledging control over his symptom, or evidence decreased depression, which also acknowledges control over his symptom. The therapist can follow through by trying to change or to circumscribe the situation further, suggesting, for instance, that the client spread out his depression throughout the week as opposed to being depressed only on the weekends.

Weakland et al. gave an example of a client who was complaining of headaches. She was told to make every effort to have more headaches at specified periods in the coming week. Again, regardless of whether the headaches got worse or disappeared, the client was bound to demonstrate that the apparently unchangeable problem could change. Weakland et al. (1974) reported that the most effective manner to give such paradoxical instructions is to play onedown or to act ignorant or confused in order to have the advice accepted. When the therapist came on strong with the paradoxical instructions, the client tended to ignore the advice.

An additional example of prescribing the symptom is a case involving a middle-aged woman and her schizophrenic son who were in a power struggle over the son's allowance (Fisch et al., 1972). The mother was reluctant to hand over much money due to her son's unstable mental state while the son was never sure he was able to meet expenses. The mother judged the amount of money she gave the son by the amount of psychotic behavior she perceived in him. The therapist instructed the son to use his psychotic behavior deliberately with the mother who was even more fearful of an expensive rehospitalization of the son than she was of his possible squandering of his allowance. The mother came through with a larger amount paid on a regular basis from which the son saved enough money to buy himself a car, thus giving himself greater independence from his mother.

Reframing, also a therapeutic double bind, involves changing the entire meaning of a situation by altering both or either its conceptual and/or emotional context in such a manner that the entire situation is experienced as completely different, i.e., the situation has been placed in a new frame (Watzlawick, Weakland, & Fisch, 1974). The therapist may frame the therapy procedures so he can work effectively, reinterpret messages from family members in a positive light (Jackson & Weakland, 1961), take a psychotic client's metaphors literally and interpreting it as evidence of his sanity (Kantor & Hoffman, 1966), define all events as being for the good of the family (Haley, 1972), and turn a family member into an observer (Minuchin, 1965). Haley (1963) used the term relabeling which essentially is a synonym for reframing. He makes the point that relabeling maladaptive patterns (or reframing) in couples therapy makes continuing those patterns more of an ordeal than changing.

The concept of reframing may be further clarified by the following examples. DeShazer (1975) reports the tactic of having an uninvolved father formally assigned the chore of keeping score in fights between the mother and child. In another case (Andolfi, 1974), a young couple whose relationship was characterized by frequent fighting was told that their fights were demonstrations of their love. They were directed to fight on a regular schedule. The couple was determined to prove the therapist was wrong, ceased fighting, and consequently began to get along better.

Luthman (1974) reports a case involving a family where the father was progressively going blind. She inquired whether he was learning Braille. The father defensively replied he was "as good a man as anyone else." She asked him, "How does it come about that the possible adding of new knowledge and skills to your repertoire would make you feel less in some way?"

The therapist may employ reframing in his own family. Guerin (Guerin & Fogarty, 1972), a Bowen trainee, reversed his usual tactic of interrogating his wife about what was the matter when she was distant. He began commenting to her that it sure is peaceful to live with some who does not burden me with personal thoughts and feelings. Or he said, "I cannot stand people who are always talking about their troubles." He would immediately leave the room before she could reply. His wife began to broach the issues that were bothering her to her husband.

TASKS

The therapeutic double bind may be in the form of an assignment or task. The therapist utilizes his clients resistance when assigning a task (Jackson & Weakland, 1961; Camp, 1973). Haley (1973) presents a case of Erickson's involving the breaking of an overt-involved mother-son dyad. The son wet his bed almost on a nightly basis. The exasperated mother brought him to Erickson who assigned a task to the two of them. The mother was to get up between 4:00 a.m. and 5:00 a.m. each morning to check her son's bed. If it was wet, he had to get up and practice his handwriting with his mother supervising him. If the bed was dry, his mother still had to get up and check. The boy went along with the task because his mother would like it less than he. The boy ended up with a dry bed, beautiful handwriting, an admiring mother, and even increased involvement with his father who now played ball with him. Hare-Mustin (1975) used a similar strategy with a four-year-old boy who threw spectacular and frequent temper tantrums. She instructed the boy to continue having his tantrums but only in a special tantrum place at home. The child and his family decided on the specific location. In the following session, the child picked a time of day he would tantrum. By the third session the tantrums had decreased to a bare minimum. Hare-Mustic expressed concern over the rapid change and asked the child to choose a day for a tantrum the following week. The child had no further tantrums.

DeShazer (1974) presents an excellent example of a task in his use of the functions of the presenting symptom in the family's interaction. A family brought in their 14-year-old son who had a stealing problem. The therapist instructed the father and son as a team to hide 5 one dollar bills around the house. If the son resisted stealing the money for one week, he was to be allowed to come in for a previously denied private session with the therapist. Otherwise the whole family was to come in. The son did come in alone and received instructions to steal two of the bills but to delay his usual dramatic confession until the next family session. At this time the son went through a dramatic display of guilt and sinfulness gaining the full attention of his family, but this time the father's open complicity was known to all. The father was able to recognize his part in his son's stealing episodes as were other family members.

The junior author remembers a difficult case with a couple where the husband demanded intercourse two or three times a week from his wife who felt resentful and angry at being used. Intercourse had become an ordeal for both. Other courses of action such as treatment of sexual attitudes and behaviors had failed. The husband was instructed to give up sex completely for the time being. The husband was reluctant, but the wife expressed great enthusiasm at the idea. For this couple the advantages of the husband's curtailment of his sexual behavior began to become apparent: (1) the pressure would be off both parties to perform sexually; (2) the wife could feel loved for herself rather than for her body; (3) the husband would be forced to think about his sexual behavior in relationship to his wife rather than take the usual route of unreflectively following his impulses; (4) by lowering the husband's dominance the couple could establish equilibrium in the relationship; and (5) the wife, who had been protesting that it was not sex *per se* that turned her off, but the manner in which her husband approached her for intercourse, would be on the spot. It would now be up to her to initiate any sexual activity.

WRITTEN INSTRUCTIONS

Both Selvini-Palazzoli et al. (1975) and L'Abate et al. (1976) have experimented with the effectiveness of using paradoxical written messages for presentation to the clients generally at the end of a session. The advantages of such a procedure are: (1) the message can be systematically thought out in advance and would serve as the major, important interpretation of the session; (2) the message would be more difficult to distort or forget by the clients than a verbal interpretation and thus assure repercussions in marital or familial homeostasis; and (3) copies of the messages could serve as progress notes for the therapist as well as a source of research data. For instance, a paradoxical message was presented to a couple whom the junior author and his wife had seen in therapy for approximately one year with minimal results. Previously, the couple had been in therapy numerous times over the years with a variety of therapists in different towns.

Dear B and J:

On the basis of our detailed and prolonged observation of your marriage and after a great deal of thought and deliberation, we have come to the conclusion that you both love each other so deeply and so dearly that any change for the better in the other is interpreted as a sign of rejection and a demonstration of disloyalty. You both are so loyal to each other that neither one can change for fear of disappointing the other one.

We can see and understand then, how it is impossible for each of you to change for the better, since changing for the better would be a sign of disloyalty and rejection. We really wonder whether each of you can change for the better without disappointing the other.

We would like for each of you to read this note each day but not to talk about it too much. We will talk about it next time we meet.

Cordially yours,
Luciano L'Abate and Bess L. L'Abate

POSITIVE INTERPRETATION

With this technique the therapist takes the stance of stressing the positive aspects of behaviors rather than the negative aspects (L'Abate, 1975; Otto, 1963). Stressing the positives is a form of relabeling or reframing.

Selvini-Palazzoli and her co-workers (1974, 1975) make use of positive connotation in their work with families. The therapists declare themselves as allies of the family and approve the behaviors of the family members—particularly those traditionally considered scapegoated by making them the family heroes, i.e., "By drawing attention to himself Giovanni has protected the whole family and especially father and mother, from looking at themselves and how they behave."

Change is produced by the therapist paradoxically aligning themselves with the family's homeostatic tendency (Selvini-Palazzoli et al., 1974, 1975). They report a case in which the martyr-like mother of a schizophrenic six-year-old boy declares herself as changed in an early session and no longer wanting to suffer. The therapist expressed concern over her premature change and described the importance of her suffering as a commendable virtue without which she would be at a severe loss. The therapist further described the husband and son as protecting the mother from suffering more than she had to, i.e., keeping her at the status quo. In essence, the therapist posed a paradox which was a metacommunication or confirmation of the pathogenic paradox by prescribing the symptom. Since the family always tries to disqualify the therapist, they must now change their game.

L'Abate (1975) writes of the choice available to the therapist in interpreting behaviors to the family and to himself. He may choose a traditional, negative orientation based on the pathology being presented to him and view the behaviors as a deficit or liability. On the other hand, the therapist may also choose to view the behaviors in terms of assets or strengths. The family expresses many strengths if the therapist is open to recognizing them and pointing them out to the family: Asking for help is a strength, expressing hurt through tears is a strength, caring for oneself and one's family is expressed by the family's presence in the therapist's office, and sharing hurt is a sign of caring. Paradoxically, the use of positive labeling can disrupt fixed, negative views the family takes for granted. For example, the parents of a ten-year-old girl complained that she is making new demands on them. Since she was initially shy and undemonstrative, the therapist praised her new demands as an indication of her positive self-assertion and increased self-esteem.

PARADOXICAL INTENTION

Paradoxical intention, a technique devised by Victor Frankl (1965, 1975a, 1976) has been used successfully in the treatment of phobias, obsessive-compulsive disorders, and anxiety states (Gerz, 1962; Solyom et al., 1972; Hand & Lamontagne, 1974). The technique is similar to that of prescribing the symptom. The therapist instructs the client to train himself to experience his symptom to an extreme degree as frequently as possible. The symptom has run its course when the client recognizes its absurdity and gains sufficient self-detachment to laugh at the symptom. Frankl (1975, 1975b) described the viciously circular nature of symptom which brings forth a fear of recurrence or anticipatory anxiety. The anxiety provokes the symptom whose recurrence reinforces the anxiety or fear. The technique of paradoxical intention is aimed at the phobic's flight from his fear and the obsessive's tendency to fight his fears. In short, the client is instructed to give up the mechanisms of resistance he has developed to avoid giving in to his fears and to face his fears head on. Frankl (1975b) reported the case of a woman who had suffered from severe claustrophobia for 15 years. She feared riding in all modes of transportation and entering buildings. She would become anxious and would fear that she would suffocate and die upon entry into a closed, confined space. As part of her desensitization treatment, she was encouraged to let the symptoms become as bad as possible and to seek out places where her symptom had previously occurred. Within a week, she was able to enter symptom-free innumerable places, first with her husband and then by herself, that she had previously been under considerable duress to enter.

HYPNOSIS

Hypnosis employs many of the paradoxical procedures mentioned in this article. The hypnotist uses reframing, emphasizing the positive, resistance, and a variety of double binds. A paradoxical injunction is given to the subject by the hypnotist who communicates two levels of messages: (1) Do as I say; (2) Don't do as I say but behave spontaneously. The subject adapts to the conflicting set of directives by undergoing a change and behaving in a way described as trance behavior (Sander, 1974; Andolfi, 1974; Haley, 1973, Haley, 1963). The hypnotist's techniques are very similar to those of the therapist who first directs his client to do things he can voluntarily do and then requests or communicates an expectation of spontaneous change (Haley, 1973).

Erickson and Rossi (1975) have identified a number of double binds used in hypnosis as well as in therapy. The first involves offering a free choice among comparable alternatives, one of which must be chosen, (i.e., "Would you like to go into a trance now or later?"). In a second, rather complex double bind, a request ostensibly made at the conscious level effects a change at the unconscious or subconscious level (e.g., "If your unconscious wants you to enter a trance, your right hand will lift. Otherwise your left hand will lift.") A third double bind uses time as a binding agent (e.g., "Do you want to get over that habit this week or next? That may seem too soon. Perhaps you'd like a longer period of time like three or four weeks?"). The fourth double bind—the reverse set double bind—is frequently used by Erickson in enabling patients to reveal material by enjoining them not to. The fifth therapeutic double bind used by Erickson is the *nonsequitur* double bind where he casually inserts a variety of increasingly absurd comments in a binding form. There is a similarity in the content of the alternatives offered by no logical connection (e.g., "Do you wish to take a bath before going to bed, or would you rather put your pajamas on in the bathroom?").

Not every case involves formal hypnosis. Joe, the eight-year-old son of a divorcee, had become the neighborhood and family terror (Erickson, 1963). His mother brought him to see Erickson who assured Joe he would change his behavior "all by himself." His mother would be told some simple things she could do so he could change himself, and he was to guess what they were. The next day, Joe arose, demanded breakfast, and when it was not forthcoming, began to tantrum. His mother prepared for the occasion with books and food for herself, sat on Joe explaining she would get up when she thought of a way to change his behavior, but unfortunately as the day progressed, she did not think she would come up with anything so it was all up to him. Joe struggled, pleaded, screamed all to no avail for most of the day. He was sent to bed without supper since he had missed lunch and breakfast had to be eaten before lunch. The next day, Joe was fed oatmeal which he hated for breakfast and had the leftover oatmeal for lunch. He accepted it gratefully. That day he spontaneously cleaned his room, canvassed the neighborhood, apologizing to the neighbors for his past behavior and making arrangements for amends. He spent the rest of the day with his schoolbooks and voluntarily went to bed. The mother explained to him she expected him to behave like a normal eight-year-old boy. All went well with the exception of one relapse dealt with by Erickson several months later. Otherwise, Joe behaved like a normal eight-year-old.

RELATED APPROACHES

Other therapists use paradoxical approaches without labeling their techniques as being paradoxical *per se*. Nelson, and her colleagues (1968) used the term "paradigm" to denote the interactions in which the therapist attempts to foster insight in the client by siding with his resistance and avoiding making interpretations. Sapirstein (1955) emphasized the importance of unconscious processes in the maintenance of paradoxical behavior. Farrelly and Brandsma (1974) labeled their brand of therapy as "Provocative Therapy" using symptom prescription and other double binding maneuvers.

Many of Rosen's (1953) techniques of direct therapy with psychotics involved a therapeutic double bind. When Rosen felt sufficient progress had been made, i.e., the client begins to let the therapist into his unconscious, a variety of techniques acknowledging the psychosis were initially employed. When a client began to make unsuccessful efforts at stopping his visions or voices, Rosen used magical gestures to stop the voices (e.g., repetitive strokes in the air, jumping and shouting, or drawings of antiwitchcraft figures posted on the wall). The client was intent on what Rosen was doing and did not hear the voices. After the client achieved some sense of reality, Rosen employed the technique of *reduction ad absurdum* which is an outright attack on the delusional system or suicidal impulses. He would observe loudly and with annoyance in front of the client who still insisted on dressing as Christ, "Isn't this the fourth Jesus Christ who's been here today?" He would portray the suicide attempt to the client who was no longer suicidal as the most absurd action he could have possibly taken. Both Haley (1955) and Andolfi (1974) viewed this technique in terms of a deliberate confusion of the symbol and the object symbolized. Rosen took his client's metaphorical statements seriously and then insisted they do the same. This technique dramatized the differences between metaphorical and literal messages leading to a clarification of the situation for the client who learned to discriminate between the two levels of messages. Haley (1955) emphasized the importance of reframing in this technique. A second technique employed by Rosen was re-enacting an aspect of the psychosis that bears some similarity to prescribing the symptom. Rosen would instruct a client who no longer heard voices but who was still in a rather shaky state to hear the voices again. The client, if all went well, insisted he did not hear anything while Rosen insisted he did. The client's coming back indignantly was a sure sign of a cure.

THE STATUS OF PARADOX-THEORETICAL AND OTHER CONSIDERATIONS

Paradox as a therapeutic technique appears to have spotty recognition. In several recent reviews of psychotherapy, paradox was not mentioned (Usdin, 1975; Barter & Barter, 1973; Bergin & Barfield, 1971). Even more surprising is the absence of mention of paradox in recent family therapy publications (Bell, 1975; Howells, 1975; Flick & Kessler, 1974; Andrews, 1974; Zuk, 1971). Fox (Weiner, 1976) also did not mention paradox as a therapeutic technique but does mention the pathological double bind as a historical note. Friedman (1974) did, however, mention prescribing the symptom and relabeling in his alphabet of family therapy techniques. Dolliver (1972) also recognized the importance of paradoxical techniques in the conceptualization of opposites in psychotherapy.

THE WHY OF USING PARADOX

Regardless of the recognition or lack of recognition by psychotherapists, important questions surround the usage of paradoxical techniques: How are paradoxes formed; how does one deliver a paradox successfully; and theoretically, why do paradoxes work? Practitioners and theorists offer a variety of answers to the questions posed which will be briefly reviewed in this section.

The basic appeal of paradox is novelty. Straightforward interpretations by the therapist, particularly with families, have little chance of "shaking-up" the family system. Straightforward interpretations are frequently expected, and, therefore, easily ignored. A paradoxical communication, by presenting the familiar in a new unexpected light, has a greater chance of being heard and, by virtue of this novelty, has a greater potential for evoking change.

A second characteristic of a paradoxical communication is the apparent craziness of the suggestion. The communication seemingly goes against common sense and can even be termed nonsense. How can a client or clients be persuaded to follow a nonsensical directive? One obvious predisposing condition is the desperateness of the client (s). Hare-Mustin (1975) reports spending a great deal of time with her inquiry about the details of the presenting symptom. After laying this ground work, she begins prescribing the symptom. Rossi (1973) points out that the therapist sets up binding conditions prior to the paradoxical prescription. For example, the client promises in advance he will follow the therapist's directive without protest. Weakland et al. (1974) comment that a high pressure approach to presenting the paradox does not work, but a confused, ignorant stance on the part of the therapist seems to facilitate client compliance. Selvini-Palazzoli et al. (1975) observe that paradoxical interventions are more effective if spaced out over time.

There are many theoretical explanations as to how paradoxes work. Social psychology contributes some explanations. Attribution theory (Jones, 1971) is concerned with how an individual explains his world. People tend to think in terms of a linear, cause-effect context and employ social consensus as a criterion for validation of explanations. The presentation of a paradox in therapy provides an alternate, circular explanation or attribution of meaning for a given event. This "reframing" affects the client's subsequent feelings and behavior about that event. The therapist and changed reactions of other family members are the social context for validating the new explanation of the event.

Laing's use of attribution and mystification in pathological situations (1963, 1971) can be translated into therapeutic paradoxes. The therapist attributes an alternate explanation of the behavior sequence at hand and then offers a cryptic prescription which he refuses to elaborate upon. The attribution denies the family's usual negative explanations of the given behavior and the mystification of the prescription keeps the clients in a state of confusion which circumvents their ignoring of what the therapist has said. Whitaker (1975) writes of the potency of the therapist's use of obscurity and absurdity in family therapy.

Transactional Analysis (TA) utilizes a straightforward approach to therapy. Steiner (1974) commented that the use of permission giving by the therapist in TA is criticized on the grounds that the client may react paradoxically and do the opposite of what the therapist indicates he should do. Steiner denies that this will result if the therapist is speaking from his Adult. Berger (1976) contends that in a deliberate paradoxical approach, an effective paradoxical message comes from the therapist's positive Parent and the client's Child does not dare comment that the message does not make sense. Hartman and Narboe (1974) reported on the protective aspects of certain pathological catastrophic injunctions.

The most widely held explanation for why the paradox works is based on the idea that some clients come to the therapist for help but are resistant to any help offered, in addition to provoking the therapist to try and fail (Adolfi, 1974). The use of paradox enables the therapist to implicitly tell the client to change by asking him not to change. This paradoxical communication, as derived from the Russellian paradoxes in classification systems (Reusch & Bateson, 1951; Haley, 1963) is not a contradiction in the sense that two levels of communication are involved. The higher level or metacommunication is an attempt to control the definition of the relationships (Anderson, 1972; Jackson, 1967). Thus, the therapist is perceived by the couple or family (each of whom have been resisting one another's attempts at defining the relationship already) as trying to define the relationship and unit to resist the therapist. To transcend this circular resistance, the therapist must use circular language (Selvini-Palazzoli et al., 1975). He makes his double binding request at the primary conscious level but effect change on the unconscious or metalevel (Erickson & Rossi, 1975).

The criticism can still be leveled that paradox, irregardless of the preceeding theoretical explanations, still lies outside of adequate theoretical explanation. Weisskopf-Joelson (1975) points out that aspects of Frankl's technique of paradoxical intention remain outside the existential tenets of Logotherapy.

CONCLUSION

From this review about the use of paradoxical practices in family therapy, it is easy to see that most evidence is still impressionistic, incomplete, and, hence, questionable. One of the greatest needs in the use of paradoxical practices lies in finding more tenable theoretical, clinical, and empirical bases.

REFERENCES

ANDERSON, E.K. A review of communication theory within the family framework. *Family Therapy*, 1972, 1, 15-34.

ANDOLFI, M. Paradox in psychotherapy. *American Journal of Psychoanalysis*, 1974, 34, 221-8.

ANDREWS, E.E. *The emotionally disturbed family and some gratifying alternatives*. New York: Jason Aronson, 1974.

BARTEN, H.H., & BARTEN, S.S. *Children and their parents in brief therapy*. New York: Behavioral Publications, 1973.

BATESON, G. The group dynamics of schizophrenia. In L. Appleby, J.M. Scher, and J. Cumming (Eds.), *Chronic Schizophrenia*. Glencoe, Ill.: The Free Press, 1960.

BATESON, G., JACKSON, D.D., HALEY, J., & WEAKLAND, J.H. A note on the double bind—1962. *Family Process*, 1963, 2, 154-61.

BATESON, G., JACKSON, D.D., HALEY, J., & WEAKLAND, J.H. Toward a theory of schizophrenia. *Behavioral Science*, 1956, 1, 251-64.

BELL, J.E. *Family therapy*. New York: Jason Aronson, 1975.

BERGER, M. What is done in trust: Conditions underlying the success of paradoxical interventions. Unpublished manuscript, Georgia State University, 1976.

BERGIN, H.E., & GARFIELD, S.L. (Eds.). *Handbook of psychotherapy and behavior change: An empirical analysis*. New York: Wiley, 1971.

CAMP, H. Structural family therapy: An outsider's perspective. *Family Process*, 1973, 12, 269-77.

DOLLIVER, R.H. The place of opposites in psychotherapy. *Journal of Contemporary Psychotherapy*, 1972, 5, 49-54.

EDWARDS, P. (Ed.) *The encyclopedia of philosophy*. New York: MacMillan Co. and The Free Press, 1967.

ERICKSON, M.H. The identification of a secure reality. *Family Process*, 1962, 1, 294-303.

ERICKSON, M.H. The confusion technique in hypnosis. In J. Haley (Ed.), *Advanced techniques of hypnosis and therapy*. New York: Grune & Stratton, 1967.

ERICKSON, M.H., & ROSSI, E.L. Varieties of double bind. *American Journal of Clinical Hypnosis*, 1975, 17, 143-57.

FARRELLY, F., & BRANDSMA, J. *Provocative therapy*. Fort Collins, Co.: Shields Publishing Co., 1974.

FELDMAN, L.B. Processes of change in family therapy. *Journal of Family Counseling*, 1976, 4, 14-22.

FISCH, R., WATZLAWICK, P., WEAKLAND, J., & BODIN, A. On unbecoming family therapists. In A. Ferber, M. Mendelsohn and A. Napier (Eds.), *The book of family therapy*. New York: Science House, 1972.

FISCHER, J. The Mental Research Institute on family therapy: Review and assessment. *Family Therapy*, 1974, 1, 105-40.

FOX, R.E. Family therapy. In I.B. Weiner (Ed.), *Clinical methods in psychology*. New York: John Wiley & Sons, 1976.

FRANKL, V.E. Paradoxical intention and dereflection. *Psychotherapy: Theory, Research and Practice*, 1975, 12, 226-37.

FRANKL, V.E. Paradoxical intention and dereflection: Two Logotherapeutic techniques. In S. Arieti and G. Chrzanowski (Eds.), *New dimensions in psychiatry: A world view*. New York: John Wiley & Sons, 1975.

FRANKL, V.E. *The doctor and the soul*. New York: Alfred Knopf, 1965.

FRIEDMAN, P.H. Outline (alphabet) of 26 techniques of family and marital therapy. *Psychotherapy: Theory, Research and Practice*, 1974, 11, 259-64.

GERZ, H.O. The treatment of the phobic and the obsessive-compulsive patient using paradoxical intention. *Journal of Neuropsychiatry*, 1962, 3, 375-87.

GLICK, I.D., & KESSLER, D.R. *Marital and family therapy*. New York: Grune & Stratton, 1974.

GUERIN, P., & FOGARTY, T. Study your own family. In A. Ferber, M. Mendelsohn, and A. Napier (Eds.), *The book of family therapy*. New York, Science House, 1972.

HALEY, J. (Ed.). *Changing families*. New York: Grune & Stratton, 1971.

HALEY, J. Paradoxes in play, fantasy, and psychotherapy. *Psychiatric Research Reports of the American Psychiatric Association*, 1955, 2, 52-8.

HALEY, J. Strategic therapy when a child is presented as the problem. *Journal of the American Academy of Child Psychiatry*, 1973, 12, 641-59.

HALEY, J. *Strategies of psychotherapy*. New York: Grune & Stratton, 1963.

HALEY, J. *Uncommon therapy*. New York: Ballantine Books, 1973.

HALEY, J. Whither family therapy? *Family Process*, 1962, 1, 69-100.

HAND, I., & LAMONTAGNE, Y. L'intention paradoxale et techniques comportementales similaires en psychotherapie a court terme. *Canadian Psychiatric Association Journal*, 1974, 19, 501-7.

HARE-MUSTIN, R.T. Treatment of temper tantrums by a paradoxical intervention. *Family Process*, 1975, 14, 481-5.

HARTMAN, C., & NARBOE, N. Catastrophic injunctions. *Transactional Analysis Journal*, 1974, 4, 10-12.

HOWELLS, J.G. *Principles of family psychiatry*. New York: Brunner/Mazel, 1975.

HUGHES, P., & BRACHT, G. *A panoply of paradoxes: Vicious circles and infinity*. New York: Doubleday & Co., 1975.

JACKSON, D.D. (Ed.). *Communication, family, and marriage*. Palo Alto: Science & Behavior Books, 1968.

JACKSON, D.D. The individual and the larger contexts. *Family Process*, 1967, 6, 139-47.

JACKSON, D.D., & WEAKLAND, J.H. Conjoint family therapy: Some considerations on theory, technique, and results. *Psychiatry*, 1961, 24, 30-45.

JONES, E.E. (Ed.). *Attribution: Perceiving the causes of behavior*. Morristown, N.J.: General Learning Series, 1971.

KANTOR, R.E., and HOFFMAN, L. Brechtian theater as a model for conjoint family therapy. *Family Process*, 1966, 5, 218-29.

L'ABATE, L. A positive approach to marital and familial intervention. In L.R. Wolberg, and M.L. Aronson (Eds.), *Group therapy 1975*. New York: Stratton Intercontinental Medical Book Corp., 1975, 63-75.

L'ABATE, L., O'CALLAGHAN, J.B., BIAT, T., DUNNE, E.E., MARGOLIS, R., PRIGGE, B., & LOPEZ, P. Enlarging the scope of intervention with couples and families: Combination of therapy and enrichment. In L.R. Wolberg and M.L. Aronson (Eds.), *Group therapy 1976: An overview*. New York: Stratton Intercontinental Medical Book Corporation, 1976, 62-73.

LAING, R.D. Mystification, confusion, and conflict. In I. Boszormenyi-Nagy, and J.L. Framo (Eds.), *Intensive family therapy*. Hagerstown, Md.: Harper & Row, 1965.

LAING, R.D. *The politics of the family*. New York: Pantheon Books, 1971.

LUTHMAN, S. Techniques of process therapy. *Family Therapy*, 1974, 1, 141-62.

MINUCHIN, S. Conflict-resolution family therapy. *Psychiatry*, 1965, 28, 278-86.

MONTALVO, B., & HALEY, J. In defense of child therapy. *Family Process*, 1973, 12, 227-44.

NELSON, M.C., NELSON, B., SHERMAN, M.H., & STREAN, H.S. *Roles and paradigms in psychotherapy*. New York: Grune & Stratton, 1968.

OTTO, H.A. Criteria for assessing family strength. *Family Process*, 1963, 2, 329-38.

PECK, B.B. Psychotherapy with fragmented (father-absent) families. *Family Therapy*, 1974, 1, 27-42.

PROSKY, P. Family therapy: An orientation. *Clinical Social Work Journal*, 1974, 2, 45-56.

ROSEN, J.N. *Direct analysis*. New York: Grune & Stratton, 1953.

ROSSI, E.L. Psychological shocks and creative moments in psychotherapy. *American Journal of Clinical Hypnosis*, 1973, 16, 9-22.

RUESCH, J., & BATESON, G. *Communication: The social matrix of society*. New York: W.W. Norton, 1951.

SANDER, F.M. Freid's "A case of successful treatment by hypnotism (1892-1893)": An uncommon therapy? *Family Process*, 1974, 13, 461-68.

SAPIRSTEIN, M.R. *Paradoxes of everyday life*. New York: Random House, 1955.

SELVINI-PALAZZOLI, M., BOSCOLO, L., CECCHIN, G.E., & PRATA, G. Paradox and counterparadox: A new model for the therapy of the family in schizophrenic transaction. Paper presented at the Fifth International Symposium on Psychotherapy of Schizophrenia. Oslo: August 14-18, 1975.

SELVINI-PALAZZOLI, M., BOSCOLO, L., CECCHIN, G.E., & PRATA, G. The treatment of children through brief therapy of their parents. *Family Process*, 1974, 13, 429-42.

SHAZER, S. de. Brief therapy: Two's company. *Family Process*, 1975, 14, 79-93.

SHAZER, S. de. On getting unstuck: Some change-initiating tactics for getting the family moving. *Family Therapy*, 1974, 1, 19-26.

SOLYOM, L., GARZA-PEREZ, J., LEDWIDGE, B.L., & SOLYOM, C. Paradoxical intention in the treatment of obsessive thoughts: A pilot study. *Comprehensive Psychiatry*, 1972, 13, 291-7.

STEINER, C.M. *Scripts people live*. New York: Bantam Books, 1974.

USDIN, G. (Ed.). *Overview of the psychotherapies*. New York: Brunner/Mazel, 1975.

WATZLAWICK, P. A review of the double bind theory. *Family Process*, 1963, 2, 132-53.

WATZLAWICK, P., BEAVIN, J.H., & JACKSON, D.D. *Pragmatics of human communication*. New York: W.W. Norton, 1967.

WATZLAWICK, P., WEAKLAND, J., & FISCH, R. *Change: Principles of problem formation and problem resolution*. New York: W.W. Norton, 1974.

WEAKLAND, J.H., FISCH, R., WATZLAWICK, P., & BODIN, A.M. Brief therapy: Focused problem resolution. *Family Process*, 1974, 13, 141-68.

WEISSKOPF-JOELSON, E. Logotherapy: Science or faith? *Psychotherapy: Theory, Research and Practice*, 1975, 12, 238-40.

WHITAKER, C.A. Psychotherapy of the absurd: With a special emphasis on the psychotherapy of aggression. *Family Process*, 1975, 14, 1-16.

ZUK, G.H. *Family therapy: A triadic based approach*. New York: Behavioral Publications, 1971.

CHAPTER 22

A COMPILATION OF PARADOXICAL METHODS

GERALD R. WEEKS

University of North Carolina, Wilmington

and

LUCIANO L'ABATE

Georgia State University, Atlanta

A compilation of paradoxical interpretations and prescriptions is presented after a short review of similar efforts. This compilation includes the following dimensions, as defined by polar opposites: individual vs. systemic; prescriptive vs. descriptive; direct insight vs. indirect insight-producing; direct vs. cryptic; time-bound vs. time-random; reframing vs. relabeling; and specific vs. general. Theoretical, empirical and clinical implications of this typology are considered, with an emphasis on the latter.

Paradoxical psychotherapy has become a major form of therapy in the last few years, especially in family therapy. Watzlawick, Beavin, and Jackson (1967) and Watzlawick, Weakland, and Fisch (1974) developed a theory of communication and change which stressed the importance of paradoxical intervention. They also offered a number of examples to demonstrate how paradoxes could be used therapeutically with individuals, couples and families. These cases were divided into categories in order to exemplify what Watzlawick et al. (1974) called "reframing." Altogether they presented ten different ways to "reframe." Most of the literature on paradoxical techniques has reported on very specific ways to use therapeutic paradoxes (see Weeks and L'Abate, 1978). The systematization of paradoxical techniques into classes, types or categories has been neglected. The purpose of this paper is to describe different types of paradoxical interventions which would be useful theoretically, empirically and clinically. The main emphasis, however, is to demystify paradoxical psychotherapy as it is presented by Erickson (Haley, 1973) and serve as a heuristic model for the clinician.

Although paradoxical techniques appear new and strange, they in fact have been in use for many years and and are embedded in many different therapeutic approaches. As early as 1928, K. Dunlap began applying a technique he called "negative practice" to problems such as nail biting, enuresis, and stammering. He would direct the patient to practice the symptom under prescribed conditions

---

Gerald R. Weeks, is an Assistant Professor of Psychology at the University of North Carolina, Wilmington. Luciano L'Abate is a Professor of Psychology and Director of the Family Studies Program at Georgia State University in Atlanta.

The authors would like to thank Kathy Weeks and Jackie Johnson for their comments and suggestions.

with the expectation of extinguishing the habit. Alfred Adler (1959) prescribed or predicted symptoms, and his technique of prosocial definition is equivalent to what is known as reframing in paradoxical psychotherapy. Victor Frankl (1967) was probably the first clinician to identify the paradoxical method. He called his approach paradoxical intention and used it in the treatment of mostly phobias and obsessions. His technique involved prescribing the symptom. John Rosen (1953) published a book entitled *Direct Psychoanalysis* that describes a method that can be construed as paradoxical. The thrust of his approach was to have clients re-enact an aspect of their psychosis. Whenever a patient threatened or began to exhibit psychotic symptoms, Rosen would intervene by demanding that the patient proceed and enact his symptoms. Paradoxical techniques are also found in behavioral approaches. Implosion, a technique where the patient is instructed to experience his fear or anxiety as fully as possible, can be conceptualized within a paradoxical framework.

Although paradoxes have been used for many years, Watzlawick et al. (1967) were the first to develop a coherent theory to explain their use. Their book marked the beginning of a new kind of therapy which appears irrational and noncommonsensical. It eventually led to the development of an entirely new approach to family therapy. This new paradigm of family therapy emerged from the work of Seivini-Palazzoli and her co-workers (1978) in Italy. The reader interested in a more complete historical review should consult a previous paper (Soper and L'Abate, 1977).

Before presenting our classification of paradoxes, it would be useful to define what is meant by the term "therapeutic paradox" and review similar efforts at classification. Watzlawick et al. (1967) described a paradoxical message as follows: "(a) it asserts something, (b) it asserts something about its own assertion, and (c) these two assertions are mutually exclusive. Thus, if the message is an injunction, it must be disobeyed to be obeyed; if it is a definition of self or the other person, the person thereby defined is this kind of person only if he is not, and is not if he is" (p. 212). As the reader can see, it is difficult to define the phenomenon clearly in an understandable way. Our approach is to define paradox operationally by specifying different types of intervention. All of our types are designed to produce what Watzlawick et al. (1974) called second-order change as opposed to first-order change. First-order change refers to change within a system which itself remains unchanged. Second-order change refers to change in the system itself (e.g., the rules of the system) and is known as paradoxical change. Interventions designed to produce second-order change are by definition paradoxical. Thus, there may be many different kinds of paradoxes which produce second-order change.

Aside from Watzlawick et al. (1974), there have been only two other attempts to produce the kind of classification we are proposing. These classifications were formulated by Andolfi and Menghi (1976, 1977) and Tennen (1977). According to Andolfi and Menghi there are two broad categories of prescriptions: 1) restructuring and 2) paradoxical. Restructuring prescriptions can be subdivided into: (a) *countersystemic* prescriptions directed toward creating an obvious contrast to the homeostasis of the family system; (b) *context* prescriptions directed toward establishing or maintaining a therapeutic context; (c) *displacement* prescriptions of either the symptom or the scapegoat; (d) *systemic re-elaboration* prescriptions directed toward a direct restructuring of present relational schemes through the utilization of already existing elements; (e) *reinforcement* prescriptions directed toward reinforcing movements already present in the family system and judged to be useful to change; and (f) *utilization* of the symptom prescriptions, either through attack or alliance. Paradoxical prescriptions are divided into those directed toward the encouragement of symptomatic behavior and those directed toward the rules that govern and are peculiar to a particular family.

Tennen (1977) formulated a simple, yet relatively encompassing, three-fold classification of paradoxes in terms of actual procedures. These interventions were 1) prescribing, 2) restraining and 3) positioning. In prescribing, the therapist urges the client to engage in the behavior that is to be eliminated. The underlying message is: (a) in order to lose your symptom, keep it and/or exaggerate it; or (b) you have an uncontrollable symptom; will it to occur. In restraining, the therapist attempts to restrain change. That is, he discourages or even denies the possibility of change. The underlying message for restraining is that in order to change, the client must give up or stay the same. In the third type of intervention, positioning, the therapist accepts and exaggerates the patient's position or assertion about himself. It is used when the therapist has attempted to be optimistic and encouraging about the patient's symptom only to find the client becoming more symptomatic. The underlying message to the client is for him to continue to be oppositional, and thus he will change behaviorally.

The types of paradoxical interventions formulated here are a beginning effort to distill the various types of paradoxes reported in the literature and those types developed by us. It should be useful for the clinician in providing a framework from which to generate therapeutic paradoxes. The first two categories of paradoxes presented are given emphasis because they have not been considered extensively in the literature. Most paradoxes will fall within two or more of the categories we present. Our types are based on an implicit dialectical metatheory which assumes that everything exists in opposition or contradiction to something else and that paradoxical psychotherapy is a dialectical approach to therapy (Weeks, 1977; Weeks & Weeks, 1978; Weeks & Wright, 1979). We have delineated seven general categories of paradoxes as shown in Table 1.

TABLE ONE

Types of Paradoxes

Individual vs. Systemic	Prescriptive vs. Descriptive	Direct insight vs. Indirect insight	Direct vs. Cryptic	Time-Bound vs. Time-Random	Reframing vs. Relabeling	Specific vs. General

TYPES OF PARADOXES

Individual vs. Systemic

One of the most critical issues in family therapy pertains to the focus of interpretation. Should the focus be directed toward the individual, or should it be directed toward the family relationship or system? The same issue is relevant for paradoxical messages or prescriptions—individual or systemic? We are aware that this is not an either-or proposition. Most family therapists use both types of interpretation. However, our review of the literature strongly suggests that most paradoxical messages have been to some extent individually oriented or *ad hominem*. We need to recognize that systemic paradoxes are an option and to ask ourselves when is it appropriate to use one type or the other?

There appear to be at least three types of paradoxes within the individual vs. systemic category (see Table 2). The first type of paradox (Level I) is strictly

TABLE TWO

Individual vs. Systemic Paradoxes

Levels	Descriptive Name	Focus on Message
I	Individual	Paradox directed toward one individual
II	Interactional	Interlocking paradoxes directed toward two or more members
III	Transactional (Systemic or Relational)	One paradox directed toward a system of behavior which focuses on a single dynamic or pattern of behavior within the system

individual. It is directed toward only one member of the family. The second type (Level II) may be directed toward all members of the family, but as individuals. That is, each member is given a paradoxical task, and each is clear about what his task is to be. The third type (Level III) is directed at the *relationship* between or among the members of a family. Level I paradoxes do not need to be described here. A number of cases are available in Haley (1973).

Level II paradoxes are a bit more complex. They require that the therapist give *two or more interlocking paradoxes* to the members of the family. For example, a husband might be told that: "Whenever he feels .... he is to do ...., and whenever the wife feels .... she is to do ...." What goes in the blanks could be the same for what each is feeling or is to do, or it could be different. Watzlawick et al. (1974) offered many examples of interactional paradoxes. A concrete example might be the prescription of symptomatic behavior, for example: "Mary, the next time you feel unloved, start a fight with John. John, the next time you feel you are getting too intimate through your fighting with Mary, get out of the fight by being logical or rational or by leaving the room."

Level III paradoxes are extremely complex and require a thorough understanding of the family relationship system. This type of paradox requires that the therapist "collapse" his Level II paradox by focusing on a single dynamic *and* avoiding naming names in giving the paradox. This means the paradox is directed toward the plural "you." For example, a couple complaining about their differences could be told "So, *you* don't have anything in common. Maybe *you* should split up." Collapsing a Level II paradox may take the form of prescribing that the members act in certain ways when they experience a certain feeling or when a certain event occurs. It could also involve giving the family a single descriptive message or relabeling a system's behavior.

The following messages demonstrate Level III paradoxes: "We have some suggestions about how to improve the ways you already fit together. The next time you are feeling powerless, make a major purchase on your own, or start an argument with your mate. At all costs you should not tell your mate when you feel powerless or out of control. In fact, if one of you asks the other whether you feel powerless or out of control, you should deny it." Note that in this paradox the issue of powerlessness is the central dynamic, and reference is made to *you,* the couple, not to the individuals. Another type of Level III message reframes the behavior of the family in positive terms and is descriptive rather than prescriptive. For example, "This family must really care about each other to come here for help," or "This is a strong family to be able to admit that (it needs help, etc.)."

In summary, Level I paradoxes are prescriptions given to the individuals. Level II or interactional paradoxes tie together the behavior of two or more individuals in the system by prescribing specific behavior to each member. Level III or transactional paradoxes are systemic: they focus on a single dynamic within the system. They are more generalized than Level II paradoxes and are not directed to any specific member of the system. In addition, transactional paradoxes usually destabilize systems by creating confusion.

Prescriptive vs. Descriptive

Most of the examples of paradoxical messages in the literature have been prescriptive; i.e., the symptom is prescribed. Watzlawick et al. (1974) presented the most elaborate scheme of prescriptive messages. Altogether they list ten different paradoxical techniques. All of these techniques utilize "reframing" to effect second-order or paradoxical change. Reframing is the process of changing the meaning attributed to a situation. The reader should consult Watzlawick et al. (1974) for their discussion of prescriptive paradoxes. Aside from prescribing the symptom, Andolfi and Menghi (1976, 1977) stated that another type of prescriptive paradox prescribed the *rules* of a family system rather than the symptoms. The "rules" paradox is directed toward the entire family system. For example, a family with an implicit rule not to fight or argue could be told: "During the next week some things will happen which will make you angry with each other, and you will want to get these feelings out in the open by fighting. We agree that this family is not strong enough for this kind of confrontation right now. We feel you should avoid fighting at all costs. The next time a fight happens, we want you to avoid it by everyone going to his own room. If you get angry you should hide it, and deny you are angry when someone asks you." This is also an example of a Level III or transactional paradox.

It may appear too dangerous to the therapist to give a paradoxical prescription, for example, to a client who engages in behavior dangerous to himself or others. In cases such as these it might be possible to use an action-fantasy prescription. That is, prescribe part of the sequence in action and another part in fantasy. For example, a client who felt lonely and depressed would: go out to singles bar, have a few drinks, get picked up by "rough" men, and later feel used and guilty. A paradox could be constructed prescribing that the next time she felt lonely and depressed she was to get dressed, get in her car, and then have a fantasy that she would get picked up by a man who would sexually abuse her, etc. If the fantasy aspect were exaggerated by the therapist, then this technique would probably be even more powerful. To our knowledge this type of paradox has not been reported in the literature, but we have had success with it in a limited number of cases.

Another form of the prescriptive paradox is the *predictive* paradox. The predictive paradox is an extension of the prescriptive paradox. A predictive paradox is designed to *maintain control* over the symptom. It is set up so that if the symptom disappears, the client has control over the symptom; and if the symptom continues, then the therapist predicted it, and it is under his control. Predicting a relapse is the most commonly used form of this type of paradox. In general, the therapist predicts that the symptom will continue or occur again. One way to increase the power of a predictive paradox is to make the prediction and discuss ways the client can make it come true or have the client think of ways to make it come true. For example, a client who does not do his homework or tasks could be told: "I'm going to give you this task to do, but I know you won't do it because each week you come in with a different excuse. I want to try something new, and I don't want to talk about why I want to do it. I want you to make a list of all the ways you can avoid doing this task. Next week when you come in, tell me your best excuse why you didn't do the task, even if by some miracle you did do it."

Descriptive paradoxical messages differ from prescriptive messages in that descriptive messages do not prescribe the symptom but *describe* the symptom. Our formulation of descriptive messages involves three basic components. First, we tell the couple or family how we like the pattern of behavior or symptomology they have established. We usually say something like: "We like . . ." "We want to congratulate . . ." or "You have a real talent, ability, etc." In short, a negative behavior is relabeled as a positive behavior. The second component of descriptive messages is to describe the nature of the family relationship to the family in dialectical terms. That is, oppositeness, contradiction, or bipolarity is pointed out in their relationship (e.g., if one spouse or member of the family is up, good or right, the other(s) must be down, bad or wrong). In other words, the polarization present in the system is described and exaggerated. In order to be an effective message, the dynamics of the system must be well understood. Our experience has shown that dysfunctional family systems are characterized by polarization. There are many different types of polarization which may exist in family systems. These polarizations have been best described in the family theories of L'Abate (1976), Stierlin (1974), and Boszormenyi-Nagy and Spark (1973). The third component of the message is a question directed toward the family about the pattern of behavior. This question usually asks if the family is really happy with the situation described and may ask them to "wonder" about different ways of relating or to suggest different ways of relating. We have given a number of these descriptive messages in written form to couples participating in marital enrichment and therapy. One complete letter and a few excerpts from these letters demonstrate how descriptive paradoxical messages may be formulated. The reader may note that these letters consist of 1) a positive reframing statement, 2) a dialectical description and 3) a restraining statement.

Dear ——————,

I am very impressed with your commitment to your marriage and how much you care for each other. Each of you is very considerate of the other's feelings, and you do not wish to hurt each other.

I think that it's very commendable that you care for each other so much that you try to be like your partner. Each of you can depend on the other to avoid confronting your differences. This has allowed you to achieve a harmonious relationship which would be too risky to change right now. Why tamper with a good thing?

* * *

It really seems like a good idea that both of you stop yourselves from confronting the other with your different points of view and avoid some of the pain coming from facing both small and large issues directly. Why stop a good thing?

* * *

How nice it is that you have worked out such a fine way of delegating authority and responsibility. One of you makes the decisions, while the other allows the decisions to be made. While we commend the achievement of the resulting stability, it concerns us that you may be achieving it at the price of retarding change in the marriage relationship.

* * *

We are very impressed by the degree to which you have given of yourselves to the marriage, even at the expense of individuality. It is really gratifying to see a couple who has resolved this dilemma of equality by maintaining and upholding the traditional status quo. It must add a lot of stability to your relationship to know what to expect from your spouse. It must really be exciting having so much predictability in your relationship.

Direct Insight vs. Indirect Insight

Insight has been recognized as an aim—if not the basic aim—of psychotherapy since Freud. Freud defined insight as intellectual understanding—coming to know the "why" of one's present neurosis. Humanistically oriented therapists such as Rogers have viewed insight as the awareness and acceptance of feelings and attitudes. The way most therapists from Freud up to the present day have attempted to produce insight in their clients has been to reflect what the client verbalizes or provide interpretations.

The kind of insight produced from a paradoxical intervention is different from that produced by reflection or interpretation (i.e., by words). A paradox produces what could be called a "pragmatic insight," that is, an insight produced through action which emerges from systemic manipulation by the therapist. The truth of the insight is utterly convincing and inescapable. It is such a powerful insight that the client may slip into a trance state as the insight occurs. It might be noted that using the term pragmatic to describe an insight is consistent with William James' (1907) pragmatic theory of truth. For James, truth referred to whether an idea worked, and whether any idea worked depended upon some form of *action*.

Haley (1976) pointed out that insight is not necessary for change to occur in therapy. The only requisite for change is that the person do the task he is given whether it is a direct task or a paradoxical task. Haley is in fact opposed to insight-oriented psychotherapy, and most of his tasks are not designed specifically to produce insight. However, insights are produced many times in spite of the therapist's bias.

The basic form of a paradox which produces insight indirectly is often "Whenever you feel, think of, hear, see, etc., I want you to (prescribe some concrete behavior)." As the person does the prescribed behavior he will automatically link that behavior to the feeling, etc. given in the paradox. For example, "Whenever you feel ignored, pick a fight with . . ." A variant of this structure which is not quite as insight-producing is: "The next time John does ...., I want you to (and prescribe the symptom)." This sub-type helps to produce insight around the impact another person has on the client. For example, "The next time your wife starts a serious discussion with you, I want you to find something to do to get out of the discussion as quickly as possible." Watzlawick et al. (1974) discussed this type of paradox in terms of making the covert overt.

Why use insight-directed paradoxes? First, they could be used with clients who expect and want insight. Second, why not? The paradox should produce a behavioral change, and insight is a bonus. The new insight might also help the client become more aware of other feelings and facilitate further change.

Direct vs. Cryptic

Direct paradoxes are given in a straightforward, easy to understand manner. The message conveyed to the client is clear—he knows exactly what has been requested at a cognitive level. However, paradoxical messages may be given with varying degrees of clarity and directness, varying the client's awareness that he is receiving a paradoxical message. In other words, some paradoxes may be cryptic. There are a number of advantages to giving cryptic messages. First, they may be especially useful with clients who are therapy-wise, or perhaps therapists themselves. Second, they are useful with intellectualizers or "computers." Since cryptic messages are unclear, the therapy-wise client or intellectualizing client cannot ignore, oppose or resist the message. Third, cryptic messages are essential to clients who would be too threatened by a more direct paradox and a straightforward confrontation. Fourth, the more cryptic the message, the more the client has to think about what was said and try to make sense of it. In the process, he may explore a number of alternative ways of looking at his situation. Fifth, cryptic messages are directed toward the unconscious.

All these reasons appear consistent with why Milton Erickson chooses to be indirect with clients. Beahrs (1977) quotes Erickson as saying "a patient himself is a person who is afraid to be direct." Beahrs further stated:

> A healthy person is direct—he defines a problem, thinks of alternatives, chooses the one that is most likely to achieve the desired outcome, and does it, facing whatever obstacles are in the course. Somehow a neurotic or any disturbed individual is afraid to do this. Neurotics are very indirect in their manner, schizophrenics even more so, and it is Erickson's profound faith that to reach a disturbed patient you have to deal in his terms. If you directly face patients, they are going to resist for the very same reasons that they resist directness in their life anyway (p. 57-58).

Cryptic messages also have another important function. Since the client is not aware of being given an injunction, he assumes that any change he makes must be of his own doing. This event enhances the client's sense of control and power and diminishes the power and importance of the therapist in solving his problems.

The most commonly described cryptic paradoxical technique is the confusion technique. This technique derives from the confusion technique in hypnosis (also see Haley, 1967). The therapist essentially says a lot of things which don't make sense, but includes one or more relatively clear statements which may be either direct or paradoxical. The client is in such a state of confusion that he is willing to accept any statement which makes sense. However, because the statement is given in the context of many other confusing statements, he does not have time to negate it or view it critically. DeShazer (1975) described the mechanics of the confusion technique and gave examples of how it can be used. Confusion was also discussed in detail by Watzlawick (1976).

A number of psychologists have considered the use of metaphor in therapy. Haley (1973, 1976) reviewed cases where Erickson used metaphor in therapy and discussed the therapeutic use of metaphorical communication. The best known example is Erickson's technique of talking about sex metaphorically by describing how men and women eat and encouraging the couple to plan a meal given their individual preferences. Ehrenwald (1966) concluded that the client's use of metaphor indicated repressed feelings, while Lenrow (1966) saw the therapist's use of metaphor as a way to unlock the client's growth potential.

However, the most interesting observation was made by Koen (1965) in describing the metaphor. He stated that the metaphor allows for transportation from one sensory modality to another (e.g., the tie was loud). This observation is directly related to Bandler and Grinder's (1975) and Grinder and Bandler's (1976) idea that people deal with problems in different sensory modalities. Dealing with a problem in one sensory modality might facilitate its resolution, while dealing with it in another would leave the person at an impasse. Thus, metaphor may facilitate second-order change by changing the frame in which the solution is attempted. A technique which emerges directly from Bandler and Grinder's (1975) work is to ask the client to conceptualize the solution to a problem using all the sensory modalities (e.g., "What does it feel, taste, smell, look and sound like?").

A metaphorical way of dealing with patients confronting difficult and anxiety-producing tasks is to find another situation in which the person is competent. For example, a client was very anxious over starting a new job. The therapist asked the client to discuss various aspects of mountain climbing (e.g., what to take, what to wear, where to climb, what to avoid in the terrain, and who to climb with). The therapist alternated between the skills used in mountain climbing and those she could use in approaching her new job. The intermeshing of these two "apparently" unrelated tasks helped the client transfer her knowledge from one area to another and reduced her anxiety over the new job.

The use of metaphor in therapy is limited only by the therapist's imagination and creativeness. All that is required is that the key elements of the message be abstracted and then integrated into another story. For example, a girl who was resistant in therapy and had a lot of secrets could be told a story about how "secret agents" work and how they always have an ally with whom to share their secrets.

Another type of cryptic message relates back to paradoxes being transactional. When a message is given to a couple or family at the transactional level (e.g., "We are impressed by how you care for each other" or "You are such a responsible family") each member wonders who is caring or being responsible. By not specifying individuals, the family is plunged into a guessing game which may help to break the set with which they had been viewing one another.

A related technique is to use statements which are unclear or perhaps words which have double meanings (e.g., "Since you enjoy bad health . . .") and to state the message very abstractly and obtusely. We have experimented a good deal with the latter type and offer the following examples of abstract and ambiguous paradoxes.

> Your relationship is very nicely complementary, but since you can only be what the other is not, you cannot really be yourselves.

* * *

> It hurts me that you seem to feel that you must either choose to keep a busy schedule or withdraw entirely in order to focus on yourselves and each other. I wonder whether you have dealt with the issue of doing vs. being?

* * *

> We are impressed by the way in which you are supporting each other's growth as lovers apart from the marriage and family. Continue to be pro-

tective of each other's individuality and growth, and continue to move slowly towards forming a new integrated relationship and facing the task of being married and being parents.

* * *

We want to congratulate you for being such an extraordinary couple by never misunderstanding each other. You both seem to have an in-depth understanding of each other's feelings. It is obvious that you have devoted much thought to this pursuit. Consequently, we feel your thoughtful understanding will enable you to continue your present degree of sharing feelings.

These paradoxes are probably too abstract to make sense to the reader. However, the couples who received these messages spent a good deal of time *working together* trying to decipher their meaning.

Time-Bound vs. Time-Random

Some paradoxes are definitely related to time and others are not. There are at least two major types of time-bound paradoxes. One type of paradox specifies that something is to happen at a specific time or on the occurrence of a specific event. The first type of time-bound paradox has been called "symptom scheduling" (Newton, 1968). This technique involves having the client schedule a time in which to enact his symptom. For example, a client who is anxious and reports worrying chronically could be instructed to set aside one hour a day in which to worry. He would be instructed to keep a list of things that worry him and save them up for his one hour session when he can concentrate all his efforts on being an effective and competent worrier. The second sub-type of time-bound paradoxes is related to the occurrence of a specific feeling state or event (also insight-producing). For example, "Whenever you feel ...., I want you to ...., or whenever one of you does x, I want the rest of you to ...." There are numerous examples in the literature of these two types of paradoxes.

Paradoxes may be unrelated to time or occurrence of a specific event. The paradoxical message may go into effect at any time or on the occurrence of a variety of events. The set up for this type of paradox could be: "Sometime during the next . . .," for example, "Sometime during the next week I want you to go ahead and experience what it is like to be furiously angry. Just let yourself go. But remember, don't do anything that would hurt yourself, anyone else, or break anything that couldn't be replaced." Another example for clients who do not express anger could be: "During the next week I want you to pretend to be angry. It can be anytime, but you will know when it is the right time because something will happen . . ."

It should also be noted that statements may be used to help unbind the client in time. These statements imply that the client is involved in some form of change *already*. For example, "As you continue to learn, change, etc." Words such as before, after, since, when and while are useful in unbinding clients in time (see Bandler and Grinder, 1975, p. 258).

Reframing vs. Relabeling

Watzlawick et al. (1974) defined reframing as changing ". . . the conceptual and/or emotional setting or viewpoint in relation to which a situation is experienced and to place it in another frame which fits the 'facts' of the same concrete situation especially well or even better, and thereby change its entire meaning" (p.)5). In short, the meaning attributed to the situation is changed. They transformed this concept into practice by the use of basically prescriptive paradoxes. They did not explore the issue of relabeling, at least not explicitly.

The purpose of this section is to differentiate the technique of relabeling. In relabeling there is the implication that the reinforcement of what the client wants to change is the vehicle of change. The therapist simply redefines what the client views as desirable or undesirable. In other words, any so-called undesirable behavior given a positive label must be desirable, and any so-called desirable behavior given a negative label must be a behavior that is either carried to the extreme or inappropriately expressed.

Relabeling a behavior changes a person's phenomenological perspective of the behavior and changes the system's view of the behavior, or symptom-bearer. It provides the client (or system) a new way of thinking and feeling about the behavior. Landfield (1975) suggested that therapists should take a positive approach to labeling behavior. He offered several examples of how behavior usually viewed as negative could be labeled positively (e.g., rigidity as a steadfast purpose, immaturity as aggressive exploration, hostility as involvement, and confusion as preparation for new growth). Weeks (1977) also offered a number of examples which once again require the therapist to be creative and break from the usual set of accepting and assigning negative labels (e.g., withdrawing, taking care of oneself; passive, ability to accept things as they are; submissive, seeking authority and direction in order to find oneself; wandering, exploring all possibilities; impulsive, able to let go and be spontaneous; crying, ability to express emotions, especially share hurt). It should be noted that all of these new labels involve some element of truth and are positive in connotation.

Selvini-Palazzoli et al. (1978) also made extensive use of positive labeling. They called this method positive connotation. In other words, the therapist positively connotes the symptom of the identified patient. The connotation is intended to preserve the homeostatic tendency of the system and serve as an obstacle to further scapegoating. The connotation has the effect of putting all family members on the same level, while placing the family in a paradoxical situation. In order to escape the paradoxical situation, the system must literally take flight into health.

The examples given up to this point deal with relabeling a negative behavior positively. It is also possible to relabel a positive behavior negatively, although this becomes more complex. L'Abate (1975) pointed out strengths which were causing liabilities or weaknesses. For example, mates may be told that they love and protect each other so much that they go to all lengths to avoid conflict, confrontation, and thus, intimacy. It should be noted that L'Abate (1977) defined intimacy as sharing hurt. The fact that the couple's problem had resulted from love and protection implies that love and protection are negative labels. However, because this couple does love and protect each other they should also be willing to change for each other in helpful ways. In the present case, the change would involve learning to fight fairly and share hurt. This strategy is especially useful in dealing with systems of behavior where pathology may have positive antecedents (Haley, 1976; L'Abate, Weeks, and Weeks, 1977).

Another way to relabel behavior is through "pretense." The client is asked to engage in his problem behavior, i.e., to pretend to be symptomatic. This request once again allows the client to gain control over a symptom that was defined as either partially or fully out of his control. It also gives the client permission to have the symptom. An excellent example of "pretense" is demonstrated in the case of "A Modern Little Hans" (Minuchin, 1974). In order to prevent a child from suffering a relapse over a dog phobia, the therapist encouraged the dog-phobic boy to pretend to be afraid of his new pet. In one of our cases, a couple was feeling helpless vis-à-vis the wife's in-laws. Her parents constantly gave them gifts and made subtle demands on them. They were instructed to begin asking for more and more from her parents (see Watzlawick et al., 1974, p. 116-119). Furthermore, they were told that they must also pretend to be very helpless and childish. The latter task was emphasized because this couple was immature. By pretending to be childish they not only became more aware of their behavior, but were, as instructed, pulled closer together in coaching each other on how to be childish in order to successfully complete this paradox.

Relabeling is a complex therapeutic technique. It may have a number of effects on a client or system of behavior such as a couple or family. In general, it should change the way a client thinks or feels about his behavior. For example, a behavior viewed as a liability may suddenly be viewed as an asset and vice-versa. This effect may occur even when no action or behavior is involved, as Haley seems to imply (Haley, 1976). Secondly, the new label may imply that the symptom is the vehicle of change. Not only may the new label give the client an expectational set for change, but it may also give him a sense of control over his symptom. Landfield's (1975) example of confusion as preparation for new growth is an excellent example in this regard. Finally, relabeling behavior demonstrates the linguistic principle that language is not reality—the map is not the territory (Bandler and Grinder, 1975). In other words, words do not represent an immutable reality. This last point is especially useful to remember when dealing with obsessive-compulsive types. It is also consistent with Kelly's (1955) position that there are many different and workable ways to construe reality.

Paradoxical and family therapists have used relabeling more than any other group of therapists. Haley (1973), for example, suggested that a therapist could relabel a couple's behavior so that they were told they were trying to get closer but going about it poorly. Jackson and Weakland (1971) pointed out how viewing positive behavior as negative could "shake up the system." Satir (1967) also advocated relabeling. More recently, Andolfi (1979) has discussed the importance of redefinition and offered clinical material for exemplification.

Before leaving this section, we would like to point out one important use of relabeling in the early phases of therapy. Families seek therapy because they are experiencing difficulties. This motivation for seeking therapy is negatively motivated, and, thus, the drop-out rate is very high. It is useful in the first session to relabel the family's motivation for therapy (L'Abate, 1975). This relabeling can be achieved by pointing out that only a strong family could admit that it needs help, or that it takes a strong family to admit that it has problems. Additionally, "the care for each other" present in the family could be "proved" by pointing to such facts as the whole family coming together to work on a problem, or finding some things that the members do for each other (e.g., the mother's protectiveness of the identified patient).

Specific vs. General

This last category of paradoxes is something of a catch-all category. Most paradoxes are fairly specific in nature. That is, they are directed toward some specific symptom or context. There are, however, a few relatively standard paradoxes which are general in their application. They are nonspecific and do not contain any specific content which requires understanding the context of the symptom.

Haley (1973) and Watzlawick et al. (1974) described several general paradoxes. Haley (1973), for example, discussed prescribing a relapse and providing a worst alternative. Before prescribing a relapse, the client will show some progress but feel unsure about continued improvement. When a relapse is then prescribed, and if the client has a relapse, it proves the therapist is still in control. If no relapse occurs, it proves the client is in control of his behavior. For example, a couple who had continued to get worse for several months showed a drastic improvement after being placed in a therapeutic double-bind. We immediately expressed our concern that things were going too well, and that in the past such improvement had always been temporary. We expressed serious doubts that their progress would continue.

Haley (1973) also talked about providing a worst alternative to whatever the symptom was or whatever the situation might be. The alternative provided may be anything that the client does not want to do. The general format of such a paradox is "Either you do X or Y." The client is given no choice about whether he does X or Y. A useful variation of this paradox can be used in overcoming resistance of family members. This type of paradox is set up as follows: "I want you (child) to do X. I know you won't like it, but your mother will like it even less."

Watzlawick et al. (1974) described another general technique called "giving in." The client is told to give in to his symptom and then it is prescribed (specific). It is possible to remain at a general level with this technique simply by instructing the client: "I want you to give in to your (name symptom). I want you to do this so we can find out just how bad it is. I want you to count how many times it happens this week." Another technique would be to say: "Your (name symptom) is trying to tell you something important about yourself. I want you to try an experiment. This week just give up trying to stop your (symptom) and observe what is happening just before, during and after your (name symptom). I want a full report next week."

Aside from these three general paradoxes there are a number of other general paradoxical statements which can be employed at various times. They take the form of: "Why should you change a good thing?" "If you must change, do so slowly and cautiously." "Don't change any faster than you can." "You're hopeless, you'll just have to learn to live with this." "Maybe I can help you learn how to live with your (symptom) and maybe even learn to enjoy it." "I'm glad you're not doing anything about (name symptom) right now. If you were to give up (name symptom) what would you do?"

Our experience and the literature show that general paradoxes tend to precede and follow specific paradoxes. General paradoxes may be used in the early stages of therapy when the dynamics of the symptom are not well understood, and after a specific paradox has been given in order to reinforce it (e.g., by prescribing a relapse).

DISCUSSION

The implications of this compilation can be directed toward (a) theory, (b) training, (c) clinical applications and (d) research.

Theoretically, the types of paradoxes can be related to an existentially free and loose, dialectically derived metatheory that conceives reality as paradoxically variable, contradictory and relative. It is this relativity of our perceptions, linguistic habits and attributions that allows us to be paradoxical. Our clients are not coming to see us to get the same interpretations and injunctions they can get from their neighbors. We do need to create an element of surprise and even shock to focus attention and energy in different directions than those already present (Watzlawick, 1976).

Describing different types of paradoxes is important for training purposes. Students and trainees achieve a better understanding of the subtle nuances and differences among possible interpretations, messages and injunctions available to them. The types presented here facilitate understanding and give a clear view of what a therapist is saying and doing when he employs a paradoxical technique. We do, however, want to caution the student learning to use paradoxical methods. First, the student should read several of the basic books about paradox, especially Watzlawick et al.'s (1974) book. The student should also read as many full-length case studies as possible before attempting to work paradoxically (see Papp, 1977). Unless a student has expert supervision, he is likely to make one intervention and then not know how to follow it up. Finally, paradoxical methods should only be used after the student has mastered basic clinical skills and developed clinical sensitivity. Even then, we suggest the beginner find a competent paradoxical supervisor.

Aside from the reasons mentioned above, a paradoxical therapist oftentimes finds himself pitted against a couple or family in a power struggle. Systems of behavior do not relinquish their pathology readily and will defeat the therapist to maintain this homeostatic system. Thus, without supervision the therapist will feel isolated and begin doubting his working method. The consequences can be disastrous for treatment. Students who view paradox as some kind of magical answer eventually abuse it and risk the clients' welfare. Moreover, the use of paradoxical methods for their shock value and the power they promise raises the issue of senseless and unethical manipulation. Paradoxical techniques can be powerfully manipulative just as any other psychotherapeutic technique. They should always be used to enhance the client's growth—not the therapist's status.

The greatest advantage of the description given here is in providing the clinician with a number of categories he can consult in choosing interventions. A description such as this one demystifies paradox. For example, a typical response to reading Haley's *Uncommon Therapy* is, "I could never do that." The techniques appear magical. The types presented in this paper are intended to serve as "mental templates." The emphasis in this paper has been on how to develop paradoxical interventions. There is still a great deal of work to be done in describing when and under what circumstances specific types of paradoxes are appropriate. We also concur with Haley (1976) that paradoxical methods should be used only after more direct or linear methods have failed. Consequently, paradoxical methods are most appropriate with difficult or resistive cases.

Finally, identifying paradoxical types provides a greater degree of specificity which in turn allows for more rigorous and vigorous research. Each type of paradox could and should be studied empirically to assess its effectiveness. At the present time, all of the data supporting the effectiveness of paradoxical methods are anecdotal. While many of the cases are quite dramatic, almost unbelievable, there is no substitute for controlled research where variables such as the placebo effect can be ruled out and maintenance of change over time (follow-up) can be established.

To our knowledge, Wagner, Weeks, and L'Abate (1979) are the only researchers to study the effectiveness of paradoxical messages experimentally. Their study used four groups of nonclinical couples. One group served as a control; another received a structured form of intervention; and the other two groups each received structured intervention, but one group received a direct letter, while the other received a paradoxical letter during treatment. The group which received the paradoxical etters evidenced no more change than the other two experimental groups.

It is clear that the greatest need in the field of paradoxical psychotherapy is empirical research.

REFERENCES

ADLER, A. *Individual Psychology.* Totowa, N.J.: Littlefield, Adams, & Co., 1959.
ANDOLFI, M. Redefinition in family therapy. *American Journal of Family Therapy,* 1979, 7, 5-15.
ANDOLFI, M. and MENGHI, P. La prescrizione in terapia familiare I. *Archivo di Psicologia, Neurologia e Psichiatria,* 1976, 37, 434-456.
ANDOLFI, M. and MENGHI, P. La prescrizione in terapia familiar: II: Il paradosso terapechico. *Archivo di Psicologia, Neurologia e Psichiatria,* 1977, 38, 57-76.
BANDLER, R. and GRINDER, J. *The Structure of Magic,* Vol. I. Palto Alto: Science & Behavior, 1975.
BEAHRS, J. Integrating Erickson's approach. *American Journal of Clinical Hypnosis,* 1977, 20, 55-68.
BOSZORMENYI-NAGY, I. and SPARK, G. *Invisible Loyalties: Reciprocity in Intergenerational Family Therapy.* Hagerstown, Md.: Harper & Row, 1973.
EHRENWALD, G. *Psychotherapy, Myth, and Model.* New York: Grune & Stratton, 1966.
DeSHAZER, S. The confusion technique. *Family Therapy,* 1975, 2, 23-29.
FRANKL, V. *Psychotherapy and Existentialism: Selected Papers on Logotherapy.* New York: Washington Square Press, 1967.
GRINDER, J. and BANDLER, R. *The Structure of Magic,* Vol. II. Palo Alto: Science & Behavior, 1976.
HALEY, J. *Uncommon Therapy.* New York: Ballantine Books, 1973.
HALEY, J. *Problem-Solving Therapy.* San Francisco: Jossey-Bass, 1976.
JACKSON, J. and WEAKLAND, J. Conjoint family therapy: Some considerations on theory, technique, and results. In J. Haley (Ed.), *Changing Families.* New York: Grune & Stratton, 1971.
JAMES, W. *Pragmatism.* New York: World Publishing, 1907.
KELLY, G. *The Psychology of Personal Constructs,* Vol. I and II. New York: Norton, 1955.
KOEN, R. An intra-verbal explication of the nature of metaphor. *Journal of Verbal Learning and Verbal Behavior,* 1965, 4, 129-133.
L'ABATEE, L. A positive approach to marital and familial intervention. In L. R. Wolberg and M. L. Aronson (Eds.), *Group Therapy.* New York: Stratton Intercontinental Medical Books Corp., 1975.
L'ABATE, L. *Understanding and Helping the Individual in the Family.* New York: Grune & Stratton, 1976.
L'ABATE, L. Intimacy is sharing hurt: A reply to David Mace. *Journal of Marriage and Family Counseling,* 1977, 3, 13-16.
L'ABATE, L., WEEKS, G. and WEEKS, K. Protectiveness, persecution, and powerlessness. *International Journal of Family Counseling,* 1977, 5, 72-76.
LANDFIELD, A. The complaint: A confrontation of personal urgency and professional construction. In D. Bannister (Ed.), *Issues and Approaches in Psychological Therapies.* New York: Wiley, 1975.
LENROW, P. The uses of metaphor in facilitating constructive behavior change. *Psychotherapy,* 1966, 3, 145-148.
MINUCHIN, S. *Families and Family Therapy: A Structural Approach.* Boston: Harvard University Press, 1974.
NEWTON, J. R. Therapeutic paradoxes, paradoxical intentions and negative practice. *American Journal of Psychotherapy,* 1968, 22, 68-81.
PAPP, P. The family who had all the answers. In P. Papp (Ed.), *Family Therapy: Full Length Case Studies.* New York: Gardner Press, 1977.
ROSEN, J. *Direct Psychoanalysis.* New York: Grune & Stratton, Inc., 1953.
SATIR, V. *Conjoint Family Therapy.* Palo Alto: Science & Behavior Books, 1967.
SELVINI-PALAZZOLI, M., BOSCOLO, L., CHECCHIN, G. and PRATA, G. *Paradox and Counterparadox.* New York: Brunner/Mazel, 1978.

SOPER, P. and L'ABATE, L. Paradox as a therapeutic technique: A review. *International Journal of Family Counseling*, 1977, 5, 10-21.
STIERLIN, D. *Separating Parents and Adolescents: A Perspective on Running Away, Schizophrenia, and Waywardness.* New York: Quadrangle, 1974.
TENNEN, H. *Perspectives on Paradox: Application and Explanations.* Paper presented at American Psychological Association, San Francisco, August, 1977.
WAGNER, V., WEEKS, G. and L'ABATE, L. Enrichment and written messages with couples. Submitted for publication, 1979.
WATZLAWICK, P. *How Real is Real?* New York: Random House, 1976.
WATZLAWICK, P., BEAVIN, J. H. and JACKSON, D. D. *Pragmatics of Human Communication.* New York: W. W. Norton, 1967.
WATZLAWICK, P., WEAKLAND, J. and FISCH, R. *Change: Principles of Problem Formation and Problem Resolution.* New York: W. W. Norton, 1974.
WEEKS, G. Toward a dialectical approach to intervention. *Human Development*, 1977, 20, 277-292.
WEEKS, G. and L'ABATE, L. A bibliography of paradoxical methods in the psychotherapy of family systems. *Family Process*, 1978, 17, 95-98.
WEEKS, G. and WEEKS, K. Paradoxical psychotherapy as applied dialectics. Unpublished manuscript, Georgia State University, 1978.
WEEKS, G. and WRIGHT, L. Dialectics of the family life cycle. *American Journal of Family Therapy*, 1979, 7, 85-91.

CHAPTER 23

ENRICHMENT AND WRITTEN MESSAGES WITH COUPLES

VICTOR WAGNER, GERALD WEEKS, and LUCIANO L'ABATE

Georgia State University, Atlanta

The field of paradoxical therapy has mushroomed in a variety of conceptual and methodological ways. One of the latest methods is the use of paradoxically worded letters that will be given to couples and families, usually at the outset of therapy. To check on the validity of this approach, 56 couples were evaluated before and after a course of six sessions of marital enrichment. One group received no enrichment. A second group received enrichment. A third group received linearly worded messages at the end of the fourth session of enrichment, while a fourth group received paradoxically worded messages. The effect of these messages on the outcome is analyzed and discussed.

INTRODUCTION

The purpose of this study was to determine whether the use of written statements or letters given to couples participating in marital enrichment would be an effective therapeutic technique and a useful adjunct to marital enrichment. The hypotheses investigated were that, in comparison to a nontreatment control group, groups receiving intervention in the form of enrichment, enrichment plus a direct, straightforward or linear letter, or enrichment plus a paradoxical letter show greater degrees of positive change. However, the primary focus of the present study was to assess the effectiveness of paradoxical letters (Selvini-Palazzoli et al., 1978). Very little empirical research has been conducted on the use of paradoxical messages or letters. In more general terms, the study was designed to assess the effectiveness of paradoxical psychotherapy, since very little empirical work has been conducted on this type of therapy (Weeks and L'Abate, 1978; Soper and L'Abate, 1977).

The use of written communication in therapy is not new (Pearson, 1965). Albert Ellis (1965) serendipitously found that when he wrote down his interpretations for his clients instead of talking (because of laryngitis), his clients seemed to progress faster. He also noted that written communications might facilitate psychotherapy research since the personal influence of the therapist was parcelled out. Burton (1965) considered both the pros and cons of written communication. On the negative side he stated that written interpretation might be:

(a) dissociative, i.e., places emphasis outside therapist-client interaction;
(b) too empathetic of intellectualization rather than feelings;
(c) used uncreatively;
(d) a defense against direct confrontation; or
(e) promoting introspection at times when externalization would be more appropriate.

On the positive side, he felt that written communication could be:

(a) a creative act and a catharsis (if written by the client);
(b) content for further analysis;
(c) more integrative of contextual factors not otherwise considered in therapy;
(d) reductive of time required for treatment if used judiciously; or
(e) used in special emergencies.

In recent years, Selvini-Palazzoli and her co-workers have become the most significant advocates of therapeutic written communication. She and her team of clinicians use paradoxical letters in working with families. They report being tremendously successful with these letters, although no empirical data to support their claims have been presented.

There are a number of reasons for investigating the use of written communications in clinical intervention. First, if anything is worth remembering, it is worth putting in writing. Verbal messages can be forgotten, ignored, repressed, confused, distorted or otherwise belittled and sidetracked. Hence, it may increase the efficiency and effectiveness of therapeutic techniques for feedback to be written. Second, written communications become a record that can be read repeatedly. A letter serves as a reminder of what the family needs to think about or do that might not otherwise be thought of or done. Further, a written communication is the basis on which most adult enterprises operate. It is more binding than a verbal communication. Finally, a written communication may serve as a model of how to state issues in as careful, concise, clear and helpful a fashion as possible.

Because written communications have these characteristics, they may be useful for couples or families in the following ways:

(a) to break impassive or repetitively destructive patterns not otherwise breakable;
(b) to confront issues not otherwise confrontable, especially when lack of awareness, externalization, denial and avoidance are present;
(c) to specify and crystallize vague and unclear issues; and
(d) to depersonalize the emotionality surrounding any issue the family might face.

The medium chosen to test the effectiveness of written communication, i.e., linear and paradoxical letters, was marital enrichment. L'Abate (1974) defined enrichment as "a process of intervention based on prearranged programmed lessons and exercises dealing with interpersonal relations between and among family members. The emphasis of this process is on the systematic arrangement of exercises and lessons in a gradual sequence that is assumed to be helpful and beneficial to the family or to family members." It is neither education, nor therapy, nor just an intellectual exercise. Enrichment differs from therapy in that it is structured, prearranged, can be administered to nonclinical couples or families and can be applied by individuals with lower levels of training than that of a therapist. The model is essentially preventive and is based on the assumption that families "learn by doing." The programs are designed to enhance overall potential and are not designed to alleviate any particular problem or symptom as in therapy.

L'Abate (1977) reviewed a number of studies on the effectiveness of structured marital enrichment and concluded that most were impressionistic and subjective. While most of the studies he reviewed found that enrichment produces favorable results, they took place under noncontrolled conditions and did not measure outcome objectively. An exception was a study conducted by Wildman (1977). Wildman found that the use of structured marital enrichment programs developed by L'Abate et al. (1975) was effective in improving marital relationships. In his study, he compared a control group, an enrichment group and a therapy group. There was a significant and positive difference between the control group and the enrichment group but not between the enrichment group and the therapy group. He concluded that both enrichment and therapy are effective forms of intervention—a finding consistent with Gurman (1973) and Beck (1975). His most dramatic finding was that therapy was no more effective than enrichment. Wildman also found that his control group made no increases, in fact decreased slightly, on pre- vs. post-assessment.

Wagner (1977) conducted a study which extended Wildman's research. Since one of the primary goals of enrichment is to improve communication, Wagner investigated the use of written homework assignments designed to enhance communication. In addition to improving communication skills, structural communication training has also been shown to enhance self-concept, increase self-acceptance and improve the marital relationship in general (Miller et al., 1976; Olson, 1976).

Wagner compared four groups of couples. One group was a control; one group received written homework assignments and instructions on effective communication, but no enrichment; one group was simply enriched; and one group received enrichment, written homework assignments and instructions on effective communication. The results showed that the couples who received written assignments evidenced the highest degree of positive change, with the enrichment plus the assignment group showing the greatest improvement.

The present research focused on two types of letters. One type is called a linear letter. These letters are written in a straighforward style that is easy to understand. They serve as direct feedback to the couple, much like the verbal feedback given by insight-oriented therapists. These letters reflect the couple's behavior as seen by the intervener.

The other type of letter is known as paradoxical. Paradoxical letters are much more complex and difficult to compose. They derive from paradoxical psychotherapy. Paradoxical approaches to therapy are fairly recent (Haley, 1973, 1976; Watzlawick et al., 1967, 1974; Weeks and L'Abate, 1978). Paradoxical therapists employ therapeutic double-binds or pragmatic injunctions to change behavior. The emphasis is on actions rather than words. The paradoxical therapist essentially prescribes the behavior causing the problem. For example, a classical prescription is "be spontaneous." It is impossible to act on this command because the behavior would no longer be spontaneous. According to L'Abate (1975), the paradoxical approach to psychotherapy implies a paradoxical view of behavior; i.e., behavior is multidetermined and has multiple meanings or possible interpretations (e.g., one person's trash is another's treasure). Thus, whether a behavior is seen as positive or negative is arbitrary; it depends on the frame of reference. In order to change behavior, it may be necessary to change the frame of reference (Haley, 1976). Thus, strengths may be interpreted as weaknesses and vice versa (Weeks, 1977).

Writing Paradoxical Letters

Since enrichers are usually paraprofessionals or beginning graduate students, the letters given to the couple should be written under supervision. The letter should not be too long—never more than a page—and it should consist of no more than two or three major points. Each point should consist of one major asset accompanied by the liability or "flip side" of the asset. If no such connection is apparent, then the asset should be listed early in the letter and "what concerns" the enricher or "what they question," "muse," "wonder about," etc. listed in the latter half, as issues for the couple to consider. Each member of the couple or family should receive a copy of the letter addressed as a personal letter. Numerous examples of these letters may be found in L'Abate (1977).

A paradoxical letter is constructed within a paradoxical frame of reference. Thus, it (a) is cryptic in nature; (b) is not prescriptive; and (c) deals with different levels of behavior and focuses on specific genotypes or underlying issues. First, the letter should possess a certain degree of cryptic obscurity, in the sense that it raises more questions than it answers. If the letter were clear and direct, the couple could easily put it aside. However, its incompleteness in terms of meaning forces the couple to think about it more actively. Second, the letter should not contain prescriptive directions (shoulds or oughts), since these could be easily construed as judgmental or evaluative. Third, the letter should discriminate between the presentational (facade), phenotypical (most frequent mode of interacting) and genotypical (underlying, inferred) levels of behavior.

The connections and relationships between these differing and sometimes contradictory levels of behavior are pondered in the letter (e.g., anger vs. hurt, caring vs. protection). Moreover, issues which occur at the genotypical level need to be focused on, since they are underlying and appear to be fairly universal. Some of these genotypic patterns include an emphasis on externals to avoid looking at self, an emphasis on thinking to avoid feeling, and an emphasis on digital thinking (i.e., on-off, black-white, true-false, good-bad, right-wrong) to avoid the complexity of increased choice and possibility. These issues should be raised in a cryptic manner. Finally, the messages in the letter should be *ad* relationship rather than *ad hominem*. That is, the letter should be systemically oriented.

It might also be noted that our letters are descriptive and not prescriptive in the sense that paradoxical therapists use. However, we recognize that to some extent all descriptions are also prescriptions (Weeks and L'Abate, 1979).

In order to demonstrate what we mean by linear and paradoxical letters, one linear and one paradoxical letter are included here.

A Linear Letter

Dear .... :

I have really enjoyed these sessions with you and am quite fond of you both. You have a good sense of humor and care a lot about how the other acts and feels. You both seem to be working on communicating effectively with each other.

I have the impression, though, that sometimes you focus on money problems to avoid confronting issues more sensitive to you both. When you blame or put each other down and fail to deal with issues directly, communication and growth of the relationship remain at a standstill. Just because one of you behaves in a hurtful way, it does not justify the other one's behaving in a similar way.

Although you do seem to have a lot of commitment in this relationship, you tend to use your friends to escape from marital responsibilities. By making your friends more important than your marriage, your involvement with them detracts from your relationship with your partner. I think you have to decide between whether you want to be married or whether you want to remain single.

Sincerely,

A Paradoxical Letter

Dear ....:

I am very impressed with your commitment to your marriage and how much you care for each other. Each of you is very considerate of the other's feelings, and you do not wish to hurt each other.

I think that it's very commendable that you care for each other so much that you try to be like your partner. Each of you can depend on the other to avoid confronting your differences. This has allowed you to achieve a harmonious relationship which would be too risky to change right now. Why tamper with a good thing?

Sincerely,

METHOD

Subjects

Fifty-six married couples participated in the study. All subjects were nonclinical volunteers drawn from introductory psychology courses who needed credit for participating in psychology experiments. The population is defined as nonclinical since none of the couples included in the study were asking for help in the form of enrichment or therapy. There were: 1) 14 couples in the control group; 2) 14 couples in the enrichment group; 3) 14 couples in an enrichment group who received linear letters; and 4) 14 couples in an enrichment group who received paradoxical letters.

Assessment

The following techniques were utilized on a pre- and postintervention basis:

1) *Revised Marital Happiness Scale.* This inventory is a modification of the Marital Happiness Scale (Azrin et al., 1973) and it allows the subjects to rate their spouses' satisfaction as well as their own, providing additional scales to rate satisfaction on specific aspects of the couple's sexual adjustment.
2) *Marital Progress Sheet.* This form is used by the subjects to rate their degree of satisfaction (on a one to ten scale) with 18 aspects of their life situation and marital and family relationships.
3) *Communication Reaction Form.* This device asks subjects to rate their degree of satisfaction with ten aspects of communication behaviors in the

marriage. As with all of the other instruments utilized in this investigation, the ratings were done on a one to ten scale. These ten dimensions are explained in detail for the subject in a sheet entitled, "Communication Behaviors," which supplements the Communication Reaction Form.

Procedure

Enrichment sessions as well as testing sessions were conducted either in the Family Study Center at Georgia State University or in the home of the couple. Arrangements were made to accommodate the needs of the enrichers as well as the enrichees. The enrichers were graduate students enrolled at Georgia State University. Different couples had different enrichers but a given enricher remained with the couple from pretest through posttest. Likewise, the group which did not receive enrichment was evaluated by the same individual on pre- and posttesting.

The programs used in enrichment were drawn from a manual of enrichment programs written by the author and his students (L'Abate et al., 1975), which contains a variety of programs. The enricher, the couple and the enrichment supervisor worked at selecting the program most suitable to each couple's needs and desires. Typically the enrichers and supervisor would select three programs that were appropriate for the couple. The enricher would then briefly describe these programs to the couple and give them the choice of selecting the program they felt best suited their needs.

Enrichment programs consist of six structured lessons. Each program has its own central theme such as negotiation, conflict resolution, assertiveness training, clarification of sexual attitudes, etc. Each lesson explores a particular aspect of the theme, building on the lesson of the previous week.

The two groups that received letters were given them at the conclusion of the fourth enrichment session. Each spouse would be handed a letter in a sealed envelope as the enricher departed. The letter was delivered as part of an agreement made at the beginning of enrichment. The letters would be discussed in a follow-up session if the couple were interested, otherwise this communication was not specifically discussed. Couples who wanted to respond to the letter earlier were allowed to do so, but the enricher would remain neutral and avoid discussing the letter until follow-up.

RESULTS

Total scores for each of the three instruments were obtained for each couple by summing the rating each couple produced on the individual scales on each test. This procedure was followed for the instruments administered both at pre- and posttesting. Missing data throughout the study was accounted for by prorating to obtain the total scores.

A mean couple change score was computed for each group on each individual instrument as well as on the total battery by subtracting pre- vs. postscores. An analysis of variance was then performed on the change scores for the four groups on each scale separately as well as on the total battery change scores. Analysis of variance on the Revised Marital Happiness Scale approached significance with an F probability of .055. The majority of the variance coming from Group 3. Analysis of variance on the Communication Reaction Form was significant at the .044 level with the major part of the variance coming from Group 2. Analysis of variance on the Marital Progress Sheet showed no trend toward significance. The analysis of variance on the Revised Marital Happiness Scale approached significance with an F F probability of .067 obtaining with the major part of the variance coming from Group 3.

A chi square analysis was computed by separating the couples into two groups on the basis of their improvement in comparison to the median change score (13.5) for all couples in the study. Couples with change scores above the median were classified as most improved while couples below the median were classified as least improved. A 2 × 4 chi square analysis of improvement × group was then computed but was not significant. Treatment groups 2, 3, and 4 were then collapsed into one

TABLE ONE

Summary Data for Each Group on All Scales

	Mean/ Standard Deviation	Group I Males	Group I Females	Group II Males	Group II Females	Group III Males	Group III Females	Group IV Males	Group IV Females
Revised Marital Happiness Scale									
Pretest	M	259.57	264.38	251.93	260.14	212.64	219.20	237.21	252.20
	S.D.	38.16	55.57	33.16	39.29	46.14	40.20	44.40	45.36
Posttest	M	263.71	257.64	263.14	268.07	234.50	244.14	247.93	260.02
	S.D.	48.58	54.60	25.05	34.39	43.47	32.13	45.08	36.71
Marital Progress									
Pretest	M	151.36	150.64	151.43	153.43	132.00	131.14	137.07	139.00
	S.D.	20.62	23.49	12.16	15.87	19.56	19.08	26.97	25.67
Posttest	M	151.29	148.07	150.57	156.38	138.21	139.07	134.79	148.79
	S.D.	21.58	26.50	9.91	14.52	21.95	19.38	31.75	27.76
Communication Reaction Form									
Pretest	M	81.07	76.43	75.14	73.43	68.14	70.43	73.64	75.21
	S.D.	11.69	12.28	12.36	15.45	11.64	11.37	14.05	12.35
Posttest	M	80.71	71.14	79.64	82.93	71.00	75.50	72.29	78.64
	S.D.	14.24	18.31	7.67	8.86	8.95	9.34	13.42	9.30

group, and a 2 × 2 chi square of most improved-least improved by treatment vs. no treatment was computed. The computed chi square value was 3.84 and was significant at the .05 level.

DISCUSSION

The significant results obtained in the chi square analysis as well as the trend toward significance in the analysis of variance of total battery change scores indicate that intervention did bring about positive change. When these results are viewed in the context of Wildman's (1977) study and those reviewed by L'Abate (1977), they suggest that inexpensive marital enrichment is useful for couples. In addition, the large mean change score for couples in Group 3 (enrichment plus linear letters) on the Revised Marital Happiness Scale and on the total battery change scores suggests that written communication in the form of linear letters may be a useful adjunct to enrichment.

A primary purpose of this research was to study empirically the effectiveness of paradoxical psychotherapy, since very little research has been conducted in this area (Weeks and L'Abate, 1978). The only other empirical study conducted on paradoxical treatment did not support its hypothesized superior effectiveness (Fulchiero, 1976). Likewise, the present study did not demonstrate the superiority of paradoxical interventions over more traditional linear interventions. Although the group receiving paradoxical letters as an adjunct to enrichment did evidence an overall positive pre and post mean change score, this overall mean change was below that obtained by both the enrichment plus linear letters group and the group receiving only enrichment.

The empirical evidence from the present study is in contrast to the strong clinical evidence of the positive effects of paradoxical letters (Selvini-Palazzoli et al., 1978; L'Abate, 1977). For example, L'Abate (1977) have observed reactions ranging from explosion of affect to strong verbal denials to simple verbal compliance with behavioral changes. They have concluded that couples or families who agree with the letters tend not to change, while those who disagree with the letters evidence the most change.

It is quite possible that the clinical observations of L'Abate (1977) on the effectiveness of paradoxical interventions are not contradictory to the results obtained in this study. In the attempt to provide empirical verification for paradoxical interventions, the instruments used to assess change required each spouse to rate various areas of their marriage. They did not ask about specific symptoms or problem areas toward which a letter may be directed. These instruments are very linear and direct in the information that they capture; however, in assessing the effectiveness of a nonlinear, indirect form of intervention, it is possible that these scales missed the mark.

The present study supports the utility of marital enrichment as an effective intervention technique with couples and indicates that linear letters can enhance the enrichment process. It is possible that these more linear forms of intervention can be assessed more effectively by the instruments used to measure change in this study than can change induced through the paradoxical letters. It is suggested that future research should use a larger sample size, include clinical as well as nonclinical couples, and assess symptom resolution or severity in more couple-specific ways.

REFERENCES

AZRIN, N. H., NASTER, B. J., and JONES, R. Reciprocity counseling: a rapid learning-based procedure for marital counseling. *Behavior Research and Therapy*, 1973, 11, 365-382.

BECK, D. Research findings on the outcomes of marital counseling. *Social Casework*, 1975, 56, 153-181.

BURTON, A. The use of written productions in psychotherapy. In L. Pearson (Ed.), *The Use of Written Communication in Psychotherapy*. Springfield, IL: C. C Thomas, 1965.

ELLIS, A. The use of printed, written, and recorded words in psychotherapy. In L. Pearson (Ed.), *The Use of Written Communication in Psychotherapy*. Springfield, IL: C. C Thomas, 1965.

FULCHIERO, C. Evaluation of a therapeutic paradox technique in brief psychotherapy. *Dissertation Abstracts International*, 1976, 26 (8-B), 4153.

GURMAN, A. The effects and effectiveness of marital therapy: A review of outcome research. *Family Process*, 1973, 12, 145-170.

HALEY, J. *Uncommon Therapy*. New York: Ballantine Books, 1973.

HALEY, J. *Problem-Solving Therapy*. San Francisco: Jossey-Bass, 1976.

L'ABATE, L. Family enrichment programs. *Journal of Family Counseling*, 1974, 2, 32-38.

L'ABATE, L. A positive approach to marital and familial intervention. In L. R. Wolberg and

M. L. Aronson (Eds.), *Group Therapy—1975—An Overview*. New York: Stratton Intercontinental Medical Books Corp., 1975.

L'ABATE, L. *Enrichment: Structured Interventions with Couples, Families, and Groups* Washington, D.C.: University Press of America, 1977.

L'ABATE, L. and collaborators. *Manual: Enrichment Programs for the Family Life Cycle.* Atlanta, GA: Social Research Laboratories, 1975.

MILLER, S., NUNNALLY, E., and WOCKMAN, D. Minnesota couples communication program: Premarital and marital groups. In D. H. Olson (Ed.), *Treating Relationships.* Lake Mills, IA: Graphic Publishing Co., 1976 .

OLSON, D. *Treating Relationships.* Lake Mills, IA: Graphic Publishing Co., 1976.

PEARSON, L. (Ed.). *The Use of Written Communication in Psychotherapy.* Springfield, IL: Thomas, 1965.

SELVINI-PALAZZOLI, M., BOSCOLO, L., CECCHIN, G., and PRATA, G. *Paradox and Counterparadox.* New York: Aronson, 1978.

SOPER, P. and L'ABATE, L. Paradox as a therapeutic technique: A review. *International Journal of Family Counseling*, 1977, 5, 10-21.

WAGNER, V. Enrichment and written homework assignments with couples. In L. L'Abate, *Enrichment: Structured Interventions with Couples, Families, and Groups.* Washington, D.C.: University Press of America, 1977.

WATZLAWICK, P., BEAVIN, J., and JACKSON, D. *Pragmatics of Human Communication.* New York: Norton, 1967.

WATZLAWICK, P., WEAKLAND, J., and FISCH, R. *Change: Principles of Problem Formation and Problem Resolution.* New York: Norton, 1974.

WEEKS, G. Toward a dialectical approach to intervention. *Human Development*, 1977, 20, 277-292.

WEEKS, G. and L'ABATE, L. A bibliography of paradoxical methods in the psychotherapy of family systems. *Family Process*, 1978, 17, 95-98.

WEEKS, G. R. and L'ABATE, L. A compilation of paradoxical methods. *American Journal of Family Therapy*, 1979, 7, 61-76.

WILDMAN, R. Structured versus unstructured marital intervention. In L. L'Abate (Ed.), *Enrichment: Structured Interventions with Couples, Families, and Groups.* Washington, D.C.: University Press of America, 1977.

CHAPTER 24

The Use of Paradox With Children in an Inpatient Treatment Setting

ED JESSEE, M.A.[†]
LUCIANO L'ABATE, PH.D.[‡]

This paper illustrates with case examples the use of paradoxical procedures in a child inpatient treatment center. Indications and contraindications for this type of intervention are discussed.

THE USE OF PARADOX in psychotherapy can frequently produce marked changes in behavior (2, 3, 6). It is of particular interest, therefore, that the literature contains no mention of paradoxical procedures on inpatient child units (7, 9). The conscious and strategic use of paradox can not only change a child's behavior but also change systemic interaction around him. In fact, paradox seems to have several definite advantages that offset the chronic difficulties found within an inpatient child setting.

One of the problems in working with children is that insight and the verbal aspect of therapy are usually restricted by the child's developmental-cognitive capacity. Paradoxical interventions require limited verbal ability and insight, are normally short-term, can include an interactional perspective, and seem to work very well with oppositional individuals. Therefore, the use of paradoxical interventions, as described below, might well be the treatment of choice in many instances in an inpatient setting.

[†] Ph.D. candidate, Family Studies Program, Psychology Department, Georgia State University, Atlanta, Georgia.
[‡] Professor of Psychology and Director, Family Studies Program, Psychology Department, Georgia State University, Atlanta, Georgia.

Case 1: To Catch a Thief

History of the Problem

Billy, age 11, was a rather overweight, immature child, the youngest of three children. He was hospitalized following repeated instances of stealing resulting in several juvenile court appearances. Both of his older siblings had been in continual difficulties with the law—the oldest sibling being in jail at the time of Billy's hospitalization. The father worked the graveyard shift at a local machinery plant and slept during the day, thus having minimal contact with the family. The mother stayed at home and reportedly had been depressed for many years. The mother usually handled all matters concerning Billy, except when he was caught stealing. At that point, the mother and father would get together, and the father would discipline Billy. Interestingly, the objects of Billy's thefts were machines very similar to the ones his father made at work.

Treatment

Soon after hospitalization Billy began to develop warm, nurturant relationships with female staff but had difficulty getting close to male staff, although he clearly desired to do so. After several weeks I was able to establish a close emotional relationship with him, and we spent much enjoyable time together playing. However, the splintered family situation, and the child's difficulties in relating to other male staff persisted. Finally, after several weeks we decided to try a tactic that would produce some change in this stalemated situation. The treatment team met with Billy and explained to him that we finally realized what a difficult time he had letting us know when he wanted to spend time with us. Therefore, from now on when he wished to spend some enjoyable time with one of the male staff he could let us know by "taking" (his language for stealing) a machinery magazine that we would leave on the counter. We also told Billy that when he took the magazine we would first have to meet with female staff members to discuss the situation, and only afterward could we get together. Furthermore, we congratulated Billy for giving male and female staff a chance to get together, since we were normally so busy that we didn't have time to talk to each other.

Billy's initial reaction to our proposal was one of astonishment and confusion—"Why are you going to do that?" After a few minutes he began to get angry and refused to follow through with the task, even though he had earlier agreed. Billy never did do the task, but he also never stole again. The following week Billy and his father spent an afternoon together for the first time in years. The next week when Billy's mother came in, she reported feeling better than she had in weeks and exhibited a much brighter affect. Billy was discharged shortly thereafter, and at follow-up several months later was functioning well and had not engaged in any stealing.

Case 2: The Protector

History of the Problem

Timmy, age 10, was a bright, physically well-developed child. He was the older of two children, with a brother age 6. Timmy was hospitalized because of his "hyperactiveness" and the family's inability to handle him. The parents reported a history of behavioral problems, including inattentiveness and misbehavior at school, defiance in speech and actions at home, and arguments and fights with peers. The mother stated that Timmy fought with her more often than with his father. The younger son was reported to be a model child. During the family sessions the parents were unable to express anger toward each other and virtually did not speak to each other. The father was rational and controlled in his speech. The mother would become embroiled in arguing with Timmy in the sessions, but the father denied all emotions—especially anger. At home, the mother would deal with Timmy's misbehavior until she became totally frustrated. Then the father would be called in, and after the mother had explained the difficulty, the father would dole out punishment.

Treatment

After hospitalization Timmy quickly became embroiled in arguments with staff and peers and in general was defiant in school and on the unit. Several weeks of individual and group therapy did not seem to be helping to change Timmy's behavior. Finally we decided to prescribe the symptom to Timmy in hopes of enabling him to get an experiential understanding of the function of his behavior in the family. A new female staff member had just started working and she and Timmy had begun arguing almost from the moment they met. He said that this staff member reminded him of his mother. We asked Timmy to help us out. We explained that we were very worried about the new staff member because she seemed depressed much of the time and was having difficulty deciding if she should stay with us or find another job. However, we observed that when Timmy misbehaved in front of her, she became so involved with him that she forgot how bad she felt and eventually had to come to us for some help.

Consequently, we asked Timmy to help us out by misbehaving in front of the female staff member whenever he thought she was depressed. We stressed the fact that he was the only one who could help and that if he refused to help we would be powerless to help her.

Timmy's reaction to the task was one of blatant anger. He violently refused the task and became extremely angry with us. Two days later during family conference the parents were again talking about Timmy's misbehavior and his inability to control it when Timmy spoke up and said, "The only reason I misbehave is to keep you together. I've heard you talk about getting a divorce. Everytime I fight with Joey (his little brother) or something, you both yell at me instead of each other." Both parents responded by denying the accuracy of Timmy's statements. However, he then began to talk about heretofore unmentionable family secrets, such as his mother's running away and hiding in the woods for a day. This development in the session allowed a shift to be made from Timmy's behavior to the marriage. After this session, Timmy's behavioral problems diminished both on the unit and at home. Two weeks later Timmy was discharged, but the family continued in therapy.

Case 3: Accidents Will Happen

Background History

Jimmy was a thin, small boy of 11 years. He was hospitalized following the accidental shooting death of his younger brother. For several years prior to this incident, however, Jimmy had been involved in dangerous and destructive play, such as breaking the windows of his home. These incidents typically occurred when no one was at home, and frequently the events were called "accidents" by Jimmy. Jimmy's father was a firm, stern man who tolerated "no nonsense," whereas the mother was tremendously distraught over the situation and blamed herself for Jimmy's actions.

Following intensive work in individual and group therapy dealing with the guilt over the accident and the grief of losing his brother, a curious pattern began to develop. Jimmy began having a large number of "accidents." At first, the accidents involved Jimmy's hurting himself by tripping, falling down, running into things, etc. Gradually, the accidents began to involve others, such as hitting a peer with a ball, tripping others, and saying offensive things to peers. Interestingly, these "accidents" seemed to occur when the patient was angry.

Treatment

The decision was made to deal with this new pattern of behavior by encouraging it. Jimmy was encouraged to have at least two accidents a day. "Accidents will happen, so we might as well try to learn to control them." Jimmy was informed also that it was my hunch that the accidents would most likely happen when he was feeling angry, "But of course, you're not expected to understand that yet." Jimmy was confused by this task but agreed to go ahead with it anyway. Within three days the accidents had disappeared completely. Also, Jimmy began responding to attempts to have him verbalize and express his anger in appropriate ways. Only two more accidents occurred during the remaining months's hospitalization.

Discussion

An interesting common denominator in most of these cases was the initial occurrence of anger on the child's part when the paradoxical prescription was given. Selvini Palazzoli et al. (5) report a common reaction of rage and anger by autistic children when the family was given an effective written paradoxical prescription. Thus, it is quite possible that the child's expression of anger is a favorable sign for the occurrence of change in the family system and therefore should be encouraged rather than inhibited. This appears to be an issue in need of further investigation.

Numerous specific behavioral problems as well as systems dynamics can be effectively dealt with through paradoxical tasks and prescriptions. One of the most effective tactics has been the use of "the winner's bet." In this instance the inappropriate behavior is verbally acknowledged, and a bet is made with the child that he will continue to act inappropriately since he obviously has no control over it. In addition to predicting the behavior, the bet is set up so that if the child does not misbehave he wins the object of the bet. If the person the child is betting against (the therapist) wins, the child must teach the therapist how he goes about misbehaving. Thus, if the child wins he has exhibited control over his behavior—which he has usually denied. If the therapist wins, the child must show how and under what circumstances he misbehaves. In doing so the child is required to think about what he is doing in a manner that detaches himself from the problem and gives new meaning to the behavior, thus allowing insight and awareness into his difficulty. No matter how the bet turns out, both the therapist and the patient ultimately win. This playful procedure has proved to be extremely effective and popular with competitive children.

A common problem on any inpatient child unit is peer conflict. In most cases the situation can be dealt with in a reasonable, logical, straightforward manner. Often behavioral contracts work very well in controlling the behavior. However, in many instances none of the above procedures work, regardless of the child's good intentions. The child frequently feels he has no control over actions and reactions with his peers. One procedure currently being tested involves giving perpetually argumentative roommates the task of arguing with each other. Each child is told he has a two-part task. The first part is to try to start an argument with his peer once daily on purpose. The second part of the task is for each child to try to figure out when the other child is trying to start an argument on purpose. Thus, each child is forced to analyze how the other child acts to set him up for an argument, as well as how he would act in order to start an argument with his peer. Again, this type of playful paradox is popular with children when framed in an understandable manner and, so far, seems to be effective. Our current evaluation indicates that within two days after the initiation of the task verbal conflict diminishes significantly below the pretask baseline.

A final general procedure that has also proved to be very effective is the concept of reframing the child's behavior in a way that makes sense out of the child's confusion about why he does what he does and, in addition, gives his actions a positive connotation. Similar to the problem-maintaining solution of the Palo Alto group (8), this type of strategy short-circuits the process that is perpetuating the problem. For instance, when a child first comes to the hospital he suffers from "homesickness" and is unable to sleep his first night away from home. One effective means of approaching this difficulty is to label the child's staying up as love and devotion to his parents and to assure the child that his parents would be very proud of him for demonstrating his caring so convincingly. The child is then encouraged to stay up until he feels like he has shown enough caring for his parents. This behavior, then, reassures the child he is cared for by his parents, labels the distress as a positive expression, and prescribes the symptom in a manner that obviates the need for it. This type of procedure has been found effective with various behavioral difficulties.

The above cases have illustrated how paradoxical procedures can be effective on an inpatient child unit. It should be remembered that from a systems viewpoint, by virtue of hospitalizing the identified patient, effective treatment is often limited or delayed in that the hospitalization of an identified patient protects and solidifies the family homeostasis. Therefore, framing the problem as a transactional one involving all members of the family frequently is difficult. As a result, many of the procedures outlined were designed to deal with and change the family system yet were implemented with only part of the family system present. The process of change then becomes more difficult but, as has been discussed, not impossible. Invariably the family system is perpetuated on the unit, thus allowing the unit system to both replicate a family and to serve as a prototype for change in the family. The crucial variable is interdicting the present problem-solving solution of the child.

Because paradox can be an extremely powerful intervention, it is important to have an understanding of when it is most applicable and least applicable, especially with impressionable children. If defiance is high, particularly with children who seem unable to tolerate being helped, paradoxical techniques might be considered the first line of approach (4). Paradoxical strategies would then be used with the expectation that the patient would rebel or react against the prescription. Compliance-based paradoxical strategies can also be very effective (4). These strategies are based on the premise that by attempting to comply with a paradoxical prescription to continue the symptom the patient will change and the symptom will cease. For example, in the case of psychosomatic headache, the therapist may prescribe that the child have headaches for an hour each day at the same time. Complying with the task implies that the child has control over his symptom. Thus he must either comply and admit control of his disorder or cease having symptoms during the prescribed time. Generally, our experience has been that the child gives up his symptom rather than admit control of it. This approach is particularly effective with somatic complaints, depressions, and phobias.

Perhaps the most important question to be addressed is when not to use paradox. Paradoxical strategies with children are usually inappropriate in situations of intense crisis. For instance, paradoxical directives given during an acute grief reaction to a death or divorce of parents could be devastatingly destructive. Paradoxes are effective with fairly normal and intact individuals. It could be inappropriate to deliver such injunctions to disorganized or mentally retarded individuals. In these cases, children are more available to direct, straightforward influence that offers structure, control, and stability. Finally, paradoxes must always be framed within the reality of the child to maximize effectiveness. Bandler and Grinder (1) eloquently discuss the concept of the client's reality. Basically, the reframing of the problem must be accomplished in a manner that the child understands and sees as part of his world. If abstract rationale or language that is not understandable is used, the child is likely not to react to the double-binding aspect of the directive and will go ahead and do what is asked in the paradox. This seems to be a particularly difficult problem with very young children, primarily under five years of age, because of developmental deficits in cognitive understanding. It should be remembered that if a paradoxical strategy can be powerful in its effectiveness, it can be equally powerful in a destructive manner.

When paradoxical intervention is used appropriately on an inpatient child unit, it can have several advantages. First, systemic paradoxical interventions, such as those cited in these case studies, can induce quick problem resolution. If the presenting problem is solved the child can usually be discharged to at least an outpatient status, thus avoiding much of the detrimental effects of long-term hospitalization. Second, paradoxical intervention enables the child and family to assume responsibility for change. The therapist receives little credit because the child has not complied with the therapist's requests. Therefore, change occurs and must be attributed to the child himself. Enabling the child to feel solely responsible for the change undoubtedly increases his self-esteem and ability to control his behavior. Third, by focusing on problems rather than diagnoses, the child is allowed to feel more "normal" and less "sick." If a child is considered in terms of "intrapsychic pathology," as is the case in most traditional child settings, it is inevitable that the child will think that something "bad" is indeed wrong with him and behave accordingly. However, if the problem is seen as just that, a simple problem that involves the system, the child does not have to feel solely responsible and his role can be "normalized." Finally, the child loses his role as identified patient in the family, if: (a) the problem is resolved; (b) the child is subsequently discharged; and (c) a change is made within the family system. Paradoxical intervention used effectively in a systemic manner achieves, or at least fosters, these goals.

Conclusion

As is true with any treatment approach, the use of paradox is not a panacea for all ills. When used appropriately, however, and framed within the reality of the child, it can be a powerful and effective tool. Although the use of paradox on an inpatient child unit has previously been unaddressed, it is the contention of this paper that paradoxically induced changes within the unit system can have profound influence on the individual child and his approach to problem-solving.

REFERENCES

1. BANDLER, R., and GRINDER, J., *The Structure of Magic*, vol. 1, Palo Alto, Science and Behavior, 1975.
2. HALEY, J., *Uncommon Therapy*, New York, Ballantine Books, 1973.
3. HARE-MUSTIN, R., "Treatment of Temper Tantrums by Paradoxical Intervention," *Fam. Proc.* 14: 481–486, 1975.
4. ROHRBAUGH, M.; TENNEN, H.; PRESS, S.; WHITE, L.; RASKIN, P.; and PICKERING, M. R., "Paradoxical Strategies in Psychotherapy," Paper presented at the American Psychological Association, San Francisco, 1977.
5. SELVINI PALAZZOLI, M.; BOSCOLO, L.; CECHIN, G.; and PRATA, G., *Paradox and Counterparadox*, New York, Jason Aronson, 1978.
6. SOLYOM, L.; GARZA-PEREZ, J.; LEDWIDGE, B. L.; and SOLYOM, C., Paradoxical Intention in the Treatment of Obsessive Thoughts: A Pilot Study," *Compr. Psychiat.* 13: 291–297, 1972.
7. SOPER, P. H., and L'ABATE, L. "Paradox as a Therapeutic Technique: A Review," *Int. J. Family Therapy* 5: 10–21, 1977.
8. WATZLAWICK, P.; WEAKLAND, J.; and FISCH, R., *Change: Principles of Problem Formation and Problem Resolution*, New York, W. W. Norton, 1974.
9. WEEKS, G., and L'ABATE, L., "A Bibliography of Paradoxical Methods in Psychotherapy of Family Systems," *Fam. Proc.* 17: 95–98, 1978.

Reprint requests should be addressed to Ed Jessee, M.A., Psychology Department, Georgia State University, Atlanta, Georgia 30303.

CHAPTER 25

COPING WITH DEFEATING PATTERNS IN FAMILY THERAPY

Luciano L'Abate*
(Georgia State University)

Lynette Farr
(Cobb County Juvenile Court)

ABSTRACT

Families engaged in family therapy exhibit defeating patterns in order to remain together unchanged in the face of external threats to homeostasis. A variety of defeating patterns are outlined and a variety of letters written to deal with these patterns are presented. The possibility of using these letters in a pre-programmed fashion is briefly discussed.

One of the major issues of family therapy is coping with *defeating patterns,* that is, how family members defeat each other as well as the therapist. It is important to deal with these patterns by recognizing: a) how and what patterns are used to defeat; b) their function in family homeostasis; and c) what therapists can do about them. It is the purpose of this paper to consider all three areas, hoping to expand this analysis to our failures rather than our successes. The literature is replete with successful cases. It takes a very courageous and strong therapist to use failures to improve his or her therapeutic functioning—as illustrated in the detailed and painstaking analysis made by Selvini-Palazzoli (1974) to switch from an individual/psychodynamic model to a systemic one. *Failures are our negative feedback.* It is on the basis of this feedback that we can improve our practices.

PATTERNS OF DEFEAT IN FAMILIES

There are many ways in which families defeat themselves and us. Among them we can consider just a few that we have found difficult to deal with.

1. *Excessive fighting and bickering:* This can be intensive and last a long period of time, dealing with almost any issue, even though most of the bickering could be reduced to issues of power and control. It is especially present in families with teenagers and it represents a level

*Reprint requests to Luciano L'Abate, Department of Psychology, Georgia State University, University Plaza, Atlanta, Georgia 30303

of deterioration that has escalated over years, since the time both spouses started agreeing to disagree and essentially established a reactive marital relationship based on sameness-oppositeness (L'Abate, 1976).

Example

One family entered counseling because of the extremely defiant attitude of their youngest daughter who was 15. Mother and father were in their early 40's and had three other children, one son aged 18 who lived at home and another older son and daughter, who were married and lived away from home.

Excessive fighting and bickering occurred each time the daughter was expected to comply with the rules of her parents. It seemed that mother and daughter were always and most intensely involved in a power struggle which generally escalated until father entered the picture. Since father had had two coronaries, mother and daughter temporarily would stop the fight—which by this time had usually reached proportions of a physical brawl. Mother was in charge of discipline. It seemed that mother and father had agreed that mother would assume the heavier, more responsible role while father would be the nicer, more passive parent. Since this agreement placed mother in the role of disciplinarian, she and daughter were in a continuous struggle over all issues.

2. *Unwillingness to cooperate and to complete assignments:* These families are on the opposite end of the continuum. Their resistance is more passive and more subtle than overt fighting. They may comply verbally but defeat one another nonverbally. In fact, this pattern again can be traced back to the marital dyad, where the wife is verbally more articulate and explosive, defeating her husband actively through her continuous complaints and diatribes. The husband, on the other hand, defeats her nonverbally. He is usually unable to articulate his feelings in words and therefore "acts out" (e.g., by drinking, watching T.V., leaving home). In both of these patterns, often present in families of rebellious teenagers, verbal agreements are not honored and transactions are left incomplete, since no one takes personal responsibility. This could be said of most self-defeating patterns.

Example

This family came to counseling because of their 16-year-old son's non-verbal aggressive behavior. According to the family, the adolescent's aggressive behavior and unwillingness to comply were unbearable. When confronted with this problem or any other issue, he pretended to be sleepy. Because of a poor relationship with the parents, an older brother and sister had left home before completing high school.

Mother and father came from very different backgrounds, which led to confusion over the way they should discipline the children and what their expectations should be. Mother attempted to be the enforcer, but felt she got no support until she exploded in rage. Although father was concerned, he could not offer much support to his wife because he either left town on work-related business or would avoid her (by not listening or by engaging in another activity) whenever his son's behavior required attention. Since mother was the most verbal in the family, she defeated both father and son by either exploding or completing statements for them. They, in turn, by not cooperating or conversing with her, also refused to take any personal responsibility for dealing with family issues.

3. *Continuation of same patterns in spite of all types of intervention:* There are families who are rigidly resistant to any type of intervention. In most of these cases the therapist may feel like hitting his or her head against a stone wall. The family will not budge.

Example

The identified patient was a 15-year-old boy whose violent antisocial behavior brought the family into counseling. This was a blended family consisting of mother, her two children ages 15 and 16, and a stepfather. Although the stepfather and mother had been married for 3½ years, the mother complained that the problem could not be altered because the stepfather would not discipline either the son or daughter. When this family was first seen, they had previously been in therapy for one year, but said they saw no evidence of change.

This was a first marriage for the stepfather who was so quiet that no one ever listened to his "mumbling." Stepfather explained that since he never had any children, he really did not know how to parent. When stepfather did attempt to move closer to his step-children, the move was interpreted by the mother as their being too independent and no longer needing her. Mother, therefore, would become overly critical of the son for not assuming responsibility for his work at home, which broke up the stepfather-son relationship. Son would then become furious with everyone, and the stepfather would again start feeling incompetent. Son and daughter "acted out" their frustrations by destroying property at school and at home and by fighting with those in authority.

In spite of numerous interventions to strengthen generational boundaries so that mother and stepfather would be supportive of each other, mother and siblings remained bound in an enmeshed relationship.

4. *Divide and conquer:* This fourth pattern is especially visible in families with teenagers, who are masters at separating the parents from each other, making hay out of whatever polarization may have been present in the marriage (Stierlin, 1974).

Example

This family of four came for family counseling because of the "acting out" of their oldest son, aged 15. Father was a truck driver and mother a shampoo girl. There was one younger sibling, a brother, aged 10, who was in the fourth grade. The IP was a large, handsome youth who towered over his father. He was neatly dressed and appropriately groomed. According to this family, the youth was doing such things as leaving home in the family car, without permission, but going only a few miles away. He was also consistently lying about his behavior and taking things that would be rather conspicuous by their absence. He would also place beer and other undesirable items in his room where they would easily be found.

Father was the disciplinarian in the family, using physical force at times to gain control of the older son, while mother's responsibility was to establish rules and report on her son's behavior to the father. Since father was away most of the week, it was the older son's responsibility to take care of his mother. Problems arose whenever mother and father attempted to set limits and administer discipline on which they did not agree. It seemed that the imposition of inconsistent, poorly identified expectations and limitations was allowing this youth to divide and conquer his parents. Consequently, everyone felt confused and defeated.

5. *Disqualifications:* This may appear as a subtle or as a very evident pattern. It can creep up on therapists very slowly and then hit them all of a sudden, or it can explode in their faces from the outset. It is an insidious as well as an entrenched pattern found in families with extreme pathology of long standing. It consists of telling others—intimates as well as non-intimates—that they do not count, they are not important. One could argue that disqualification of others means essentially a disqualification of the self. Then one could talk about low self-esteem and other intrapsychic concepts that are of questionable usefulness in dealing with self-defeating families. The ultimate disqualification, for the therapist of course, is the family dropping out of therapy suddenly, without proviso.

In looking at this pattern one sees that members enjoying it are usually hypercritical and perfectionistic, i.e., no one can satisfy them, including the therapist, who should be on the lookout for this pattern whenever the family shows up with a long series of previously defeated therapists.

Example

This family was first seen in counseling because of the extreme antisocial behavior of the 16-year-old daughter who had been expelled permanently from school for persistent drug use and disrespect to teachers. There was one other younger daughter, age 15, at home, who engaged in equally destructive behavior but was never caught. Father held an administrative level position and mother was a housewife, who reported that her husband wanted her to find work away from home. However, she could not do so because of the trouble with her older daughter. The mother reported also that they all felt very insecure and scared about being in counseling, because they had been in counseling before and no one had ever helped. The mother, in particular, doubted from the very outset that they could continue in therapy.

Mother verbalized excessively critical comments of the daughter's behavior and commented that she received no support from the father. Although father tended to be withdrawn and quiet, he was extremely critical of the way in which mother handled problems with the older daughter. Father reprimanded the daughter in the counseling session, whenever mother reported that she received no support from him. Daughter was extremely critical of her mother and other authority figures but was easier on father and her younger sister.

In this family each member talked about what they needed to do, but it was quite evident that no action had been taken. For instance, they administered no punishment when rules were broken; mother made no movement to find work; and father and mother never showed their daughters that they were supportive of each other.

6. *Depression:* Depression is another self-defeating pattern frequently found in family therapy. Most approaches to the treatment of depression are linear; very little has appeared in the literature concerning a *circular* treatment approach. Once it appears or surfaces—and often that takes time because it is usually disguised by the individual as well as the family—it is important to reframe it positively in two different aspects: 1) as a protection of the family, e.g., "As long as you are depressed, no one in the family has to change," and 2) as "A blessing rather than a curse:" e.g., "You are lucky that you can feel and be whole;" or, "Depression is the royal road to selfhood," comparing people

who cannot get depressed as being the unfortunate ones. "People who cannot get depressed do not ask for help. They can be found in cemeteries, morgues, and hospitals."

Once the positive reframing is done, we usually have found it helpful to *prescribe it in a ritualized fashion* (Selvini-Palazzoli et al., 1978). "I want you to get depressed on Mondays, Wednesdays, and Fridays from 9:00 to 9:15 p.m." It is important to link this prescription systemically by having the mate or a parent remind the individual that they have to get depressed and use the kitchen timer set for 15 minutes to "get with your depression so you can learn something about yourself." The depressed person should do this alone, usually in the bedroom. "Make notes of everything that comes into your head as you feel depressed." If more than one intimate (usually a spouse) is involved in the depression, assign that person to remind the reminder about the time of prescribed depression.

7. *The ultimate defeat:* This, of course, occurs when the family drops out of therapy, usually without much warning and without previous discussion. Here the therapist is left completely helpless since there is nothing that can be done about it. On one hand, the therapist is relieved that a difficult problem has been terminated. On the other hand, his or her therapeutic effectiveness has been brought into question by the family's dropping out. No matter what the reasons and rationalizations a therapist may have when a family drops out, *it still hurts!*

Undoubtedly, there are many other patterns of defeat that could be outlined. We have not tried to enumerate them systematically. Each family has its own unique and specific style of defeating. LaFave (1980) found correlates of dropping out of treatment which apparently went beyond any issue of therapeutic effectiveness. These correlates were: a) age of the identified patient—the older the patient, the greater the chance of dropping out; b) the greater the number of children, the greater the chance of dropping out; c) family's prior involvement with community agencies; d) pressure or absence of antisocial acting out; and e) attendance of father at both the initial intake interview and early treatment services (L'Abate, 1975).

THE FUNCTIONS OF DEFEATS

Defeats have two major classes of function: one relates to families and the other relates to therapists.

Families

As long as the family works actively or passively at defeating themselves, it means that they are involved with each other and, if they are involved, it means they are maintaining the homeostatic *status quo,* as discussed elsewhere (L'Abate, Weeks, & Weeks, 1979). Whatever these defeats may produce, *they do keep the family together.* Furthermore, we must remember that, from a dialectical as well as human viewpoint, for every defeat there is a success, or at least presumed success. We need to discover the specific, functional payoffs of defeating behaviors. Each family succeeds in defeating, and may even enjoy the success of defeat! As paradoxical or far-fetched as this may seem, accounts of defeats are often reported with someone in the family smiling. Defeats should not be regarded negatively. They have many important functions that can be reframed positively, i.e., a) *protectiveness* ("As long as you defeat each other, you are also protecting everybody in the family"); b) *caring* ("As long as you continue bickering, you keep everybody in the family from having to take on further responsibility"); c) *keeping things the same;* d) producing *excitement* and even enjoyment ("You certainly don't want to get bored") in an otherwise repetitious and dull routine; and e) *keeping the family close.*

Therapists

Because we learn from failures, our defeats are more important than our successes. Yet, defeats need to be anticipated before they happen—although this same awareness may prevent us from doing anything about them, as the Milan group has recognized (Selvini-Palazzoli et al., 1978). Defeats have a way of keeping us humble—no matter how successful and effective we may be with some families, attrition and dropouts are part of doing therapy. In fact, most of us, after a few years of practice, learn to accept a certain percentage of defeats, usually rationalizing them in terms of negative externalizations about families. Externalizations are an avoidance of coming to critical terms with ourselves. Instead of using defeats to sharpen our creativity, instead of using them to spur us toward a more differentiated practice, we submit to a critical resignation and passive rationalization. Rather than externalize blame, we can begin to use ourselves to come up with more creative and interesting patterns of coping with defeat. *Coping* rather than solving is the more proper term, because it is doubtful whether we can ever "solve" patterns of defeat. We are vulnerable and fallible human beings and therapists. Anyone who claims to more than this bottom line is asking to be defeated.

PATTERNS OF COPING WITH DEFEAT

1. *Admission of defeat and helplessness:* This is the favorite ploy

used by the Milano group (Selvini-Palazzoli et al., 1978).Such an admission seems to mobilize family members into an attempt to do the opposite, that is, win. Even better, one should start therapy with the full realization (Andolfi, 1980) that underneath the pleas for help there is a hidden agenda that pulls for defeat in each and every family. This hidden agenda is present from the outset of each therapy. Should a therapist lose sight of his or her vulnerability and the possibility of defeat, that therapist *will* be defeated.

Example

This verbal message was given to the family described under *Disqualification:*

> "I am aware that, because of the power of this family, I am feeling a real sense of defeat and helplessness. I do know I have power that you cannot speak to, but yours is also special. You are a special family that I cannot fight with. I don't know where I could have found a better family than you to defeat me."

This verbal message provided this family with an incentive for continuing their therapy. Not only did this admission of defeat on the therapist's part assure their continued participation in counseling (in order to win), but the parents learned something about the strength of their influence when they were united.

2. *Congratulating the family:* The family should be congratulated for their involvement with each other: "As long as you defeat each other, it means that you really care for each other." Hence, admiration for the family should be expressed positively and repeatedly: "You are a really tough family."

Example

The family described under *Divide and Conquer,* was given the following letter:

> "I am impressed with the ability you have developed to defeat each other. This keeps your family together and unchanged. To succeed by defeating is hard to master, but when instructions are unclear and not negotiated, then it is easier not to follow through.
> I admire you for wanting every family member to feel the power of defeat. You are assured of this power as long as instructions are given without everyone having an investment in them. One person can then use this against another, and in this way keep the family the same.

I want to congratulate the family for knowing how to be happy by defeating and by being defeated. Since this seems successful, I would encourage you to continue doing what you are doing and by no means would I encourage Mother and Dad to share authority and responsibility with each other, because this change could break up the family."

This circular letter not only gave this family a more positive description of their relationship, but promoted an evaluation of their family system. In very resistant families this is a way to begin establishing and strengthening parental boundaries.

Both mother and father decided that they did not need to feel the power of defeat as much. They noticed that when they agreed on clearly stated expectations, disciplines and consequences, their two sons did not "act out" as frequently. They did not really understand what was happening, but they all agreed that when the siblings did "act out," it would be up to the parents to show more authority and responsibility together.

3. *Reframing positively:* The pattern of defeat needs to be reframed positively—tying it to success, enjoyment, caring, protectiveness, closeness. Once this positive reframing is made, one can go on to the next step.

Example

The family described under *Fighting and Bickering* was given a letter with the following instructions:

1. Father will read this letter to other members of the family.
2. The letter will be read after dinner on Monday, Wednesday, and Friday evenings.
3. Mother will remind Father to read the letter.
4. Please do not discuss content of this letter with anyone outside of counseling:

"We are appreciative of your protecting us because as long as you act up neither Mother nor I will need to look at ourselves and deal with our middle age. You will also help your brother to stay the way he is.

Consequently, we will understand that any time you blow up it will be to protect us and your brother. We hope, therefore, that you will continue protecting us, because we need it."

This descriptive letter was used to reframe positively the general patterns of relating observed in this family and to relabel negative behavior as positive. The nature of the family's relationship is described dialectically, in other words, as passivity and aggressiveness.

4. *Prescribing the defeat:* Since defeat is now a positive expression, it follows that the family should assist, continue, and even escalate

whatever they are doing to defeat each other. To make sure that the reframing and prescription will not be ignored or forgotten, the therapist puts them into writing and ritualizes them, i.e., "Read this letter after supper on alternating days, either Mondays, Wednesdays, and Fridays, or Tuesdays, Thursdays, and Saturdays." This is the Milano group's recommendation (Selvini-Palazzoli et al., 1978).

Example

This letter was given to the son in a family that *continued the same patterns in spite of all intervention,* to read to his parents following these instructions:

1. To be read by son to other members of the family.
2. Please read on Mondays, Wednesdays, and Fridays after dinner.
3. Mother is to remind son to read and if she forgets, stepfather and daughter are to remind her.
4. Do not discuss contents outside of counseling.

"I am impressed with the way in which you show how much you care about this family and especially your mother. I feel you need to be congratulated for having violent temper tantrums, because these tantrums serve as a safety valve for what your father and mother cannot do. I admire you for the way in which you show your loyalty to your mother.

If this is the way you want to protect your parents from each other and continue keeping them apart, you should continue to blow up, but do this on Monday, Wednesday, and Friday of each week. Be sure to break some inexpensive item in your home and continue these outbursts, because if you stop, they might get back together."

After our prescribing and ritualizing the behavior, this youth found that if he could control outbursts part of the week, he could exhibit more control in general. No one really understood why mother was now accepting responsibility in her relationship with stepfather, nor why the son was getting along so well with him. This was an opportunity to unhook son from mother and move him closer to stepfather.

5. *Balancing the family upset:* After the therapist gives the first letter changing the role of the family IP from that of "victim" or "victimizer" to "rescuer" and putting the responsibility back on the rest of the family (Selvini-Palazzoli et al., 1978), it is often important to follow up by helping the children praise their parents, thus giving the children something to think about. Therefore, a second letter should be given after the first. The children should thank their parents for giving up part of themselves and their marriage to deal with the raising of children, and express the hope that they, the parents, will be able to pick up and make up for lost time.

Example

This letter was given to the mother of the family described as *unwilling to cooperate and to complete assignments:*

1. To be privately read on Monday, Wednesday, and Friday.
2. Please read after dinner and in the privacy of your room.
3. Please be reminded not to read this to other members of your family.

"The job of raising two children without a father has been hard, but you are to be commended for the wonderful way in which you have sacrificed yourself to take care of your daughter and son. You are to be congratulated for the work and sacrifices that have gone into protecting your children. Because of the special way in which you care for your son, you are assured of raising him to be like his father. It is especially clear that you need to keep protecting your son from further involvement with men, because that will insure that he be more like his father.

I am also impressed by your commitment to keeping tight reins on your family, because as long as you do this it will stay together and unchanged. I think you should continue doing this and should also give more of yourself by knowing what your son and daughter are doing at all times."

6. *Dealing with disqualifications:* With the family that used disqualification, after the therapist sent the first letter admitting to helplessness, another letter was given. In this case, it was important to reframe the family's pattern in terms of "high standards" of performance:

"Your standards for living are so high that few individuals, including me, can really live up to them. You should be congratulated for your search for perfection (and equating perfection to goodness and imperfection to badness). In spite of all the pressures to lower your standards, we hope that you can keep them up because this world needs people like you who can uphold standards against all pressures both inside and outside the family. We doubt whether we can live up to your standards and wonder whether we will ever be able to meet them anytime in the future. Keep up the good work! We will fail to meet your standards and wonder whether we really can help you."

In another instance, the following letter was given:

"We would like to congratulate you on your clear, organized and fixed perception of the world and of each other. You call a spade a spade and know black from white and erase all the grey areas of the world, making your lives much less confusing, less conflictual, and more stimulating than are most people's.

Similarly, you have learned to be perfect complements for each other. Where one of you is weak, the other is strong. When one is indecisive, the other knows "the way." It is clear that you each have in the other your better half, and it becomes even more important to stay close and together—for each of you would be in a state of confused excitement if you were to find yourself grappling alone with the problems of life."

These messages had the purpose of forcing the family to reconsider their extreme and destructive critical behavior and introduce a greater degree of acceptance of themselves and others.

DISCUSSION

One of the major shortcomings of this paper lies in our inability to report as yet on the outcome, whether immediate or long-range, of these letters on the families that received them. Subjectively, we know that it is questionable whether they would have remained in therapy otherwise. From the viewpoint of the therapist, these letters provide one more way of dealing with seemingly unresolvable impasses and pessimistic prognoses. Thus, this is another approach in an area where alternatives often seem lacking.

CONCLUSION: TOWARD A SELECTIVE USE OF PRE-PROGRAMMED WRITTEN MESSAGES

As the work of Wagner and L'Abate (1977), and Clark and L'Abate (1977) indicated, it is possible to obtain therapeutic changes with a minimum of personal contact and a maximum of homework assignment. Both studies suggest that, given a variety of problems that repeat themselves as self-defeating patterns (e.g., perfectionism, disqualifications, hypercriticalness, externalizations, put-downs, blaming), it is possible to tailor-make any one of the foregoing messages to suit the individual needs of families and therapists. Far-fetched and far-reaching as such a suggestion may appear at first, it would not be too impractical to use similarly written interpretations and assignments with different families. Clearly, this is an area of clinical application in which to test the usefulness of paradoxical techniques (Weeks & L'Abate, 1979). A selective use of such letters may both shorten the process of therapy and decrease the likelihood of defeat in therapy at the same time. Of course, we will need all of the feedback we can get in order to verify this approach.

REFERENCES

Andolfi, M. "Prescribing the Family's Own Dysfunctional Rules as a Therapeutic Strategy," *Journal of Marriage and Family Therapy*, 1980, 6, 29-36.

Clark, D., & L'Abate, L. "Enrichment and Tape Recordings with Couples," in L. L'Abate (Ed.), *Enrichment: Structured Interventions with Couples, Families, and Groups*. Washington, D.C.: University Press of America, 1977, 203-213.

L'Abate, L., Wagner, V., Lockridge, J., Hardin, S., Gallope, R. H., & Sloan, S. "Linear and Circular Models: Combination of Enrichment and Written Interpretations with Couples," in L. L'Abate (Ed.), *Enrichment: Structured Interventions with Couples, Families and Groups*. Washington, D.C.: University Press of America, 1977, 214-237.

LaFave, M. K. "Correlates of Engagement in Family Therapy," *Journal of Marriage and Family Therapy*, 1980, 6, 75-81.

Selvini-Palazzoli, M. *Self-starvation: From the Intrapsychic to the Transpersonal Approach to Anorexia Nervosa*. London, England: Human Context Books, 1974.

Selvini-Palazzoli, M., Boscolo, L., Cecchin, G., & Prata, G. *Paradox and Counter Paradox: The Family in Schizophrenic Transaction*. New York: Jason Aronson, 1978.

Selvini-Palazzoli, M., Boscolo, L., Cecchin, G., & Prata, G. "The Problem of the Referring Person," *Journal of Marriage and Family Therapy*, 1980, 6, 3-9.

Stierlin, H. *Separating Parents and Adolescents*. New York: Quadrangle/The New York Times Book Co., 1974.

Wagner, V., & L'Abate, L. "Enrichment and Written Homework Assignments with Couples," in L. L'Abate (Ed.), *Enrichment: Structured Interventions with Couples, Families, and Groups*. Washington, D.C.: University Press of America, 1977, 184-202.

Weeks, G.R., & L'Abate, L. "A Compilation of Paradoxical Methods," *The American Journal of Family Therapy*, 1979, 7, 61-76.

SECTION VI

IMPLICATIONS FOR TRAINING

CHAPTER 26

LUCIANO L'ABATE, MICHAEL BERGER, LARRY WRIGHT, AND MICHAEL O'SHEA

Training Family Psychologists: The Family Studies Program at Georgia State University

The rationale and background for the Family Studies Program at Georgia State University is given in terms of the need for academic (scientific) and professional (clinical) leadership in this new horizon that challenges the profession of clinical psychology and, as a new paradigm shift, most of psychology as well.

"All beginnings are difficult"
     The Midrash

Family therapy is a treatment orientation and modality to which no single professional discipline or theoretical orientation can lay claim, yet to which many can and have contributed. Indeed, the relevance of families to so many different disciplines may be one of family therapy's greatest assets; there are so many fields of study from which we can learn about the family. However, to the extent that these interdisciplinary connections have prompted the neglect of family therapy by clinical psychology, they have also been an important liability.

Psychologists have been underrepresented in the family therapy field until very recently. The Group for the Advancement of Psychiatry report (1970), based on a survey conducted during 1965 and 1966, of clinicians practicing family therapy, found that social workers represented 40% of the respondents, psychiatrists and psychologists together made up another 40%, and the remaining 20% included clergymen, physicians, nurses, and others in related disciplines. Though these figures may represent the makeup of those involved in psychotherapy by discipline or professional training in 1966, they also suggest that psychology was somewhat underrepresented among family therapists at that time. This state of affairs has apparently not changed appreciably since 1970, as Olson, reviewing a decade of development in family therapy stated:

> One field related to marital and family therapy which has not been adequately tapped is clinical psychology. Since the early 1950's, this field has placed major emphasis on developing an empirical base from which to develop theoretically and clinically. Considerable effort has been spent developing and evaluating various methods and research designs for use in psychotherapy research. (p. 528)

Perhaps one area where clinical psychologists can make an important contribution to family therapy is in that of systematic theory and research. Gurman (1973) noted that, although there has been a dramatic increase in the number of articles related to research in the areas of process, outcome, and techniques in marital therapy, the quality of this research has not been consistently good. Training in family therapy in clinical psychology programs could help to close this apparent gap between practice and research.

Whereas the number of psychologists involved in family therapy may be on the increase, as suggested by the increased application of behavior modification techniques to marital functioning (Gurman, 1973), doctoral clinical psychology training programs that include exposure to theory and techniques of marital and family therapy remain relatively few. Bodin, in a 1969 survey, listed three graduate psychology departments offering family therapy training. A neglect of family therapy by clinical psychology is suggested by the lack of references to family therapy in recent articles on clinical psychology training and practice (Rotter, 1973; Seeman & Seeman, 1973; Simmons, 1971) and is addressed directly by Stanton (1975a). Some slight evidence of a change is provided by Stanton (1975b), who surveyed graduate psychology programs and found 10 programs that incorporated, in varying degrees, family therapy theory and practice.

Some of this lack of involvement in the family therapy movement by clinical psychology may be the result of what Hobbs (1964) refers to as a lack of willingness on the part of psychologists to become involved in interdisciplinary activities in the field of mental health.

Another factor that may have contributed to the estrangement of family therapy from psychology in general and from clinical psychology doctoral training programs in particular is that the theoretical orientations that have proved to be the most useful

---

LUCIANO L'ABATE *is a professor of psychology, Chairman of the Family Studies Program, and Director of the Family Study Center at Georgia State University. An American Board of Examiners in Professional Psychology Diplomate and Approved Supervisor of the American Association of Marriage and Family Therapists, his interests lie in the theoretical and applied aspects of the familial context. He has contributed about 100 articles, book reviews, and chapters to professional psychological journals. He is the author or coauthor of five books in psychology.*

MICHAEL BERGER *is an assistant professor of psychology and Assistant Director of the Family Study Center at Georgia State University. His research interest is in how adults relate their individual destinies to their work, marriage, and parental careers. He is also a family therapist and trainer of family therapists.*

LARRY WRIGHT *is a doctoral candidate at the Family Study Center at Georgia State University. His primary interests are family, marital, and individual psychotherapy. His current research interests include how couples integrate work and family responsibilities, how working-class families survive, and how death affects families.*

MICHAEL O'SHEA *is a graduate student in psychology and family studies. He holds a master's degree in counseling from Springfield College. His areas of interest include the role of fathers in family intervention, family crisis intervention, and the use of videotape playback as a therapeutic technique.*

REQUESTS FOR REPRINTS *should be sent to Luciano L'Abate, Psychology Department, Georgia State University, University Plaza, Atlanta, Georgia 30303.*

to family therapists, such as communication theory and systems theory, are interpersonal in their focus and are derived from disciplines other than psychology (L'Abate, Note 1). As Beels and Ferber (1969) pointed out:

> This goal of changing the family system of interaction is family therapy's most distinctive feature, its greatest advantage and, especially to those who came to it from other disciplines, its greatest stumbling block. (p. 283)

By and large, in-depth exposure to these theories has not been a typical part of traditional training programs in clinical psychology. These programs have emphasized psychology's medical, biological, and philosophical roots to the neglect of sociology and anthropology and have thus been oriented toward the behavior of the individual *in vacuum* or "in culture," but seldom "in the family" context (L'Abate, 1976). The closest that most students in traditional programs come to family interaction theory is a course in social psychology or a practicum in group psychotherapy. Both of these courses, however, focus on the behavior of the individual as a function of group influence rather than on the behavior of a group of individuals acting as an intimate system, with a history and a future of day-to-day emotional relatedness and interdependency, which characterize the family unit.

Concomitants of this shift from intrapsychic to interpersonal dynamics in family therapy are many. For instance, other factors influencing the relative exclusion of family therapy theory and technique from clinical psychology training are the system's transactional and ecological orientation and the view of the family unit as more than the sum of its members (Bateson, 1972; Bertalanffy, 1969; Spiegel, 1971). The emphasis on a whole new set of variables makes long established, individually oriented psychological tests inadequate or obsolete, if not entirely irrelevant (Cromwell, Olson, & Fournier, 1976). In fact, as Haley (1971) and the Group for the Advancement of Psychiatry report (1970, p. 55) discussed, diagnostic evaluation in family therapy consists of the therapist's observing and assessing how the family responds to his interventions. Diagnostic evaluation is not viewed by the majority of family therapists as a preliminary, standardized, information-gathering phase that precedes the treatment phase and in which the therapist assumes an uninvolved, objective role. To the extent that their diagnostic testing skills help to define their professional identity, clinical psychologists may not know how to involve themselves in the areas of family assessment and therapy.

The Family Studies Program at Georgia State University

The Family Studies Program at Georgia State University was developed in recognition of the fact that family therapy has been and will continue to be a flexible and effective treatment modality. The program at the PhD level is one of the three specialty areas within the doctoral program in clinical psychology; the other two specialties are psychotherapy and behavior modification. The Family Studies Program was implemented as a specialty within clinical psychology in recognition of the need for a radically different conceptual framework of experiences, in addition to the intrapsychic orientation of traditional clinical psychology training. The Family Studies Program attempts, through course work, pratica, theses, dissertations, and internships to embody the concept of the clinician–researcher.

At present, the Family Studies Program has two full-time faculty members and a third part-time member with extensive experience in family therapy. Their interests include family theory and therapy, child clinical psychology, family assessment, family enrichment (L'Abate, 1977), supervision of family therapy, family network therapy, interventions aimed at families with handicapped children (Berger & Foster, 1976), and the interrelationship between work and family life in dual-worker and dual-career families (Berger, Foster, & Wallston, 1978; Berger & Wuescher, 1975). Teaching and practicum supervision responsibilities are shared by these and other members of the clinical faculty, when appropriate. In addition, members of the general clinical faculty teach relevant courses and provide supervision in individual assessment and psychotherapy.

Students at the master's level select 30–35 hours of courses from the major core areas and methodology, with the remaining 15–20 hours devoted to the family studies sequences of courses and to master's thesis research. Students at the PhD level, in addition, obtain substantial supervised practicum experience in enrichment and therapy and may develop a minor in addition to dissertation research.

Ferber and Mendelsohn (1969) listed seven basic assumptions that, in their view, are characteristic of adequate, realistic training in family therapy, and these are incorporated to varying degrees in the Family Studies Program. Their first two principles refer to the status of family therapy theory described above and state that no "single, systematic, or comprehensive" theory of family process or family therapy has yet emerged, nor have all the relevant phenomena yet been identified or conceptualized. Eight years later, these observations are still valid (L'Abate, 1976). The Family Studies Program maintains a theoretical eclecticism, but a systems orientation is implicit. The two courses in theories of personality development in marriage and in the family, which initiate the family studies sequence at the master's level, expose the student to anthropological, sociological, and psychological perspectives of marriage and family and preserve the open-endedness of theory in this area. A course in family assessment teaches techniques of objective family evaluation and includes the use of projective tests and self-descriptive measures of family functioning. Similar to the orientation of Lewis, Beavers, Gosset, & Phillips (1976), the assessments are with normal (nondysfunctional) families as well as with families in treatment, to insure control-group data for research purposes and to acquaint students with nonpathological family processes.

Ferber and Mendelsohn (1969) stressed that "the learning achieved by first hand contact with family units, when the trainee has some defined responsibility vis-à-vis these family units, is far superior to that achieved by reading about, hearing or seeing families for which the trainee has no responsibility .... These first hand contacts with families must be experienced within a framework of didactic and supervisory experiences" (p. 26). Shapiro (1975) supported this view with his experience as a family therapy trainer, in which he found that psychology graduate and postgraduate students, as compared with psychiatric residents, more readily accept a systems theory intellectually but are less adept than residents in "taking a role of therapeutic responsibility with the whole family unit" (p. 43). This shortcoming may well be a reflection of research and academic orientation at the expense of applied clinical experience of the doctoral training of his psychology trainees.

This program offers a two-phased clinical practica format that combines theory and practice. Students first take a course in the theory and techniques of enrichment (L'Abate, 1977), a series of programmed exercises and lessons designed to improve various aspects of communication and interaction and enhance relationships among family members. Enrichment is taught and applied according to the "laboratory method" (L'Abate, 1968, 1973). This training approach allows for a clear separation and delineation of responsibilities between a professional (instructor-clinician) who uses "unstructured, impressionistic procedures" and paraprofessional personnel (graduate students) who use structured techniques and exercises outlined in a manual (L'Abate, 1977). Enrichment is followed by a course in theories of family therapy, with a subsequent or concurrent sequence of practica in family therapy. A 1-year internship, preferably at a facility that offers family treatment services, is required and is seen as an extension of the students' practica experience.

The advantages of this format include a gradual, structured exposure to the family orientation and to intervention in families, with an incremental increase in clinical responsibilities. Both enrichment and family therapy are usually conducted in teams of two students of opposite sex. Therapeutic interventions with clients are dependent on the nature of the dysfunction and may include both structural change and communication and affect clarification. Supervision of students for both enrichment and therapy is didactic and instructional, as opposed to quasi-therapeutic in nature, as recommended by Ferber and Mendelsohn (1969, p. 29). The context of this supervision moves from group supervision and individual supervision of intervention teams to live supervision via a one-way mirror and videotapes during the process of intervention. In line with Fox's (1976) recommendation, students are given both the opportunity and assistance in obtaining individual or marital therapy for themselves during their graduate careers.

Beck (1975) noted that because of the makeup of typical clients of university-affiliated clinical services, clinical experiences and research data derived from this population tend to have limited applicability to clients in the community social-service network. The Family Study Center at Georgia State University, therefore, has expanded its target population from student couples and families who are self-referred or referred from the university counseling center to include limited referrals from social-service facilities in the metropolitan Atlanta area.

In spite of the differences in theory and technique between family therapy and the conventional individual psychotherapies, students in the Family Studies Program are encouraged to gain experience with individual psychotherapy and psychological testing. There are several reasons for this practice; among them is that in lieu of a comprehensive, systematic theory of family process and treatment, many of the approaches to individual psychotherapy must be regarded as compatible with a family approach in the sense that therapeutic change in one member can bring about changes in the entire family system (Bowen, 1965). Another factor is that the advancement of family therapy and family research can best be served by the Family Studies Program's preserving its ties to the larger body of clinical psychology, given the stature of clinical psychologists in the contemporary mental health field and the need for their particular skills in the family area.

The Family Studies Program attempts to formalize what has already begun, the involvement of clinical psychologists in family theory and practice. But in discovering new horizons, traditional expertise must not be automatically abandoned, regardless of theoretical antagonisms. To do so would be to perpetuate the rigidity and professional isolation discussed by Olson (1976). The issue of whether training in individual psychotherapy enhances or impedes one's effectiveness in family therapy is largely an empirical one and remains unresolved (Winter, 1971). In the meantime, the Family Studies Program assumes that the broader the students' therapeutic exposure, the more potentially competent they will be as family leaders and interveners.

In addition to course work and practica, students in the Family Studies Program assume administrative responsibility for the day-to-day running of the laboratory. Students are elected by their peers to handle such matters as intake of new cases, liaison with community mental health agencies, public relations, maintenance of equipment, availability of needed supplies, billing of clients, and so forth.

Conclusion

The Family Studies Program at Georgia State University has attempted to create an atmosphere in which students may learn the intricacies of becoming family therapists. The program is broad, eclectic, and flexible in meeting the needs of both individual students and the profession of psychology. The format of this program is by no means completed or fixed. The program will change as our knowledge of families and family practice increases.

REFERENCE NOTE

1. L'Abate, L. (Ed.). *Models of clinical psychology* (Research Paper No. 22). Atlanta, Ga.: Georgia State University, 1969.

REFERENCES

Bateson, G. *Steps to an ecology of mind.* New York: Ballantine Books, 1972.

Beck, D. Research findings on the outcomes of marital counseling. *Social Casework,* 1975, *56,* 153-181.

Beels, C. C., & Ferber, A. Family therapy: A view. *Family Process,* 1969, *8,* 280-318.

Berger, M., & Foster, M. Family-level interventions for retarded children: A multivariate approach to issues and strategies. *Multivariate Experimental Clinical Research,* 1976, *2,* 1-21.

Berger, M., Foster, M., & Wallston, B. Dual-worker couples and joint job-seeking. In R. Rapoport and R. Rapoport (Eds.), *Working couples.* New York: Harper & Row, 1978.

Berger, M., & Wuescher, L. The family in the substantive environment: An approach to the development of transactional methodology. *Journal of Community Psychology,* 1975, *3,* 246-253.

Bertalanffy, L. *General systems theory.* New York: Braziller, 1969.

Bodin, A. Family training literature: A brief guide. *Family Process,* 1969, *8,* 272-279.

Bowen, M. Family psychotherapy with schizophrenia in the hospital and in private practice. In I. Boszormenyi-Nagy & J. Framo (Eds.), *Intensive family therapy: Theoretical and practical aspects.* New York: Harper & Row, 1965.

Cromwell, R., Olson, D., & Fournier, D. Diagnosis and evaluation in marital and family counseling. In D. Olson (Ed.), *Treating relationships.* Lake Mills, Iowa: Graphic, 1976.

Ferber, A., & Mendelsohn, M. Training for family therapy. *Family Process,* 1969, *8,* 25-32.

Fox, R. Family therapy. In I. Weiner (Ed.), *Clinical methods in psychology.* New York: Wiley, 1976.

Group for the Advancement of Psychiatry. *Treatment of families in conflict: The clinical study of family process.* New York: Aronson, 1970.

Gurman, A. The effects and effectiveness of marital therapy: A review of outcome research. *Family Process,* 1973, *12,* 145-170.

Haley, J. (Ed.). *Changing families.* New York: Grune & Stratton, 1971.

Hobbs, N. Mental health's third revolution. *American Journal of Orthopsychiatry,* 1964, *34,* 822-833.

L'Abate, L. The laboratory method in clinical psychology: An attempt at innovation. *Clinical Psychologist,* 1968, *21,* 182-183.

L'Abate, L. Psychodynamic interventions: A personal statement. In R. Woody & J. Woody (Eds.), *Sexual, marital and familial relationships: Therapeutic interventions for professional helping.* Springfield, Ill.: Charles C Thomas, 1973.

L'Abate, L. *Understanding and helping the individual in the family.* New York: Grune & Stratton, 1976.

L'Abate, L. *Enrichment: Structured interventions with couples, families, and groups.* Washington, D.C.: University Press of America, 1977.

Lewis, J., Beavers, W., Gosset, J., & Phillips, V. *No single thread: Psychological health in family systems.* New York: Brunner/Mazel, 1976.

Olson, D. Marital and family therapy: Integrative review and critique. *Journal of Marriage and the Family,* 1970, *32,* 501-538.

Olson, D. (Ed.). *Treating relationships.* Lake Mills, Iowa: Graphic, 1976.

Rotter, J. The future of clinical psychology. *Journal of Consulting and Clinical Psychology,* 1973, *40,* 313-321.

Seeman, J., & Seeman, R. Emergent trends in the practice of clinical psychology. *Professional Psychology,* 1973, *4,* 151-157.

Shapiro, R. Problems in teaching family therapy. *Professional Psychologist,* 1975, *6,* 41-44.

Simmons, W. L. Clinical training programs, 1964-1965 and 1968-1969: A characterization and comparison. *American Psychologist,* 1971, *26,* 717-721.

Spiegel, J. *Transactions: The interplay between the individual, family, and society.* New York: Science House, 1971.

Stanton, M. Psychology and family therapy. *Professional Psychology,* 1975, *6,* 45-49. (a)

Stanton, M. Family therapy training: Academic and internship opportunities for psychologists. *Family Process,* 1975, *14,* 433-439. (b)

Winter, W. Family therapy: Research and theory. In C. Spielberger (Ed.), *Current topics in clinical and community psychology.* New York: Academic Press, 1971.

Received September 9, 1977

CHAPTER 27

TRAINING IN FAMILY PSYCHOLOGY*

Abstract

The general, theoretical, and technical background for training in family psychology is introduced. Academic curriculum requirements, clinical practicum, internship, and experiences are described. Some of the products of this program are also presented.

The purpose of this chapter is to elaborate on the training program in family psychology developed at Georgia State University. A previous paper (L'Abate, Berger, Wright & O'Shea, 1979) described the general, conceptual, and practical background; it is the purpose of this chapter to elaborate on and to specify in detail the nature of this training.

Although the emphasis of this chapter is on training, we should not lose sight of the term "family psychology." Why not, as fashion has it, "family therapy"? As will be made abundantly clear, the term "family therapy" is unduly restrictive. It does not convey, for instance, the need to combine theory with practice, evaluation with intervention, and research with intervention. Furthermore, there are countless and ever-growing programs in family therapy. It has been a personal conviction of this author (L'Abate, 1964, 1968, 1969, 1973) that more progress is made when therapy, theory, evaluation, and research are combined than when they are separated.

General Background

In a recent survey of training in applied developmental psychology (Rau-Ferguson, 1980), of 148 respondents representing most graduate programs in this area of training, 5 (Georgia State, Nova, Penn State,

---

*An earlier draft of this chapter was presented to the Mailman Winter Conference on Applied Developmental Psychology, Miami, Florida, January 8, 1982.

Syracuse, and Michigan State) acknowledged the family as their major goal of training.

Some of the issues relevant to training in family therapy have been considered by Little, Vance, and Pastershot (1979) as well as in the symposium by Green, Rau-Ferguson, Framo, Shapiro, and LaPerriere (1979). These issues, considered in greater detail by Rau-Ferguson (1979), Framo (1979), Shapiro (1979) and LaPerriere (1979), help to bring about a distinction that is crucial to the purposes of this chapter: that is, the difference between family psychology as an academic discipline and as a distinct branch of social psychology, and family therapy as a clinical method of treatment used by a variety of professionals. The former, as a discipline, is a part of psychology as a science and as a profession. The latter is available to any professional who wants to claim it as a specialization. Thus, family therapy is one form of intervention that any family psychologist should master; however, it is by no means the only available form of family intervention. Any family psychologist worthy of the calling should also be knowledgeable of preventive, social skill-oriented approaches that would supplement, if not supplant, family therapy (L'Abate, 1980, 1981).

Cooper, Rampage, and Soucy (1981) surveyed the status of family therapy training in graduate clinical psychology. With a 79% response rate, they found that 10% of the faculty of these training programs identified themselves as family oriented; 32% of the responding programs had no family-oriented faculty members; while 18% of all psychotherapy courses were on family therapy. Of these programs, 21% had no family therapy course. These authors listed 8 programs that awarded to family therapy the highest importance rating and that reported offering and requiring at least one family therapy course. These programs were: (a) Brigham Young, (b) DePaul, (c) East Texas State, (d) Georgia State, (e) Southern Illinois, (f) Delaware, (g) Utah, and (h) Virginia Polytechnic Institute. Schools that included family therapy in their clinical curricula were also listed (p. 159).

Again, this survey indicates the need to continue distinguishing between <u>family therapy</u> as a course, or a series of courses, that make it (or them) indistinguishable from other courses for mental health professionals (Bloch & Weiss, 1981) and <u>family psychology</u>, a term that implies an academic curriculum dedicated to studying the relationship between the individual and the family. The former is concerned with theories, techniques, and applications of a method (i.e., family therapy). The latter is concerned with a whole discipline, which implies a much greater emphasis on academic preparation in theory and research as well as clinical evaluation, prevention, and intervention. Thus, the term family psychology is a much broader and, for psychologists, a much more relevant term than family therapy. Many people can call themselves family therapists; however, how many can call themselves family psychologists and support this claim with: (a) relvant curriculum and coursework; (b) specific clinical practica and internships with families rather than individuals, and (c) research related and relevant to individuals in their families rather than individuals out of their family context or to families without individuals (as sociological research emphasizes)?

Once these three criteria are used to evaluate training in family psychology as a complete Ph.D. curriculum, the number of institutions and programs devoted to such an undertaking becomes very small: Michigan State University (Rau-Ferguson, Note 1, Note 2) and Georgia State University. The fact that only, at most, a handful of programs can boast a curriculum in family psychology may be an indictment of our academic and professional narrowness and conservatism. As has been found elsewhere (Thaxton & L'Abate, in press), psychologists have been quite late in joining the family therapy movement. Although we have made great strides in the last decade, we have been slow in creating a whole new and much-needed discipline of family psychology.

First among the various factors that have accounted for a shift from a traditional practice of clinical child psychology to a family emphasis has been a disenchantment with individual approaches, both diagnostically and interventionally. After all, how many times can one administer the WISC, the Rorschach? No matter how exciting this activity may be, one cannot help reaching a certain degree of "burn out." How many clinicians are burned out on testing and lose a sense of enjoyment and excitement by the time they evaluate the 500th client?

Training and practice in individual therapy and play therapy show distinct economic and professional limitations when dealing with children. How often does the individual therapist hear about one's spouse, parents, siblings, lovers, with a sense of helplessness and frustration? How can we help our clients deal better with these intimates? How can we deal with the scapegoating process, especially after one has accepted the child as the "identified patient"? In fact (L'Abate, Weeks & Weeks, 1978, 1979), the individual approach, under certain conditions, could become a collusion with one spouse against the other spouse (the monster) and a collusion with parents against the child.* By accepting the child in our offices as the "patient," have we not agreed that indeed s/he is the one in need of treatment? Telling the parents to get treatment in parallel begs the question of costs, effectiveness, and fragmentation of treatment efforts. The author reached the limit when he evaluated a child whose parents and three siblings were working with different therapists, all working at cross-purposes! Under these conditions, one needs to consider the madness of an individual approach with children: ineffectiveness and extreme costs.

In theory, the need for a perspective more transactional and ecological (L'Abate et al., 1978) than the one available from traditional psychology brought out the fallacy of considering the <u>individual in a vacuum</u>, void of contact with intimate others (L'Abate, 1976). Hence, the family can now be considered the legitimate unit of psychological study and practice (chap. 1). Consequently, the Family Psychology Program developed at Georgia State University incorporates some of the foregoing biases and positions (L'Abate, Berger, Wright & O'Shea, 1979). Administratively, this program is one of the five subspecialties in the clinical program at Georgia State. The other subspecialties are: (a) general, (b) child clinical, (c) psychotherapy, and (d) behavior modification.

Academic Curriculum

To enter and to stay in the Family Psychology Program, the graduate student needs to fulfill departmental requirements in core courses, both experimental and clinical. Most of the students accepted in this program do fulfill additional requirements in individual evaluation to satisfy entrance requirements in the psychotherapy specialization, in order to qualify for

---

*To this point, see the recently published <u>The Psychotherapeutic Conspiracy</u> by Robert Langs.

competitive internships.

After a few years of uncertainty and indecision, we have finally decided to offer a locked-in sequence of courses. The first-year curriculum consists of an Introduction to Theories of Family Therapy (Fall), Personality Development in Marriage (with laboratory experience in role-playing of enrichment, Winter), Marital Interventions (with laboratory experience in Marital Contracting, Spring). The second year consists of courses in Family Evaluation (Fall), Personality Development in the Family (Winter), and Family Enrichment (Spring). The third-year curriculum consists of a seminar (Fall and Winter) on Advanced Theory and Therapy Techniques, a sociology course on Family Theory, and a course on Family Law. The fourth year includes an internship in a family-oriented clinical setting, possibly APA-approved. The Ph.D. dissertation is sandwiched somewhere between the third and fourth or even the fourth and fifth years. Some of our students stay on for a fourth year to complete coursework requirements or electives and the Ph.D. research before going on to their internships.

Clinical Curriculum

This part of the curriculum is organized according to the criteria of structure and gradualness (to be discussed in the next chapter), consisting of six steps in sequence.

First-Year Practica Experience

Most Structured: Enrichment

This approach consists of following verbatim instructions from three manuals (L'Abate, 1977; L'Abate & Sloan, 1981). Even within this first step there are steps: (a) students start role-playing couples and trainers (Jessee & L'Abate, 1981); (b) they then progress to nonclinical couples; (c) to clinical couples; (d) to nonclinical families; and (e) to clinical families (L'Abate, 1977; L'Abate & Rupp, 1981).

Structured: Covenant Contracting

This approach helps students deal with the whole issue of <u>contracting as a process</u> rather than as a fait accompli, or a given. Obviously, this approach is a trifle more complex than simple behavioral contracts and the like. It is based on contracting as a process of treatment rather than a baseline or an outcome.

Less Structured: Intimacy Workshops

Up to now, students have worked in teams of two, with only one couple at a time. In this approach, students will have a chance to deal with couples in one group in a one-day sitting rather than in single one-hour sessions over periods of weeks (L'Abate & Sloan, Note 3), as done in enrichment.

Second-Year Experience

Least Structured: Therapy

Eventually, the student reaches what s/he has been waiting for all along: to become a therapist and to work with clinical couples or families, using video and audio tapes for supervision (Soper & L'Abate, 1977; Weeks & L'Abate, 1982) and learning the variety of family therapy approaches (Hansen & L'Abate, 1982).

Third-Year Experiences

During this year, each student is assigned to various family-oriented agencies in the metropolitan Atlanta area, where they receive practicum experience and supervision in situ. This experience provides the bridge between the protective university atmosphere and the real-world experience of the internship.

Outcome

Even though we have graduated Ph.D. students in the last decade whose experience was in part as described, only in the last three years have we graduated students who can rightfully call themselves Family Psychologists by virtue of having fulfilled the three major criteria used at the outset of this chapter: (a) a family-oriented academic curriculum; (b) clinical experiences with families; and (c) at least one piece of research related to family, usually, but not limited to, the Ph.D. dissertation. By these criteria we have graduated five full-fledged family students.

Conclusion

As we have argued elsewhere (L'Abate & Thaxton,

1981), clinical psychology is now ready to break away from traditionally monolithic, individually-oriented training, to make the jump to specializations. One of these specializations is now family psychology. The program just described continues to subscribe in spirit and in letter to the Boulder scientist-practitioner model, with leeway along these two polarities. Instead of two aspects of the same training, there are many choices along the continuum of scientist-practitioner. We want our students to choose responsibly what they find exciting.

Reference Notes

1. Rau-Ferguson, L. The family perspective in the training of clinical child psychologists. Paper read at the First National Conference on Applied Developmental Psychology, Mailman Center, Miami, Florida, January 8-9, 1981.
2. Rau-Ferguson, L. Training program in child and family clinical psychology. Unpublished ditto. Department of Psychology, Michigan State University, East Lansing, Spring, 1980.
3. L'Abate, L., & Sloan, S. Z. A workshop format for increasing intimacy in couples. Research in progress, 1982.

References

Block, D. H., & Weiss, H. M. Training facilities in marital and family psychology. Family Process, 1981, 20, 133-146.

Cooper, A., Rampage, C., & Soucy, G. Family therapy training in clinical psychology programs. Family Process, 1981, 20, 155-166.

Dunne, E. E., & L'Abate, L. The family taboo in psychology textbooks. Teaching of Psychology, 1978, 5, 115-117.

Framo, J. A personal viewpoint on training in marital and family therapy. Professional Psychology, 1979, 10, 868-875.

Green, R. J., Rau-Ferguson, L., Framo, J. L., Shapiro, R. J., & LaPerriere, L. A symposium on family therapy training for psychologists. Professional Psychology, 1979, 10, 859-862.

Hansen, J. C., & L'Abate, L. Approaches to family therapy. New York: Macmillan, 1982.

Jessee, E., & L'Abate, L. Enrichment role-playing as a step in training family therapists. Journal of Marital and Family Therapy, 1981, 7, 507-514.

L'Abate, L. Principles of clinical psychology. New York: Grune & Stratton, 1964.

L'Abate, L. The laboratory method in clinical psychology: An attempt in innovation. The Clinical Psychologist, 1968, 21, 183-184.

L'Abate, L. The continuum of rehabilitation and laboratory evaluation: Behavior modification and psychotherapy. In C. M. Franks (Ed.), Behavior therapy: Appraisal and status. New York: McGraw-Hill, 1969.

L'Abate, L. The laboratory method in clinical child psychology: Three applications. Journal of Clinical Child Psychology, 1973, 2, 8-10.

L'Abate, L. Understanding and helping the individual in the family. New York: Grune & Stratton, 1976.

L'Abate, L. Enrichment: Structured interventions with couples, families, and groups. Washington, DC: University Press of America, 1977.

L'Abate, L. Toward theory and technology for social skills training: Suggestions for curriculum development. Academic Psychology Bulletin, 1980, 2, 207-228.

L'Abate, L. Skill training programs for couples and families. In A. S. Gurman & D. P. Kniskern (Eds.), Handbook of Family Therapy. New York: Brunner/Mazel, 1981.

L'Abate, L., Berger, M., Wright, M., & O'Shea, M. Training in family studies: The program at Georgia State University. Professional Psychology, 1979, 10, 58-64.

L'Abate, L., & Collaborators. Manual: Enrichment programs for the family life cycle. Atlanta,GA: Social Research Laboratories, 1975.

L'Abate, L., & Rupp, G. Enrichment: Skill training for family life. Washington, DC: University Press of America, 1981.

L'Abate, L., & Sloan, S. Z. Workbook: Enrichment programs for families and couples. Atlanta: Georgia State University, 1981.

L'Abate, L., & Thaxton, L. The differentiation of resources in mental health delivery: Implications for training. Professional Psychology, 1981, 12, 761-768.

L'Abate, L., Weeks, G. R., & Weeks, K. Psychopathology as transaction: A historical note. International Journal of Family Counseling, 1978, 6, 60-65.

L'Abate, L., Weeks, G. R., & Weeks, K. Of scapegoats, strawmen and scarecrows. International Journal of Family Therapy, 1979, 1, 89-96.

LaPerriere, L. Toward the training of broad-range family therapists. *Professional Psychology*, 1979, 10, 880-883.
Little, H. A., Vance, S., & Pastershot, R. J. Family therapy training opportunities in psychology and counselor education. *Professional Psychology*, 1979, 10, 760-765.
Rau-Ferguson, L. The family life cycle: Orientation for interdisciplinary training. *Professional Psychology*, 1979, 10, 863-867.
Rau-Ferguson, L. Survey of training in applied developmental psychology. *Newsletter: Division 7 Developmental Psychology*, Fall 1980, pp. 47-49.
Shapiro, R. J. The problematic position of family therapy in professional training. *Professional Psychology*, 1979, 10, 876-879.
Soper, P. H., & L'Abate, L. Paradox as a therapeutic technique: A review. *International Journal of Family Counseling*, 1977, 5, 10-21.
Thaxton, L. M., & L'Abate, L. The second wave and the second generation: Characteristics of new leaders in family therapy. *Family Process* (in press).
Weeks, G. R., & L'Abate, L. *Paradoxical psychotherapy: Interventions with individuals, couples, and families*. New York: Brunner/Mazel, 1982.

CHAPTER 28

STRUCTURE AND GRADUALNESS IN THE CLINICAL
TRAINING OF FAMILY PSYCHOLOGISTS

James A. Kochalka and Luciano L'Abate

The past several years have witnessed a proliferation in the literature describing training programs for family therapists (Cleghorn & Levin, 1973; Falicov et al., 1981; Flomenhaft & Carter, 1974; Goldenberg & Goldenberg, 1980; Rosenbaum & Serrano, 1979). We are in agreement with Kniskern and Gurman's (1979) statement of the field's empirical ignorance concerning the relevant aspects of family therapy training. However, in spite of the paucity of research evidence, we wish to comment on those aspects of family training programs which, when used exclusively, appear intuitively to be seriously lacking. We have identified five training models that appear to be somewhat inappropriate when used as single methods of clinical training: (a) the "book" model, (b) the "guru" model, (c) the "individual" model, (d) the "sink-or-swim" model, and (e) the "high tech" model. A consideration of these models will provide a backdrop for a description of the clinical training program in family psychology at Georgia State University. The reader is referred to L'Abate, Berger, Wright, and O'Shea (1979) for descriptions of the course work and curricula of the family psychology program.

The "Book" Model

Reading has been considered the sine qua non for learning psychotherapy, a condition that reflects the context of traditional academic training. We are, of course, in agreement with the need for reading widely to gain rudimentary theoretical skills. It is axiomatic that all disciplines have idiosyncratic language that represents a distinctive element of professional socialization. Basically, this mode of training allows the student to become inducted into the training experience and "talk therapy" with trainers and fellow students. One must, of course, be able to distinguish between talking about therapeutic interventions and actually doing interventions with couples or families.

We appeal to the principle of behavioral relevance (Ayllon & Azrin, 1968), which suggests that training should be specific to the tasks to which one wishes to generalize. The intellectual and cognitive material provided through readings is a necessary but insufficient condition for learning how to intervene with couples and families. One might also argue that too much book learning may inhibit the student's development of clinical expertise because of the inability to process and translate the wealth of information derived from books and also because of the great perceived discrepancy between how it "should be" done and what the student is actually able to do. The gap may act as a great deterrent to the self-confidence of the trainee.

The "Individual" Model

Little is known about the effects of learning an individual model of psychotherapy either before or concurrent with learning a family therapy model. A study by Shapiro and Budman (1973) suggested that family therapy clients who terminated prematurely negatively valued the therapist's lack of activity within a session. Conversely, those clients who remained in therapy made positive comments about their therapists' being active. Few statements were made about the therapists' lack of empathy and interest. The implication, if one assumes individual therapy methods to be less active relative to family therapy, is that these forms of training would not be particularly helpful to the trainee. Many trainees whose experience lies in the individual model find it extremely difficult to switch from the rather passive role of active listener to the more conductive posture often required in various forms of couple and family intervention.

There is no intent to indict the individual model in toto since empirical evidence exists (Gurman & Kniskern, 1981) to suggest the importance of the therapist's relationship skills in attaining a successful treatment outcome. This model does, however, often lack skills considered relevant to family interventions, e.g., any number of structuring skills (Cleghorn & Levin, 1973; Flomenhaft & Carter, 1974; O'Hare, Heinrich, Kirschner, Obershave & Ritz, 1975; Tomm & Wright, 1979; Weeks & L'Abate, 1982).

The "Guru" Model

This is a very pervasive form of training experience

that often appeals to those persons not enrolled in any
formal training program. The field of family therapy is
full of workshop afficianados who go to hear the visit-
ing gurus with the same fervor of the attenders at tent
revival meetings of not too long ago. This form of
observational learning can offer no more than a brief
slice of the therapeutic pie; yet, participants will
often bill themselves as having received training in
family therapy as a result of these gatherings. The
status of these meetings is elevated when one considers
that professional social convention allows a place for
workshop attendance on a vita!

It is likely that the influence of these gurus on
trainees is probably very little and largely directly
proportional to the degree of activity that the facilitator requires of the audience. The more the audience
actively participates through role playing or actual
intervention, the greater the learning. In some cases,
this model confuses method with style or technique.
The former is a set of repeatable procedures that can
be acquired through experience (Haley, 1976). The latter is a matter of personal style and, as such, is not
repeatable. Yet, the gurus often sell only this
aspect, i.e., themselves. Since, of course, they are
non-repeatable events, it is no wonder that we cannot
learn from them (Liddle, 1980; Liddle & Halpin, 1978)!

The "Sink-or-Swim" Model

This method of training involves putting a trainee
with a clinical family and letting him/her do whatever
interventions can be conjured up. Even though this
statement may be exaggerated, it is not uncommon to see
it applied to some degree. The jump for the trainee is
sudden and often traumatic, with little logic to make
it a compelling form of training. Further, one must
also question its usefulness for families who are presenting with serious problems (Cohen et al., 1976;
Tomm & Leahey, 1980).

The "High Tech" Model

A number of potentially useful devices, such as
one-way mirrors, video cameras, "bug-in-the-ear,"
define this approach. All of these paraphernalia are
intended to justify, mystify, and increase the mystique
of therapy. As useful as all of these mechanical con-
trivances can be, they are not substitutes for systematic and graduated approaches to training.

Additionally, the use of video feedback may raise the trainee's anxiety to inordinately high levels. Finally, although families may permit their use, we really do not know how they are influenced by the use of these technological aids.

The GSU Training Program in Family Psychology

The framework of the GSU training program falls under the rubric of family psychology versus that of family therapy. As discussed in the two preceding chapters, this training presumes that the clinician will be capable not only of conducting marital and family therapy from a systems orientation but will also creatively provide and evaluate services for normal families in a variety of mental health delivery contexts. Given this orientation, a clinical training sequence has been devised that allows the trainee to acquire distinct intervention strategies while developing a wide range of clinical skills. These strategies include the following: (a) Structured Enrichment, (b) Covenant Contracting, (c) Intimacy Workshop, and (d) unstructured therapy.

Gradualness in Structure: A Rationale for Sequence

Goldenberg and Goldenberg (1980), in reviewing training aids, considered: (a) didactic course work, (b) videotapes, (c) marathons, (d) live supervision, (e) films, and (f) looking at one's own family (of origin and the present). However, they failed to give a sequential order to all these aids: What should come first, before which course, and why? Theirs, as well as the presentations of many others, such as Liddle (1980), indicates that no attention has thus far been given to the systematic sequencing of various steps in the training of family therapists.

Regardless of how one views the relative merits of these various training models, none of them contains an approach to a systematic sequencing of training. Our training program attempts to order these training experiences by casting them within the framework of structure and gradualness.

The first concept, structure, has been used by social scientists rather than by mental health workers or family therapists. Strauss's (1978) comments bear mention in this regard:

Structure is not "out there"; it should not be

reified. When we talk about <u>structure</u>, we are, or should be, referring to the structural <u>conditions</u> that pertain to the phenomenon under study. Those conditions surely do obtain but they just as surely need to be discovered and analytically linked with their consequences.

We propose that the concept of structure is the thread that interweaves the elements of the GSU training program. The salient aspect of utilizing training elements that range from maximal to minimal structure is rooted in the assumption that a great deal of structure would simplify the trainee's demands, therefore decreasing the amount of perceived conflict and anxiety. Conversely, a novice's initial experience of very little structure would provoke a great deal of conflict and anxiety. Although empirical evidence does not exist for much of what is done in the name of family therapy training, we can imagine no scenario in which a great deal of initial anxiety would assist the trainee.

The second concept, gradualness, is hypothesized to suggest that the structure be decreased in a systematic fashion. As the trainee becomes more experienced and confident of the ability to interact in a variety of treatment contexts, more is demanded of the trainee to produce spontaneously in the setting.

The concept of gradual structure (or structured gradualness?) follows along broad lines the original framework set by Tomm and Wright (1979), distinguishing among perceptual, conceptual, and executive skills. If one were to consider these three sets of skills sequential, one could conceivably relate the framework presented here to Tomm and Wright's framework by suggesting that enrichment provides primarily the learning of perceptual skills, covenant contracting and intimacy workshops provide maximal learning of conceptual skills, and, eventually, therapy training and supervision provide learning of executive skills. Of course, such a sequence is selective; that is, one cannot learn one set of skills without receiving some experience in the other two.

Maximal Structure - Enrichment

Structured Enrichment (SE) originated within a training context (L'Abate, 1974, 1977; L'Abate & Allison, 1977; L'Abate & L'Abate, 1977) designed to give students an introductory experience with normal couples and families. A fortunate secondary gain has been the demonstrated usefulness of these programs with both normal and clinical populations, thus making SE a legitimate intervention apart from its training value. The basic procedures of SE were described in Chapters 26 and 27. This section will focus primarily on those aspects which characterize its structure and gradualness.

The student basically interacts with a couple or a family for eight one-hour sessions: one hour each of pre- and post-testing; six hours of actual enrichment lesson participation. Structure is provided in a very concrete way through use of a manual that contains verbatim instructions for the student to follow in administering the program to the clients. The student is allowed to bring this manual into the session as a visible display to the clients that s/he is not an expert but a facilitator of the canned program, thus keeping performance anxiety to a minimum. The student is also instructed to defer to the supervisor and the enrichment content when clients bring up matters that the student feels incapable of addressing. For example, if one spouse begins to initiate overtly aversive comments to the other spouse, the student is expected to encourage the clients to return to the exercises. The student would report to the supervisor and be advised how to proceed with the clients.

Another element of SE, with respect to the two-tiered supervisory format, is that the trainees are supervised in a group format by an advanced graduate student, who in turn is supervised by a faculty member. This arrangement allows the trainees to have a first supervisory experience with a fellow student, who by virtue of lower status than faculty, will likely evoke much less anxiety in the trainee as s/he struggles to develop an understanding of family interactions.

Beginning skills in conceptualization of family process are developed through the supervisory context of SE. Trainees read concurrently a number of theorists and practitioners (e.g., Haley, 1976; L'Abate, 1976; L'Abate & McHenry, in press; Minuchin, 1974) and use these readings as grist for discussing what is occurring in the family and how one might intervene therapeutically. This encouragement to think about families from various theoretical and therapeutic orientations is congruent with our belief that this exposure breeds a healthy skepticism for all frameworks. Furthermore, it allows the student eventually to select from a strong knowledge base of various orientations that perspective(s) to which s/he feels allied. This perspective is in contrast to the monolithic approach that fosters unfailing loyalty to a single ideology and an arrogant appropriation of "reality," with a concomitant put-down of alternative viewpoints.

The sequence of a trainee's participation in SE follows the same principle of gradualness noted earlier. First, trainees conduct SE with a mock couple, fellow graduate students who first play the role of client and then play the role of enricher. In the second experience, trainees conduct enrichment with "normal" undergraduate student couples who are either married or involved in a committed relationship. These students participate voluntarily as experimental subjects. Finally, trainees conduct SE with "normal" nonclinical families who are also obtained through the experimental subject pool (L'Abate & Rupp, 1981; L'Abate, Note 1).

Intermediate Structure - Covenant Contracting

The term "covenant contracting" describes a specific method of treatment developed by Sager (1976), by which the couple, with the aid of the trainee, works toward the goal of fulfilling a negotiated behavioral contract. We have modified the format of Sager for our own training purposes by imposing an eight-session limit (i.e., one session each for pre- and post-testing and six sessions devoted to the completion of contracts). Briefly stated, the spouses construct individual contracts that concern self, spouse, marriage, and children. The goal of our form of covenant contracting is the negotiation between spouses of a mutually agreed single contract.

Although the trainee is operating with procedures that can be used by therapists with clinical couples, several elements of our unique adaptation of Sager provide a more comfortable structure for the trainee. The major factor concerns the client population, who are married undergraduates participating in "research for experimental credit." This feature tends to mitigate the potential burden of having to intervene effectively with couples who are presenting in distress. To be fair, however, several couples have participated with thinly veiled relational problems, in hopes of ameliorating their difficulties. The supervisory tactic has been to monitor the trainee's conduct closely during the process and make a recommendation for marital therapy if that seems appropriate.

Structure is built into the procedures that the trainee follows in the conduct of covenant contracting through session guidelines requiring the completion of certain aspects of the contracts in specific sessions. This adherence to the written and verbalized tasks provides the thrust for each session and allows the trainee a "handle" for each session, both procedurally and tangibly. The tangible element is the actual contract that each partner has written from the previous week. The verbal sharing of these contracts during each session allows the trainee to observe marital interaction of a sometimes intense nature while providing an effective means of keeping the session under control. The trainee does this by deferring to the task at hand (i.e., completion of the contracts).

Supervision is conducted by a faculty member with a group of trainees. The supervisory focus tends to elicit from the trainees various conceptualizations of marital process as determined by the contract responses of each partner. The trainees also receive initial evaluation of their ability to structure the session, as judged by the completion of contracts, and also of their ability to conduct interventions suggested by the supervisor. Although the brevity of our adaptation of Sager's techniques limits the depth of exploration of various relevant dyadic issues, the conduct of this strategy offers the trainee a rich clinical experience. As the student becomes more sophisticated clinically, s/he may conduct a more intensive version of covenant contracting as one component of unstructured marital therapy. This more intense format would include attempts toward resolving, as opposed to merely specifying, the items of conflict generated by each partner.

Use of the covenant contracting procedures has been well received by both trainees who have had much prior therapy experience and by those who have had little previous therapy experience.

Less Structured - Intimacy Workshops

An Intimacy Workshop is a training strategy in which a male and a female trainee facilitate theme-centered discussions with a group of four to six committed couples. This one-day workshop lasts from four to six hours. The theoretical basis for this procedure comes from L'Abate (1976; L'Abate & L'Abate, 1977, 1979). The trainees are guided by the following themes in their conduct of the workshop: (a) acceptance of personal responsibility, (b) differentiation and priorities, (c) learning to negotiate, (d) learning to problem-solve together, and (e) sharing hurts and fears of being hurt. Although the sequence and intended substance of these themes are provided, the trainees must utilize their own resources to carry them out, thereby making this experience the most unstructured in terms of interpersonal demands. The fact that the trainees are leading a group of several couples also adds to the potential for performance anxiety.

The inclusion of a group format within the context of a family psychology training program is essential when one considers the increasing need to provide mental health services at reduced costs (L'Abate & Thaxton, 1981). Family clinicians may use the Intimacy Workshop experience as a springboard for creating other theme-focused group activities in which couples and families can engage.

Minimal Structure - Therapy

The therapy practicum for family psychology students consists of four quarters of weekly group supervisions of marital and family therapy cases that are conducted in the GSU Family Study Center. This is a research and treatment facility which provides services to GSU students and community residents.

Initial telephone contacts are handled by a designated graduate student who obtains basic demographic and problem-related information. A faculty member who acts as supervisor then assigns the case to a student, based on case load and appropriate problem-skill match.

Various therapeutic configurations are utilized in the conduct of marriage and family therapy. For example, during the year, the student may see a case alone, with a student co-therapist, be supervised live by a faculty member, or be assisted by a student consultant behind the mirror.

Participation in therapy is, of course, the least structured form of intervention that the student conducts during training and, as such, demands the widest range of skills. Although each of the four supervisors with whom the student comes into contact during this phase of training promotes an eclectic approach, a systems view of problem maintenance and resolution is implicit. Therefore, interventions often require task assignments and homework containing symptom prescriptions and paradoxical injunctions (Soper & L'Abate, 1977; Weeks & L'Abate, 1978, 1982). Clinical supervisors meet regularly to discuss the student's progress.

Clinical Training and the Laboratory Method

A critical element of the clinical training in family psychology at GSU concerns the pervasiveness of the spirit of the laboratory method (chaps. 16 & 17). The basic principle of the laboratory method, which underscores the training sequence, is the rigorous adherence to a pre- and post-testing format for all clinical interventions that are conducted in the lab. This adherence to evaluation creates an expectation of accountability, which appears to be a necessary, though sometimes neglected, component of clinical training. This focus on evaluation has resulted in student interest in process and outcome research in SE (for a review, see L'Abate, 1981; L'Abate, Note 1), covenant contracting (Caiella, 1982; Flores, 1982) and intimacy workshops (Sloan, Note 2). Laboratory method procedures have also been utilized in community settings with paraprofessional volunteers (Kochalka et al., 1982).

Consumers' Reactions

Graduate students in training, and clients and students who participate in the range of services in the Family Psychology program compose the constituency of the family psychology faculty. Each group's reactions concerning their involvement have generally been favorable, though often constructively critical of discrete components.

Reaction by graduate students to the structure of the clinical training has basically been positive, with some exceptions noted, depending on the previous experience of the trainee. Those trainees who have had clinical experience prior to entering GSU often chafe at the great degree of structure at the outset of their clinical work. They see themselves as therapists already and are sometimes not interested in learning strategies that can be useful with normal couples or families. Reports from more inexperienced trainees indicate satisfaction with the degree of structure, as the amount of anxiety does not interfere with clinical training.

As for clinical reactions, we have a great deal of data on SE (L'Abate, 1977) but, so far, only some case reports of covenant contracting and Intimacy Workshops. We will continue to establish a larger data base with all of these intervention strategies.

Conclusions

This chapter has presented the current state of clinical training in Family Psychology at GSU. The program comprises methods of training that are responsive to the changing demands of trainees and receptive to new developments in the training literature. Current concerns for this training program include a more complete explication of Tomm and Wright's (1979) classifications with respect to our training components. Another concern is the development of trainee assessment devices that will allow a better trainee-program fit: How many repetitions of each of the various components are necessary for each trainee? Must all trainees begin the sequence with a mock role play of SE or would some trainees make better use of their time by moving to more advanced stages? These are questions which we will continue to answer.

Reference Notes

1. L'Abate, L. Structured Enrichment (SE) with couples and families. Manuscript submitted for publication, 1982.

2. Sloan, S. An intimacy workshop for couples. Ph.D. dissertation research in progress, 1982.

References

Ayllon, T., & Azrin, N. The token economy. New York: Appleton, 1968.

Caiella, C. The process and effects of marital contracting with married couples. Unpublished master's thesis, Georgia State University, 1982.

Cleghorn, J., & Levin, S. Training family therapists by setting learning objectives. American Journal of Orthopsychiatry, 1973, 43, 439-446.

Cohen, J., Gross, S., & Turner, M. A note on developmental model for training family therapists through group supervision. *Journal of Marriage and Family Counseling*, 1976, *2*, 48.

Falicov, C., Constantine, J., & Breunlin, D. Teaching family therapy: A program based on training objectives. *Journal of Marital and Family Therapy*, 1981, *7*, 497-505.

Flomenhaft, K., & Carter, R. Family therapy training: A statewide program for mental health centers. *Hospital and Community Psychiatry*, 1974, *25*, 789-791.

Flores, J. *The process and effects of marital contracting with unmarried couples*. Unpublished master's thesis, Georgia State University, 1982.

Goldenberg, I., & Goldenberg, H. *Family therapy: An overview*. Monterey, CA: Brooks/Cole, 1980.

Gurman, A., & Kniskern, D. Family therapy outcome research: Knowns and unknowns. In A. Gurman & D. Kniskern (Eds.), *Handbook of family therapy*. New York: Brunner/Mazel, 1981.

Haley, J. *Problem-solving therapy*. San Francisco: Jossey-Bass, 1976.

Kniskern, D., & Gurman, A. Research on training in marriage and family therapy: Status, issues, and directions. *Journal of Marital and Family Therapy*, 1979, *5*, 83-94.

Kochalka, J., Buzas, H., L'Abate, L., McHenry, S., & Gibson, E. *Training paraprofessionals in the use of structured enrichment with couples and families*. Paper presented at annual meeting of the National Conference of Family Relations, Washington, DC, October 13, 1982.

L'Abate, L. Family enrichment programs. *Journal of Family Counseling*, 1974, *2*, 32-38.

L'Abate, L. *Understanding and helping the individual in the family*. New York: Grune & Stratton, 1976.

L'Abate, L. Intimacy is sharing hurt feelings: A reply to David Mace. *Journal of Marriage and Family Counseling*, 1977, *3*, 13-16.

L'Abate, L. Skill training programs for couples and families. In A. Gurman & D. Kniskern (Eds.), *Handbook of family therapy*. New York: Brunner/Mazel, 1981.

L'Abate, L., & Allison, M. Planned change intervention: The enrichment model. *Transactional Mental Health Newsletter*, 1977, *19*, 11-15.

L'Abate, L., Berger, M., Wright, L., & O'Shea, M. Training in family studies: The program at Georgia State University. *Professional Psychology*, 1979, 10, 58-64.

L'Abate, L., & L'Abate, B. L. How to avoid divorce: Help for troubled marriages. Atlanta: John Knox Press, 1977.

L'Abate, L., & L'Abate, B. L. The paradoxes of intimacy. Family Therapy, 1979, 6, 175-184.

L'Abate, L., & McHenry, S. Methods of marital intervention. New York: Grune & Stratton, in press.

L'Abate, L., & Rupp, G. Enrichment: Skill training for family life. Washington, DC: University Press

L'Abate, L., & Thaxton, L. Differentiation of resources in mental health delivery: Implications for training. Professional Psychology, 1981, 12, 761-768.

Liddle, H. On teaching a contextual or systemic therapy: Training content, goals, and methods. American Journal of Family Therapy, 1980, 8, 58-69.

Liddle, H., & Halpin, R. Family therapy training and supervision: A comparative review. Journal of Marriage and Family Counseling, 1978, 4, 77-98.

Minuchin, S. Families and family therapy. Cambridge, MA: Harvard University Press, 1974.

O'Hare, C., Heinrich, A., Kirschner, N., Obershave, A., & Ritz, M. Group training in family therapy: The student's perspective. Journal of Marriage and Family Counseling, 1975, 1, 157-162.

Rosenbaum, I., & Serrano, A. A rationale and outline for a training program in family therapy. Journal of Marital and Family Therapy, 1979, 5, 77-82.

Sager, C. Marital contracts and couple therapy. New York: Brunner/Mazel, 1976.

Shapiro, R., & Budman, S. Defection, termination, and continuation in family and individual therapy. Family Process, 1973, 12, 55-67.

Soper, P., & L'Abate, L. Paradox as a therapeutic technique: A review. International Journal of Family Counseling, 1977, 5, 10-21.

Strauss, A. Negotiations: Varieties, contexts, processes, and social order. San Francisco: Jossey-Bass, 1978.

Tomm, K., & Leahey, M. Training in family assessment: A comparison of three teaching methods. Journal of Marital and Family Therapy, 1980, 6, 453-458.

Tomm, K., & Wright, L. Training in family therapy: Perceptual, conceptual, and executive skills. Family Process, 1979, 18, 227-250.

Weeks, G., & L'Abate, L. A bibliograph of paradoxical therapy literature. Family Process, 1978, 17, 95-98.

Weeks, G., & L'Abate, L. Paradoxical psychotherapy. New York: Brunner/Mazel, 1982.

CHAPTER 29

Enrichment Role-Playing as a Step in the Training of Family Therapists

Ed Jessee*
Luciano L'Abate**

In recent years increasing attention has been devoted to the training of family therapists. This paper focuses on the difficulties inherent in such training, and the benefits provided by an alternative model based on enrichment role-playing. This technique provides a much needed step in the systemization of family therapy training. Specific benefits include: (a) an optimal environment for teaching basic relationship skills, (b) security for the student and clarity of perceptions for the supervisor, and (c) an opportunity for the trainee to learn family diagnostics. A brief review of family therapy training, marital and family enrichment, and role-playing precedes discussion of the enrichment role-playing technique. Case material is presented to illustrate the trainee's experience.

The field of family therapy has recently experienced a quarter century of growth and popularization that has propagated numerous theoretical approaches. Unfortunately, the question of training has not been approached in such a concentrated manner. Liddle & Halpin (1978) concluded that the training and supervision literature was "fragmented and disorganized," and suggested that there was a dire need to specify learning objectives and expectations in empirical terms. Haley (1975) commented on training difficulties due to an inherent clash in theoretical orientations. A variety of models of family therapy training have emerged in recent years, all of which contain certain disturbing aspects (Liddle & Halpin, 1978). What are these problems and what is the nature of their origin?

One frequently cited difficulty lies in trainee resistance to learning a new viewpoint. As Liddle (1978) commented, "trainees with some prior training and experience tend to be more rigid in their ways of thinking and behaving than less experienced and younger students." Haley (1975) felt that this rigidity can lead to disorientation and disorganization of a staff that is attempting to master a family treatment approach. A second problem concerns what Barton & Alexander (1977) described as a neglect of interpersonal skills training. They maintained that currently much family training is in danger of over-emphasizing technique, and consequently the importance of acquiring basic interpersonal skills is not stressed. Russell (1976) commented that perhaps the most popular mode of training, live supervision, is too intrusive and distracting to the learning process to be effective. Several authors (Tucker & Liddle, 1976; Miyoshi & Liebman, 1969) have identified a variety of predictable problems students experience in going from didactic to experiential training. Initially most students exhibit caution, anxiety and competitiveness. At times students become defensive to the point of being unable to accept sugges-

---

*Ed Jessee is a PhD candidate, Family Studies Program, Psychology Department, Georgia State University.
**Luciano L'Abate, PhD, is Professor of Psychology and Director, Family Studies Program, Psychology Department, Georgia State University, Atlanta, Georgia 30303.

tions. Also, despite theoretical training to the contrary, students often unwittingly engage in side-taking in the family. This side-taking frequently accompanies a tendency to focus on an individual rather than on interactional patterns.

Maloref and Alexander (1972) exemplify in their crisis intervention model a possible improvement on the basic didactic-experiential model. After didactic training, they require the student to engage in a period of observation of experienced therapists at work before they themselves attempt therapy. Tomm and Wright (1979) proposed a training format that involves specification of stages in the therapy process and the concommitant executive and perceptual skills inherent in each stage. This approach is particularly useful in terms of providing a systematic approach to training. The supervisor can determine by observation whether the therapist possesses the requisite executive skill. If he does not, the supervisor can pinpoint the perceptual/conceptual skill underlying his deficit. Tomm and Wright (1979) do not, however, address the issue of students receiving this training at the expense of their patients.

The training of competent family therapists must itself be systematized in a manner that illustrates and maximizes the interrelationship between theory and practice. According to Liddle & Halpin (1978), "the family therapy field is more sophisticated developmentally in its therapeutic methodologies than in the areas of training and supervision." The following is a first step at developing a systematic training model for family therapists through the technique of role-playing in marital and family enrichment.

Marital and Family Enrichment

Mental health needs of the present and the future indicate that therapy and therapeutic approaches, whether with individuals, groups, or families, can only deal with a small percentage of the population in need of some kind of intervention. In an attempt to fill this vacuum, the last decade has seen the upsurge of what have been called structured, interpersonal, or social skills training programs. These skills training programs for couples and families are for those who: (a) do not need nor require prolonged treatment; (b) want a preset, preselected topic that will meet some of their needs; (c) want a definite number of sessions, and (d) want a clear fee with no surprises (L'Abate, 1980). For every couple and family in therapy there are many others who could profit by such skill training. Because of these needs, Marriage and Family Enrichment Programs were developed in the Family Study Center of the Psychology Department of Georgia State University. As part of their training, graduate students learn to conduct enrichment programs with couples and families mostly drawn from the undergraduate population (L'Abate, 1977; L'Abate & Rupp, 1981).

The Nature of Enrichment Programs

Any notion, idea, concept and theory can be broken down into small steps and set into a sequential order that will allow learning through progressive and gradual steps from the simplest idea to the most complex. This practice has been the technological basis of our Enrichment Programs. An extremely large number of programs for couples and families have been written and published, ranging from expecting the first child to adolescence, marriage, divorce and death. The two available manuals of Enrichment contain 27 programs for a total of hundreds of lessons, designed to meet the various needs faced by most couples and families. Each lesson gives the trainer(s) verbatim instructions on how to ask a particular question and what to do whenever certain predictable issues come up during the course of enrichment. A written contract describing the program is given to a couple or family and is signed to safeguard the couple and family's confidentiality, and meet standards of research set for human subjects. Each couple or family is evaluated objectively pre- and post-enrichment. A follow-up session after post-testing is given to assess the couple or family's reactions, give them feedback, and discuss with them what works well for them and what they need to work on (L'Abate, 1977; L'Abate & Rupp, 1981).

After the initial interview and testing, each couple or family is given two or three programs that seem to meet their needs, and asked to choose one from the three. Each program contains six lessons which are usually broken down so that one lesson is dealt with each week. If, during enrichment, a given program does not seem to be effective, another program is substituted.

Our training program attempts to equip the student trainee with an experiential and theoretical basis for understanding couple and family relationships. The untrained student is initially provided with a great deal of program structure which gradually diminishes as the student familiarizes himself with theoretical and experiential understanding of a family. Specifically, the trainee begins with marital enrichment role-play followed by marital enrichment with non-clinical families. The progression continues with the student enriching clinical families and beginning marital contracting (Sager, 1976). After the student has gained a basic understanding of couples' relationships he/she begins family enrichment role-playing, followed by non-clinical and clinical family enrichment. The final phase of training focuses on the unstructured process of therapy. Thus the sequential structure of our training modes involves working with: (a) simulated couples and families; (b) non-clinical couples and families; and (c) clinical couples and families. The actual training modes include: (a) enrichment; (b) contracting; and (c) therapy. The latter two modes will be considered elsewhere while here we will consider the role of role-playing and enrichment.

Role-playing

Role-playing is a popular and widely used technique in the facilitation of training both clinicians and non-clinicians (Weingarten, 1979; Raasoch and Laquer, 1979). The term "role-playing" has been applied to a wide variety of procedures, including: (a) having people predict the results of deception experiments; (b) using role-playing as an attitude-change induction; (c) involvement in simulation studies; and (d) having subjects enact scripts based on planned variations of environmental situations. However, all of the above share the common feature of asking individuals to act "as if" they were engaged in special social situations that are largely outside of the specific social context they are normally engaged in (Forward, *et al.*, 1976). Numerous individuals (Perry, 1975; Osmond, 1979; Raasoch & Lacquer, 1979) reported on the effectiveness of role-playing as a training technique for therapists. Frequently cited advantages include the usefulness of experiential vs. theoretical learning, protection against beginning therapist mistakes on "real" clients, and limited time and expense. In addition to these advantages, some results (Osmond, 1979; Weingarten, 1979) indicate that students prefer role-playing as a way of learning. One consistently cited problem is that professionals tend to simulate excessive pathology in the early stages of the simulation (Raasoch & Lacquer, 1979).

Role-Playing Enrichment

In an effort to remedy many of the aforementioned training problems, we have altered our program to include role-playing of marital and family enrichment. After initial theoretical classes, students engage in role-playing the enrichers and the clients. For example, a student may role-play a member of a couple for an entire enrichment program, after which he will switch and become one of the co-enrichers for couples enrichment.

Role-playing enrichment experiences have been added in order to aid both students and supervisors. Numerous advantages of this approach can readily be seen. First, as

Table 1*

Clinical Relationship Skills Taught in Enrichment Role Playing

1. Explain the rationale for the couple or family's involvement in the process, e.g., "Since you all live together, whatever one person does is going to affect everyone else. Therefore, if you are going to be part of the problem, you need to also be part of the solution."
2. Introduce yourself in a personal way and clarify the enricher's role as a facilitator rather than an "expert."
3. Engage each family member in direct interaction.
4. Find something you like about each person and let them know it.
5. Clearly lay out all the rules of enrichment and what can be expected in the coming weeks.
6. Ask for special permission for any procedure not covered in the rules.
7. Discuss individual's initial anxiety with warmth and sensitivity and label it as normal and healthy.
8. Reframe the couple or family's problems in positive terms, e.g., "You mean your arguing with each other has enabled you to finally seek the help you've been needing to make this the kind of marriage you really want."
9. Respond to all individuals on their cognitive/developmental level. For example, do not use large words when talking to a young child.
10. Maintain clear distinctions between roles. For example, do not make the enrichment session into a social hour. Remain theme focused.
11. Use the same type of language and metaphors used by the clients.
12. Encourage involvement from all members. Make an attempt to reach out and engage the most distant individual.
13. Establish an atmosphere of honesty and caring by modeling these traits with your co-enricher.
14. Explore ambiguous and unclear statements in order to clarify communication as much as possible.
15. Discover the situational and personal context of the problem—who is doing what, when, and where.
16. Identify patterns of communication, e.g., "I notice you change the subject every time your wife starts crying."
17. Stay in control of the flow of information. When necessary guide and refocus the conversation back to the lesson topic.
18. Do not participate in destructive interaction patterns, e.g., "If I agree with you I'll be siding against your husband and will be unable to help the both of you."
19. Maintain and exhibit a sense of humor.

*Some of these items were paraphrased from Tomm and Wright (1979).

Barton and Alexander (1977) indicated, all therapeutic relationships require certain basic relationship skills that are often neglected in experiential training programs. We find that these basic skills are often incomplete or lacking in our beginning students, even though they may have had extensive previous therapeutic experience. These basic relationship skills (see Table 1) are what Tomm and Wright (1979) call the executive and perceptual/conceptual skills needed in the first two stages of therapy—engagement and problem identification. The mastery of the basic relationship skills is essential to the development of a relationship therapist. The structured environment of enrichment role-playing provides the student with ample opportunity to learn such skills, and allows the supervisor to have adequate feedback on the student's progress.

A second major aspect of this approach is that role-playing provides a secure environment in which students can attempt mastery. The anxiety and defensiveness (Tucker and Liddle, 1977) is greatly diminished. At the same time, student therapists cannot "fake good" because they are being evaluated by their peers as well as their supervisor. Since the supervisor supervises both the role-playing couple and the role-playing therapists, the effectiveness of the student therapist is laid bare. The supervisor does not have to struggle with the perennial question of whether to attribute problems in therapy to the pathology of the couple or to the inadequacy of the therapists. The strengths and weaknesses of the student therapists become self-evident. In our experience this process increases the efficiency and effectiveness of training.

A third basic training advantage is that it gives the student the opportunity to see theory in action without placing undue pressure on him to intervene (do therapy). The student can observe family dynamics, learn how relationship systems function, and discover how to evaluate family and couples functioning. The structured format of enrichment enables the student to distance himself enough to focus on relationships without being enmeshed in the family system himself. As one student remarked, "I don't feel the awesome responsibility for helping these people that I've felt before."

For many years we have experienced a dilemma as to how to provide adequate client service as well as good student training. Often we have felt client service has been adversely affected because of beginning therapists' mistakes. Role-playing provides ample opportunity for the student to develop some basic competencies before working with real clients, and therefore should eliminate many predictable problems involved in training and service. Since initiating this training process, we have observed fewer mistakes by beginning therapists.

Tucker and Liddle (1978) concluded their review of training programs by stating, "the outcome of training is determined by the therapist's willingness to constructively deal with his own reactions, feelings, and motivations, as well as his area of weakness." Role-playing both sides of the therapeutic relationship provides the student with an increased awareness of both clients' and therapists' feelings and reactions. The student is encouraged to deal with these feelings before he is thrust into being a "real" therapist. Students are ultimately faced with their own inadequacies in relationships, and consequently their ability to be a therapist. This process is not undertaken solely by the student, but by design involves the supervisor and the student's peers. Thus, a supportive and information-rich feedback system is built into this model of training.

Student Reactions

The enrichment role-playing model is by no means an easy concept for students or supervisors. Adoption of this model necessitates an intense commitment in time and energy for both the student and supervisor. In order to gain a more complete understanding of the nature of this process, participants' reactions and problematic issues will be addressed.

Student reaction to this model has not been entirely positive. Criticism has ranged from calling it an unpleasant experience to stating it creates animosity among students. Significant problems have included initial anxiety and uncomfortableness due to being placed in a therapeutic relationship position with peers, and/or difficulty assuming the role-playing position. One student remarked, "I found that elements of the role-play were uncomfortably close to reality." Students invariably brought aspects of themselves into the role-playing. Another frequent comment centered on the fact that students were not allowed to debrief until the conclusion of the process. Most students felt that the experience became too interpersonally intense, and at times conflictual—"it creates an intolerable situation where the student is expected to exhibit proficiency to his supervisor and maintain relationships with his peers."

These problems are ultimately assets in a training program. The design of this procedure is to create a realistic therapeutic intensity for the participants within the "safe" confines of role-playing. In so doing, the student is placed in an admittedly difficult role, but one that is analagous to the binds of the family therapist. The role-player must learn to divorce himself of loyalties, overcome performance anxiety, and deal with uncomfortable personal feelings awakened by the process of these tasks. Students appear to exhibit the most difficulty with the task of dealing with their feelings. Yet, this experience has also been the source of positive experience—"these sessions provided a vehicle through which I could articulate these disillusionments and anger brought about from real life experience." Another remarked, "I recognized my own fear of anger and failure to deal with it effectively in myself or in others."

A majority of students felt the feeling aspect of the experience had both positive and deleterious effects: "At times I began to speak and feel as I had in real life. I am unsure if this is a blessing or a curse. On the one hand, perhaps these problems would have one day surfaced on their own and it is good to get them out before resentment builds, but, on the other hand, by opening it up to examination we can create a bucket of worms." Obviously this kind of student self-exploration is troublesome, but it is also the underlying foundation of an effective family therapist. Personal or marital therapy, which is strongly suggested in most training programs (Liddle & Halpin, 1978), is helpful when the student must deal with personal relationship issues in the course of role-playing. However, interestingly, whether or not a student has had personal therapy previously has not seemed to be an important variable in his/her ability to perform in role-play situations. Also, we have discovered, as Liddle (1978) indicated, often trainees with prior therapeutic training experience have more difficulty than inexperienced students—primarily due to a lack of adequate relationship skills (see Table 1).

Positive reactions to enrichment role-playing appear to support our contention that it is a viable training model:

"I gained insight and awareness of my own role-playing stereotypical expectations and sometimes overreactions."

"The major impact of this experience has been in a better understanding of marital dynamics."

"I found enrichment to be an asset in two respects: (1) for my role-play marriage, and (2) for my professional growth as a family counselor."

"The opportunity to role-play as a couple can serve to sensitize students toward key areas of human interaction far better in some ways than can role-playing as enrichers. Noteworthy among these is the ability to empathize with future clientele as a result of having been somewhat in their shoes."

Perhaps one student summed it up best when he stated, "It was a learning experience—both painful and enjoyable."

One danger that needs to be faced from the onset is the tendency for students to overplay pathological roles (Raasoch & Lacquer, 1979). Often this tendency can be distracting or can create unnecessary conflicts. In one case this tendency manifested itself to such a degree that enrichers and clients became furious with each other. The supervisor had to intervene in order to re-establish a realistic portrayal of roles by both parties. Hence, it is important for the supervisor to exercise control and monitor this process to avoid escalation to an uncomfortable and destructive extreme. At the same time the supervisor must encourage realistic role-playing, even if that realism becomes uncomfortable.

Making distinctions between realism and excessive pathology can be difficult. For example, in one foursome we supervised the couple appeared to exhibit undue pathology, yet did so as a result of the interaction with the enrichers. Initially the simulated couple presented themselves in a somewhat reserved, distant and passive-aggressive manner. The simulated enrichers failed to observe these aspects, and did not adequately master the necessary relationship skills. Unprofessional behavior and undue intrusion by the enrichers interacted with the couple's defensiveness and non-verbalized expectations to precipitate negative feelings on both sides. It was decided to continue the experience "as if" it were the real thing. Accordingly, the couple opted to end enrichment and a termination session was conducted. Afterwards, a debriefing session was utilized to help all individuals de-role. Some might say this experience was a failure since the enrichment was prematurely terminated, but from a training viewpoint it was an unqualified success. The students involved all had an experience of understanding and owning their responsibility for an emotionally painful experience. The interactional aspect of this experience was stressed in order to avoid attributing excessive pathology to the couple or excessive negligence to the enrichers.

Conclusion

Marital and family enrichment role-playing is a powerful and dynamic training model. Research is currently underway to determine its ultimate effectiveness. Preliminary results indicate this model successfully addresses many of the training program flaws cited in the literature. Although enrichment role-playing is only one step in our overall training program, it appears to have provided the missing link in terms of systematizing and ordering the training process.

REFERENCES

Barton, C. & Alexander, J. F. Therapist's skills as determinants of effective systems-behavioral family therapy. *International Journal of Family Counseling*, 1977, 5, 11–20.

Forward, J., Canter, R. & Kirsch, N. Role-enactment and deception methodologies—Alternative paradigms? *American Psychologist*, 1976, 31, 595–604.

Group for the Advancement of Psychiatry. *Treatment of families in conflict: The clinical study of family process.* New York: Aronson, 1970.

Haley, J. Why a mental health clinic should avoid family therapy. *Journal of Marriage and Family Counseling*, 1975 1, 3–12.

Kohlberg, L. Development of moral character and moral ideology. In M. L. Hoffman and L. W. Hoffman (Eds.). *Review of child development research.* Vol. 1. New York: Russell Sage Foundation, 1964.

L'Abate, L. Skill training programs for couples and families: Clinical and non-clinical applications. In A. S. Gurman and D. P. Kniskern (Eds.), *Handbook of family therapy.* New York: Brunner/Mazel, 1980.

L'Abate, L. *Enrichment: Structured interventions with couples, families, and groups.* Washington: University Press of America, 1977.

L'Abate, L. & Rupp, G. Enrichment skill training for family life. Submitted for publication (1981).

Liddle, H. A. The emotional and political hazards of teaching and learning family therapy. *Family Therapy*, 1978, 1, 1–11.

Liddle, H. A. & Halpin, R. Family therapy training and supervision literature: A comparative review. *Journal of Marriage & Family Counseling*, 1978, 4, 77–98.

Maloref, F. E., & Alexander, J. F. Family crisis intervention: A model and technique of training. Paper presented at the National Conference on Training in Family Therapy, Philadelphia Child Guidance Clinic, November 1972.

Miyoshi, N., & Liebman, R. Training psychiatric residents in family therapy. *Family Process,* 1969, *8,* 97-105.

Osmond, M. W. The use of simulation games in teaching family sociology. *Family Coordinator,* 1979, *28,* 205-215.

Perry, M. A. Modeling and instructions in training for counseling empathy. *Journal of Counseling Psychology,* 1975, *22,* 173-180.

Raasoch, J., & Lacquer, H. P. Learning multiple family therapy through simulated workshops. *Family Process,* 1979, *18,* 95-98.

Russell, A. Contemporary concerns in family therapy. *Journal of Marriage and Family Counseling,* 1976, *2,* 243-250.

Sager, C. *Marriage contracts and couple therapy: Hidden forces in intimate relationships.* New York: Brunner/Mazel, 1976.

Tomm, K. M., & Wright, L. M. Training in family therapy: Perceptual, conceptual, and executive skills. *Family Process,* 1979, *18,* 227-250.

Tucker, B., Hart, G., & Liddle, H. A. Supervision in family therapy: A developmental perspective, *Journal of Marriage and Family Counseling,* 1976, *2,* 269-276.

Tucker, B., & Liddle, H. A. Intra- and interpersonal process in the group supervision of family therapists. *Family Therapy,* 1978, *1,* 13-27.

Uhleman, M. R., Lea, G. W., & Stone, G. L. Effect of instructions and modeling on trainees low in interpersonal-communication skills. *Journal of Counseling Psychology,* 1976, *23,* 509-513.

Weingarten, K. Family awareness for nonclinicians: Participation in a simulated family as a teaching technique. *Family Process,* 1979, *18,* 143-150.

SECTION VII

CONCLUSION

CHAPTER 30

FAMILY PSYCHOLOGY: THE PRESENT AND THE FUTURE

A recent survey (Thaxton & L'Abate, in press) has shown that psychologists are becoming more and more involved in the field of family therapy. Hence, psychology as a science and as a profession may be ready to pay more attention to the family than has been the case in the past (as discussed in chaps. 1 & 2). As a result of this involvement, it is inevitable that theories and theoretical models, as discussed in Section I, will proliferate and profit by healthy competition.

At least two sections of this book have been devoted to the role of feelings in intimacy as well as in therapy. Even though feelings and emotionality may be considered primary in the development of functionality and dysfunctionality, their role will continue to be controversial. Yet, the evidence from a couple of English studies (Brown, Birley & Wing, 1972; Vaughn & Leff, 1976) with families of relapsed and nonrelapsed schizophrenics does suggest that the major determinant of a relapse was a "negative emotional" climate in the house. Furthermore, these studies and the work of Fallon (1981) do indicate that family therapy for some of these families is not the best method of treatment and that a skills training approach is more relevant and effective (L'Abate, 1980, 1981). The future will thus see a more rapid growth of structured, <u>linear</u>, skills-training methods based on educational models (L'Abate & Milam, in press) rather than circular therapeutic models.

As has been made abundantly clear in Section VI, training in family psychology cannot consist of an occasional course and seminar on family therapy. The definition of a family psychologist does consist of an individual who has: (a) followed an appropriate academic curriculum; (b) fulfilled at least two years of clinical part-time practica and one full-time year of clinical internship; plus (c) completed a dissertation based on research relevant to the family or at least to the interface between individuals and the family (L'Abate, 1976).

Clinical family psychology as a formal specialization in the field of clinical and applied psychology is still in its infancy. It has not been acknowledged officially by the profession, either as a Section in the formal structure of the American Psychological Association or as a visible and relevant part of an academic curriculum anywhere. Fortunately, this sad state of affairs will change. The entry of more and more psychologists into the field of family therapy will (should?) bring about more and more courses and, eventually, curricula. How long this process will take is anybody's guess. It may take longer than one expects but not so long as one fears (L'Abate, in press).

In conclusion, this collection of writings has attempted to bridge the gap between individual and family psychology. It is by no means a statement on the only pathway that the field of family psychology can and will follow. It is merely one of many pathways. It is hoped that in following it the reader may have developed some ideas about how to create his/her own pathway in this field.

References

Brown, G. W., Birley, J. L. T., & Wing, J. K. Influence of family life on the course of schizophrenic disorders: A replication. British Journal of Psychology, 1972, pp. 241-258.

Fallon, I. R. H. Communication and problem-solving skills training with relapsing schizophrenics and their families. In M. R. Lansky (Ed.), Family therapy and major psychopathology. New York: Grune & Stratton, 1981.

L'Abate, L. Understanding and helping the individual in the family. New York: Grune & Stratton, 1976.

L'Abate, L. Toward a theory and technology for social skills training: Suggestions for curriculum development. Academic Psychology Bulletin, 1980, 2, 207-228.

L'Abate, L. Skills training program for couples and families. In A. S. Gurman & D. P. Kniskern (Eds.), Handbook of family therapy. New York: Brunner/Mazel, 1981.

L'Abate, L. (Ed.). Handbook of family psychology. Homewood, IL: Dow-Jones-Irwin (in press).

L'Abate, L., & Milam, M. (Eds.). Handbook of social skills training and research. New York: Wiley & Sons (in press).

Thaxton, L. M., & L'Abate, L. The second wave and the second generation: Characteristics of new leaders in family therapy. Family Process (in press).

Vaughn, C. E., & Leff, J. P. The influence of family and social factors on the course of psychiatric illness: A comparison of schizophrenic and depressed neurotic patients. British Journal of Psychiatry, 1976, 129, 125-137.